P9-ARE-278

Cooking Basics

5th Edition

by Bryan Miller and Marie Rama with Eve Adamson

for
dummies®
A Wiley Brand

Cooking Basics For Dummies®, 5th Edition

Published by: **John Wiley & Sons, Inc.**, 111 River Street, Hoboken, NJ 07030-5774, www.wiley.com

Copyright © 2020 by John Wiley & Sons, Inc., Hoboken, New Jersey

Published simultaneously in Canada

No part of this publication may be reproduced, stored in a retrieval system or transmitted in any form or by anymeans, electronic, mechanical, photocopying, recording, scanning or otherwise, except as permitted under Sections107 or 108 of the 1976 United States Copyright Act, without the prior written permission of the Publisher. Requests tothe Publisher for permission should be addressed to the Permissions Department, John Wiley & Sons, Inc., 111 RiverStreet, Hoboken, NJ 07030, (201) 748-6011, fax (201) 748-6008, or online at http://www.wiley.com/go/permissions.

Trademarks: Wiley, For Dummies, the Dummies Man logo, Dummies.com, Making Everything Easier, and related trade dress are trademarks or registered trademarks of John Wiley & Sons, Inc., and may not be used without written permission. All other trademarks are the property of their respective owners. John Wiley & Sons, Inc., is not associated with any product or vendor mentioned in this book.

LIMIT OF LIABILITY/DISCLAIMER OF WARRANTY: THE PUBLISHER AND THE AUTHOR MAKE NOREPRESENTATIONS OR WARRANTIES WITH RESPECT TO THE ACCURACY OR COMPLETENESS OF THE CONTENTS OF THIS WORK AND SPECIFICALLY DISCLAIM ALL WARRANTIES, INCLUDING WITHOUT LIMITATION WARRANTIESOF FITNESS FOR A PARTICULAR PURPOSE. NO WARRANTY MAY BE CREATED OR EXTENDED BY SALES OR PROMOTIONAL MATERIALS. THE ADVICE AND STRATEGIES CONTAINED HEREIN MAY NOT BE SUITABLE FOR EVERY SITUATION. THIS WORK IS SOLD WITH THE UNDERSTANDING THAT THE PUBLISHER IS NOT ENGAGED IN RENDERING LEGAL, ACCOUNTING, OR OTHER PROFESSIONAL SERVICES. IF PROFESSIONAL ASSISTANCE IS REQUIRED, THE SERVICES OF A COMPETENT PROFESSIONAL PERSON SHOULD BE SOUGHT. NEITHER THE PUBLISHER NOR THE AUTHOR SHALL BE LIABLE FOR DAMAGES ARISING HEREFROM. THE FACT THAT AN ORGANIZATION OR WEBSITE IS REFERRED TO IN THIS WORK AS A CITATION AND/OR A POTENTIAL SOURCE OF FURTHER INFORMATION DOES NOT MEAN THAT THE AUTHOR OR THE PUBLISHER ENDORSES THE INFORMATION THE ORGANIZATION OR WEBSITE MAY PROVIDE OR RECOMMENDATIONS IT MAY MAKE. FURTHER, READERS SHOULD BE AWARE THAT INTERNET WEBSITES LISTED IN THIS WORK MAY HAVE CHANGED OR DISAPPEARED BETWEEN WHEN THIS WORK WAS WRITTEN AND WHEN IT IS READ.

For general information on our other products and services, please contact our Customer Care Department within the U.S. at 877-762-2974, outside the U.S. at 317-572-3993, or fax 317-572-4002. For technical support, please visit www.wiley.com/techsupport.

Wiley publishes in a variety of print and electronic formats and by print-on-demand. Some material included with standard print versions of this book may not be included in e-books or in print-on-demand. If this book refers to media such as a CD or DVD that is not included in the version you purchased, you may download this material at http://booksupport.wiley.com. For more information about Wiley products, visit www.wiley.com.

Library of Congress Control Number: 2020931188

ISBN 978-1-119-69677-3 (pbk); ISBN 978-1-119-69558-5 (ebk); ISBN 978-1-119-69546-2 (ebk)

10 9 8 7 6 5 4 3 2 1

641.5
mil

Contents at a Glance

Recipes at a Glance

Main Dishes

Vegetables and Side Dishes

Sauces, Dressings, and Garnishes

Sweets and Desserts

Beverages

Table of Contents

Introduction

Welcome to *Cooking Basics For Dummies,* 5th Edition. Taking into consideration recent cooking trends, this updated edition includes new information on Asian and Mediterranean cuisine, cooking techniques like pan-roasting and steaming in foil pouches, and how to get the best from farmers' markets. We've also added shorter recipes, including some that call for eight or fewer ingredients and are complete meals. Unlike most cookbooks, this one is more than a compilation of tasty recipes. We also focus on traditional cooking techniques, like broiling, steaming, braising, and roasting. This edition carries expanded information on grains and pastas and offers recipes for trendy new ingredients, like kale and bacon.

You discover the best way to mince garlic, peel a tomato, and truss a chicken. After you master these techniques, you're no longer a slave to recipes. You can cook with imagination and creativity — and that's the sign of a skilled cook.

Furthermore, this book is structured around the way you live. For example, it includes information about cooking economically, making a delicious meal when you don't even have time to get to the market, and throwing a party or celebrating a holiday when you have the time to make it special.

Most of all, you actually have fun as you explore the endless pleasures of cooking. And that, after all, is what this book is all about.

About This Book

We start at the very beginning: your kitchen and your equipment. What basic tools do you need? How do you use these things? We help you stock your pantry, refrigerator, and freezer with basic staples so you know what to have on hand. Then we move on to cooking techniques to get you up and running as soon as possible. Doing simple things well offers great personal satisfaction.

Depending on your needs and cooking skills, you can start at the beginning of the book and work your way through, go straight to the chapters that interest you most (the table of contents and index point you in the right direction), or read the book backward if that's your thing.

Before charging ahead to make any of the recipes in this book, you should know a few things about the ingredients and instructions:

>> **Milk is always whole.** You can substitute low-fat or skim milk, or even soy or rice milk, but these products give soups and sauces a thinner, less creamy consistency and may influence the texture in other dishes (although not necessarily in an undesirable way).

>> **Butter is unsalted so you can control the amount of salt in a dish.** We don't recommend substituting margarine, which has just as many calories and just as much fat as butter, unless you're avoiding dairy products. Margarine's flavor is generally inferior to butter.

>> **Unless otherwise noted, all eggs are large.**

>> **All dry ingredient measurements are level.** Brown sugar is measured firmly packed.

>> **All measured salt is common table salt, and black pepper is freshly ground.** We don't mind if you use sea salt or kosher salt when a recipe calls for salt "to taste."

>> **All oven temperatures are Fahrenheit.**

And keep the following general tips in mind:

>> Read through each recipe at least once — including any tips at the end — to make sure you have all the necessary ingredients and tools, understand all the steps, and have enough preparation time. You can also consider whether you want to try any variations.

>> Be sure to use the proper size pan when a measurement is given.

>> Preheat ovens and broilers at least 10 minutes before cooking begins and preheat grills for at least 15 minutes. Place all food on the middle rack of the oven unless the recipe says otherwise.

🍅 If you're looking for vegetarian recipes, you can find them in the Recipes in This Chapter list, located at the beginning of every chapter. Vegetarian recipes are marked by the tomato bullet shown here.

Foolish Assumptions

We wrote this cookbook with some thoughts about you in mind. Here's what we assume about you, our reader:

» You love the *idea* of cooking. You're a crackerjack at boiling water. But you just aren't quite sure how to actually organize a meal, make lots of things at once, or combine foods or flavors in ways that make your family members sigh with satisfaction after they put down their forks.

» You've cooked before. Sometimes it was pretty darn good. Sometimes you were glad you didn't have company. Sometimes the fire department had to be called. But really, sometimes it *was* pretty darn good! You're almost positive you have potential.

» You sometimes daydream about going to cooking school or impressing people with the way you chop garlic with your very expensive chef's knife. But you don't yet own a very expensive chef's knife.

» You have basic kitchen equipment on hand, including pots and pans and measuring cups, but you aren't sure whether you have all the right things you need for efficient cooking, and you probably don't know what all those different pots and pans are called.

» You bought this cookbook for yourself so you can finally gain the skills you need to earn the title of "really great cook." Or somebody gave you this cookbook as a gift, and you assume that it was a hint somehow related to that interesting casserole-type thing you attempted last week.

Icons Used in This Book

Icons are those nifty little pictures in the margin of this book. They each grab your attention for a different reason, and we explain those reasons here.

TIP

When there's an easier way to do something, a step you can take to save money, or a shortcut you can take to get yourself to the dinner table faster, we let you know by marking the tip with this icon.

WARNING

The kitchen can be a dangerous place. This icon, like a flashing yellow light, steers you clear of potentially dangerous mishaps.

REMEMBER

We hope that you remember every valuable piece of information in this book, but if your brain can hold only so much, make sure you hang on to the tidbits marked by this icon.

**RECIPE
ALERT**

When we describe cooking techniques, we often refer to recipes later in the chapter that put them to the test. This chef's hat lets you know that a related recipe awaits!

Beyond the Book

In addition to the material in the print or e-book you're reading right now, this product also comes with some access-anywhere goodies on the web. When you want some quick pointers about cooking, check out the free Cheat Sheet at www. dummies.com/cheatsheet/cookingbasics. There you'll find a list of tips for reading recipes; suggestions for cutting fat, calories, and carbs when cooking; tips for saving time while cooking; and a list of staples for your pantry, refrigerator, and freezer, which you can access on your smartphone while you're grocery shopping.

You can find additional recipes and cooking information in articles that supplement this book. Head to www.dummies.com/extras/cookingbasics for recipes for Southwestern Chili and Steak au Poivre, pointers on planning dinner menus, and tips about putting out and preventing kitchen fires.

Where to Go from Here

You can start enjoying *Cooking Basics For Dummies,* 5th Edition, with any chapter you like. Even if you know your way around a kitchen pretty well, we recommend that you start by reading Chapter 2, just to be sure you have all the equipment to cook the recipes in this book, and Chapter 3, which talks about all the basic ingredients every well-stocked kitchen pantry, freezer, and refrigerator should contain.

If you're in the process of buying a house, remodeling a kitchen, or just dreaming about your perfect kitchen, check out Chapter 1, where you can read all about kitchen design. Wary about safety? Check out the end of Chapter 1. Or maybe you just want to start cooking. In that case, check out any of the other chapters in this book. Some are arranged around techniques; others are arranged around menus for parties, for economy, or for times when you need to prepare a meal on short notice. But all these chapters are chock-full of delicious recipes with simple instructions.

One place to check out that *isn't* in this book is www.dummies.com/go/cooking. The site features lots of cooking-related videos, many of them that are directly connected with what we discuss in this book. So if you're reading our instructions for how to carve poultry or how to mince garlic, check out the website for videos that bring the steps to life.

We know you'll enjoy cooking with us. Cooking doesn't have to be complicated, as long as you know the basics. So come on in to the kitchen, grab a pot (we tell you which one), and get cooking.

1

Getting Started with Cooking

Figure out what's what in your kitchen, and get tips on staying safe in all sorts of kitchen situations.

Know what devices and implements you need when you're just starting out as a cook.

Stock your pantry, refrigerator, and freezer with ingredients that you'll be glad to have on hand.

Chapter **1**

Cooking with Confidence

RECIPE IN THIS CHAPTER

🍳 **Scrambled Eggs**

Cooking is fun and interesting and can be relaxing, exciting, and even therapeutic. Cooking is a life skill, but it can also be a hobby and a passion. When you cook at home, you can eat for less money than you'd spend ordering take-out or dining in a restaurant every night, and *you* control the ingredients, flavors, and health profile of your food so you know exactly what you're eating.

Cooking gives you options, allowing you to adapt your meals to suit your own nutritional and taste preferences. When you cook, you can always get exactly the food you want. Plus, cooking the food you eat makes you more aware of your food, your health, and your environment.

Whether you have a cramped apartment kitchen with counter space the size of a cereal box or a sprawling country kitchen with a commercial stove and a work island, this chapter helps you set up an efficient and comfortable environment. Knowing how to use what you have efficiently is even more important than square footage. You'd be surprised to see how small some restaurant kitchens are; they work, however, because everything is in its place and is easily accessible.

In this chapter, we give you a broad overview of what you need to know to be an effective cook. We talk about how to set up your cooking space and introduce you to the major appliances of a kitchen. Then we discuss kitchen safety and help you get started with a nice, easy, practical recipe.

Creating a Cook-Friendly Kitchen

You don't need a fabulous kitchen to prepare fabulous food, but a well-designed workspace sure makes cooking easier and more pleasurable. Chances are, you aren't in the process of remodeling your kitchen, and you have to make do with the basic kitchen design you have. However, if you are at liberty to shift some things around or you're designing your cooking space, consider the concept of *access.* If you want to spend the day running, join a health club. If you want to enjoy an efficient and pleasurable cooking experience, consider where your main appliances are located and where you store the equipment and ingredients you use the most. Do you have to walk 10 feet from the stove to get the salt? That's not efficient. Although nothing is wrong with a large, eat-in kitchen, the design of the cooking area in particular should be practical.

REMEMBER

You should be able to move from your working counter space to the stove/oven, refrigerator, and sink in a smooth, unobstructed fashion. This working space actually has a name: the *kitchen triangle* (see Figure 1-1). It applies whether you have a long narrow kitchen, a U-shaped kitchen, or an L-shaped kitchen. Consider the positioning of these three major appliances and jettison any obstacles — if a table, plant, or small child is blocking the way, move it. Even if you can't redesign your kitchen space or move your refrigerator to another wall, you can arrange what you need in a way that works for you. Here's how to do that.

FIGURE 1-1:
One example of an efficient kitchen triangle.

Illustration by Elizabeth Kurtzman

Declutter your countertops

You can't chop vegetables, slice meat, or whip up a cake batter if you can't even fit a cutting board or a mixing bowl on your counter, so take a good look at your countertops. What's on them? Coffeemakers, blenders, food processors, racks of spice jars or canisters of flour and sugar, stacks of bills, permission slips, and grade school art projects? Is your countertop doubling as a magazine rack, plant holder, or wine rack? Consider this: Your kitchen counters aren't meant to be storage units. They are meant to be *food preparation areas.* A clean, clear counter space can inspire the creation of a great meal. A cluttered one is more likely to inspire a call to the pizza delivery guy. If your kitchen counter is cluttered with paraphernalia beyond usefulness, that's a problem you can fix.

The ultimate test for whether something should be allowed valuable countertop real estate is how often you use it. If you use an appliance or food ingredient (like coffee or flour) *almost every day,* then go ahead and give it hallowed ground. Otherwise, stow it. Be ruthless. Put away the mixer, the food processor, the bread machine, and the rice cooker. Away with the herb and spice rack, the bottles of nut oil and fancy vinegar. Find a better spot for the mail and the bills. As you rid your counters of this clutter, you also get rid of your excuses for not having the space to cook dinner.

WARNING

In addition to keeping your countertops clutter free, take steps to care for them. Use cutting boards for cutting and trivets for hot pots and pans, and wipe up spills quickly to prevent stains. The nicer your counters look, the more you'll enjoy being in the kitchen. (Flip to Chapter 22 for more information about countertop care.)

Let there be lighting

Efficient kitchens should be well lit so you can see what you're doing. Poor lighting increases mistakes, especially over the workspaces and stove. Lights under the stovetop hood can really help when stirring sauces or browning meat, and a nice bright oven light makes it much easier to assess the state of doneness of your casserole or cookies. You haven't replaced those burned-out bulbs in years? Time to do it! Get out your screwdriver and remove the panel over the lights. Unscrew the bulbs and take them with you to the store so you're sure to get the right replacement.

Another option is to have special lighting for the cooking area, either inset into overhead cabinets or in the ceiling. If your kitchen is poorly lit over the cooking area, the least expensive solution is a wall-mounted supplementary light — or a hard hat with a built-in flashlight.

Organize your pantry

The pantry is the place where you store your basic cooking staples, as well as other dry goods. (*Dry goods* are foods that aren't refrigerated or frozen, including staples like flour and sugar, and packaged foods like crackers, cookies, pasta, and rice.) If you're lucky enough to have an entire room or closet dedicated to a pantry, keep it well organized so you can see and easily reach the staples you use most, like flour, sugar, and cooking oil. Even if you have only a cabinet or two for your pantry, organization is the key to efficiency. (For tips on what to keep in your pantry, turn to Chapter 3.)

The first thing to consider in organizing your pantry is the kind of closet or cabinet you decide to use and whether the food you store inside of it is easily accessible.

We've seen many ingenious kitchen cabinets on the market, such as those that have extra storage shelves on swing-out doors; Lazy Susan–type cabinets that rotate for full access to round shelves; and cabinets with shelves, drawers, and baskets that roll out on tracks so you can easily reach even those things you store at the back. If your cabinets don't have these convenient features, you can improvise by mounting racks on the inside of the doors or installing those handy roll-out shelves yourself. Look for such kits in hardware or kitchen stores.

A good cabinet or closet system enables you to see exactly what's in your pantry, thus helping to inspire your culinary creativity and allowing you to grab what you need without knocking over vinegar bottles and stacks of spice jars. Store dried beans, pasta, different kinds of rice, flour, sugar, tea, and coffee in large glass or clear plastic jars with lids, or in containers with clear labels — it's practical and looks professional, too.

If you use something all the time, consider taking it out of the pantry and storing it closer to your stove or workstation, in a "satellite" pantry like a cabinet or shelf. You may want to do this with your cooking oils and sprays, your spice rack, or (if you like to bake) your baking supplies, such as baking soda, baking powder, and vanilla.

TIP

Kitchen islands are efficient food preparation stations, and they can also house considerable storage space. Moreover, they can double as a kitchen table or a place to serve party food. If you don't have an island (and you have the space), consider buying a butcher block–style table to act as one — with shelving underneath to store your stuff for easy access.

Introducing Major Appliances: Friends, Not Foes

Major appliances are your allies in good cooking if you work with them, not against them. Until you make friends with your stove, oven, refrigerator, and small appliances (which we discuss in Chapter 2), you'll never really feel at home in the kitchen. To know your appliances is to love them, and knowing each appliance's relative strengths and weaknesses can help you make the most of what they can do for you.

REMEMBER

Most major appliance companies have websites and toll-free customer service numbers with appliance experts on hand to answer questions about using and caring for any major appliance.

Stovetop and oven

Whether you have an old gas stove that looks like it belonged to your grandma or a fancy space-age-looking glass cooktop, your stovetop may be the cooking appliance you use the most. Right under it, or sometimes over it, or possibly off to the side, is your oven, which you'll probably use almost as much for baking, roasting, and warming up leftovers. Your stove and oven are your best friends in the kitchen, and if you're buying new ones, you have all kinds of new technology to choose from. Even if you won't be going appliance shopping any time soon, knowing exactly what kind of stovetop and oven you have and how to use them may help your cooking efforts.

Gas

Most serious cooks prefer gas stoves because the gas flame is ultimately adjustable, allowing you to turn the heat up or down quickly and to make minute variations in the size of the flame. Commercial gas ranges can cut your cooking time by as much as one-fourth, but simple home ranges work just fine for most purposes. New cooks may feel intimidated by gas because they fear the presence of gas in the kitchen, and that cooking flame is *actual fire*. Because gas stoves can produce higher heat than some electric stoves, they take a little more practice to use; it's easier to burn the food when you cook with gas. However, when you know what you're doing, there is no substitute for gas. When you can confidently proclaim, "Oh, I much prefer my gas stove," you know you've reached a whole new level of culinary prowess.

WARNING

Newer gas ranges should not smell of gas from flaming pilot lights. Newer models no longer have standing pilots. They ignite electronically; therefore, gas doesn't flow through the system unless the range is turned on. If you do smell gas, you have a leak in your system. This situation is dangerous — call your gas company immediately. Do *not* use the stove or any other electrical appliances, even your lights, because doing so can spark an explosion. This situation is rare but possible. Older gas ranges smell like gas, but the smell shouldn't be overpowering. Have your gas range serviced periodically to guard against any problems.

Electric heat

After all our fancy-shmancy talk about gas stoves, you may be eyeing your electric range with suspicion: Can it really produce anything worth eating? Of course! If you have an electric range, you can still love your stove and cook anything on it. You just have to realize that the burners will warm up (and cool down) more slowly and you may not be able to get quite the heat intensity you could on gas. But that's no big deal if you're used to cooking on electric.

Electric ranges became all the rage after World War II. They were considered clean, easy to use, and modern. The drawback to electric ranges is their slow response time. Reducing heat from high to low can take a minute; gas can do it in seconds. However, many professional chefs prefer electric ovens, especially for baking, because they're very accurate and consistent. Today's gas and electric ovens generally hold and maintain oven temperature within a variance of about 5 degrees. If you have a choice, gas is slightly preferable for stoves and electric slightly preferable for ovens.

Induction

Some professional chefs prefer *induction* heat, and some even predict it will soon replace all other systems. Whether that is true, induction cooking is pretty cool. Basically, it works on a *magnetic transfer* principle — heat passes via magnetic force from the burner to the pan. If you place a paper towel between the burner and the pan, the towel doesn't get hot. For that matter, neither will your hand — an induction burner turned on high will not burn you. Induction is just as adjustable and quick as gas, if not more so. A 2-quart pot of water comes to a boil in about a minute.

REMEMBER

An induction cooktop uses only selected metal pans to which a magnet adheres, such as stainless steel. Copper and glass cookware, for example, don't work. Induction cooktops run on electricity, so they're a great option when you want precision in your range but don't want to install a gas line. They are expensive, however, and can cost twice as much as an equivalent standard electric or gas cooktop. Even so, plenty of home cooks say they are worth every penny.

Convection ovens

Convection ovens cook food more rapidly and evenly than standard gas or electric ovens due to a small fan in the rear of the oven that circulates air all around the food. This efficient circulation means that your cooking time and/or temperature setting may be reduced. For example, a cake meant to bake for 30 minutes may be done after 20, or you may be able to set that 350-degree oven to 325 degrees. You always adjust recipes according to the manufacturer's instructions for your individual unit (and check for doneness at least 15 minutes earlier than you would when using a standard oven). Some oven manufacturers offer both regular and convection cooking at the flick of a switch. Do you need a convection oven? No. But if you bake often, you may learn to love one.

TIP

If a convection wall oven is over your budget, consider the smaller, less expensive convection toaster oven, especially if you're cooking for one or two. It can toast, bake a cake, broil a burger, and roast a small chicken. And cooking times are shorter than in conventional ovens. Small convection ovens can cost as little as a few hundred dollars, while larger, full-sized convection ovens can range from a couple thousand dollars to $10,000 or more, depending on the model and brand.

Microwave ovens

Microwave cooking is unlike any other kind of conventional cooking. You must follow a different set of cooking rules. Although more than 90 percent of American kitchens have a microwave, most people use the microwave only as a reheating and defrosting device — and maybe to make popcorn. If this is your intention, you don't need an expensive, fancy microwave with a lot of different settings. If you're short on counter or wall space, consider a microwave–convection oven combination that allows you to cook by using either method.

Microwaves can't pass through metal, so you can't cook with traditional metal cookware. You can, however, use flameproof glass, some porcelain and ceramic, paper, and some plastics. (Be sure the plastic container or plate says "microwave safe"; recent research suggests that plastics can leach chemicals into the food and shouldn't be used in the microwave.) Some microwaves permit you to use aluminum foil to cover dishes, as long as the foil doesn't touch the oven walls or the temperature probe. Check your operating manual to see whether your appliance allows using foil in this way.

TIP

A microwave isn't a replacement for conventional cooking of grilled meats, baked breads, cakes and cookies, and other foods that need browning — unless it has a browning unit. Use your microwave for what it does best in combination with other appliances. For example, you can precook chicken in minutes in the microwave and finish it under the broiler or on an outdoor grill. Following are some other microwave tips:

>> Recipes that require a lot of water, such as pasta, don't work as well in a microwave and probably cook in less time on your stovetop, although microwave rice cookers are efficient.

>> Foods must be arranged properly to cook evenly. Face the thickest parts, like broccoli stalks, outward toward the oven walls. Arrange foods of the same size and shape, such as potatoes, in a circle or square or like the spokes of a wheel.

>> Covering dishes eliminates splattering, and it also cuts down on cooking time. Use paper towels or waxed paper. Frequently stirring, turning, and rotating foods ensures an even distribution of heat.

>> As with conventional cooking, cutting foods into smaller pieces shortens cooking time.

>> Before cooking, pierce with a fork any foods that have skins, like potatoes, hot dogs, and sausages. Doing so releases steam that can lead to sudden popping and splattering (or a hotdog with an exploded end like a firecracker).

>> A number of variables, including the type of microwave, can affect a recipe's cooking time, so check for doneness after the minimum cooking time. You can always cook food longer. Also, always observe the recipe's "standing" time, because microwaved food continues to cook after you remove it from the oven.

>> Be sure to use the defrost power setting (30 to 40 percent of full power) when thawing food to ensure slow and even defrosting; otherwise, the outside of the food may start to cook before the inside is thoroughly thawed.

HOW DOES A MICROWAVE COOK?

Every microwave has an energy box called a *magnetron,* which produces microwaves (from electricity). The microwaves pass through materials like glass, paper, china, and plastic to convert to heat when they come in contact with food molecules. The microwaves cause the water molecules in the food to rotate so rapidly that they vibrate, creating friction and heat.

A major misconception is that microwaves cook from the inside out. They do not. Microwaves penetrate primarily the surface and no farther than 2 inches into the food. The heat spreads by conduction to the rest of the food.

Read your microwave manual carefully before using it. One woman we know ruined her microwave oven because she used the cooking-time button as a kitchen timer, not realizing that you should never run an empty microwave — a warning found in just about every manual.

Refrigerator

Refrigerators are the black holes of the kitchen — objects drift in and are never seen again, at least until the next thorough cleaning. At that time, your leftovers may resemble compost. And what's in this little ball of aluminum foil? *Do not open!*

Refrigerators come in many sizes and shapes. A family of four needs a minimum of 16 cubic feet and should probably buy one that's at least 18 cubic feet (unless you have a teenage boy, in which case you need a second refrigerator). If you use the freezer a great deal, having the freezer compartment on the top or to the side is more convenient. If you are more of an "open the fridge and see what looks good in there" type, you may prefer a model with a bottom freezer, maybe even with expansive French doors. Make sure that the doors open in the most convenient way for your kitchen. If the entrance to the kitchen is blocked every time you open the refrigerator door, you're going to get irritated. Also check the door compartments to see whether they can hold a bottle of wine or a jug of milk. Door space should be spacious, not cluttered with little compartments that just eat up space.

TIP

Try not to pack the refrigerator too densely. Cold air needs space to circulate around and cool the food. Store foods in the same spot each time so you don't have to search for that little jar of mustard or jelly every time you open the door. Most refrigerator shelves are adjustable, so play around with the spacing until it works for the items you generally keep on hand. Transparent shelves and bins make it even easier to see where everything is.

The bottom drawers are usually the coldest and should be used for storing meat, poultry, and fish. Fresh vegetables are usually stored in the *crisper* drawer, which is often located just above the meat bin. Salad greens and leafy herbs can be washed, thoroughly dried, and wrapped in paper towels to extend their storage life. Other vegetables, like broccoli and cauliflower, should be washed just before serving. Excess water on any vegetable in storage can hasten its deterioration.

Liberate old food from the refrigerator every two weeks or so, and give the fridge a good soap-and-water bath every few months. An open box of baking soda at the back of a shelf soaks up odors. Remember to replace the baking soda every few months, when you do your major clean-out. Keeping your refrigerator clean, organized, and filled with fresh food you love is one of the most effective and inspiring ways to get excited about cooking.

Freezer

Most of us buy more at the store than we can eat in a week. What you won't eat this week, your freezer can keep for you until later. It can also keep leftovers fresh longer so you can reheat them on days when you want a home-cooked meal but don't have time or energy to make one from scratch. Package your leftovers in individual serving-sized containers or in freezer-friendly baking pans you can slide straight into the oven.

If you're lucky enough to have a stand-alone freezer, you can take advantage of sales on meat, frozen vegetables, and fruits. You can also cook in bulk, freezing leftover soups, stews, sauces, and desserts. You'll always have food handy at the touch of the microwave's defrost button.

TIP

Not everything freezes well (milk, lettuce, and block cheese are poor candidates for the freezer, for example), but many things do, especially if they're properly sealed or wrapped to keep out oxygen. To get the most use of the freezer space you have, stack things neatly and use bins to keep things organized. If you just toss everything in there randomly, you may not find things again until they've been in there for too long and are freezer burned or stale.

Finally, while you want your refrigerator/freezer within easy reach of your workspace, you can store a stand-alone freezer in another room off the kitchen or even in the basement or the garage.

Dishwasher

Because you probably have better things to do with your evening than wash the dishes, you likely want a dishwasher, especially if you cook for more than one or two. Your dishwasher may be built in, or it may be portable. You can even buy tabletop dishwashers for modest dishwashing needs. Dishwashers use a lot of water and electricity, but for people who'd rather load the dishwasher and then relax with their families after a good meal, the expense is probably well worth it.

Most major brand dishwashers get the job done in more or less the same fashion. Some have more controls for cycles, times, and power. Top-line machines use less water and power and, not insignificantly, are quieter.

Today, some models sanitize 99.9 percent of bacteria, which may be desirable if you have infants or are concerned about the cold and flu season. And if you don't like prewashing items before placing them in the dishwasher, ask about models that have a steaming function. Some machines even come with soil sensors, which measure the amount of food particles in the batch and automatically adjust power, temperature, and timing.

Garbage disposal

Garbage disposals are handy for the home cook. These grinders, housed in the underbelly of your sink drain, grind up the food that goes down the drain. If all you eat are frozen dinners and take-out, you probably won't need a disposal very often, but if you're always peeling, chopping, and wiping counters of the residue of cooking a good meal, you'll appreciate the convenience of a garbage disposal. *Note:* This doesn't mean that garbage disposals are the lazy man's trash bin. They're designed for only small scraps of food that can be ground up easily. Never toss in hard root vegetables, tough skinned foods like leeks, mounds of coffee grinds, or socks.

TIP

To keep your garbage disposal smelling good, grind up a few orange or lemon peels every so often. To keep the drain clean, once a month pour ½ cup baking soda down the drain, followed by 1 cup white vinegar. Let it sit, bubbling and foaming for 15 or 20 minutes, and then pour a pot of boiling water down the drain.

Kitchen Safety 101

Cooking is fun, but it also requires certain precautions. You're continually maneuvering around hot, sharp, slippery things, and it's easy to lose concentration.

WARNING

Always pay attention to what you're doing because one slip can cause great pain. (Keep in mind that dull knives can be even more dangerous because they force you to apply too much pressure, and you can lose control of the blade.) For more on kitchen safety and preventing or dealing with kitchen disasters, check out Chapter 22. Here are some basic rules of safety:

>> Store knives in a wooden block or on a magnetic bar mounted out of reach of children, not in a kitchen drawer. For more information about knives and knife safety, see Chapter 4.

>> Never cook in loose-hanging clothes that may catch fire, and keep long hair tied back for the same reason (not to mention keeping hair out of the food!).

>> Never cook while wearing dangling jewelry that can get tangled around pot handles or lost in the garbage disposal.

>> Professional chefs have hands like asbestos from years of grabbing hot pots and pans. You don't. Keep potholders nearby and use them.

>> Turn pot handles away from the front of the stove, where children may grab them and adults can bump into them.

>> Don't let temperature-sensitive foods sit out in your kitchen, especially in warm weather. Raw meat, fish, and certain dairy products can spoil quickly, so

refrigerate or freeze them right away. Put away hot foods within two hours after a meal.

>> Wipe up floor spills immediately so no one slips and falls, and wipe up counter spills to keep counters sanitary (and unstained).

>> Don't try to cook if your mind is elsewhere, because your fingers may wind up elsewhere as well.

>> Separate raw meat, especially poultry, from produce and other items in your refrigerator to avoid cross-contamination of harmful bacteria from one food to another. Never put cooked food or produce on a cutting board where you were just cutting raw meat.

>> Wash your hands before handling food. Hands can be a virtual freight train of bacteria, depending, of course, on what you do during the day. Also wash thoroughly after handling meat or poultry.

>> To avoid panic-stricken searches, always return utensils to the proper place. Always return a knife to its holder when you're finished with it.

>> Clean up as you work. We know people who can make a tuna salad sandwich and leave the kitchen looking as if they just served a lunch to the Dallas Cowboys. Clean and put away knives and other utensils, wipe down counters, and return food to the refrigerator between steps in a recipe — doing so keeps you thinking clearly and keeps your kitchen neat and organized. Plus, cleaning up as you go frees up that spatula or whisk for the next step of the recipe, so you don't have to use a new one and double the dirty dishes.

>> Every kitchen needs a fire extinguisher. It's inexpensive (about $20), easy to use, and mounts on the wall (or can be stowed under the sink). This device may not do much for your cherries jubilee, but it can avert a disaster.

Now Get Crackin'!

If you're eager to jump in and start cooking, try your hand at this quick and easy recipe for scrambled eggs, which you can enjoy for breakfast, lunch, or dinner. Eggs are a healthy and nutritious protein source, and cooking them is easy (see Chapter 11 for more egg recipes). If you know how to cook scrambled eggs, then you *know how to cook.* At least, a little.

TIP

If you want to make excellent scrambled eggs, don't overbeat the eggs before you cook them. Some scrambled egg recipes call for cream, which adds a nice smoothness to the eggs; others call for water, which increases the volume by stimulating the whites to foam. You can use either ingredient, or milk, or nothing but the eggs. Try it different ways and see which you prefer. This recipe can be doubled or halved.

Scrambled Eggs

INGREDIENTS

8 eggs

¼ cup light cream, half-and-half, milk (whole or low-fat), or water

2 tablespoons chopped chives (optional)

½ teaspoon salt (optional)

Few dashes black pepper (optional)

2 tablespoons butter

DIRECTIONS

1 Break the eggs into a medium bowl. With a fork or a wire whisk, beat the eggs just until they're blended to incorporate the yolks and whites.

2 Add the cream (or milk or water) and chives, salt, and black pepper (if desired), and beat a few seconds to blend.

3 Heat a 10-inch (preferably nonstick) skillet or omelet pan over medium heat. Add the butter. As it melts, tilt the pan to cover the surface with butter. Pour in the egg mixture.

4 Stir the eggs, pulling them gently across the bottom and sides of the pan with a spatula or wooden spoon as they set. Cook to desired doneness (from creamy to dry). Taste just before serving to determine whether you need more salt and/or black pepper.

PER SERVING: *Calories 228 (From Fat 167); Fat 19g (Saturated 8g); Cholesterol 450mg; Sodium 133mg; Carbohydrate 2g (Dietary Fiber 0g); Protein 13g.*

VARY IT! For a lower-fat option, eliminate the butter and spray the pan with cooking spray. You can dress up this basic scrambled eggs recipe by adding to the liquid egg mixture 2 tablespoons of chopped fresh herbs, like parsley or basil, a dash of Tabasco sauce, or a sprinkling of shredded cheese (¼ to ½ cup).

IN THIS CHAPTER

» Gathering the cookware you really need

» Uncovering pots and pans

» Getting the bakeware basics

» Finding out how small appliances can be a big help

» Discovering other kitchen gadgets

Chapter **2**

Investing in the Essential Tools

O wning kitchen equipment is like having a car. When you first get your driver's license, a dented 10-year-old Honda Civic is nirvana. But as you become a more experienced driver, you start dreaming of something better, maybe a Lexus. When you enter the wonderful world of cooking, you can do fine with just a few basic tools — the ride may not be as luxurious, but you'll get to the prom on time. You can always upgrade later.

This chapter is all about the kitchen equipment you really need and how to use it correctly. Learning how to use kitchen equipment properly is time well spent.

If you're just getting started or are on a tight budget, we suggest some essential tools. As you become more proficient, you may want to expand your repertoire — and, for that reason, we let you know about more luxurious equipment, too.

Note that the one type of equipment we don't cover in detail here is knives. That's because they're so important that we gave them their own chapter: Chapter 4.

Collecting Your Cookware Basics

Here is our short list of bare-bones-all-I-can-spend-now kitchen equipment. (You can find more detailed descriptions of some of these items later in this chapter.) See Chapter 1 for information on appliances. This is our list of pots, pans, and other tools no home cook should be without:

» **10-inch chef's knife:** You can perform more than 80 percent of all cutting and slicing chores with this knife.

» **9- to 12-inch serrated bread knife:** Invaluable for cutting slices of fresh bread without squishing the loaf and also for slicing other delicate foods like fresh tomatoes.

» **Paring knife:** For peeling, coring, and carving radish roses and miniature replicas of the Eiffel Tower from rutabagas. (Or just for peeling and coring.)

» **10-inch nonstick skillet:** Your go-to pan for sautéing or frying just about anything.

» **3-quart saucepan:** For cooking vegetables, rice, soups, sauces, and small quantities of pasta.

» **10-quart stockpot with lid:** For making stocks or large quantities of soup, pasta, and vegetables. You'll be surprised by how often you use this pot.

» **Heavy-duty roasting pan:** For cooking everything from beef brisket to your Thanksgiving turkey. Roasting pans have high sides to keep in all those juices you can use to make gravy.

» **Liquid and dry measuring cups and measuring spoons:** So you don't botch recipes by using too much or too little of something.

» **Strainer:** Essential for straining sauces and soups, rinsing pasta, or cleaning and draining lettuce and fruit.

» **Meat thermometer:** Why guess? We talk about a couple different kinds in the "Graters and Mashers and Peelers, Oh My!" section, later in this chapter.

» **Vegetable peeler, heatproof rubber spatula, and a few wooden spoons:** Don't go off the deep end buying little kitchen gizmos; these tools are all you need to get started.

» **Gravy separator:** Pours gravy and other liquids while solid fats remain on top.

Picking Pots and Pans

Have you ever wondered what the difference is between a pot and a pan? If it has two opposite-set handles and a lid, it's classified as a *pot. Pans* have one long handle and come with or without lids. This section gives a rundown of important pots and pans and how to evaluate them, including the must-haves listed in the previous section and lots of other types of fancy pots and pans you don't need but may decide to acquire anyway.

Doing some comparison shopping

Pots and pans come in all kinds of materials, from aluminum with a nonstick coating to heavy-duty stainless steel to expensive copper to muscle-building cast iron coated with enamel. The more you cook, the more uses you'll find for different kinds of pots and pans, and the more you'll develop your own tastes and preferences for different types of pots and pans and different materials.

Here are some things to keep in mind when buying cookware:

>> **Consider going the nonstick route.** Nonstick coatings are the best aid to novice cooks since grocery stores started selling spaghetti sauce in jars. If you do a lot of fat-free and low-fat cooking, this is the way to go. Nonstick pans don't brown foods as well as regular pans do, but they're easier to clean, and the convenience may be worth it.

In recent years, nonstick pans have improved tremendously. A few new varieties even work with metal utensils and have lifetime guarantees. Be careful not to scour nonstick pots and pans because the surface can scratch and eventually lose their nonstick quality. Use plastic or nylon spatulas and whisks.

Nonstick aluminum is light, durable, and a great conductor of heat. Look in restaurant supply stores where you can buy a nonstick 10-inch sauté pan for as little as $20. It won't last as long as its pricier cousins (after two or three years of heavy use, the nonstick coating may wear thin), but the price makes it easy to replace.

If you decide to invest more money in longer-lasting pieces, consider your choice of materials. Copper (lined with stainless steel or tin) provides the best heat control of all metals. That control is the secret of well-textured sauces. Stainless steel with copper or aluminum sandwiched in the base works very well, too, and is less expensive than the all-copper variety.

>> **Think twice about purchasing whole sets, even if they're on sale, unless you can use every piece.** Sets are limited to one type of material and one style, whereas you may be better off with various styles and materials — for example, a nonstick skillet, a cast-iron stockpot, and a stainless steel saucepan.

>> **Grasp the handle of the pan in the store.** It should sit comfortably in your hand. Ask yourself whether having a heat-resistant handle is important or whether you'll always remember to grab the handle with a potholder. Also consider whether the handle is ovenproof. Some recipes, such as frittatas, require both stove time and oven time. Look for a pan that can do it all.

>> **Don't assume that the higher the price tag, the better the choice for you.** Want to know a secret? Restaurant cooks don't always use expensive equipment. They do, however, insist on quality. No loose handles or spatulas that bend and break! You want a strong pot or pan with a comfortable handle, a thick base, and if nonstick, a durable coating with a guarantee. Restaurant supply stores can be your best source for affordable, high-quality cookware. As you get more experienced, you can spend more based on the way you like to cook. For example, you may try stainless steel pots and pans with a copper core for superior heat distribution, which can lead to a better texture in fancy sauces. For now, though, just go for quality and the basics as you build your skills.

Buying the essentials

The following list of different kinds of pots and pans isn't exhaustive, but it will get you started. These are the pots and pans we think you'll use the most.

Skillets and sauté pans

You'll probably use this skillet all the time, so get a good, heavy-duty one. (See the preceding section for tips on what to buy.) You may wonder, as you browse through your options, why some skillets have rounded, curved sides and some have straight sides. To be more specific, a *sauté pan* has straight sides, while a *frying pan* or *skillet* has rounded sides. You may prefer one or the other. The rounded sides facilitate fast cooking and flipping food around (like when those fancy chefs flip the food into the air by tapping the handle). The curved sides help you turn the food. The straight sides of a sauté pan are better for enclosing liquids like hot oil and broth so they won't slosh over the sides, and they're good for braising and stewing. Sauté pans are also more likely to come with lids.

Your skillet or sauté pan (see Figure 2-1) should be at least 10 or 12 inches in diameter and 2 inches deep, which is ideal for sautéing, braising, frying, and making quick sauces.

FIGURE 2-1:
A nonstick skillet
or sauté pan
helps you cook
with very little fat.

Illustration by Elizabeth Kurtzman

Cast-iron skillet

The cast-iron skillet, shown in Figure 2-2, has been a standard in American and European kitchens for hundreds of years and still outperforms contemporary cookware in some respects (for example, browning, blackening, and searing). Better yet, a cast-iron skillet is one of the most inexpensive pans you can find, and it will outlast most other skillets as well. Tag sales and antique shops are loaded with them.

FIGURE 2-2:
You use a
cast-iron skillet
for browning,
searing, and
more.

Illustration by Elizabeth Kurtzman

TIP

Before using a cast-iron skillet for the first time, season it by wiping it with vegetable oil and then heating it on the range on a medium setting for about 2 minutes. In addition, you must thoroughly wipe the skillet dry after washing it to prevent rust. Clean the skillet gently with water and a plastic scrubber. Never scour with metal pads, and never put soap into a cast-iron skillet because it can penetrate the coating and affect the flavor of the food you cook in it later. Look for a skillet with a spout for pouring off fat, if you think you'll use it for frying. Before storing, wipe the skillet with a few drops of vegetable oil to keep the surface seasoned and to help develop that characteristic nonstick coating of well-used cast iron. For recipes and more details on choosing and caring for cast-iron cookware, check out *Cast-Iron Cooking For Dummies,* by Tracy Barr (Wiley).

Saucepans

A saucepan can be stainless steel with a copper or aluminum core or a combination of metals. It's an all-around pan used for cooking vegetables, soups, rice, and sauces for pasta and other dishes (see Figure 2-3). You'll want to own two or maybe three saucepans in different sizes. A 1- to 1½-quart saucepan is perfect for melting small quantities of butter or chocolate or for warming milk. A medium 2- to 3-quart saucepan is essential for making sauces. And saucepans that are 4 quarts or larger are suitable for making soups, steaming vegetables, or boiling a moderate amount of pasta or rice.

FIGURE 2-3:
You use a saucepan to boil foods and make sauces.

Illustration by Elizabeth Kurtzman

Roasting pans

A well-equipped kitchen should have one oval roasting pan, about 12 inches long, and a large rectangular one, about 14 x 11 inches. An oval roasting pan is suitable for poultry and small roasts; a 14-inch rectangular one can handle two chickens, a large roast, or a load of vegetables from the farmers' market. The oval one should be enameled cast iron so it can double as a gratin pan (which we describe later in this section); the rectangular pan can be heavy-gauge aluminum or stainless steel. If you can afford only one roasting pan right now, the covered oval pan is probably the most versatile.

9-x-13-inch baking dish or casserole with lid

Another classic you want to own is the versatile 9-x-13-inch baking dish or covered casserole. Whether made of aluminum, glass, or ceramic, it's great for making casseroles; roasting winter vegetables; or baking brownies, other bar cookies, and cakes.

Enameled cast-iron stew pot (Dutch oven)

This attractive, all-around stew pot, also called a *Dutch oven,* is ideal for slow-cooking stews, soups, and all sorts of hearty winter meals (see Figure 2-4).

TIP

You may want to brown or sear meat in a separate pan before adding it to the Dutch oven because enamel doesn't brown food as well as cast iron or plain stainless steel. A 4-quart version made by Le Creuset and a similar one from Copco are excellent.

FIGURE 2-4:
Use a stew pot, or
Dutch oven, for
cooking stews
and soups.

enameled cast-iron
stew pot

Illustration by Elizabeth Kurtzman

Stockpot

A stockpot is indispensable in any kitchen (see Figure 2-5). It can serve many functions: soup making, braising, steaming, and poaching, to name a few. Look for a tall, narrow, 10- to 14-quart heavy-gauge pot with a tight-fitting lid that can hold a steamer basket. (Inexpensive circular steamers open and close like a fan to fit different sizes of pots and pans.) Heavy aluminum is fine for a stockpot; stainless steel costs twice as much.

stockpot

FIGURE 2-5:
You make soups
and much more
in a stockpot.

Illustration by Elizabeth Kurtzman

Getting fancy

If you really want to go to town with this pots-and-pans thing, you could probably buy a hundred different ones, each with its own specialized function. But is your kitchen really that big? You can do just about any cooking chore with the pots and pans we've listed so far. However, if you want to take it to the next level, you may consider acquiring some of these additional handy pans. They aren't essential, but they are pretty cool — and some of them even give you the opportunity to spout French to your guests. Who's not impressed by that?

Rondeau (shallow, straight-sided pot)

A rondeau (pronounced ron-*doe*) is great to have on hand when you entertain — and of course you will! A straight-sided pot with two handles and a lid, as shown in Figure 2-6, a 12-inch rondeau (the size we recommend) can hold enough food to serve eight people or more. If you just got a raise (a whopper, that is), consider heavy-gauge copper. It's so beautiful you may want to set it out on the front lawn when guests are coming for dinner.

FIGURE 2-6:
A rondeau can go from oven to table.

Illustration by Elizabeth Kurtzman

A rondeau has many uses, among them braising, stewing, and browning large quantities of meat, poultry, or fish. Look for brands like All-Clad, Calphalon, Cuisinart, Magnalite, Paderno, and Sitram.

Sauteuse evasée (slope-sided saucepan)

This Gallic mouthful refers to a little pan that is the workhorse of the French kitchen. If you ever splurge on a piece of copper cookware, we recommend a sauteuse evasée (pronounced saw-*tooz* eh-va-*say*), which is 8 to 9 inches in diameter with a volume of about 3 quarts (see Figure 2-7). A sauteuse evasée may be referred to as simply a saucepan, which is its major role. Its sloped sides (*evasée* refers to the sloped sides) make for easy whisking.

FIGURE 2-7:
You use a sauteuse evasée mainly as a saucepan.

Illustration by Elizabeth Kurtzman

Wok or stir-fry pan

A wok is a large, bowl-shaped pan with a rounded bottom that sits inside a disk that fits over your heat source. Woks work best over a gas flame, but you can still use them if you have an electric stove. In a wok, the very bottom gets super hot, while the sides are cooler, so woks cook meat and vegetables very quickly, leaving vegetables bright and crispy and meats crisp on the outside and tender on the inside. You can cook meat and vegetables in a stir-fry–like technique by using a sauté pan, but for authentically cooked Chinese food, use a wok (or go to a Chinese restaurant).

Pasta pot

A large, 8-quart stainless steel pot fitted with a lid is the perfect size for cooking ½ to 2 pounds of pasta (or you can use your stockpot instead).

Pancake griddle

This flat, nonstick griddle is well suited for pancakes, grilled cheese sandwiches, bacon, and the like. Of course, you can always use the sauté pan for these chores.

Omelet pan or skillet

An 8- or 10-inch omelet pan, like the one shown in Figure 2-8, is handy to have around if you love your eggs. It's also handy for sautéing potatoes and other vegetables (see Chapter 6 for more information about sautéing), but you can do any of these tasks in your go-to skillet, too.

FIGURE 2-8:
Omelet pans are great for more than just omelets.

Illustration by Elizabeth Kurtzman

Gratin pan

Novice cooks tend to make many one-pot dishes. To give these entrées a delicious finishing touch, often by broiling to crisp the top, you should have a gratin dish, shown in Figure 2-9. Unlike Dutch ovens, gratin dishes are shallow, measure from 10 inches long and up, and don't have a lid. A 12-inch dish can feed six or more people. These pans are ideal for macaroni and cheese, turkey casserole, gratin of potatoes, and many other simple dishes. Some are attractive enough to go from oven to table.

FIGURE 2-9:
A gratin pan is handy for finishing one-pot dishes.

Illustration by Elizabeth Kurtzman

Selecting Tools for Mixing and Baking

Baking requires a wide assortment of pots, pans, bowls, spoons, whisks, and spatulas. Although there is some crossover — for instance, you may make lasagna in your 9-x-13-inch baking pan — you'll probably reserve many of your baking pans, mixing bowls, and stirring equipment for baking because baking tools and equipment are designed specifically for that purpose.

Whether you're making bread, birthday cake, muffins, or your mother's killer recipe for homemade brownies, the right baking equipment makes these jobs easier. Here's what you need:

>> **A kitchen scale:** For the home baker, most name-brand digital scales will do the trick. Get one that can hold 3 or 4 cups of flour. It should be sturdy and feature bright, easy-to-read numbers.

>> **Stainless steel, glass, or ceramic mixing bowls:** Mixing bowls are among the most frequently used items in every kitchen. Buy bowls with flat bottoms for good balance in these sizes: 8 quarts, 5 quarts, 3 quarts, and 1½ quarts. Buy them in sets that stack and store easily. You can use these bowls to mix batters for cakes, cookies, or muffins; whip egg whites or whipped cream; let bread dough rise; or even toss salads, whip up sauces and dressings, or store leftovers (if you buy bowls that come with handy plastic lids).

>> **Whisks:** Whisks may be made of stainless steel or heat-proof plastic (for use with nonstick cookware). Two types we recommend:

- **Sauce whisk:** This stiffer type of whisk is about 8 to 10 inches long and perfect for blending sauces, such as béchamel and some cream sauces (see Chapter 14).

- **Balloon whisk:** This larger, rounder whisk is generally 12 to 14 inches long and is better shaped for whipping and incorporating air into egg whites and heavy cream.

>> **Spoons, spatulas, long-handled forks, and tongs:** You'll need a few of these, for example:

- A few **wooden spoons** of various sizes work best for hand-mixing batters, scraping food bits off the bottom of a simmering casserole, or stirring anything cooking in nonstick cookware.

- You may also like to have a solid, one-piece **stainless steel spoon,** about 12 to 15 inches long, for stirring food in larger pots, such as stockpots or pasta pots.

- A **slotted, stainless steel spoon** removes solid foods from hot liquid — use it to scoop pasta or vegetables from boiling water.

- Use a **long-handled, stainless steel ladle** for doling out soups, sauces, stews, or chili, or for putting pancake batter onto a griddle or into a waffle iron.

- A **heatproof rubber spatula** will scrape batter and sauce from bowls or measuring cups.

- A **square-tipped, hard plastic turner** can flip burgers and other foods cooking on nonstick pans.

- **Metal tongs** can turn over tender pieces of meat or fish and can double as serving items at the table (for salad or spaghetti).

» **Baking (or cookie) sheet:** For baking cookies, biscuits, and breads, a heavy-duty steel or nonstick baking sheet is essential. Some are flat, and some have raised or flared edges to keep butter and juice from spilling into your oven.

TIP

Baking sheets come in different sizes. Buy two large ones that fit in your oven, leaving a 2-inch margin on all sides to allow an even flow of heat during baking.

» **Round cake pans:** Standard layer cake recipes call for two 8-x-2-inch or 9-x-2-inch pans. Choose anodized or nonstick aluminum.

» **Square cake pan:** For making brownies or gingerbread, you need an 8- or 9-inch square, 2-quart capacity pan. Anodized aluminum and other nonstick materials make removing the brownies easier.

» **Muffin tins:** For baking muffins and cupcakes, most recipes call for a 12-cup or two 6-cup tins of nonstick or heavy-gauge aluminum (or try stoneware or even nonstick silicone). It's handy to have paper muffin liners on hand, too, for recipes (like chocolate cupcakes) that tend to stick. No oil necessary!

» **Pie pan:** A glass or aluminum pan that is 9 inches in diameter suits most standard recipes.

» **Rolling pin:** You don't need an arsenal of rolling pins like professional pastry chefs have. For home baking, get a two-handled, hardwood or marble rolling pin that is about 15 inches long.

» **Cooling racks:** Cookies and cakes removed from the oven need to cool. Racks allow air to circulate around them. Buy one or two 12- to 14-inch racks.

» **Silicone pastry mats:** These thin mats go on top of your cookie sheet to prevent baked goods from sticking without oil. You can also use them to roll out pie crust to transfer to your pie plate.

- » **Loaf pan:** For baking breads, terrines, and meat loaf, you want a sturdy, 6-cup loaf pan (see Figure 2-10). Look for heavy-duty aluminum or stoneware.

- » **Springform pan:** With its hinge-release and detachable bottom, a springform pan easily unmolds cheesecakes, delicate tarts, and cakes with crumb crusts. Get a 9- to 10-inch pan of heavy-gauge aluminum (see Figure 2-11).

- » **Flour sifter:** Not all baking recipes call for sifted flour, but when they do, you need a sifter to aerate the flour and eliminate lumps. A 3-cup sifter is handy, or just use a fine-mesh strainer (see Figure 2-12).

- » **Pastry brush:** To apply glazes and coatings to breads and cakes, use an all-purpose, 1½-inch pastry brush with natural bristles. Pastry brushes are also essential for basting food with pan drippings or sauces. Buy several brushes at a time because they wear out quickly. Clean the brushes with mild dish soap, rinsing thoroughly.

- » **Metal or plastic dry measuring cups:** To follow precise recipes, you need a set of dry measuring cups — ¼ cup, ⅓ cup, ½ cup, and 1 cup.

- » **Glass or plastic liquid measuring cup:** Get one with a 1-cup and one with a 2-cup capacity, each with a spout for pouring liquids. Four-cup and 8-cup liquid measuring cups come in handy, too.

- » **Metal or plastic measuring spoons:** These items are essential for baking. Make sure the set you purchase comes with ¼ teaspoon, ½ teaspoon, 1 teaspoon, and 1 tablespoon capacities.

FIGURE 2-10:
You can bake all sorts of foods in a loaf pan.

Illustration by Elizabeth Kurtzman

FIGURE 2-11:
Use a springform pan to make delicious desserts.

Illustration by Elizabeth Kurtzman

How to Sift Flour If You Don't Have a Sifter

1. Pour flour into a strainer.

2. Use your hand to lightly tap the strainer

— OR —
tap the strainer on the inside of the bowl.

FIGURE 2-12: You can sift flour by using a strainer.

Illustration by Elizabeth Kurtzman

Considering Small Appliances

TIP

You don't need to own every small appliance on the market, but some are essential and others can be useful and time-saving. Here is your guide to the basic small appliances.

» **Toasters and toaster ovens:** Everybody needs either a toaster or toaster oven; you probably don't need both. A toaster oven is more versatile but takes up more counter space. If you use your toaster for, well, toast (or bagels, English muffins, or toaster pastries), just pick one that matches your kitchen décor. If you also want to be able to broil little meals for yourself, the toaster oven is nifty.

» **Mixers, beaters, and blenders:** Mixers, beaters, and blenders are necessary for the home cook. You'll use these all the time, to mix up cake and cookie batters, blend homemade smoothies or milkshakes, or whip up a fluffy meringue. Here are your choices:

- **Stand-alone mixers:** Strong and durable, these workhorses come with a deep mixing bowl and attachments for whisking, beating, and bread making. Use the beater for batters, the whisk for egg whites and whipped cream, and the dough hook to knead bread dough while you kick back and read a magazine.

- **Beaters, or hand mixers:** These are great for mixing batters, beating egg whites, and making whipped cream. Most hand mixers aren't sturdy enough to handle bread dough or thick cookie dough.

- **Blender:** The blender is definitely a must-have. Even if you don't enjoy protein shakes for breakfast or daiquiris on the weekends, you'll certainly use your blender for many kitchen chores, from chopping a cup of walnuts to making homemade salsa. Blenders and food processors can do many of the same chores, but for beverages and really smooth purées, you can't beat a blender. Go for the high-quality, heavy-duty blender because it will last for years. A cheap plastic blender can burn out in a few months.

- **Immersion blender:** This appliance, a cross between a hand mixer and a blender, is very popular in professional kitchens. You immerse it in a saucepan of soup or anything else you want to purée in the pan without having to transfer it to a blender.

>> **Slow cookers:** Slow cookers (or, as people often refer to the brand-name, Crock-Pot) consist of stoneware crocks that sit in heated metal containers. They cook your chicken, roast, rice, veggies, soup, chili, beans, and so on for a long time at a low temperature. Incredibly handy for the time-pressed cook, slow cookers allow you to pop the food in before work in the morning and come home eight to ten hours later to a piping hot meal. Turn to Chapter 16 for more about how to use the slow cooker.

>> **Pressure cookers:** For many years, pressure cookers were considered about as fashionable as dickies, but now they're making a comeback. For one, these culinary speedsters appeal to family cooks on the run and can handle large cuts of meat, vegetables, and even whole chickens. They work by trapping and pressurizing steam in a tight-lidded container with a release vent, creating a super-hot environment that cooks food with moisture rather than dry heat, as in an oven. The result is similar to that of braising, which can take hours.

>> You can cook a 3- to 4-pound pork or lamb shoulder, for example, in 40 to 60 minutes. A whole chicken is ready in about 20 minutes. Pressure cookers range from $25 to more than $200, depending on size and composition — stainless steel is more expensive than aluminum, although both do the same thing.

>> **Food processor:** A food processor (see Figure 2-13) is a versatile kitchen machine that used to be a luxury but has become a necessity for anybody who cooks a lot. Food processors have steel blades that can whip up pie crust dough in seconds, not to mention sauces, soups, and finely chopped nuts, herbs, or vegetables. Other attachments on the same machine can grate cheese or carrots; slice tomatoes; and chop celery, onions, garlic, or just about anything else. Although your blender can do some of these things, it isn't as versatile. We recommend owning both so you can make great smoothies *and* flaky pie crusts.

FIGURE 2-13:
Food processors can do a wide variety of tasks.

food processor

Illustration by Elizabeth Kurtzman

VACUUM PACKAGING MACHINES

Vacuum packaging is the process of removing oxygen from an impermeable sealed bag, usually plastic. Vacuum packaging preserves food three to five times longer than refrigeration. Vacuum packaging doesn't kill all harmful bacteria — it just slows its rate of growth — so follow conventional safety measures and cook thoroughly. Removing air also prevents freezer burn. Dry, solid foods, such as brown sugar, won't become hard; ingredients high in fats and oils don't turn rancid.

Vacuum packing is particularly useful for large families that hurdle through prodigious amounts of food and generate lots of leftovers. And think how handy it would be for those Costco runs when you drop in for six food items and depart with 60 pounds.

Good vacuum sealing machines begin at around $50. A cheaper option is a hand-held device that sucks air out of storage bags, but for the marginal savings, you're better off with the automatic unit.

Graters and Mashers and Peelers, Oh My!

Just when you thought you had everything you need, we're giving you more! These miscellaneous tools can be useful for all kinds of reasons.

» **Bulb baster:** Using this tool is the most convenient way to coat a roast or chicken with pan juices. A large spoon also works as a basting tool, but a bulb baster is quicker and safer for removing hot grease from the bottom of a roasting pan.

» **Colander:** Buy one made of stainless steel or plastic for draining pasta and rinsing salad greens, vegetables, and berries.

» **Cutting boards:** Use cutting boards to save your counters from sharp knives and hot pots and pans. Plastic or composite boards are easier to clean than wooden ones and can be washed in the dishwasher. Chefs clean their wooden boards with a solution of water and bleach or rub them with lemon juice. Excessive soaking or placing wooden boards in the dishwasher causes them to splinter, warp, and crack.

>> **Kitchen timer:** Don't stand in front of the oven staring at the clock. Set a timer and go watch something on HGTV. Many ovens and microwaves have built-in kitchen timers, so you may not even need to buy a separate one.

>> **Meat thermometer:** Most people can't tell that a roast has finished cooking by pressing its surface. You can use two types of meat thermometers to check (see Figure 2-14):

- An *instant-read thermometer,* our favorite, has a thin rod that lets you pierce into the roast periodically to test for doneness.

- An *ovenproof thermometer* remains inside the meat or poultry from beginning to end of cooking.

Meat thermometers, like the bathroom scale that you tamper with to make you appear slimmer than you are, aren't perfect. You can check their accuracy by calibrating them, which is easy (although you may need small pliers). Bring water to a boil and submerge the stem. It should read 212 degrees. If it doesn't, adjust the small nut or screw where the face meets the probe until it does (some inexpensive thermometers lack this). Then plunge the probe into a bowl of ice water. It should read 32 degrees.

>> **Steamer pots or basket:** The conventional steamer model is a pair of pots, the top one having a perforated bottom and a lid. You can also buy bamboo steamers or little metal steamer baskets that fit inside saucepans.

FIGURE 2-14:
Meat thermometers are essential for determining whether a roast is done.

meat thermometers

Illustration by Elizabeth Kurtzman

Following are more handy utensils to have around your kitchen:

- Citrus juicer
- Lemon and cheese grater
- Mortar and pestle
- Multipurpose kitchen shears
- Oven thermometer
- Pepper mill
- Pie server
- Potato masher
- Salad spinner
- Shrimp deveiner
- Vegetable peeler

Chapter **3**

The Bare Necessities: Stocking Your Pantry and Fridge

You could probably survive for quite some time on a diet of peanut butter, canned tuna, and saltines, but eventually you'd get bored (and you might get scurvy). When you've got interesting ingredients in your pantry, you can always whip up a satisfying meal. Shopping thoughtfully not only cuts down on trips to the market but also saves you money — those 8 p.m. dashes to 7-Eleven for grated cheese add up. When you don't have time to make it to the market, what's for dinner often depends on the ingredients you have in the fridge and cupboard.

Add some vegetables and meat to a can of chicken broth for soup or to pasta or rice for a quick and delicious dinner. Add a salad, some bread, and a glass of good wine, followed by cheese and fruit for dessert, and you'll see how wonderful it is to have your pantry at your service.

Following are some checklists of pantry and fridge basics. Foods such as milk, cheese, eggs, and bread are obvious items to keep stocked. Less common staples such as sun-dried tomatoes, fruit chutney, dry sherry, anchovies, and artichoke hearts are important, too, because they can instantly impart flavor and dress up everyday dishes like tossed salads, omelets, and pasta. You won't need all of these, but if you always have a few exotic ingredients on hand, you'll feel ready for just about anything.

Dry Goods: The Pantry's Backbone

Every pantry should be well stocked with dry goods. You probably consume these foods at least once a week, so buy them in bulk to save on packaging costs. When possible, keep pantry items in airtight containers for freshness and to prevent *weevils* (those little bugs that like to feed on dry goods):

>> **Bread, English muffins, bagels, tortillas, pita breads, and so on:** Keep what you will eat that week in the pantry. If you buy more (when bread is on sale), keep the extra loaves in the freezer and defrost as needed.

>> **Coffee:** Buy ground or whole-bean coffee in small batches for freshness, or keep it in the freezer.

>> **Cold and hot cereals:** Always tightly reseal cereal boxes after opening to keep them fresh.

>> **Dry beans and grains:** See Chapter 17 for more information about the various types of dried beans and Chapter 13 for more information about the various types of grains, such as rice, oats, polenta, barley, and quinoa.

>> **Herbal and regular teas:** After you open a box or other container of tea, store it in a sealed canister or enclose it in an airtight plastic bag.

>> **Macaroni and other pasta:** Spaghetti and a short, stubby pasta like penne should meet most of your needs, but see Chapter 13 for more pasta possibilities.

Stocking Up on Baking Supplies

No one expects you to bake a cake when you get home from work at 7:30 p.m. But if you like to bake — if you even find it relaxing — you'll want the essential supplies when the mood strikes. Keep all baking supplies in a cool, dry place, tightly sealed for freshness. Here's what to keep in stock:

>> **Baking powder:** This leavening agent is used in some cake, cookie, and quick bread recipes to lighten texture and increase volume. Check the sell-by date to ensure that the powder is fresh before buying. (Baking powder eventually expires, losing its effectiveness.)

>> **Baking soda:** It's used as a leavening agent in baked goods and batters that contain an acidic ingredient such as molasses, vinegar, or buttermilk. Baking soda is also good for putting out grease fires and flare-ups in the oven or on the grill and for keeping your refrigerator and freezer deodorized.

>> **Chocolate:** You may want unsweetened and bittersweet squares, semisweet chips, and cocoa powder for chocolate sauces, chocolate chip cookies, and hot chocolate.

TIP

When the temperature climbs above 78 degrees, chocolate begins to melt, causing the cocoa butter to separate and rise to the surface. When this happens, the chocolate takes on a whitish color called *bloom.* Bloomed chocolate is perfectly safe to eat but rather unappealing in appearance, so to prevent bloom, store the chocolate in a cool, dry place (not the refrigerator), tightly wrapped.

>> **Cornmeal:** Choose either yellow or white cornmeal for corn muffins, corn bread, polenta, and for use as a thickener.

>> **Cornstarch:** You'll use it for thickening.

>> **Cream of tartar:** This staple can stabilize egg whites and add tang to sugar cookies.

>> **Flour:** All-purpose flour will do for most jobs, but it's nice to have bread flour and cake or pastry flour on hand, too. You could also try other flours for new flavors, such as oat flour and whole wheat flour. Flour is a must-have for dredging meats, fish, and poultry, and for pancakes, biscuits, and waffles, as well as baking.

TIP

Gluten-free flours, such as brown rice flour, soy flour, and nut flour, don't act exactly like wheat flour because they don't contain protein-rich gluten that gives baked goods their classic texture and ability to rise. When baking with gluten-free flours, be sure to follow a gluten-free recipe.

>> **Gelatin:** Stock unflavored and powdered gelatin for molded salads and cold dessert mousses.

>> **Sugar:** White granulated sugar, light and dark brown sugar, and powdered sugar should fulfill most of your sweetening needs.

>> **Vanilla and almond extracts:** Both are used for flavoring whipped cream, desserts, and baked goods. (You can buy hundreds of extract flavors, so experiment if you feel daring. Some we like: orange, lemon, rum, hazelnut, and maple.) Avoid inferior imitation vanilla extract.

Spicing Up Your Life with Herbs, Spices, and Seasonings

Herbs and spices are essential flavoring ingredients. *Herbs* are produced from the leaves and stems of a variety of plants; *spices* can come from a plant's roots, seeds, bark, buds, or berries. If you stock the following, you will have the basics for most recipes:

>> **Dry herbs:** Basil, bay leaves, dill, marjoram, oregano, parsley, rosemary, sage, tarragon, and thyme

>> **Salt and pepper:** Table salt, kosher salt, sea salt, or other gourmet or flavored salts, as your taste dictates; whole or ground black pepper; whole or ground white pepper; cayenne pepper; and red pepper flakes

>> **Spices:** Allspice, chili powder, cinnamon, whole and ground cloves, ground cumin, curry powder, ginger, dry mustard, nutmeg, and paprika

Working with herbs

While you want to always keep the essential dry herbs on hand, some herbs (such as cilantro) are best purchased fresh, refrigerated, and used within a few days. Others can be purchased in either dry or fresh varieties. Fresh herbs have a brighter, lighter, fresher taste than dried herbs, which have a more intense, concentrated flavor. As a rule, if a recipe calls for one tablespoon of dried herbs you should double the quantity when using fresh.

Table 3-1 can help you decide which herbs go best with which kinds of dishes. (Also see Figure 3-1.) After you become familiar with the properties of these flavor enhancers, you can toss the chart and navigate on your own.

TABLE 3-1   **Some Herbs You Should Know**

Herb	Description
Basil	Essential to Mediterranean cooking, especially Italian and French cuisine. Excellent with tomatoes, eggs, pasta, poultry, fish, and in vinaigrette.
Bay leaf	Add the dried leaves to long-cooking dishes like soups, stews, poaching liquid, marinades, and pot roasts. (Remove the leaf before serving the dish.)
Chervil	Use with fish and shellfish, eggs, chicken, tomatoes, asparagus, summer squash, eggplant, and herb butter.

Herb	Description
Chives	Try them in cream sauces or soups; with chicken, eggs, shellfish, or marinated salads; or sprinkled over cottage cheese.
Cilantro	Dried versions pale in comparison to fresh. Good with Mexican and Asian dishes, especially on rice, fish, and pork or in salsa and guacamole.
Dill	Use seeds in pickling recipes; use leaves on fish and shellfish, chicken, and omelets, and in salad dressing.
Marjoram	Add to almost any vegetable dish.
Mint	The most common varieties are standard peppermint and spearmint. Terrific with fresh fruit, in cold fruit soups and sauces, and in cold drinks like iced tea or mojitos.
Oregano	An essential ingredient in Italian and Greek cooking. A little goes far with poultry, tomato sauce, eggs, and vegetable stew.
Parsley	Better fresh than dried. An all-purpose herb as well as a pretty plate garnish.
Rosemary	Excellent with grilled meat, especially lamb, and in herb bread, or to flavor oils and marinade.
Sage	Try it in poultry stuffing, in pâté, with fish and chicken, and in herb butter.
Savory	Comes in two types: winter and summer. Try it in fresh or dried bean salads, fish and shellfish dishes, omelets, rice dishes, and on tomatoes, potatoes, and artichokes.
Tarragon	This herb turns a Hollandaise sauce into a Béarnaise sauce. Also try it on chicken, pork, lamb, veal, fish, and shellfish, and as flavoring for white vinegar and hot or cold potato dishes.
Thyme	Add to vegetables, meat, poultry, fish, soups, stews, and cream sauces.

TIP

To get the most flavor from dried herbs, crush them between your fingers before adding them to a dish.

Studying spices

Spices, which are almost always sold dried, have been a vital element in international cooking since Byzantine times. Most spices come from the East, where they were introduced to Europe during the Crusades.

Store spices in a cool, dry place and try to use them within six to ten months. Whole spices, such as peppercorns, nutmeg, cinnamon sticks, cumin seeds, and coriander seeds, are more aromatic and flavorful than their pre-ground counterparts, so grind them yourself as needed. A coffee grinder reserved for spices works well for this purpose. Whole spices also can be wrapped and tied in a piece of cheesecloth, added to soup, stew, braises, and marinades, and then removed before serving.

Table 3-2 lists the more common spices.

FIGURE 3-1:
Types of herbs.

Illustration by Elizabeth Kurtzman

TABLE 3-2   A Few Spices You Should Know

Spice	Description
Allspice	Spice berries with tastes of cinnamon, nutmeg, and cloves — hence the name. Excellent in both sweet and savory dishes, from pâtés and meatballs to fruit pie fillings, chutneys, and gingerbread.
Caraway	Common in German cuisine. Essential for rye bread and also in some cheeses.
Cardamom	Excellent in baked goods and pumpkin pie. One of the main ingredients in *garam masala*, an essential spice mixture in Indian cooking.
Cayenne or red pepper	A hot, powdered mixture of several chile peppers. Use sparingly for extra spice in any cooked dish.
Chili powder	A spicy mixture of dried chiles, cumin, oregano, garlic, coriander, and cloves. Use to flavor meat, bean dip, barbecue sauce, and, of course, chili.
Cinnamon	Sweet and aromatic spice from the bark of a tropical tree. Common as a baking spice and in Mexican chocolate, molé sauce, and Grecian cuisine.
Clove	Adds intense spice flavor to sweet or savory dishes — use sparingly!
Coriander	Seeds used for pickling; powder used for curries, sausage, and baked goods.
Cumin	Essential to Middle Eastern, Asian, and southwestern U.S. cuisine.
Curry powder	A blend that can include more than a dozen different herbs and spices. Use to season lamb, chicken, rice, and sautéed vegetables, and in Indian curries.
Ginger	Essential in Asian cooking and in spice cakes and gingerbread. Use ground or grate the fresh root.
Nutmeg	Delicious in white sauces, sweet sauces, and glazes, over eggnog, in fruit and pumpkin pies and spice cakes. Best freshly grated.
Paprika	Varieties range from sweet to hot or smoked. Adds flavor and red color to dip, creamy salad, dressing, stew (like goulash), sautéed meat, chicken, and fish.
Peppercorns	Black pepper is perhaps the world's most popular spice, used to accent nearly every savory dish. Use white pepper to enrich cream sauces and white dishes for an unadulterated white color. Also try other colored peppercorns for a variety of flavor.
Saffron	The world's most expensive spice, made from dried stigmas handpicked from a special variety of purple crocus flowers. Available as powder or whole threads. A little goes a long way. Essential to classic Mediterranean dishes like bouillabaisse and paella. Imparts a rich yellow color to cream sauces and rice dishes.
Turmeric	Yellow-orange powder that is intensely aromatic and has a bitter, pungent flavor; gives American-style mustard its color. Sold as a powder. Essential ingredient in Middle Eastern cuisine.

Peanut Butter and Beyond: Bottled and Canned Goods

With a well-stocked pantry full of useful bottled and canned food, you can jazz up a salad, spice up a soup, or make an entire dinner in a pinch. Stock your larder with these ready-to-heat-or-eat items:

- **Broth:** Chicken, beef, and vegetable broth, stock, or bouillon cubes add flavor and form the base for delicious homemade soup or sauce. Always have at least one can or carton at the ready.

- **Canned beans:** Pinto, white, black, kidney, garbanzo, and baked beans add quick and easy protein to soups, salads, and quick side dishes. Refried beans for tacos, burritos, and nachos come in handy, too.

- **Canned clams and clam juice:** Use them for quick pasta sauce or as a substitute for homemade fish stock.

- **Canned fish:** Tuna, crab, salmon, sardines, anchovies, and kippers make good snacks, quick sandwiches, or fancy salads.

- **Chutney, fruit relish, and cranberry sauce:** Serve with grilled meats and poultry or use as a basting sauce.

- **Condiments:** Ketchup, mustard, mayonnaise, barbeque sauce, and soy sauce are the basics, but there are lots of other possibilities: Tabasco, chipotle sauce, tamari, hoisin sauce, Asian chili sauce, brown mustard, hot mustard, and more.

- **Jam, jelly, or preserves:** Jars of preserved fruit spread make peanut butter and jelly sandwiches possible but can also be used on breakfast breads and in many desserts and sauces.

- **Marinated vegetables:** Artichoke hearts, olives, red peppers, asparagus, pickles, olives, and capers all add jazz to salads and platters of vegetables, or put them on sandwiches or into pasta for a gourmet flair.

- **Nut butters:** Peanut butter is always great to have around, but also try almond, cashew, and sesame butters.

- **Oils:** Extra-virgin olive oil, canola oil, grapeseed oil, and peanut oil work for cooking, frying, and dressing salads. For extra dashes of flavor, try toasted sesame oil, chili oil, walnut oil, or other gourmet oils that look interesting to you.

- **Syrup:** For sweetening desserts and drizzling over pancakes and waffles, keep real maple syrup and honey on hand. Also try brown rice syrup, agave nectar, and fruit-flavored syrups.

MOVING BEYOND THE BASICS

After you're familiar with common ingredients, such as those listed in the "Peanut Butter and Beyond: Bottled and Canned Goods" section earlier in this chapter, you can explore dishes that require more-exotic ingredients. Here are a few more pantry items we suggest you consider. If you can't find some of them locally, you can find them online. (Also see Chapter 18 for tips on stocking an Asian pantry.)

- **Aged Parmesan cheese:** Commonly grated over pasta, this versatile cheese makes a delicious quick appetizer with assorted crackers. It has unlimited uses like grating into soups, tossing into omelets, even sprinkling on roasted vegetables like asparagus and cauliflower. Save the rind to toss into a pot of homemade soup; it adds a nutty and slightly salty creaminess to the broth.

- **Chipotle peppers in adobo sauce:** These preserved jalapeño peppers can be chopped up and used to enhance beef, turkey, or vegetable chilies, stews, and bean soups. Be sure to remove and discard their hot seeds. Transfer to a plastic container after opening and refrigerate or freeze.

- **Dried mushrooms:** Soak these in hot water to reconstitute, and then chop and toss into pan sauces, soups, or stews to add a pleasant woody flavor. Most available are shiitakes, porcini, chanterelles, and morels.

- **Edamame:** Sold frozen in their pods or shelled, these make great snacks when you're sitting in front of the TV watching the game and don't want to overload on chips and sour cream dip. They're also terrific tossed into green salads or tossed with butter served hot as a simple side dish.

- **Fresh chili peppers (jalapeño, habanero, or serrano):** Use these when you want to add a bit of bite to staples like macaroni and cheese, frittatas, dips and marinades, stuffings, and pasta dishes. The heat and flavor vary from one kind of pepper to the next.

- **Herbes de Provence:** Packaged in little earthenware crocks, this fragrant blend of dried Mediterranean herbs adds a sunny, nuanced flavor to all kinds of dishes. Especially good on sautéed seafood or seafood stews.

> **» Tomato paste, sauce, and canned tomatoes:** You'll be glad to have canned Italian plum tomatoes and crushed tomatoes for making pasta sauces when fresh tomatoes are pale and tasteless. Tomato paste and sauce add flavor and texture to your Italian dishes and form the base of a good spaghetti sauce.

- >> **Vinegar:** Apple cider, white, and red wine vinegar are three basics to have on hand, but you can also try Balsamic, champagne, white wine, and other flavored vinegars for making your own salad dressings and marinades.

- >> **Wines:** Keep a dry white and a dry red wine for adding to sauces, stews, and long-simmering casseroles and soups. Dry sherry, Port, and Madeira are nice to have, too.

REMEMBER

Condiments such as relishes, jellies, pickles, mayonnaise, mustard, and salsa keep for months in the refrigerator after you open them. Steak sauce, peanut butter, oil, vinegar, honey, and syrup don't require refrigeration after you open them and can be stored on a shelf or in a cool cabinet for months, away from heat and sunlight. When in doubt, always follow the storage instructions on the product's label.

TIP

Purchase dried herbs and spices in small quantities. After a year or so of storage, their potency diminishes. Keep all dried herbs and spices tightly sealed and away from direct sunlight and heat (don't store them directly over the stove).

Cooling It with Refrigerated and Frozen Staples

Refrigeration extends the life of most fresh foods. Items that you want to keep very cold — milk, juice, stocks, beer, leftovers, and seafood, for example — should be placed in the back. And what about those crisper drawers? When closed, they create higher humidity, which is good for vegetables, especially lettuce and fresh herbs. And those little butter compartments prevent butter from drying out.

TIP

Don't keep dairy and other highly perishables on the fridge door. Every time you open it — this can be 250 times or more a day if you have teenage boys — food warms up a bit. And, of course, don't leave the door open for longer than is absolutely necessary.

Following are a few essential items to stock in the refrigerator or freezer:

- >> **Eggs:** Never be without them, for omelets, breakfast foods, and quick dinners. (See Chapter 11 for handy egg recipes and other egg tips.) Refrigerate eggs in the shipping carton to keep them from picking up odors and flavors from other refrigerated foods, and use them before the expiration or "use by" date stamped on the carton.

>> **Fresh pasta:** Stock various stuffed pastas, such as ravioli, in the freezer for quick dinners. You can wrap fresh pasta in freezer bags and store it for six to eight months. Don't defrost before cooking; simply drop frozen pasta into boiling water and cook until *al dente* (tender but still pleasingly firm to the bite).

>> **Milk:** We make our recipes with whole milk, which has about 3.5 percent butterfat. If you prefer, use 1 percent (low-fat), 2 percent (reduced fat), or skim (nonfat) milk, with the understanding that the recipe may not have as creamy a consistency. If you don't like milk or avoid dairy products, you can substitute soy, rice, coconut, or almond milk for regular milk in most recipes.

>> **Sweet (unsalted) butter:** Use unsalted sweet butter in all recipes so you can control the amount of salt. Butter has a refrigerator shelf life of about 2 to 3 weeks and can be frozen for 8 to 12 months in the original unopened carton or, if opened, in plastic freezer bags.

These items are nice to have, too:

>> **Cottage cheese, ricotta, and cream cheese:** Keep them on hand for adding to dressings and dips, snacking, spreading on bagels or toast, and for cheesecakes. Store in the original, covered container or foil wrapping and consume within 1 to 2 weeks.

>> **Hard and semihard cheeses:** Cheese has enjoyed somewhat of a renaissance in the United States, with a proliferation of artisanal cheese producers and cheese shops offering hundreds of types, so it's easy to become a connoisseur if you so desire (and don't mind asking questions at your local cheese counter). For starters, stock mozzarella, Parmesan, cheddar, and blue cheeses for salads, casseroles, omelets, white sauces, and sandwiches; to grate into pasta; and just to snack on! Then, we strongly suggest expanding your cheese horizons by tasting different cheeses whenever you can to determine what you like.

Wrap all cheese in foil, a resealable plastic bag, or plastic wrap after opening. Trim off any mold that grows on the outside edges of hard cheeses. Depending on its variety, cheese keeps in the refrigerator for several weeks to months.

TIP

Pre-grated Parmesan or Romano cheese quickly loses its potency and absorbs the odors of other refrigerated foods. Instead of buying pre-grated, keep a tightly wrapped wedge in the fridge and grate as needed. Or, if you'll use it all right away, save time with a high-quality Parmesan or Romano that has been freshly grated at the deli.

>> **Heavy cream, light cream, or half-and-half:** They're great for making quick pan sauces for fish, poultry, and pasta. Use within a week of purchase or freeze for longer storage. Heavy cream (not half-and-half or light cream) is used for making whipped cream.

>> **Ice cream or frozen yogurt:** Instant dessert (and great for eating guiltily in bed at midnight)! After you open it, you should eat ice cream and frozen yogurt within 2 weeks. You can freeze unopened containers for up to 2 months.

>> **Plain yogurt:** This is a good ingredient for quick dips and low-fat sauces. It also makes pancake batters lighter. Follow the expiration date on the package.

>> **Sour cream:** You can use standard (18 percent fat), low-fat, and nonfat sour cream interchangeably in recipes. As with all dairy products, heed the expiration date.

Squeezing the Melon: Buying and Storing Fruits and Vegetables

Fruits and vegetables add color, flavor, vitamins, minerals, and fiber to your diet, and the quality of the produce you buy directly impacts the quality of the dishes you prepare. Always seek out the best sources for produce. If you have a local farmers' market featuring seasonal produce, browse the stalls and choose what looks best. You can plan a whole meal — or at least a memorable side dish — around a really ripe carton of tomatoes and a dewy bin of fresh lettuce, or what about those blushing peaches bursting with juice for dessert?

When choosing and storing fruits and vegetables, a few rules apply across the board. Avoid fresh produce with brown spots or wrinkled skin or produce that doesn't look so healthy. Squeeze them to make sure they're not overripe. Here are a few other produce rules to live by:

>> **Apples:** Should be crisp and firm. Refrigerate or store in a cool, dark place. Keep for several weeks. Some varieties keep for several months.

TIP

Apples release a gas that makes other fruits ripen more quickly, so if you don't want your fruit to ripen too fast, keep it away from the apple bowl and don't store it with apples in the refrigerator.

>> **Artichokes and asparagus:** Refrigerate and use within 2 to 3 days of purchase.

>> **Avocados:** These tropical delights should yield just slightly to pressure when ripe. Keep at room temperature until fully ripened. If you won't eat them right away, refrigerate them to keep for several more days.

>> **Bananas:** Eat them before they turn completely brown. You can refrigerate them to slow down their ripening. Their peel continues to darken in the refrigerator, but not their flesh.

>> **Bell peppers:** Store in the refrigerator for up to 2 weeks.

>> **Broccoli and cauliflower:** Refrigerate and consume within a week.

>> **Cabbage:** Keeps for 1 to 2 weeks in the refrigerator.

>> **Carrots:** Best when firm, not rubbery, without a lot of little roots growing all over them. They keep in the refrigerator for several weeks.

>> **Celery:** Fresh celery is crisp and firm. Old celery flops around like a rubber pencil. Keeps for 1 to 2 weeks in the refrigerator.

>> **Cherries and berries:** Keep refrigerated. For best flavor, consume them the same day you purchase them. Cherries and berries get soft and moldy quickly.

>> **Citrus fruits (such as lemons, grapefruits, and oranges):** When refrigerated, citrus fruits (which don't ripen further after they're picked and are relatively long-storage fruits) keep for up to 3 weeks.

>> **Corn:** Refrigerate and use the same day of purchase. After corn is picked, its sugar immediately begins converting to starch, diminishing its sweetness.

>> **Cucumbers and eggplant:** The skin should be firm, shiny, and smooth, without soft brown spots. Keep for up to 1 week in the cold crisper drawer of the refrigerator.

>> **Garlic:** Garlic should feel firm, not soft, and should be without any green sprouts. Once it sprouts, it turns bitter. Keep garlic at room temperature, in a small bowl within reach of your food preparation area, to encourage you to use the fresh stuff. Garlic will last longer in the refrigerator, however, so if you don't use it often, keep it chilled to inhibit sprouting.

>> **Grapes:** Fresh, ripe grapes are full and juicy looking with a powdery bloom on the skin. Keep in the refrigerator for up to a week.

>> **Green beans:** Refrigerate and use within 3 to 4 days of purchase.

>> **Leafy greens (beet tops, collards, kale, mustard greens, and so on):** Very perishable. Refrigerate and consume within 1 to 2 days.

>> **Mushrooms:** Store in a paper bag in the refrigerator. Use within a week.

>> **Onions, potatoes, shallots, and hard-shelled winter squash (like acorn and butternut):** Keep at room temperature for several weeks to a month. Store onions, potatoes, and winter squash in a cool, dry, dark drawer or bin. Onions, shallots, and potatoes should be firm. If they are soft or rubbery, they are past their prime.

- » **Pineapple:** It doesn't ripen after it's picked and is best if eaten within a few days of purchase. Keep at room temperature, away from heat and sun, or refrigerate whole or cut up.

- » **Salad greens:** Rinse thoroughly, trim, and dry completely before storing wrapped in paper towel or in plastic bags in the refrigerator crisper drawer. They keep for 3 to 4 days. (See Chapter 12 for more information.) Do we have to tell you not to buy slimy lettuce?

- » **Spinach:** Trim, rinse, and dry thoroughly before storing in the refrigerator for 2 to 3 days.

- » **Summer squash (zucchini and yellow squash):** Store in the refrigerator for up to a week.

- » **Tomatoes:** Store at room temperature for more flavor. Keep in a cool, dark place or in a paper bag to ripen fully. Once ripe, eat them right away. If you can't, refrigerate them for two or three more days, although this can compromise the texture, making them mealier. Return them to room temperature before eating.

- » **Tropical fruits:** Mangoes, papaya, and kiwi should be firm but yield slightly to pressure and should smell fruity. Store at room temperature for more flavor, but refrigerate when they're ripe and then return to room temperature before eating.

- » **Unripe melons and tree fruits (such as pears, peaches, and nectarines):** Keep at room temperature so they can ripen and grow sweeter. After they're fully ripe, you can store them in the refrigerator for several more days. Melons are ripe when they smell melon-y at the stem end.

Where to purchase produce

The biggest cooking trend of recent years is the locavore movement. This essentially means buying foods that are grown and produced as close to home as possible — preferably within field-goal range of your backyard. Doing so not only supports local agriculture and increases the supply of organic goods, but it also yields more flavorful and healthful nutrition. This isn't to say that everything from a farmers' market or local garden is superior in taste and appearance than the commercial stuff grown hundreds or thousands of miles away. Vegetables are only as good as the soil they're grown in.

Farmers' markets

Farmers' markets have been blossoming like zucchini in August (there are now more than 8,000 nationwide), and their appeals are many, particularly to garden-deprived city dwellers. For one, they support local, small-scale farmers, many of whom grow organically. In addition, the produce (and other foods) is fresher and more wholesome than that grown thousands of miles away by an industrial scale operation that may use lots of pesticides and herbicides. And we can return to eating seasonally, according to the calendar, not a supermarket contract.

For the most part, these colorful markets sell products that have been fed, nurtured, grown, caught, harvested, cooked, baked, brewed, pickled, or canned by the vendors. This doesn't mean that everything is delicious — for example, always sample berries before buying a carton. And you'll hear about all kinds of *heirloom* produce, a term for strains of vegetables that have been passed down over generation for their unique qualities. (Sometimes those ugly, malformed tomatoes taste the best!)

Community supported agriculture (CSA)

Above all an urban phenomenon, a CSA is a group of individuals who form a club of sorts to pay one or more farmers in advance for a season's worth of food. This provides growers with seed money, literally, and a guaranteed market. As the harvest progresses, members receive batches of fresh food, usually on a weekly basis. CSAs may also include herbs, cut flowers, honey, eggs, dairy products, cider, and so on.

WARNING

Unlike shopping at a farmers' market, where you buy only what you need, in a CSA, you could find yourself with an armful of Swiss chard one week, and the following, enough kale to cover a major league infield. Ascertain at the outset what products you'll be receiving and when.

Going organic

The term *organic* is clearly defined by the United States Department of Agriculture (USDA) National Organic Program. It states that organic plant foods are produced without using most conventional pesticides, fertilizers made with synthetic ingredients, bioengineering or ionizing radiation. Organic meat, poultry, eggs, and dairy products come from animals that are given no antibiotics or growth hormones. A government-approved certifier must inspect the farm to ensure that these standards are met. Organic foods in the supermarket carry an official USDA label.

WARNING

Some food companies attach largely meaningless labels that resemble the official seal. And the term *organic* is a little tricky when you're buying fresh produce from farmers' markets. Unlike supermarkets, which must adhere to strict FDA rules, farmers' markets are outdoor markets that are kind of free-wheeling. Anybody can call anything organic. For the most part, growers are honest, although some of them may sneak in a little herbicide or pesticide now and then.

Organic food comes at a cost, usually 10 percent or more above conventionally grown food. You may consider going organic with foods you consume regularly: milk, eggs, poultry, meat, and produce.

Selecting, Buying, and Storing Meat, Poultry, and Fish

Meat, poultry, and fish are highly perishable foods that need to be stored in the coldest part of your refrigerator. Keep them tightly wrapped, preferably in their own drawer, to prevent their juices from dripping onto other foods.

REMEMBER

Always check expiration dates (avoid items that are older than your car's last oil change), and never allow meat, poultry, or fish to thaw at room temperature, where bacteria can have a field day. Always thaw them in the refrigerator, which takes more time (and planning) but is by far the safest method.

Beef

Beef is rated according to the animal's age and the amount of fat (or *marbling*) in the cut (the more marbling, the more moist and tender the meat) as well as its color and texture. *Prime* meat is the highest grade and the most expensive. In general, the most tender and flavorful meat falls under this category. Aging has an effect, too. If possible, buy from butchers who still age their own beef. You pay a little more, but the increased tenderness and superior flavor are worth the price.

Choice is the second tier of meat grading, leaner (and therefore a little tougher) than prime. *Select* meats are best for stewing and braising for long periods, which dissolves the tough connective tissue in these cuts.

The more tender cuts of meat include steaks such as porterhouse, sirloin, shell, New York strip, Delmonico, and filet mignon as well as roasts like rib, rib eye, and tenderloin. Tender meats are usually cooked by the dry heat methods of roasting, broiling, grilling, and sautéing. (See Chapter 8 for roasting, Chapter 9 for broiling and grilling recipes, and Chapter 6 for sautéing recipes.)

Less tender cuts, such as brisket, chuck, shoulder, rump, and bottom round that have more muscle tissue and less fat are usually cooked by braising and stewing. (See Chapter 7 for braising and stewing recipes.) Figure 3-2 illustrates where the various cuts come from.

FIGURE 3-2:
Various cuts
of beef come
from different
parts of a steer.

Illustration by Elizabeth Kurtzman

TIP

When choosing meat, look for cuts that are bright red, never dull or gray. Excess juice in the package may indicate that the meat has been previously frozen and thawed — don't purchase it. Boneless, well-trimmed cuts are slightly more expensive per pound but have more edible meat than untrimmed cuts, so in the long run they generally cost about the same.

Use raw meat within two days or by the "use by" date on the package, or freeze it. To freeze, rewrap in aluminum foil, heavy-duty plastic wrap, or freezer bags, pressing out as much air as possible and dating all packages. Freeze ground meat for a maximum of 3 months; freeze other cuts for up to 6 months. Defrost in the refrigerator or microwave.

Chicken

The tenderness and flavor of fresh poultry vary somewhat from one commercial producer to the next, so you should buy and taste a few different brands to determine which you like. Grade A poultry is the most economical because it has the most meat in proportion to bone. Skin color isn't an indication of quality or fat content. A chicken's skin ranges from white to deep yellow, depending on its diet.

Here are five kinds of chicken to know:

>> **Broiler/fryer:** A 7- to 9-week-old bird weighing between 2 and 4 pounds. Flavorful meat that's best for broiling, frying, sautéing, or roasting. A whole broiler/fryer is always less expensive than a precut one.

>> **Capon:** A 6- to 9-pound castrated male chicken. Excellent as a roasting chicken because of its abundance of fat. Just to be sure, pour off or scoop out

excess melted fat as the chicken roasts — especially if you don't have an exhaust fan — or your kitchen could resemble the Towering Inferno. Not widely available in supermarkets (it usually needs to be special-ordered).

>> **Roaster or pullet:** From 3 to 7 months old and between 3 and 7 pounds. Very meaty, with high fat content under the skin, which makes for excellent roasting.

>> **Rock Cornish game hen:** A smaller breed of chicken weighing 1 to 2 pounds. Meaty, moist, and flavorful for roasting.

>> **Stewing chicken:** From 3 to 7 pounds and at least 1 year old. Needs slow, moist cooking to tenderize. Makes the best soups and stews.

Remove the package of giblets (the neck, heart, gizzard, and liver) in the cavity of a whole bird and then rinse under running cold water and dry before cooking it. Also trim away excess fat. After preparing poultry, wash your hands and work surfaces (counters and cutting boards) with soap and water to prevent cross-contamination from bacteria (see the next section).

TIP

Consume whole or cut-up poultry within 1 to 2 days of purchase. A whole, raw chicken may be wrapped and frozen for up to 12 months; parts can be frozen for up to 9 months. Defrost in the refrigerator, never at room temperature. Be sure to place the thawing package in a pan or on a plate to catch any dripping juices. A 4-pound chicken takes 24 hours to thaw in the refrigerator; cut-up parts between 3 and 6 hours. If you use your microwave to defrost poultry, do so on a very low setting and be sure to cook the poultry immediately after thawing it.

Minimizing the risks of salmonella infection

You've read the scary reports about salmonella outbreaks in restaurants, schools, catering facilities, and on cruise ships. This isn't surprising, because the vast majority of raw poultry (and to a lesser extent raw meat) carries the harmful bacteria. So far, the industry hasn't come up with a way to eradicate it because bacteria can come from the soil on which animals are raised, their feed, fecal material, and the processing system.

Although salmonella is rarely fatal, it can sure spoil your picnic (and the hours after). And it isn't limited to poultry and meat. Some of the largest outbreaks have originated in produce.

Salmonella is killed by heating food to 167 degrees for 10 minutes (or longer at lower temperatures). Fortunately, you can take certain measures at home to minimize the risk. Foremost — and this may come as a surprise — *do not* rinse raw poultry in the sink. Rinsing raw poultry only risks contaminating the sink, faucets, countertops, floor, and clothing. (A safer way would be outside with a garden hose, but it's really not necessary.)

Here are a few other ways you can reduce your chances of getting sick from salmonella:

- >> When purchasing poultry, make sure it's securely packaged with no leaks. At the checkout counter, ask that it be double-wrapped in plastic bags.

- >> When you get home, immediately refrigerate the chicken. Cook it within two days.

- >> *Never* defrost chicken on the counter! The correct way is to thaw it in the refrigerator (a 4-pound chicken takes up to two days; boneless breasts, less than a day) or microwave (if you use the microwave, cook it immediately after thawing).

- >> Don't handle raw chicken with dish towels that may touch other surfaces.

- >> Keep in mind that freezing doesn't kill bacteria — it just makes them shivering mad.

- >> Thoroughly wash cutting boards and knives. Inspect your clothing for drips,

- >> Wash your hands thoroughly with soap. Anti-bacterial dish soap is a good idea.

Checking how your chicken was raised

The conventional way to raise mass numbers of chickens is in long lines of wire cages, about eight to a cage. Their movement is severely limited, and they have no access to the outdoors. *Cage-free chicken* (and cage-free eggs) stands for birds that are raised on some type of floor system, typically an open barn, shed, or coup. The hens have bedding material, like wood shavings, and access to perches and nest boxes to lay their eggs. This doesn't necessarily ease overcrowding. And this doesn't mean that they're free of antibiotics.

Chickens can also be raised as free-range chickens. In many cases, free range is a bit of an exaggeration. Most free-range chickens are enclosed in fenced areas with very limited room to maneuver or inside buildings with the door open. That doesn't mean they go outside.

Because it costs more to produce cage-free and free-range chickens, they're generally more expensive — sometimes a whole lot more depending on the store, the brand, and the source. Whether they're more flavorful is a matter of taste. Or go a step further and purchase organic free-range chickens. By law, they must be fed organic food and be treated according to certain humane standards that don't apply to conventional chickens. These generally have firmer and tastier meat.

Fish and other seafood

Fish falls into two broad categories: lean and oily. Lean fish include mild-tasting sole, flounder, snapper, cod, halibut, and haddock. Oily fish have more intense flavor, higher levels of heart-healthy essential fatty acids, and generally darker flesh. These include bluefish, mackerel, salmon, swordfish, and tuna. As a general rule, purchase fillets of oily fish with the skin intact so the fish holds together better during cooking. Lean fish are usually packaged without the skin.

TIP

When buying fish, always ask your fish dealer what is the freshest that day. To break out of the salmon-or-tuna rut, try some of these other types of delicious fish:

>> **Bluefish:** Rich flavor, especially when fresh and under 2 pounds. Bake or broil.

>> **Catfish:** Dense, relatively mild fish. Usually cooked in a strong sauce or deep-fried.

>> **Cod:** Mild-flavored, white, firm flesh. Can be broiled, baked, fried, or braised.

TIP

Right now, we're loving black cod, sometimes called *sablefish* or *butterfish*. This rich fish is high in heart-healthy fat and is a treat not to be missed, if you can find it. It costs more than regular cod, but oh how delicious it is!

>> **Haddock:** Meaty, white flesh, mild flavor. Good pan-fried or braised.

Hake: In the cod family, hake is mild flavored and low in fat, which means you must be careful not to overcook it. Cook any way you would cod.

>> **Porgy:** Firm, low-fat, white-fleshed fish with delicate flavor. Excellent grilled or broiled.

>> **Tilapia:** A popular and affordable farm-raised fish with a mild flavor. Tilapia holds together well and can therefore be cooked in many different ways, making it a favorite of restaurant chefs.

>> **Whiting (silver hake):** Fine, semifirm white flesh. Subtle and delicious when broiled or pan-fried.

Freshness is the most important factor in purchasing fish. Learn to recognize it. In a whole fish, the eyes should be bright and clear, not cloudy. The gills of fresh fish are deep red, not brownish. The skin should be clear and bright with no trace of slime. Really fresh fish shouldn't smell like fish, either. Fish may smell briny but shouldn't smell fishy.

If possible, have your fishmonger cut fresh fillets from whole fish while you wait. Purchase precut fillets only if they're displayed on a bed of ice, not sealed under plastic, which can trap bacteria and foul odors. Fillets should look moist and lie flat, with no curling at the edges. Consume fresh fish and seafood as soon as possible, ideally on the day of purchase. You can freeze freshly caught and cleaned fish for 2 to 3 months if they're wrapped well in two layers of freezer wrap. Although some fish merchants will tell you that you can refreeze shrimp, salmon, and other types of seafood, refreezing compromises the flavor and texture of many kinds of fish. We recommend never refreezing fish after thawing it.

Buying shellfish

Shellfish should be firmly closed and odorless when purchased. If clams or mussels don't close when tapped on the counter, toss them. Eat fresh clams, oysters, and mussels as soon as possible. Store for no more than 24 hours in the refrigerator in a plastic bag poked with small holes, allowing air to circulate. It's best to purchase shrimp in the shell. Eat shrimp the same day you purchase it. Most of all, never overcook shellfish because it gets rubbery.

When buying shrimp, pay no attention to the vague terms *jumbo* and *extra large.* Instead, look for the count number on the seafood display or label. This tells you how many shrimp comprise 1 pound, so the lower the count, the bigger the shrimp. A pretty standard size is 21 to 25 count. Choose the count that's recommended for the dish you're making.

When buying scallops, you follow a similar method. Designating scallops as 20/30 means that it takes between 20 and 30 to make up a pound. Bay scallops are among the smallest, corresponding to double that or more.

WARNING

Some unscrupulous markets have been known to sell expensive "bay scallops" that are really stamped out meat, cookie-cutter fashion, from very large sea scallops. Some have pulled this off using shark. Your only protection is to frequent a quality retailer.

Considering where your seafood came from

Approximately half of the seafood eaten worldwide today is farm-raised. Because so many types of fish and shellfish are endangered, aquaculture is widely recognized as the method by which we'll be able to meet the growing demand for seafood. And don't think that anything farm-raised is inferior or bad for you.

Aquaculture — also known as fish or shellfish farming — refers to the breeding, rearing, and harvesting of plants and animals in all types of water environments, including ponds, rivers, lakes, and the ocean. Tilapia, catfish, salmon, striped bass, rainbow trout, mussels, scallops, oysters, and more are all farm-raised in massive quantities.

To confuse matters, you can also purchase fish and seafood that is *wild-caught* or *sustainably fished.*

» *Wild-caught fish* aren't farmed but caught in their natural habitats. Proponents of wild-caught fish claim that farmed fish contains fewer beneficial omega-3 fatty acids than wild-caught fish and that because of crowded conditions in "factory fish farms," farmed fish are dosed with antibiotics and other drugs and even dyed to look more appetizing. Fish farming also poses some environmental concerns. However, wild-caught fish can be a problem, too, if they're caught in a way that puts other fish at risk or if they're overfished and in danger of becoming endangered or extinct.

» *Sustainably caught* fish are carefully fished with an eye for sustaining populations and not putting other species in harm's way.

If these issues matter to you, download a Seafood Watch Pocket Guide from www.montereybayaquarium.org/cr/cr_seafoodwatch/download.aspx or check out the Natural Resources Defense Council Sustainable Seafood Guide at www.nrdc.org/oceans/seafoodguide.

Does farm-raised seafood taste different from wild seafood? Yes and no. If you compare a wild salmon from Scotland to a farmed salmon from Washington state side by side, you may well detect a difference. With certain shellfish, like mussels, you probably wouldn't. It's mostly a matter of personal taste.

2
Know Your Techniques

Figure out which knives you really need in your kitchen, and master skills like mincing, chopping, and slicing.

Submerse yourself in information about boiling, poaching, and steaming — in other words, how to cook in liquids.

Grab a frying pan and figure out the secrets to sautéing. It's simpler than you think.

Take it easy when making your evening meal by using the slow-cooking approaches of braising or stewing.

Draw your family to the dinner table with the delectable aromas of roasting meat.

Head to the back yard and grill your entire meal — meat, veggies, and even dessert — over an open flame.

Satisfy your sweet tooth with delicious desserts you'll want to make again and again.

Chapter **4**

The Cutting Edge: Working with Knives

This chapter is all about understanding and using the most important pieces of kitchen equipment you'll ever own: knives. Professional chefs revere their knives the way jockeys respect horses, and those knives can last for decades. A really high-quality, super-sharp knife that feels well balanced and comfortable in your hand can practically give you kitchen superpowers. Seriously! A really great knife is one of the secrets of a really great cook.

In this chapter, we explain everything you need to know about kitchen knives, from buying and maintaining them to holding them and cutting with care. Whether you want to chop an onion, cube a potato, or carve a turkey, you find the how-tos in this chapter.

TIP

To supplement our instructions for mincing, julienning, carving, and so on, be sure to check out www.dummies.com/go/cooking. Search for the knife skill you're wondering about (such as "julienne" or "dice") and watch a video that brings it to life. And check out www.dummies.com/go/knives for a primer on the knives you need to have in your kitchen.

Buying Knives for All Occasions

Investing in quality knives yields dividends for years. A good chef's knife will be your constant companion in the kitchen, although as you progress you'll likely need several others.

Investing in the three essentials

REMEMBER

Most home cooks can get along with three versatile knives: a 10- to 12-inch chef's knife, an 8- to 10-inch serrated (bread) knife, and a small paring knife.

Chef's knife

A *chef's knife* (shown in Figure 4-1) can be used for all sorts of chopping, slicing, dicing, and mincing. This knife is really the workhorse of the kitchen, so investing in a quality chef's knife always pays off.

TIP

A 10-inch chef's knife is the best choice for a home cook. It should feel comfortable in your hand and be *balanced,* which means the handle should not be significantly heavier than the blade, or vice versa. You'll know a suitable one when you hold it.

FIGURE 4-1:
A chef's knife is handy for all sorts of chopping chores.

Illustration by Elizabeth Kurtzman

Serrated knife

Have you ever tried to slice a baguette with a regular knife? It's not only frustrating but also dangerous. For this reason (and many others), we include a serrated knife on our list of essentials.

A *serrated knife* (shown in Figure 4-2) generally has an 8- to 10-inch blade, and you want to find one that has *wide teeth* (meaning the pointy edges along the blade aren't too close together). This type of knife is essential for cutting bread; a chef's knife can do the job if you're in a pinch, but a hard-crusted bread dulls a chef's knife quickly. A serrated knife is also handy when slicing tomatoes and other foods that have thin but resistant skins.

Illustration by Elizabeth Kurtzman

Paring knife

A *paring knife* (shown in Figure 4-3) has a blade from 2 to 4 inches long. You use it for delicate jobs like peeling apples and other fruits, trimming shallots and garlic, removing stems from strawberries, coring tomatoes, and making vegetable or fruit decorations.

FIGURE 4-3:
Use a paring knife for delicate cutting tasks.

Illustration by Elizabeth Kurtzman

Adding to your knife block

As your cooking skills develop, you may want to consider buying one or more of these knives as well:

>> **Boning knife:** This one, used to separate raw meat from the bone, is generally 8 to 10 inches long and has a pointed, narrow blade.

>> **Fish filleting knife:** With a 6- to 11-inch blade, this knife resembles a boning knife, but its blade is thin and flexible to perform delicate tasks.

>> **Slicer:** This type of knife is mostly used to slice cooked meat. It has a long, smooth blade — 8 to 12 inches — with either a round or pointed tip.

>> **Cleavers:** These knives feature rectangular blades and look almost like hatchets. They come in many sizes, with some cleavers heavy enough to chop through bone and others intended for chopping vegetables.

REMEMBER

Stores often sell knives in sets of four or six, which means the set includes one or more of the nonessentials in this list. You can usually save money if you buy a quality knife set instead of individual knives. The catch is that you need to be confident that you're actually going to *use* all the knives in the set. If you're a vegetarian and quite certain that you're never going to separate raw meat from any critter's bone, you most likely don't need a boning knife. If you don't like seafood, don't bother buying a set that features a filleting knife.

Shopping wisely

When you're ready to go knife shopping, you need to know a thing or two about what knives are made of as well as how to compare those on the shelf.

Knowing the knife composition

Knives come in several types of materials, each of which has its advantages and disadvantages:

>> **High-carbon stainless steel:** This material is the most popular choice for both home cooks and professionals because it combines the durability of stainless steel with the sharpening capability of carbon steel. It's also easy to clean and doesn't rust.

>> **Carbon steel:** Used primarily by chefs who want an extremely sharp edge, carbon steel has the disadvantage of getting dull quickly. It also gets discolored from contact with acidic food.

>> **Ceramic:** Made from superheated zirconium oxide, ceramic knives are denser, lighter, and sharper than steel. In fact, ceramic knives stay razor sharp for years. The main drawback is that the blades can shatter when dropped. They're comparable in price to other knives.

Homing in on what you want

Every department store carries kitchen knives these days, and many of them look quite impressive. But not all knives are the same. Some look great but are lightweights with thin, insubstantial blades that just won't last. How do you find knives that will still be part of your life years from now? When you're shopping for knives, keep the following tips in mind:

TIP

>> **Before you buy a knife, hold it in your hand.** If the knife is well constructed, it should feel substantial and balanced for you.

>> **Assess the knife handles.** When shopping for large knives, like chef's knives and cleavers, look for those with riveted handles featuring three circular bolts that provide stability.

>> **Consider only knives whose blades are *forged*.** This means that the blades taper from the tip to the base of the handle.

>> **Look for reputable brands.** Here are some to consider:

   - ChefsChoice

   - Global

- Henckels
- Hoffritz
- International Cutlery
- Kyocera (ceramic knives)
- Sabatier
- Wüsthof

Caring for Your Knives

After you invest in quality knives, you want to make sure they give you peak performances for many years. The advice in this section can help.

Storing and washing

Here's rule number one: Don't store your good knives in the same drawer with other cutlery where they can be damaged. You don't want your good chef's knife getting into a wrestling match with a pizza cutter! Instead, keep your knives in a wooden knife holder or on a magnetic strip mounted on the wall (out of the reach of children).

Wash your knives with warm soap and water, using a sponge or plastic scrubber. Don't put them in the dishwasher, and don't scrub them with steel wool.

Also, because you want your knives to look shiny and nice, never leave acid such as lemon juice or vinegar on a knife blade; it can discolor the surface.

Sharpening twice a year

Quality knives are only as good as their sharpened cutting edges. To keep your knives in peak condition, you may want to have them professionally sharpened a couple times a year. Don't have them sharpened more often than that because oversharpening wears down the blade. Your local butcher, gourmet retailer, or restaurant supply store may sharpen your knives or put you in touch with someone who does. You can also ask a professional chef to sharpen your knives for you.

An alternative is a home sharpening machine. You can find these devices, which start at about $40, at knife retailers. They do a fairly decent job, but they definitely don't match the quality of professional sharpening.

You can also use a sharpening stone, which professional chefs typically use. These flat, rectangular stones, about 8 to 10 inches long, come in various types and grits. The technique: Apply one edge of the knife to the stone, moving the blade across the surface as though you're cutting a thin slice off of it. Then do it in reverse. Stones cost from $25 and up.

Honing before each use

To help maintain a knife's sharp edge, you should *hone* its blade — move it across a sharpening steel — before every use. A *sharpening steel* is a long (up to 12-inch) rod of steel or ceramic with a handle. The rod has ridges on it, and when you run a knife blade across at a 20-degree angle, it removes tiny fragments that dull the edge.

REMEMBER

Keep in mind that despite its name, a sharpening steel doesn't actually sharpen a knife. To sharpen requires removing a certain amount of steel from the knife. Honing simply removes any rag-tag bits of steel that may be hanging on the knife's edge because of everyday wear and tear. Honing regularly can definitely help you extend the sharpness of your blade.

Honing a knife before you use it takes less than a minute. The following steps walk you through the process and are illustrated in Figure 4-4:

1. **Grab a sharpening steel firmly and hold it slightly away from your body at a slight upward angle. Hold the knife firmly with the other hand.** The sharpening steel doesn't move during this process; only the knife does.

2. **Run the knife blade down the steel rod, toward the handle (don't worry, it has a protective lip on the top of the handle) at about a 20-degree angle.**

3. **Repeat Step 2, alternating sides of the blade.** This may be nerve-racking at first because the technique has the knife coming at you, but with practice you'll get the hang of it.

4. **Keep alternating for at least 10 times until the blade is sharp.** Tip: To test for sharpness, run the blade lightly across the skin of a tomato. It should slice through effortlessly. Whatever you do, don't test it by running your finger along the blade!

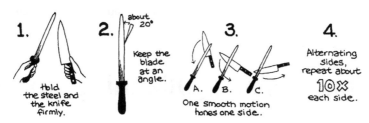

How to Use a Honing Steel

1. Hold the steel and the knife firmly.

2. about 20° Keep the blade at an angle.

3. A. B. C. One smooth motion hones one side.

4. Alternating sides, repeat about 10✕ each side.

FIGURE 4-4:
Honing a knife.

Illustration by Elizabeth Kurtzman

Using Knives Correctly (and Safely)

WARNING

Many knife injuries are the result of rushed, hungry people doing dumb stuff, like trying to separate frozen hamburgers or slicing through hard bagels. So rule number one is, don't do dumb stuff! (Or maybe it should be, don't use knives when you're starving!)

Seriously, you can avoid any knife-related accidents by following some simple rules:

>> **Always slice away from your hand.** Notice the word *slice* here. If you're using a paring knife to peel an apple, the blade is going to be facing the hand holding the apple; you can't get away from that. But when you slice or chop or mince (all of which we explain in the next section), the blade should never be turned toward the hand holding the food.

>> **Keep your fingers clear of the blades.** Before you say "well, duh!" consider how often we take unnecessary chances. If you're slicing a tomato and get down to a half-inch piece remaining, what do you do? That half-inch piece is too thick to put on your sandwich, and you don't want to waste it, so don't you go ahead and slice it in two? Well, exactly how far away can your fingers get in this situation? Until you're really skilled at using a knife, let the tomato go — and find some other way to use it that doesn't require that final slice. And if you insist on making that final cut, at least use a serrated knife (which slices through tomato skins effortlessly).

>> **Always use a cutting board, and don't let it slide around on the counter.** Either use a cutting board with rubber feet that help the board grip the counter, or put your cutting board on a moist dish towel so it won't slip.

>> **Keep your fingertips curled under when slicing.** The knife should not move toward or away from the food; rather, you nudge the food toward the blade. This way, if you do misfire, you're more likely to hit a hard knuckle than a soft fingertip.

So how exactly do you hold and move the knife? That depends on what you're cutting and how you want the finished product to look. Keep reading to find out more.

Chopping, Mincing, Julienning, and More

In this section, we define the terms you're most likely to see in a recipe that calls for you to prepare vegetables, fruits, herbs, and meats. We explain how to chop, mince, cube (or dice), julienne, and slice.

Chopping and mincing

Chopping food means to use your chef's knife to cut it into pieces. Those pieces don't have to be exactly uniform, but the recipe will often tell you whether you need to chop something finely, coarsely, or somewhere in between. Another word for chopping something very finely is *mincing*. You're most often asked to chop or mince veggies or herbs.

To chop or mince, hold the knife handle in a comfortable manner and cut the food into thin strips. Then cut the strips crosswise (as thickly as desired), rocking the blade with your hand and applying pressure on top. Your best bet is to grip the handle with one hand and place your other hand on top of the blade.

Practicing on an onion

Want to practice chopping? Many recipes call for chopped onions, so they're a good place to start. Follow these steps, which are shown in Figure 4-5:

1. **Chop off the stem, and then cut the onion in half lengthwise through the bulbous center and peel back the papery skin.**

   Leave the root end intact. As you slice through the onion, the intact root end holds the onion half together while you slice and chop.

2. **Place each half cut-side down and, with your knife tip just in front of the root end, slice the onion lengthwise in parallel cuts, leaving ⅛ to ¼ inch between the slices.**

3. **Make several horizontal cuts of desired thickness, parallel to the board.**

4. **Cut through the onion crosswise, making pieces as thick as desired.**

5. **Finally, cut through the root end and discard.**

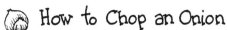

How to Chop an Onion

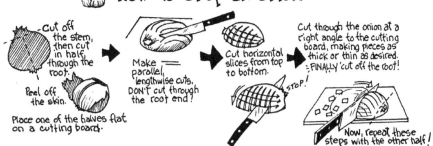

Cut off the stem, then cut in half, through the root.

Peel off the skin.

Place one of the halves flat on a cutting board.

Make parallel, lengthwise cuts, DON'T cut through the root end!

Cut horizontal slices from top to bottom.

Cut through the onion at a right angle to the cutting board, making pieces as thick or thin as desired. FINALLY cut off the root!

STOP!

Now, repeat these steps with the other half!

FIGURE 4-5:
Chopping an onion.

Illustration by Elizabeth Kurtzman

At www.dummies.com/go/choppingonion, you can find a video that shows you what we've just described.

TIP

No matter how you slice it, an onion releases intense flavor and juice, which is why so many recipes call for chopped or minced onion. The fumes they emit when sliced raw, however, can be irritating to the eyes. To minimize chopped onion tears, use a sharp knife that reduces cutting time, and frequently rinse off the onion in cold water as you go. Better yet, have someone else cut it.

Mincing garlic

Mincing garlic simply means chopping it very finely. In this section, we explain how.

First, a quick explanation of terms: In your grocery store, you find garlic bulbs. (Buy garlic that feels firm and hard, not soft.) A bulb is covered by papery skin. When you peel it off, you discover that the bulb contains multiple cloves with thin skins. If you have difficulty removing individual cloves, take a butter knife and pry them out. Then, here's what you do:

1. **Peel the cloves.**

   To help you get the skin off easily, set the cloves on your cutting board, and lay your chef's knife across them with the blade facing away from you. Hold the knife handle with one hand, and use your other hand to whack the side of the blade above the cloves. Doing so should break the skins and let you slip them off easily.

2. **Hold the garlic clove on the cutting board, with the knuckles of your index finger and middle finger leaning against the side of the knife blade.**

   Keep your fingertips folded inward to prevent cutting yourself.

3. **Keeping the tip of your knife on the cutting board, pump the handle up and down while you move the clove under the blade.**

   You've probably seen this technique used by the pros on cooking shows.

4. **Slowly move your knuckles toward the other end of the garlic as you mince.**

Using fresh garlic really is worth a couple extra minutes of prep time because the flavor is so superior to the stuff that comes pre-chopped in a jar. That ingredient works in a pinch, however, so it doesn't hurt to keep a jar in the refrigerator.

Julienning

Don't let the French accent scare you: Julienned vegetables are as simple as they are attractive. Just trim a vegetable, like a radish or carrot, so it's flat on all sides. Slice it lengthwise into ⅛-inch thick pieces. Stack the pieces, and slice them into strips of the same width. See Figure 4-6 for an illustration of this technique and visit www.dummies.com/go/juliennecarrots to watch a chef in action.

Julienne a Carrot!

Now, stack the slices and make even cuts through the stack.

we're all julienned!

Slice lengthwise to make slices of even thickness.

FIGURE 4-6: Julienning a carrot.

Illustration by Elizabeth Kurtzman

Cubing (or dicing)

If you can julienne vegetables, cubing is a breeze. Think of a potato. Trim all the sides until it's flat all around. Cutting lengthwise, slice off ½-inch-thick pieces (or whatever thickness you desire). Stack all or some of the flat pieces and cut them vertically into even strips. Cut them crosswise into even cubes.

Dicing is the same as cubing, except that your pieces are smaller: ⅛ to ¼ inch, usually.

Halving tough-skinned vegetables

With their nearly impervious skins and odd shapes, winter squash, such as butternut squash, is difficult to cut open. We recommend using a Chinese cleaver and a mallet or hammer rather than a chef's knife, which can slip. The squash will be fresher and cheaper if you cut and peel it yourself. But for convenience's sake, many markets now sell precut butternut squash. Follow these steps, which are shown in Figure 4-7:

1. **Place the squash on a cutting board.**

   If needed, place a damp kitchen towel underneath the cutting board to help stabilize it.

2. **Place the cleaver on the squash so its blade runs lengthwise from stem to end.**

3. **To make your first cut, hit the top of the blade with the mallet, pounding several times until the cleaver completely severs the squash in half.**

4. **Using an ice-cream scoop or a large spoon, remove and then discard all the seeds and fibers.**

FIGURE 4-7:
A safe and easy way to cut a winter squash.

Illustration by Elizabeth Kurtzman

Slicing

Slicing is the most common — and most important — knife task. There are really only two things to keep in mind:

>> If you're slicing a hard, round vegetable, like an onion or a winter squash, trim one side flat first so it doesn't roll around on the cutting board.

>> Take your time to assure evenly thick pieces, whether you're slicing an onion or a pineapple. Doing so makes the food look better and cook more evenly.

Figure 4-8 shows how to slice a scallion. As you can see, you can slice with the knife straight in front of you or at a slight angle with the blade moving away from you.

HOW TO SLICE A SCALLION

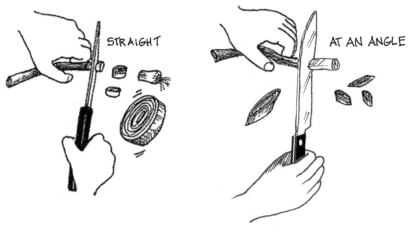

STRAIGHT

AT AN ANGLE

FIGURE 4-8:
Slicing a scallion.

Illustration by Elizabeth Kurtzman

Paring

Paring is one of the only cutting tasks you perform while holding the ingredient in your hand. Don't worry — you don't need the first-aid kit nearby! Your hands are designed for this kind of work. *Paring* means to remove skin from fruits and vegetables as well as to sculpt them into decorative shapes. They can be small items, like shallots and garlic, or larger ones, like apples and tomatoes. Above all, a paring knife must be razor sharp to perform well.

CUTTING PAPER-THIN WITH A MANDOLINE

A *mandoline* is one of those kitchen gizmos that many home cooks believe is too compli-cated to bother with. Think again. This little wonder tool can be so much fun that you may give away your toaster to make room for it on the counter. It comes in various sizes, compositions, and price, and it's fundamentally a tool that can slice vegetables more precisely even than any mere mortal could accomplish with a chef's knife. It can also make slicing soft vegetables like tomatoes easier and has attachments for paper-thin slicing and other special effects, like slicing potatoes with ridges. The mandoline itself is a long, low-sided contraption made of plastic or steel with a blade in the center of a long flat plate. The food holder slides up and down over the blade, precisely slicing or otherwise perfectly processing its prey and dropping the pieces onto your cutting board. Always use the safety handle — trust us, you don't want to run your finger over that blade.

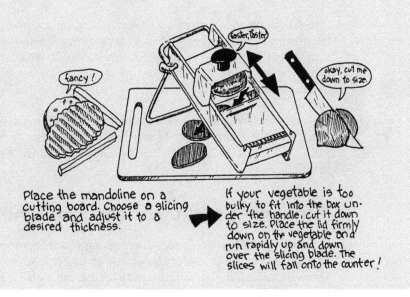

To pare an apple, for example, hold it in one hand, barely pressing it into your palm, with fingers bracing the surface (outside of where the cutting proceeds). Pierce the skin of the apple with the paring knife and carefully peel it toward you, slowly turning the apple with your thumb. Spiral all the way to the bottom (see Figure 4-9). Although fruits and vegetables come in different shapes, this tech-nique of holding food and slicing toward you is the same. Need a visual to help you figure out the best way to pare? Be sure to check out www.dummies.com/go/paring.

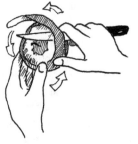

PARING AN APPLE

FIGURE 4-9:
Go round and round when paring an apple.

Illustration by Elizabeth Kurtzman

Carving Poultry and Meats

If you're daring enough to cook a whole chicken, turkey, roast, leg of lamb, or ham (all of which we show you how to do later in this book), you're definitely up to cutting your masterpiece in preparation for serving it. We offer illustrated instructions in this section, and you can find videos at www.dummies.com/go/cooking that put these steps into action.

TIP

Although we don't include the steps here for cutting apart a whole raw chicken, that's a skill that can definitely save you some money. We have a step-by-step video available at www.dummies.com/go/cuttingchicken. Won't your mother be so proud!

Showing a turkey or chicken who's boss

If the thought of carving your Thanksgiving masterpiece or even your Sunday dinner staple gives you the chills, we're here to help. Because chickens and turkeys are anatomically similar, this technique works for both. Here are the steps to follow, which are illustrated in Figure 4-10:

1. **Place the chicken or turkey, breast-side up, on a carving board.**

2. **Remove one leg by slicing through it where it meets the breast.**

   Pull the leg away from the body, cut through the skin between the leg and body, and then cut through the joint.

3. **Separate the drumstick from the thigh.**

   On a cutting board, place the drumstick and thigh skin-side down. Look for a strip of yellow fat at the center. That's the joint. Cut through the joint.

4. **Remove the wing on the same side of the bird.**

   Cut as close to the breast as possible, through the joint that attaches the wing to the body.

5. **Carve the breast meat.**

   Hold your knife parallel to the center bone and begin slicing halfway up the breast. Keep the slices as thin as possible. Continue slicing parallel to the center bone, starting a little higher with each slice.

6. **Repeat the whole process on the other side.**

TIP

Visit www.dummies.com/go/carvingturkey to see a video that shows you these steps.

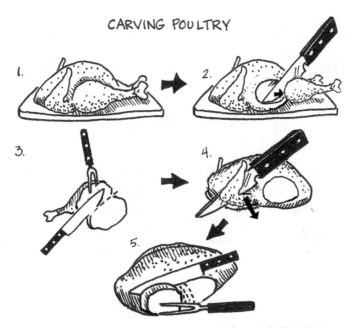

CARVING POULTRY

FIGURE 4-10:
Carving a chicken
or turkey.

Illustration by Elizabeth Kurtzman

Cutting a pot roast

When it comes to serving a pot roast, you need to follow one simple rule: Cut it against the grain so the meat holds together and doesn't shred. Figure 4-11 shows how to do it, as does www.dummies.com/go/carvingroast.

Cutting Pot Roast Across the Grain

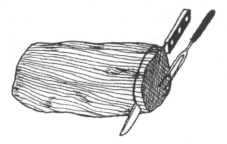

FIGURE 4-11:
Cut across the grain to avoid shredding the meat.

Illustration by Elizabeth Kurtzman

Slicing a leg of lamb

You may not make lamb as often as you do poultry, but won't your family or guests be impressed when you show off your expert carving skills! Figure 4-12 illustrates how to properly carve a leg of lamb. A chef's knife is best for this task, although you may use a boning knife for hard-to-get pieces.

Carving a Leg of Lamb

1. Cut out a narrow wedge of meat.

2. Carve the meat from either side of the wedge, down to the bone.

3. Slice through cuts to form pieces.

4. Turn the leg over. Trim off the fat and carve off slices parallel to the bone.

FIGURE 4-12:
The proper technique for carving a leg of lamb.

Illustration by Elizabeth Kurtzman

Handling a ham

When you prepare a gorgeous ham (see Chapter 8 for a delicious recipe), you want to be sure to serve it thinly sliced rather than chopped into chunks. You can use a chef's knife or a serrated knife. Figure 4-13 offers a ham-carving primer as does the video at www.dummies.com/go/carvingham.

Carving a Ham

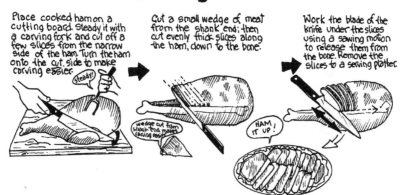

Place cooked ham on a cutting board. Steady it with a carving fork and cut off a few slices from the narrow side of the ham. Turn the ham onto the cut side to make carving easier.

steady!

Cut a small wedge of meat from the shank end; then cut evenly thick slices along the ham, down to the bone.

wedge cut from shank end makes carving easier

Work the blade of the knife under the slices using a sawing motion to release them from the bone. Remove the slices to a serving platter.

HAM IT UP!

Illustration by Elizabeth Kurtzman

FIGURE 4-13: How to carve a ham.

Chapter **5**

Boiling, Poaching, and Steaming

Water can be your friend or your foe in the kitchen — but mostly, it's your friend. Too much water can dilute a soup or make some dishes soggy, but it can also boil, blanch, poach, or steam your favorite foods to tender and succulent perfection. Who knew such simple stuff could do so much . . . and it comes right out of your tap, practically for free!

In this chapter, we cover several basic cooking techniques that employ the almost magical powers of good ol' H_2O. From eggs and veggies to melt-in-your-mouth seafood, let water woo you. (For more recipes that involve boiling, flip to Chapter 13 to discover how to boil pasta, rice, and other great grains. And for visual aids to supplement this chapter, check out www.dummies.com/go/cookingwithliquid.)

Water, Water Everywhere . . . Now What?

Relax — even home ec dropouts can figure out the basic cooking techniques of using water and other liquids. Cooking with liquid is simple, but it helps to understand the process to get the best results. Here are some terms to know:

>> **Boiling:** Bringing water to 212 degrees Fahrenheit in a high-sided pot, like a saucepan, soup pot, or tea kettle. Let the water come to a *full rolling boil* (when the bubbles are rapidly breaking the surface). Covering the pot speeds the process by trapping surface heat. And here's a tip based on our recent research: A watched pot *does* prevent water from boiling. We suggest you look out the window or start chopping veggies. (Just don't leave the kitchen because an unsupervised pot will definitely boil over!)

>> **Parboiling and blanching:** Precooking tough or salty foods to soften their textures and sometimes to remove harsh flavors or soften tough skin. Rice is sometimes parboiled (or "converted") and then packaged to shorten cooking time and retain nutrients. Tomatoes can be blanched to loosen their skins.

Blanch tougher vegetables like broccoli and cauliflower to make them more palatable and attractive than the raw versions in cold salads. You can even blanch bacon for use in recipes to get rid of some of the salt. After vegetables are blanched, they should be submerged in a large bowl of ice water to stop the cooking and thus retain their color.

>> **Simmering:** Bringing liquid to a gentle preboil. In a simmer, tiny bubbles break the surface gently — like a soft summer shower on a still lake. (Are we going overboard? That really is what it looks like!) Simmering occurs at a lower temperature — just below a boil, or 180 degrees Fahrenheit — and is used for long, slow cooking and braising. (Chapter 7 talks more about braising.)

REMEMBER

By the way, *poaching* is cooking something like eggs or fish in simmering water or other liquid. *Simmering* is usually used to describe what the liquid itself is doing. You poach eggs, but you simmer soup.

>> **Reducing:** Boiling down stock or other liquids to thicken and to intensify flavors. This technique is typically used for sauce making (see Chapter 14). Great care must be taken not to overreduce and burn the reduction.

>> **Steaming:** The gentlest way to cook. Steaming is better than boiling or poaching for retaining a food's color, flavor, texture, shape, and nutrients. Steaming often involves placing food over simmering water on a perforated rack in a covered pot.

When you steam foods set in a pan of water in the oven, it's called a *water bath.* Cheesecakes and custards are often baked this way. Sometimes this technique is also called a *bain marie,* or Marie's Bath. (You don't want to know where that term came from.)

Making Hard- and Soft-Cooked Eggs

Sometimes the dishes that look the easiest can really trip you up in the kitchen. If you've ever had trouble making boiled eggs, we're here to show you the light!

A quick language primer: Eggs really should never be hard-*boiled* or soft-*boiled* but rather hard-*cooked* or soft-*cooked.* That's because rigorous boiling causes eggs to jostle and crack, leaving the whites tough.

Here are the steps to follow to get the perfect hard-cooked egg, which are also available in video form at www.dummies.com/go/hardcookeggs:

1. **Place the eggs in a saucepan large enough to hold them in a single layer. Add cold water to cover by about 1 inch.**

2. **Cover the saucepan and bring the water to a boil over high heat as fast as possible.**

3. **Remove the pan from the heat and let eggs stand in the pan, still covered, for 15 minutes for large eggs, 18 minutes for jumbo, and 12 minutes for medium.**

4. **Drain the eggs in a colander and run cold water over them until completely cooled.**

For soft-cooked eggs, follow Step 1 to measure how much water to use, but remove the eggs before heating the water. After the water is boiling, follow with these steps:

1. **Carefully lower the eggs into the boiling water with a slotted spoon and cook for 2 minutes with the pan covered.**

2. **Turn off the heat. If your stove is electric, remove the pan from the burner.**

3. **Let the eggs stand in the pan, still covered, for 5 minutes.**

4. **Remove the eggs from the water with a slotted spoon. Put them in a bowl or colander and run cold water over them until they're cool enough to handle.**

If you have one of those retro egg cups, you can try putting your soft-cooked egg in it and knocking the top off with a knife — in one fell swoop, like they do in the movies. (But don't blame us if the top of your egg ends up on the other side of the kitchen.) Or, for a more reliable result, cut the top one-third of the egg off with scissors and eat the yummy yolk and white with a little egg spoon.

While you eat soft-cooked eggs right away, hard-cooked eggs have numerous uses. You can slice them into tossed green salads or potato salads, make deviled eggs, mash them for egg salad sandwiches, or simply peel and eat them with a little salt. Always refrigerate hard-cooked eggs and eat them within a week to ten days.

TIP

Now, about peeling that egg. . . . The fresher the egg, the more difficult it is to peel, although running cold water over the eggs as you work can help separate the egg white from the shell slightly, making peeling easier. For perfect peeling, follow these steps:

1. **As soon as your hard-cooked egg is cool enough to handle, tap it gently on a table or countertop to crackle the shell all over.**

2. **Roll the egg between your hands to loosen the shell.**

3. **Peel off the shell, starting at the large end of the egg.**

Giving Your Veggies a Hot Bath

It's not that they are dirty. It's that a hot bath can make veggies melt-in-your-mouth tender. Water and veggies are a match made in veggie heaven, but forget boiling them to death in the manner you may remember from childhood (sorry, Mom, but it's what you did!). Instead, more sophisticated techniques for applying hot water to fresh veggies yield superior results. You can even use some of these techniques on fruit.

Parboiling, blanching, and steaming veggies

Sometimes a recipe calls for parboiling vegetables. Certain dense vegetables, such as carrots, potatoes, and turnips, may be parboiled (cooked briefly in boiling water) to soften them slightly before another method finishes cooking them. This technique guarantees that all the ingredients in the dish finish cooking at the same time. You may, for example, parboil green peppers before you stuff and bake them. Or you may parboil pieces of broccoli, carrots, and cauliflower before tossing them into a stir-fry of egg noodles and shrimp. (See the Crispy Roasted Root Vegetables recipe in Chapter 8 for an example of this technique.)

Blanching, or plunging vegetables or fruits into boiling water for a few seconds and then into cold water to stop the cooking process, helps cooks remove the skins from tomatoes, nectarines, and peaches. (See Chapter 12 for instructions on removing the skins of tomatoes.) Some vegetables, like green beans, are blanched before they're frozen or canned to help retain their color and flavor.

Steaming is the gentlest way to cook vegetables (as well as seafood). It's also one of the most healthful because no nutrients are lost in the cooking liquids. You can steam in two ways: in a perforated steamer set over simmering water (and covered) or in a deep, covered pot or saucepan holding about 1 to 2 inches of water. The latter method works especially well for vegetables like broccoli and asparagus.

If you steam foods often, you may want to invest in some sort of steamer. The conventional steamer model is a pair of pots, the top one having a perforated bottom and a lid. You can also buy bamboo steamers or little metal steamer baskets that fit inside saucepans you already own.

RECIPE ALERT

When you're ready to try cooking vegetables in water, check out two recipes that appear later in this chapter: Homemade Mashed Potatoes and Steamed Broccoli with Lemon Butter.

TIP

Something to keep in mind whenever you make mashed potatoes: Baking potatoes (like Russets, sometimes called Idaho potatoes) make fluffier, smoother mashed potatoes than "boiling" potatoes like red or yellow potatoes. Boiled potatoes contain a lot of moisture, so they get gluey when mashed, but they're great for recipes that call for firm cubes or slices, like potato salad and gratins.

Boiling and steaming a dozen fresh vegetables

All sorts of seasonal vegetables benefit from boiling and steaming. When it comes to choosing between the two techniques, remember that steaming is more gentle and better retains the texture and color of vegetables. Boiling is a more aggressive process and tends to break down the texture of vegetables, which is desirable if you're making purees or mashed potatoes. Following are specific instructions for boiling and steaming common vegetables:

>> **Artichokes:** Lay the artichokes on their side on a wooden cutting board. Using a sharp chef's knife (see Chapter 4), trim about ½ inch off the top. Use scissors to trim the prickly tips off each leaf. Pull off any very thick or tough leaves (but no more than 3 or 4) at the bottom of the artichoke. Place the artichokes in a deep pot with cold water to cover. (They should fit snugly to keep them from bobbing in the water.) Add about a teaspoon of salt per quart of water plus some black pepper and the juice of one lemon, and bring to a boil. Boil gently for 30 to 40 minutes, depending on size. When the artichokes are done, you should be able to pierce the bottom with a fork or easily pull off a leaf. Use tongs to remove the artichokes and drain upside down on a plate or in a colander. Serve hot with a sauce of lemon juice and melted butter. Or marinate for several hours in a vinaigrette dressing (see Chapter 12) and serve at room temperature.

>> **Asparagus:** Snap off the thick, woody stems at the natural breaking point. (If very coarse, use a vegetable peeler to remove some of the outer green layer at the thick end of each spear.) Rinse the stalks under cold water or soak them for about 5 minutes if they seem especially sandy. Place the spears in a covered skillet in one layer, if possible (and never more than two). Add boiling water to cover and salt to taste. Cover and boil gently until crisp-tender, about 8 minutes for medium spears. Cooking time varies with the thickness of the stalks. Drain and serve immediately with butter, lemon juice, salt and black pepper, and, if desired, grated Parmesan cheese.

>> **Brussels sprouts:** With a sharp paring knife (see Chapter 4), trim the tough outer leaves and trim a very thin slice off the stem end. Then cut an X in the stem end to ensure even cooking of the stem and leaves. Cook them in a covered saucepan with about 1 inch of water for 8 to 10 minutes or until crisp-tender. Test for doneness by tasting. Drain and serve with about ¼ cup melted butter mixed with the juice of half of a fresh lemon and a dash of salt.

To steam Brussels sprouts, place trimmed sprouts in a steaming basket over about 1 inch of boiling water. Cover the pot and steam for about 8 minutes, depending on size.

>> **Cabbage:** Cut the head into quarters and cut out the hard core. Add the quarters to a large pot of lightly salted boiling water, cover, and boil gently for about 12 minutes. Cabbage should remain somewhat crisp.

RECIPE ALERT

To steam, place the quarters in a large deep skillet or saucepan with about ½ inch of water and cook, covered, over low heat until crisp-tender. Cabbage is also quite delicious when braised. (See the recipe for Braised Cabbage with Apple and Caraway later in this chapter.) Or cook it in your slow cooker with a splash of chicken broth and some diced ham.

>> **Carrots or parsnips:** Trim off the ends and peel with a vegetable peeler. Place them sliced into a pot with lightly salted water just to cover. Cover the pot and boil gently for about 12 to 15 minutes for sliced carrots or about 20 minutes for whole ones. Or place in a steaming basket and steam in a covered pot over about 1 inch of boiling water. Sliced carrots or parsnips steam in 5 minutes; whole and large, 2- to 3-inch pieces need about 12 minutes. Serve with butter sauce flavored with lemon juice and grated lemon or orange zest or a sauce of melted butter and minced fresh dill.

>> **Cauliflower:** First, cut a whole head into *florets,* using your chef's knife: Cut the whole head in half, and then separate the head into individual buds, or small clusters, keeping a little of their stems. Boil gently in enough lightly salted water to cover for about 8 to 10 minutes, or until crisp-tender. Adding the juice of half a lemon to the cooking water helps to retain cauliflower's whiteness.

To steam, place florets in a steaming basket over about 1 inch of boiling water. Cover the pot and steam for about 5 minutes or until desired doneness. Toss in a sauce of melted butter, lemon juice, and chopped fresh parsley.

>> **Corn:** Don't husk or remove the ears from the refrigerator until you're ready to boil them. (The sugar in corn rapidly turns to starch at room temperature. To retain sweetness, keep ears cold and cook the same day of purchase.) Heat a large pot filled with enough water just to cover the corn, add the husked corn, cover the pot, and boil for about 5 minutes. Remove with tongs and serve immediately with butter.

>> **Green beans:** Trim by snapping off the stem ends. Add the beans to lightly salted boiling water to cover and cook for 8 to 10 minutes, or until crisp-tender. They should retain their bright green color.

To steam, place a steaming basket over about 1 inch of boiling water. Add beans, cover the pot tightly, and check for doneness after 5 minutes. Serve hot beans with a simple butter sauce or toss in a vinaigrette dressing and chill before serving.

>> **Pearl onions:** Peel and boil in a covered pot with lightly salted water to just cover for about 15 minutes or until tender but still firm. Don't overcook, or they'll fall apart. Serve smothered in a sauce or gravy or mixed with other vegetables.

>> **Snow peas:** Rinse the peas, snap off the stem ends, and lift the string across the top to remove it. Place in boiling water to cover and cook for 2 minutes. Drain in a colander and run cold water over them to stop the cooking and retain their green color.

>> **Sweet potatoes or yams:** Scrub and peel the potatoes using a vegetable peeler, trim the tapered ends, and cut out any bruised spots. (Cut very large sweet potatoes in half crosswise, or quarter them.) Place in a large pot, add cold water to cover the potatoes, cover the pot, and simmer for about 35 to 40 minutes for whole potatoes or 20 to 25 minutes for halved or quartered potatoes. Potatoes are done when you can pierce them easily with a fork. Don't overcook, or they'll fall apart in the water. Drain and cool slightly before peeling. Mash or serve in large chunks with butter, salt, black pepper, and ground ginger or nutmeg to taste, if desired.

>> **Yellow squash and zucchini:** Scrub clean and trim the ends. Slice into ½-inch-thick rounds. Place in a steaming basket over about 1 inch of boiling water and steam in a covered pot for about 4 minutes or just until crisp-tender. These tender vegetables are also delicious sautéed.

TIP

Fresh vegetables have more flavor and retain their nutrients better if you cook them only until *crisp-tender,* or firm to the bite. The B vitamins and vitamin C are water soluble and leach into the cooking water as the vegetables cook, so save the vitamin-packed cooking liquid to add to other dishes you're cooking, such as soups and stews.

Making vegetable purées

Vegetable *purées* are simply cooked vegetables (usually boiled or steamed but sometimes roasted) that are mashed, blended, or processed to a thick consistency. Starchy root vegetables like potatoes, sweet potatoes, rutabagas, parsnips, and carrots generally make the best purées, but broccoli, cauliflower, and roasted red peppers are also wonderful, especially when mixed with a dense root vegetable.

Thick purées make a great side dish. When thinned with water, broth, or sauce, they make delicious toppings for meat, potatoes, pasta, or rice.

To make a purée, put any soft-cooked vegetable or combination of vegetables in a blender or food processor with a bit of water or broth, and purée it. Serve it warm (you can reheat the purée in a saucepan over low heat if it's cooled off too much). Or use an immersion blender and purée the vegetables right in the pan where you steamed or boiled them. Season with salt and black pepper and your favorite herbs or spices, or in the case of sweet potatoes or winter squash, a bit of honey, maple syrup, or cinnamon. Mmm, comfort food!

Poaching and Steaming Seafood

Poaching seafood is a fabulous way to preserve its flavor and texture, especially with firm-textured fish like salmon, tuna, halibut, cod, and swordfish. The only drawback is that it takes on no flavors while cooking, as it does when seasoned and sautéed. Therefore, poached seafood usually calls for a sauce of some sort (see Chapter 14). But if you poach seafood in seasoned vegetable broth, fish broth, or water with a splash of clam juice, it will take on a subtle, herby flavor.

You have to watch the clock to prevent overcooking and keep the poaching liquid to a gentle simmer. Vigorous boiling breaks up the fish's tender flesh.

RECIPE ALERT

Later in the chapter, we show you how to make Poached Salmon Steaks with Orange Coriander Vinaigrette. Sound too fancy to be easy? It's not — we promise.

IS THAT FISH DONE OR JUST RESTING?

One traditional guideline for cooking fish is the so-called Canadian Fish Rule: Measure the whole fish steak or fillet at its thickest point and cook it (whether you're boiling, steaming, baking, broiling, or poaching) for 10 minutes per inch. Personally, we've found that 8 to 9 minutes per inch works a little bit better, so we recommend that after about 8 minutes, you check for doneness. Using this guideline, if the thickest part of the fish is ¼-inch thick, you cook it for 6 to 7 minutes.

Whole fish is easiest to check. If the dorsal fin comes out easily, it's done; if not, it needs more cooking. However, as a beginning cook, you probably won't be cooking a whole fish just yet. A fish fillet or steak is done when it flakes easily with a fork. Scallops turn opaque when done, and shrimp, which takes only a couple of minutes to cook, turns pink. Salmon and tuna are darkish pink at the center when medium. White fish should be glistening and wet looking only at the innermost core. Unless the recipe instructs you to do otherwise, remove all cooked fish from the heat or the poaching liquid immediately.

Mussels, clams, and oysters give you a clear indication that they're cooked: Their shells open when they're done, no matter how you cook them.

CLEANING MUSSELS AND CLAMS

Most mussels sold today are farm-raised, cultivated on long ropes in the ocean; hence, they're usually grit-free as opposed to those harvested on the sea bottom. To clean mussels or hard-shelled clams, place them in a colander and scrub them with a vegetable brush under running cold water to remove grit. Pull out the protruding stringy "beard." Discard any mussels or hard-shelled clams that are cracked.

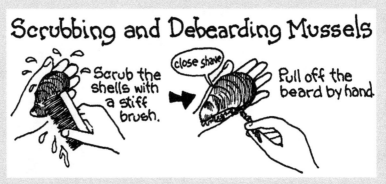

Scrubbing and Debearding Mussels

Scrub the shells with a stiff brush.

close shave

Pull off the beard by hand.

Illustration by Elizabeth Kurtzman

The best way to cook seafood in the shell — clams, mussels, and lobster — is to steam or boil it. We've found that the former yields a slightly better texture and flavor. Steaming calls for a trivet or basket to keep the food off the bottom of the pot.

RECIPE ALERT

The recipe for Steamed Mussels is as basic as it gets and is also suitable with littleneck or cherrystone clams. Cherrystone clams are the largest of these bivalves. Depending on their size, they take 8 to 10 minutes to steam open. When you've mastered this cooking technique, you can season the broth any way you like it.

Homemade Mashed Potatoes

PREP TIME: ABOUT 15 MIN	COOK TIME: ABOUT 20 MIN	YIELD: 4 SERVINGS

INGREDIENTS

4 large Idaho potatoes, about 2 pounds total

½ teaspoon salt

½ cup milk

3 tablespoons butter

Salt and black pepper

DIRECTIONS

1 Peel the potatoes and cut them into quarters.

2 Place potatoes in a medium saucepan with cold water to barely cover and add the ½ teaspoon salt.

3 Cover and bring to a boil over high heat. Reduce heat to medium and cook, covered, for about 15 minutes or until you can easily pierce the potatoes with a fork.

4 Drain the potatoes in a colander and then return them to the saucepan. Shake the potatoes in the pan over low heat for 10 to 15 seconds to evaporate excess moisture, if necessary.

5 Remove the pan from the heat. Mash the potatoes a few times with a potato masher, ricer, or fork.

6 Add the milk, butter, and salt and black pepper to taste and mash again until smooth and creamy.

PER SERVING: *Calories 263 (From Fat 88); Fat 10g (Saturated 6g); Cholesterol 27mg; Sodium 315mg; Carbohydrate 41g (Dietary Fiber 4g); Protein 5g.*

TIP: Mashed potatoes are best when mashed by hand with a potato masher or fork or when pressed through a ricer (a round, metal device with small holes through which foods are pressed). Blenders and food processors can leave them pasty.

GO-WITH: Try these potatoes with Roasted Fillet of Beef or Smoked Ham with Apricot Glaze (both in Chapter 8), and don't forget to serve them with the Thanksgiving turkey (see Chapter 21)!

VARY IT! For garlic mashed potatoes, wrap a whole, medium head of garlic in aluminum foil and roast it in a 350-degree oven for 1 hour. Remove the foil, allow the garlic to cool slightly, and then press the soft cloves to release the pulp. Mash the pulp into the potatoes with the butter and milk; then season with salt and black pepper to taste. You can mash other cooked vegetables, such as broccoli, carrots, turnips, or sweet potatoes, and blend them into the potato mix.

Steamed Broccoli with Lemon Butter

PREP TIME: ABOUT 15 MIN | COOK TIME: ABOUT 10 MIN | YIELD: 4 SERVINGS

INGREDIENTS

1 head broccoli

Salt and black pepper

3 tablespoons butter

Juice of half a lemon

DIRECTIONS

1   Wash the broccoli thoroughly. Trim off the thickest part of the stems and the large leaves. Divide the larger florets by slicing through the base of the flower and straight down through the length of the stem.

2   Place the broccoli in a 3- or 4-quart saucepan holding about 2 inches of water. (The stalks should stand on the bottom with the florets facing up.) Add salt and black pepper to taste and cover the pan.

3   Bring to a boil over high heat and then reduce the heat to low and simmer, covered, for about 8 minutes or until the stalks are tender but not soft.

4   While the broccoli steams, melt the butter in a small saucepan and add the lemon juice. Stir to blend.

5   Using tongs, carefully remove the broccoli to a serving dish. Pour the lemon–butter sauce over the broccoli and serve.

PER SERVING: *Calories 109 (From Fat 80); Fat 9g (Saturated 5g); Cholesterol 23mg; Sodium 176mg; Carbohydrate 6g (Dietary Fiber 3g); Protein 4g.*

TIP: Trim and cut the vegetables into equal-sized pieces so they cook evenly.

VARY IT! You can substitute vegetables like cauliflower and asparagus for the broccoli in this recipe.

GO-WITH: Fresh broccoli adds color and flavor to innumerable meals, including Roasted Fillet of Beef and Glazed Leg of Lamb with Pan Gravy and Red Currant Glaze (both in Chapter 8).

Steamed Mussels

PREP TIME: ABOUT 20 MIN	COOK TIME: ABOUT 15 MIN	YIELD: 2–3 SERVINGS

INGREDIENTS

2 tablespoons unsalted butter, at room temperature

1 tablespoon olive oil

1 small onion, chopped (about ½ cup)

1 large ripe tomato, peeled, seeded, and chopped, or 1 cup canned chopped tomatoes

4 medium cloves garlic, chopped

1½ cups dry white wine or chicken broth

3 long sprigs fresh thyme

Large pinch red pepper flakes

Pinch salt

2 pounds mussels, scrubbed and debearded

⅓ cup chopped fresh parsley leaves

Crusty French baguette or Italian bread, sliced

DIRECTIONS

1 Heat 1 tablespoon of the butter and the olive oil in a large 6- to 8-quart pot over medium until the fat starts to shimmer. Add the onion and cook about 3 minutes or until transparent, stirring occasionally. Add the tomato and garlic and cook about 2 minutes until the garlic is fragrant and the tomato has softened.

2 Add the wine or chicken broth, thyme sprigs, red pepper flakes, and salt; cover the pot, raise the heat to high and bring the broth to a simmer. Lower the heat and simmer, uncovered, for about 4 to 5 minutes to blend the flavors and reduce slightly.

3 Increase the heat to high and add the mussels. Cover and cook until the mussels open, 4 to 6 minutes, gently turning them over once in the broth. Discard any mussels that don't open.

4 Use a slotted spoon to transfer the mussels to a large serving bowl.

5 Add the remaining 1 tablespoon butter and parsley to the broth and stir over medium heat until the butter melts. Pour the hot broth over the mussels and serve with the bread to soak up the sauce.

PER SERVING: *Calories 617 (From Fat 180); Fat 20g (Saturated 7g); Cholesterol 105mg; Sodium 1,282mg; Carbohydrate 46g (Dietary Fiber 3g); Protein 43g.*

VARY IT! Substitute 1 medium chopped shallot or 4 chopped scallions for the onion. Substitute fresh chopped basil for the parsley. Add a large pinch of saffron threads to the steaming broth. Substitute beer or bottled clam juice for the white wine. Add 2 teaspoons chopped fresh ginger to the poaching liquid. Instead of serving with bread, toss the shellfish and the broth over a bowl of hot, cooked pasta.

Poached Salmon Steaks with Orange Coriander Vinaigrette

PREP TIME: ABOUT 25 MIN	COOK TIME: ABOUT 10 MIN	YIELD: 4 SERVINGS

INGREDIENTS

1½ quarts (6 cups) vegetable broth or water

4 salmon steaks or fillets, about 6 ounces each, with skin

Water (if necessary)

Orange Coriander Vinaigrette (see the following recipe)

DIRECTIONS

1 Bring the vegetable broth or water to a boil over high heat in a large skillet. Submerge the salmon steaks or fillets in the boiling liquid. Add more water if there isn't enough stock to just cover the steaks.

2 Return to a boil; then lower the heat to a simmer and cook, uncovered, for about 5 minutes.

3 Turn off the heat and let the steaks stand in the poaching liquid about 3 to 5 minutes. Remove a steak from the water and cut into the center delicately to check for doneness.

4 Remove the poached steaks to a platter. Drizzle some of the Orange Coriander Vinaigrette over each salmon steak and serve immediately.

Orange Coriander Vinaigrette

2 teaspoons Dijon-style mustard

1½ tablespoons fresh lemon juice

⅓ cup olive oil

1 tablespoon red wine vinegar

⅛ teaspoon red pepper flakes

Salt and white or black pepper to taste

1 tablespoon minced fresh cilantro

2 tablespoons julienne of orange zest

Combine the mustard and 1 tablespoon of the lemon juice in a small bowl. Beat briskly until the mixture begins to thicken. Whisk in the olive oil then the remaining ½ tablespoon lemon juice and vinegar. Add the red pepper flakes, salt, white or black pepper, cilantro, and orange zest. Mix well. Serve at room temperature

PER SERVING: *Calories 418 (From Fat 225); Fat 25g (Saturated 7g); Cholesterol 30mg; Sodium 837mg; Carbohydrate 3g (Dietary Fiber 0g); Protein 36g.*

Chapter 6

Simply Sautéing

Sautéing, also referred to as *pan-frying*, is generally associated with French cuisine. But in fact, many other nationalities sauté routinely to sear steaks, cook fillets of fish, glaze vegetables, and quick-cook shellfish. Sautéing is a technique you should master because it's the quickest and easiest way to put together a meal, and you'll use it more than any other.

Sautéing is little more than cooking food in a hot pan, usually with a little fat (butter or oil, for example) to prevent sticking. Sautéing imparts a crispy texture to foods and brings out all sorts of flavors from herbs and spices.

If you drop a steak onto a roaring-hot pan (maybe with a little oil to prevent sticking), it develops a dark crust in a few minutes. This effect is desirable because it intensifies any seasonings on the surface of the meat and gives it a pleasant crunchy texture. (Contrary to popular belief, sautéing has nothing to do with locking in meat juices. Cookbooks say this all the time, but it's not the case.) Seafood and vegetables glazed with butter benefit from sautéing in the same way; sautéing gives them texture and flavor.

The French word *sauté* translates literally as "to jump." Chefs shake the sauté pan back and forth over the heat, tossing the food to expose it evenly to the heat. You can actually practice this technique in a cold skillet with small candies! (Just do it when no one's watching.)

WARNING

Because sautéing is done at high or medium-high heat, you have to be careful to keep your eye on the food because it can burn in two seconds flat.

In this chapter, we discuss sautéing and provide some helpful tips and delicious recipes. Also be sure to visit www.dummies.com/go/sauteing for a video that demonstrates the technique.

Knowing When to Use Oil or Butter

When you sauté something, even in a nonstick pan, you need to use some kind of fat. But which one — butter or oil? Each is best suited for different kinds of sautéing:

>> When cooking over very high heat, use oil, which is less likely to burn.

>> When sautéing with medium-high heat, you may opt for butter, which adds a nice flavor. However, the milk solids in the butter can burn, or brown, affecting the color and taste of your food.

REMEMBER

Typically, meats are sautéed in oil because they need a higher heat, while vegetables are sautéed in butter to impart a pleasant buttery flavor. Seafood may be sautéed in either one. Many chefs opt to use half butter and half oil when sautéing seafood: They get the benefit of the buttery flavor, but the added oil helps to keep the butter from burning as easily.

TIP

Just like the professionals do, you can prevent butter from burning in a sauté pan by adding a few drops of vegetable oil or any neutral-tasting oil.

If you decide to use oil in your sautéing, it's helpful to know that some oils have a higher *smoke point* than others, which means they start to smoke at a hotter temperature (and so are preferable for sautéing). Good oils for sautéing include canola, corn, and peanut oil. If the recipe doesn't specify what type of oil to use, go with one of these three neutral-flavored oils.

Oil alone should be hot but not smoking in the pan before you add food. Butter alone should foam at its edges but not brown.

When sautéing in oil, use a minimal amount of oil. The steam created from the hot oil in the pan helps to cook the food inside while the outsides brown. Without the presence of steam, pan-fried foods would taste greasy and be soggy rather than crispy. Care must be taken to keep the cooking oil hot enough. Nonstick skillets work best; however, a well-oiled cast-iron skillet can do the job as well.

CLARIFYING BUTTER

Some chefs prevent burning when sautéing by using *clarified butter*. Quite simply, clarified butter is unsalted butter that slowly melts, causing water to evaporate and its milk solids, which burn over high heat, to sink to the bottom.

If you want to try your hand at making clarified butter, follow these steps:

1. **Put two or more sticks of unsalted butter in a saucepan over low heat.** Do not stir. Allow the butter to melt. It will begin to foam, and its milk solids will fall to the bottom of the pan. Continue to cook the butter until the foaming stops. Remove from the heat.

2. **Let the butter cool for 20 to 30 minutes.**

3. **Skim the foam from the surface and gently pour the clarified butter into a container. Refrigerate and use for several months.**

Combining Sautéing with Roasting

Thin cuts of meat, 1 to 1¼ inches thick, are best grilled or pan-seared on top of the stove. If you try to sauté thick meat, there's a good chance you'll burn the surface before the center is cooked. So thicker steaks and pork chops benefit from a combination of pan-searing and roasting, called *pan-roasting*. Pan-roasting involves searing meat or poultry in a very hot pan on both sides to give it some crispiness and then finishing the meat by putting the pan in the oven.

TIP

To create a good sear, let the steaks cook without moving them around in the hot pan, unless it's to turn them over.

The advantage to pan-roasting over basic sautéing is that sautéing draws out moisture. The longer the food is in the pan, the dryer it gets. With pan-roasting, you limit the length of time the food is in the pan, preventing it from drying out. It's particularly good for lean cuts of meat like pork and chicken; the outside gets nicely browned but more moisture is retained.

REMEMBER

When you pan-roast meat, you can't use a nonstick skillet because nonstick skillets can't go in the oven. You must use a cast-iron or stainless steel skillet that can withstand the high temperatures needed to pan-roast meat in the oven. The coating on a nonstick skillet will melt in the oven. (See the Pan-Seared and Roasted Turkey Burgers and Pan-Roasted Steaks with Simple Herb-Butter Sauce recipes later in this chapter.)

Making Great Sauce from Bits in the Pan: Deglazing

A very hot sauté pan begins to cook meat, poultry, or fish right away, browning the juices that flow from it and leaving bits of food sticking to the bottom of the pan. These browned bits (called *fond*) are loaded with flavor. If *deglazed* (moistened and scraped up) in the pan, they become transformed into a delicious sauce.

Just follow these easy steps, illustrated in Figure 6-1, if you want to deglaze:

Deglazing a Pan

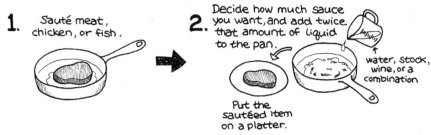

1. Sauté meat, chicken, or fish.

2. Decide how much sauce you want, and add twice that amount of liquid to the pan.

water, stock, wine, or a combination

Put the sautéed item on a platter.

3. Raise the heat to HIGH, scrape off all of the brown particles clinging to the bottom of the pan, and boil until sauce is reduced by half.

4. Spoon the sauce over the meat or fish.

Illustration by Elizabeth Kurtzman

FIGURE 6-1:
Deglazing a pan enables you to intensify the flavor of your sauce.

1. **Remove the meat, poultry, or fish from the pan onto a serving platter and immediately add liquid — you can use water, wine, stock, or a combination.**

    The liquid should be twice the amount of sauce you want to make. For example, if you want to make 1 cup of sauce, add 2 cups of wine.

TIP

   As a rule, the wine you use for deglazing depends on what you're sautéing: Use white wine for poultry and seafood, and red wine for meat.

2. **Raise the heat to high, bringing the liquid to a boil while you stir and scrape the browned bits off the bottom of the pan until they dissolve into the sauce.**

   This stirring and scraping is the key to deglazing — all those delicious little caramelized bits of cooked meat infuse the liquid, making it taste fantastic.

3. **Keep boiling and stirring until the sauce is reduced by half the volume or, in other words, until those 2 cups of wine (or water or broth) have boiled down to about 1 cup.**

   How can you tell? Just eyeball it. When it looks like you have half as much liquid as you did, it's time to take a taste.

And the verdict? Does your sauce taste delicious, or does it need more salt and/or black pepper? Maybe a dash of fresh herbs? Add more seasoning if you think the sauce needs more flavor. You might also stir in a teaspoon or more of butter just before you drizzle it over your main course — this adds a smooth texture.

Getting Versatile with Your Sautéing

You can sauté just about any meat, fish, or vegetable, so experiment and enjoy some delicious meals. Later in this chapter, we offer several recipes for sautéed veggies, fish, chicken, and beef. Here, we offer just a quick overview of how to sauté each.

Vegetables

RECIPE ALERT

Vegetables are excellent when blanched or steamed until about 90 percent done (see Chapter 5 for details on steaming and blanching) and then transferred to a skillet to be finished by sautéing in butter and maybe fresh herbs. Many classic recipes for potatoes call for sautéing; thinly sliced raw potatoes are delicious when cooked this way. In the Sautéed Skillet Potatoes recipe later in the chapter, you cut the potatoes into fine cubes and toss them in a hot pan until crispy.

WARNING

Be very careful when you put rinsed vegetables (or other foods) into a pan of hot fat. The water that clings to the vegetables makes the fat splatter, which can cause serious burns. Always dry vegetables before sautéing.

Firm, rich fish

RECIPE
ALERT

Rich fish — those with a high fat content, such as salmon, tuna, and bluefish — are exceptionally good when sautéed. And you can enhance them with countless sauces that you can make in 15 minutes or less (see Chapter 14). Because these fish have relatively high fat content, they also stand up to spicy sauces. The recipe for Tuna Steaks with Ginger-Chili Glaze later in the chapter is a perfect example.

Keep in mind that a spicy sauce paired with a delicate fish, like sole or snapper, can be a flop. In general, firm-fleshed fish (or fatty fish) stands up best to spiciness.

Chicken and turkey

Sautéing is a great way to impart flavor to poultry. It stays juicy with a flavorful outside, especially with the addition of different herbs and spices. Sautéing is particularly good with the chicken or turkey's skin left on. You can also make a delicious sauce with the leftover oil (or butter) and herbs in the pan by adding wine, juice, or chicken broth to the pan after cooking the poultry and reducing the liquid to concentrate the flavor.

RECIPE
ALERT

Want to try some wonderful recipes to see what we mean? Check out the Sautéed Chicken Breasts with Tomatoes and Thyme later in this chapter, as well as the Lemon-Rubbed Chicken with Rosemary.

Beef

When sautéing beef, you want to choose thin cuts to allow the meat to cook through over the high heat. Thicker cuts may not cook all the way through, leaving the middle pink (or red).

To create a good sear, let the steaks cook without moving them around in the hot pan, unless it's to turn them over. Don't crowd meat in a pan when cooking on the stovetop; instead leave ¼ to ½ inch between each piece in the pan. Crowding the meat can cause it to steam and turn gray.

TIP

Always let steaks and other meats rest 5 to 10 minutes after cooking, covered, to allow juices to distribute evenly.

TIP

The doneness of steaks is defined by the meat's interior color. Rare meat is bright red and juicy. Medium meat has a light pink center with light brown edges. Well-done, which we don't recommend, is brown-gray and dry throughout. Check for doneness with a meat thermometer.

Sautéed Skillet Potatoes

| PREP TIME: ABOUT 15 MIN | COOK TIME: ABOUT 20 MIN | YIELD: 4 SERVINGS |

INGREDIENTS

2 large baking potatoes, about 1½ pounds total

¼ cup canola or corn oil

2 tablespoons butter

1 medium yellow onion, peeled and chopped

½ green bell pepper, cored, seeded, and chopped

½ teaspoon dried oregano

½ teaspoon or less of salt

Few dashes black pepper

⅛ teaspoon cayenne pepper or red pepper flakes (optional)

DIRECTIONS

1 Cut any eyes and bad spots out of the potatoes. Scrub them with a vegetable brush to remove dirt, but leave them unpeeled. Cut potatoes into ¼-inch cubes.

2 Place the potato cubes in a colander in the sink. Run very hot water over the potatoes for about 10 seconds to remove the starch. Drain well and dry on paper towels.

3 Heat the oil in a large, nonstick skillet over high heat. Add the potatoes and cook, stirring often, for about 10 minutes.

4 With a slotted spoon, remove the potatoes from the pan to a large bowl. Remove the oil from the skillet, and wipe the skillet with paper towels.

5 Melt the butter in the skillet over medium-high heat.

6 Sauté the onion, bell pepper, oregano, salt, black pepper, and cayenne pepper, if desired. Cook, stirring occasionally, for 4 to 5 minutes until the vegetables begin to soften.

7 Add the potatoes back into the skillet and sauté everything together until the potatoes are browned and crisp, about 5 more minutes. Serve immediately.

PER SERVING: *Calories 325 (From Fat 180); Fat 20g (Saturated 5g); Cholesterol 15mg; Sodium 307mg; Carbohydrate 35g (Dietary Fiber 4g); Protein 4g.*

GO-WITH: These potatoes are a delicious side dish to omelets (see Chapter 11), Roasted Fillet of Beef (see Chapter 8), or Roasted Loin of Pork (see Chapter 8).

Sea Scallops Sautéed in Clarified Butter

PREP TIME: 5 MIN	COOK TIME: ABOUT 6 MIN	YIELD: 4 SERVINGS

INGREDIENTS

12 large sea scallops
(1 to 1¼ pounds)

Salt and black pepper

4 tablespoons unsalted butter,
cut into 1-inch pieces

Lemon wedges (optional)

DIRECTIONS

1 Pat the scallops dry with paper towels and sprinkle them lightly on both sides with salt and black pepper to taste.

2 Melt the butter in a small saucepan over very low heat without stirring. Use a spoon to skim off and discard the foamy layer that rises to the top. Carefully pour off the clear yellow clarified butter into a 10- to 12-inch stainless steel skillet (not a nonstick skillet). You should have at least 2 tablespoons.

3 Set the skillet over medium-high heat and heat the clarified butter just until it begins to ripple.

4 Add the sea scallops to the skillet, flat-side down, without any of them touching. (If necessary, cook the scallops in two batches). Sauté the scallops without moving them until their bottoms are a rich golden brown, about 2 minutes. Using tongs, flip the scallops and cook until golden brown on the other side, 1 to 2 minutes more, depending on the size of the scallops. When cooked, the scallops will be mostly opaque with a slightly translucent center and firm sides. Serve immediately with lemon wedges (if desired).

PER SERVING: Calories 202 (From Fat 117); Fat 13g (Saturated 7g); Cholesterol 66mg; Sodium 300mg; Carbohydrate 3g (Dietary Fiber 0g); Protein 19g.

VARY IT! After sautéing the scallops, remove them to a plate and cover with foil to keep warm. Heat 1 tablespoon butter over medium heat in the skillet used to cook the scallops, and stir with a wooden spoon to scrape up the brown bits. Add ¼ cup chicken broth or white wine and 2 tablespoons parsley; stir a few seconds or until just heated through. Pour the pan sauce over the scallops before serving.

Tuna Steaks with Ginger-Chili Glaze

PREP TIME: ABOUT 15 MIN	COOK TIME: ABOUT 15 MIN	YIELD: 4 SERVINGS

INGREDIENTS

4 tuna steaks, each about 6 to 7 ounces and ¾ inch thick

Few dashes of salt and pepper for each steak

2 tablespoons butter

1 cup white wine or white grape juice

1 tablespoon red chili paste

½ teaspoon dried ground ginger

1 tablespoon brown sugar

1 tablespoon dark sesame oil

DIRECTIONS

1 Season both sides of the tuna steaks with salt and pepper. Melt the butter over medium-high heat in a nonstick skillet or sauté pan large enough to hold the steaks in one layer.

2 Add the tuna to the pan and cook until lightly browned on both sides, about 3 minutes per side.

3 Transfer the steaks to a warm platter and cover with foil. Leave the cooking butter in the skillet and scrape the bottom of the pan with a wooden spoon to loosen the browned bits clinging to the pan.

4 Add the wine or grape juice, turn up the heat to high, and cook until about half the liquid in the pan evaporates (less than a minute).

5 Lower the heat to medium. Add the chili paste, ginger, brown sugar, and sesame oil. Stir continuously until the ingredients are well combined.

6 Add the tuna steaks (and any of their juices on the platter) back into the pan, and bring the liquid to a simmer. Cook for about 1 minute or until warmed through, turning once to coat the steaks in the glaze. Don't overcook.

7 Using a flat metal spatula, remove each tuna steak to an individual plate. Spoon a little of the sauce over each steak and serve immediately.

PER SERVING: *Calories 274 (From Fat 96); Fat 11g (Saturated 4g); Cholesterol 89mg; Sodium 305mg; Carbohydrate 4g (Dietary Fiber 0g); Protein 38g.*

TIP: If you don't have a pan big enough to cook all the tuna steaks at once, use a smaller skillet and cook the tuna in batches. If you do so, be sure to save enough sauce for all the steaks.

TIP: Find red chili paste with the Asian food ingredients in your grocery store.

Sautéed Chicken Breasts with Tomatoes and Thyme

PREP TIME: ABOUT 20 MIN	COOK TIME: ABOUT 15 MIN	YIELD: 4 SERVINGS

INGREDIENTS

4 boneless, skinless chicken breast halves

Salt and black pepper

2 tablespoons olive oil

1 medium yellow onion, chopped

1 large clove garlic, chopped

2 medium tomatoes, peeled, seeded, and chopped

1 teaspoon chopped fresh thyme, or ¼ teaspoon dried

2 tablespoons chopped fresh basil, or 2 teaspoons dried (optional)

⅓ cup white wine or chicken stock

DIRECTIONS

1   Place the chicken breasts on a cutting board, season generously on both sides with salt and black pepper, cover with wax paper, and pound them lightly so they're of equal thickness. (Use the bottom of a heavy pan or a meat mallet.)

2   Heat the olive oil in a large sauté pan or skillet over medium-high heat. Add the chicken and sauté for about 4 to 5 minutes per side or until done. Remove the pieces to a platter and cover with foil to keep warm.

3   Add the onion to the pan over medium heat. Stir for 1 minute, scraping the bottom of the pan. Add the garlic, stirring occasionally for another minute. Add the tomatoes, thyme, basil (if desired), and salt and black pepper to taste. Stir for 1 minute.

4   Add the wine or stock, increase the heat to high, and cook, stirring occasionally, for about 2 to 3 minutes until most of the liquid evaporates. (You want moist, not soupy.)

5   Place the chicken on a plate and spoon equal portions of sauce over each piece.

PER SERVING: *Calories 170 (From Fat 47); Fat 5g (Saturated 1g); Cholesterol 63mg; Sodium 203mg; Carbohydrate 6g (Dietary Fiber 1g); Protein 24g.*

VARY IT! You can modify this recipe in many ways. For example, use turkey breasts or slices of veal instead of chicken; add 1 cup fresh, frozen, or canned corn kernels with the chopped tomatoes; add 2 tablespoons heavy cream with the stock or wine; substitute tarragon, marjoram, or other herb of choice for the thyme; or grate some Parmesan cheese over the top of each serving.

Lemon-Rubbed Chicken with Rosemary

PREP TIME: 10 MIN	COOK TIME: 35–40 MIN	YIELD: 4 SERVINGS

INGREDIENTS

4 whole chicken legs, with drumsticks, trimmed of excess fat (about 1½ to 2 pounds)

2 lemons, quartered

Salt and black pepper to taste

1½ tablespoons minced fresh rosemary leaves, or 3 teaspoons dried

2 tablespoons olive oil

2 cloves garlic, coarsely chopped

5 tablespoons chicken broth or water

DIRECTIONS

1 Rinse the chicken and pat dry with paper towels. With a large knife, separate the drumsticks from the thighs.

2 Rub the chicken pieces with four of the lemon wedges. Squeeze juice from those wedges over the chicken. Season with salt, black pepper, and 1 tablespoon of the fresh rosemary (or 2 teaspoons of dried rosemary).

3 In a 10-inch fry pan over medium-high heat, heat the oil and cook the chicken pieces, skin-side down, until golden brown, 7 to 10 minutes. Flip the chicken pieces and squeeze remaining lemon juice over them.

4 Reduce to medium-low heat and cook, covered, for 25 to 30 minutes or until the meat in the center along the bone is no longer pink. Transfer to serving plates.

5 Return the skillet to medium-high heat. Add the garlic and remaining rosemary. Cook for 45 seconds to a minute (the garlic should be barely golden — don't let it burn).

6 Add the chicken broth or water. Scrape the dark bits clinging to the bottom of the pan and cook about 45 seconds, stirring. Drizzle over the chicken.

PER SERVING: *Calories 551 (From Fat 339); Fat 38g (Saturated 9g); Cholesterol 161mg; Sodium 313mg; Carbohydrate 6g (Dietary Fiber 1g); Protein 46g.*

TIP: To separate drumsticks from thighs, place the chicken pieces on a cutting board, fat-side down; use your finger to locate the joint between the thigh and the drumstick and cut through.

Pan-Roasted Steaks with Simple Herb-Butter Sauce

PREP TIME: ABOUT 5 MIN	COOK TIME: ABOUT 15 MIN	YIELD: 4 SERVINGS

INGREDIENTS

Two 12- to 14-ounce boneless New York strip steaks, 1½ inches thick

1 tablespoon vegetable oil, plus more for coating steaks

Salt and black pepper

2 tablespoons butter

2 teaspoons fresh chopped thyme

2 teaspoons fresh finely chopped rosemary leaves

1½ teaspoons Worcestershire sauce (optional)

DIRECTIONS

1 If necessary, let the steaks set out of the refrigerator for about 30 minutes to bring to room temperature.

2 Preheat the oven to 400 degrees with a rack in the middle position.

3 Use paper towels to pat the steaks dry on both sides. Rub them generously with oil and season with salt and black pepper to taste.

4 Place a large cast-iron or other heavy skillet (not a nonstick!) over medium-high heat for 1 to 3 minutes or until very hot. Add the vegetable oil and heat until just smoking. (When the oil begins to smoke, you know it's reached a temperature of about 450 degrees, which is perfect for searing.)

5 Lay the steaks in the skillet without them touching and cook about 3 minutes, or until the steak releases easily from the pan and its bottom side has a dark brown crust. Use tongs to turn and cook another 1 to 2 minutes to lightly brown the other side.

6 Place the skillet in the oven, and cook 8 to 10 minutes, or until an instant-read thermometer inserted into the thickest part of each steak registers 125 to 130 degrees for medium rare or 135 to 140 degrees for medium.

7   Transfer the steaks to a cutting board, cover with foil, and let rest 5 to 10 minutes while making the pan herb-butter sauce.

8   Allow the hot skillet to cool about 3 to 4 minutes, and then remove and discard all but 1 tablespoon of fat from the skillet. Place the skillet over medium heat; add the butter and herbs, and stir until the butter melts, scraping up any browned bits on the bottom of the pan and incorporating them into the sauce. Stir in the Worcestershire sauce (if desired).

9   Slice the steak against the grain and transfer the slices to a serving platter. Add any juices on the carving board to the pan sauce and stir to combine. Drizzle the sliced steak with the pan sauce and serve immediately.

PER SERVING: *Calories 299 (From Fat 126); Fat 14g (Saturated 6g); Cholesterol 117mg; Sodium 233mg; Carbohydrate 0g (Dietary Fiber 0g); Protein 43g.*

Pan-Seared and Roasted Turkey Burgers

PREP TIME: 15 MIN	COOK TIME: ABOUT 25 MIN	YIELD: 4 SERVINGS

INGREDIENTS

1¼ pounds ground turkey meat (93% lean)

2 slices bacon, ends trimmed of fat, cut into ¼-inch pieces

⅓ cup diced onion

⅓ cup diced celery

1 teaspoon finely chopped jalapeño pepper, seeded

2 teaspoons peeled and finely chopped fresh ginger (optional)

2 teaspoons chopped fresh parsley or thyme

1 tablespoon Worcestershire sauce

1 tablespoon ketchup

Salt and black pepper to taste

1 tablespoon extra-virgin olive oil

4 burger buns, lightly toasted

Lettuce, ripe tomato slices, ketchup, and mustard for garnishing each burger (optional)

DIRECTIONS

1 Position an oven rack in the middle of the oven and preheat the oven to 350 degrees.

2 Mix together the ground turkey, bacon, onion, celery, jalapeño, ginger (if desired), parsley or thyme, Worcestershire sauce, ketchup, salt, and black pepper in a large bowl. (**Note:** The diced bacon adds salt, so salt lightly or not at all.)

3 Shape the mixture into four patties, each about 1 inch thick. Heat the olive oil in a large cast-iron or other heavy skillet (not a nonstick!) over medium-high heat until it begins to shimmer. Add the patties to the skillet and cook without moving them, until the bottom is seared brown, 3 to 5 minutes. Use a wide spatula to turn the burgers over and cook 4 to 5 minutes longer. (Adjust the heat as necessary so the burgers brown without burning.)

4 Place the skillet in the preheated oven and cook 12 to 18 minutes. After 10 minutes, insert an instant-read thermometer through the side and into the center of the burgers to check for doneness. The burgers are ready to eat when the internal temperature reads 165 degrees.

5 Serve on toasted buns with lettuce, tomato slices, ketchup, and mustard (if desired).

PER SERVING: *Calories 375 (From Fat 153); Fat 17g (Saturated 6g); Cholesterol 104mg; Sodium 547mg; Carbohydrate 26g (Dietary Fiber 1g); Protein 33g.*

VARY IT! Skip the buns and serve the burgers over a bed of arugula tossed lightly with a dressing of extra-virgin olive oil, balsamic vinegar, Dijon mustard, and salt and black pepper to taste.

NOTE: In most households, where dinner is often a last-minute thought, turkey burgers are a go-to choice. Ground turkey meat is much leaner than ground beef, making it a healthy alternative. However, that same leanness, and the fact that you must cook a turkey burger to 165 degrees or until the juices run clear, can result in a dry patty. A little raw, diced bacon added to the patty mix overcomes this problem. The bacon releases its fat as the burger cooks, adding just the right touch of moisture and a subtle smoky flavor.

Snapper Fillets with Tomatoes

PREP TIME: ABOUT 15 MIN | COOK TIME: ABOUT 15 MIN | YIELD: 4 SERVINGS

INGREDIENTS

2 tablespoons olive oil

5 plum tomatoes, peeled, seeded, and chopped

1 large leek, white and light green part only, finely chopped

½ cup chopped fennel bulb

2 large cloves garlic, finely chopped

1 teaspoon turmeric

Salt and black pepper

½ cup dry white wine or white grape juice

½ cup fish stock or bottled clam juice

1 bay leaf

4 sprigs fresh thyme, or 1 teaspoon dried

⅛ teaspoon Tabasco sauce

4 snapper fillets with skin on, or other white-fleshed fish, about 6 ounces each

2 tablespoons Ricard, Pernod, or other anise-flavored liqueur (optional)

2 tablespoons chopped basil or parsley

DIRECTIONS

1 In a medium saucepan over medium heat, combine 1 tablespoon of the olive oil and the tomatoes, leek, fennel, garlic, and turmeric. Season with salt and black pepper to taste. Cook, stirring often, about 3 minutes.

2 Add the wine, stock, bay leaf, thyme, and Tabasco sauce. Bring to a boil, reduce heat, and simmer for 5 minutes.

3 In a large sauté pan, add the remaining tablespoon of oil and arrange the fillets of fish in one layer, skin-side down. Season with salt and black pepper to taste.

4 Pour the leek-tomato mixture evenly over the fish fillets. Sprinkle on the Ricard or Pernod (if desired), cover, and cook over medium heat for about 5 minutes, until the fish is opaque in the center.

5 Discard the bay leaf and sprinkle with the basil or parsley before serving.

PER SERVING: *Calories 264 (From Fat 85); Fat 9g (Saturated 1g); Cholesterol 61mg; Sodium 302mg; Carbohydrate 9g (Dietary Fiber 2g); Protein 35g.*

Chapter **7**

Braising and Stewing: Slow and Seductive

f you're like most people, you have precious little time, especially during the week, to stand at the stove or even the microwave. This chapter is for you. Braising and stewing are slow cooking methods that allow you to put all the ingredients in a pot, turn the heat to low, and do something else for an hour or two — maybe read last week's newspaper or shampoo the dog.

Braised and stewed foods have exceptional depth of flavor. Slow cooking allows seasonings to infuse the main ingredients, and it breaks down sinewy fibers. Also, over time, vegetables release their natural sugars. The result? Sublime simplicity, or (to use an overworked cliché) comfort food.

TIP

Because braising and stewing take time, these dishes are best made in big batches so you can freeze individual portions in tightly sealed containers. They'll last several months. Stews are unquestionably better the next day. We should point out that inexpensive braised and stewed dishes make great party vittles with a few condiments on the side (like beer).

Most meat dishes in this chapter use the less expensive front cuts of beef: the chuck, brisket, shank, and plate. (See Chapter 3 for an illustration of the various cuts of beef.) These more muscular cuts don't make much of a steak, but when you braise them for hours, their fibers break down and they become succulent. In some ways, these cuts are more flavorful than expensive tenderloin.

Slow cookers also use the concepts of braising and stewing, but they do it automatically. We talk about slow cooking in Chapter 16, and if you want even more information, check out *Slow Cookers For Dummies*, by Tom Lacalamita and Glenna Vance (Wiley).

Cooking in Liquid

Both braising and stewing involve long, slow cooking in liquid. The major difference is that in *braising,* foods lie in a few inches of liquid, not quite submerged, so they stew and steam at the same time. *Stewing* involves submerging ingredients in a liquid and simmering the mixture for a long time.

Braising involves larger cuts of meat, whereas cut-up meat is stewed. For example, you braise a pot roast but stew cubed beef. Both methods make meat very, very tender. Here, we further define braising versus stewing.

Browning before braising

Larger cuts of meat — and the very toughest — tend to be braised. The meat is usually browned in hot oil first, to give it a toothsome texture and appealing color. You can braise a beef roast, a pork roast, or any other large piece of meat, including a whole chicken, by browning it on all sides in hot oil to color it and add flavor, and then cooking it in a liquid.

RECIPE ALERT

Braising is so easy to do that you may as well jump right in and try it. Later in the chapter, we show you how to make delicious Beer-Braised Beef with Onions. One of the easiest and most basic things to braise is a good old classic pot roast, so we also offer a great recipe for Pot Roast with Vegetables. When you're shopping, keep in mind that the best cut of beef for a pot roast is the *first-cut* brisket. Sometimes referred to as the *flat cut,* the first-cut brisket has just the right amount of fat so it's not too dry after it's cooked. Ask your butcher for the first cut.

Taking time to stew

Dollar for dollar, meat goes a long way when you stew it. For instance, few dishes are more economical than beef stew, yet who would know it from the taste? More expensive ingredients such as seafood can make a stew seem luxurious, but you don't need nearly as much shrimp, crab, or fish per person as you would if you were serving these dishes on their own. You can also use cut-up boneless chicken or turkey breasts, cubed pork, or sliced sausage.

RECIPE ALERT

Lean, boneless chuck is one of the least expensive cuts of beef, and we show you a great way to prepare it with the Old-Fashioned Beef Stew recipe later in the chapter. The root vegetables (carrots and turnips) that surround it are also economical — and healthful. Other good cuts to ask for when stewing are the neck, brisket, and shank.

RECIPE ALERT

If beef isn't your thing, and you're wondering whether stew has any place on your menu at all, be sure to check out the Mediterranean Seafood Stew recipe later in this chapter. It just may change how you think about stew forever! Before you make it, you'll need to know how to devein shrimp; Figure 7-1 shows you the easy steps to take using a tool called a *deveiner*.

Cleaning and Deveining Shrimp

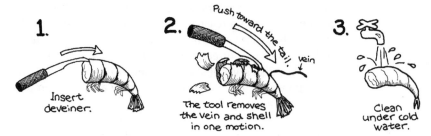

1. Insert deveiner.

2. Push toward the tail. vein
The tool removes the vein and shell in one motion.

3. Clean under cold water.

FIGURE 7-1:
How to clean and devein shrimp.

Illustration by Elizabeth Kurtzman

Braising greens

Braising is not just for meat. Certain vegetables benefit from this cooking method as well. Keep in mind that not all leafy greens are the same. Spinach and beet greens hold a lot of moisture and cook quickly in little or no liquid (sometimes a little olive oil is a nice touch). On the other hand, kale, mustard greens, and collard greens are tougher and dryer. They're best braised in chicken stock or vegetable stock (covered).

RECIPE ALERT

Sometimes, two different techniques are used to cook greens like kale. In the recipe for Sautéed and Braised Kale with Rosemary and Garlic, you lightly sauté the trimmed kale in some rosemary-flavored oil and garlic until the kale is wilted. Then you add a little chicken broth and lemon juice to the pot. You don't add enough liquid to boil or overwhelm the kale; just enough to gently braise, break down, and tenderize the leave's tough fibers.

Before you can braise thick greens like kale, Swiss chard, and collard greens, you need to remove the tough, thick stems. See Chapter 12 for details on removing stems and cutting greens into ribbons.

Keeping Herbs and Spices in Check

Many braising and stewing recipes call for a blending of herbs and spices. Because the rainbow of herbs and spices available to home cooks is so exciting (see Chapter 3), you may be tempted to overdo it. The best way to get to know herbs and spices is to cook dishes that contain only one herb or spice — see how it interacts with different foods, watch how it intensifies with cooking, and find out whether you really like it.

For example, with rosemary, you can make a quick sauce for sautéed or grilled chicken breast by combining 3 parts chicken stock to 1 part white wine in a saucepan. Then add a teaspoon of minced fresh rosemary (or ½ teaspoon dry), some very thin slices of garlic, and salt and black pepper to taste. Cook the liquid until it's reduced by three-quarters. Then strain the sauce and serve it over the chicken. This dish gives you a pure rosemary flavor. If you like it, you can refine it by adding more or less rosemary or even by adding a complementary herb, such as thyme, tarragon, or chives.

TIP

Here's a tip for recipes that call for using fresh herb sprigs: Tie them together with a little kitchen twine. Doing so makes removing the herb sprigs easier, and you get the benefit of the flavor without any stringy herb stems.

Got a recipe that calls for a dried herb? Before adding it to your stewing pot, crush the brittle leaves in a mortar and pestle or with your fingers into smaller, more palatable pieces. Doing so also releases more of the herb's flavor.

You may notice that some recipes, such as for Mediterranean Seafood Stew in this chapter, call for you to add an herb to a dish at the very last minute (in the case of this stew, the herb is cilantro). That's because fresh herbs are at their most fragrant that way. Cooking delicate chervil, cilantro, or parsley mutes their flavors. Moreover, herbs are more colorful when added at the last minute.

Beer-Braised Beef with Onions

PREP TIME: ABOUT 10 MIN	COOK TIME: ABOUT 2 HR 30 MIN	YIELD: 8 SERVINGS

INGREDIENTS

One 4-pound piece of beef chuck roast, cut into 1-inch cubes

Salt and black pepper to taste

2 tablespoons vegetable oil

1½ pounds onions, peeled and thickly sliced

1 tablespoon minced garlic

2 tablespoons flour

24 ounces dark beer

⅛ teaspoon cinnamon

4 whole cloves

1 tablespoon tomato paste

1 bay leaf

½ teaspoon dried thyme

1 cup fresh or canned beef or chicken broth

DIRECTIONS

1 Preheat the oven to 325 degrees.

2 Season the meat with salt and black pepper. Heat the oil in a Dutch oven over high heat and brown the meat on all sides. Remove the meat from the pot.

3 Add the onions and garlic to the pot and stir periodically until the onions brown, about 7 minutes. Season with salt and black pepper.

4 Stir in the flour and then the beer. Add the cinnamon and cloves. Bring to a boil.

5 Add the tomato paste, bay leaf, thyme, and broth. Return the meat to the pot and bring to a boil.

6 Cook, covered, in a 325-degree oven for about 2 hours and 15 minutes, or until the meat is tender (easily pierced with a carving fork). Slice it crosswise and serve in a deep dish with the cooking liquid.

PER SERVING: *Calories 336 (From Fat 121); Fat 14g (Saturated 4g); Cholesterol 119mg; Sodium 279mg; Carbohydrate 10g (Dietary Fiber 2g); Protein 41g.*

Old-Fashioned Beef Stew

PREP TIME: ABOUT 25 MIN	COOK TIME: ABOUT 1 HR 40 MIN	YIELD: 8 SERVINGS

INGREDIENTS

¼ cup olive or vegetable oil

4 pounds lean, boneless chuck, cut into 2-inch cubes

2 large yellow onions, coarsely chopped

6 large cloves garlic, chopped

6 tablespoons flour

Salt and black pepper

3 cups dry red wine

3 cups homemade or canned beef or chicken stock

2 tablespoons tomato paste

4 whole cloves

2 bay leaves

4 sprigs parsley, tied together

4 sprigs fresh thyme, or 1 teaspoon dried

1 tablespoon minced fresh rosemary, leaves only, or 1 teaspoon dried

1 pound small turnips, trimmed and cut into 2-inch pieces

6 large carrots, trimmed and cut into 1-inch lengths

DIRECTIONS

1 Heat the oil in a large stew pot over medium-high heat and add the beef cubes. Cook, stirring and turning the meat as necessary, for 5 to 10 minutes until evenly browned.

2 Add the onion and garlic and cook over medium heat, stirring occasionally, for about 8 minutes. Sprinkle the flour, salt, and black pepper over everything. Stir.

3 Add the wine, stock, and tomato paste, and stir over high heat until the cooking liquid thickens as it comes to a boil.

4 Add the cloves, bay leaves, parsley, thyme, rosemary, and turnips. Cover and reduce the heat to low. Simmer for 1 hour, occasionally stirring and scraping the bottom of the pot.

5 Add the carrots and cook until the meat and carrots are tender, about 20 minutes more. Remove the herb sprigs and bay leaves before serving.

PER SERVING: *Calories 409 (From Fat 155); Fat 17g (Saturated 5g); Cholesterol 119mg; Sodium 237mg; Carbohydrate 18g (Dietary Fiber 4g); Protein 43g.*

Mediterranean Seafood Stew

PREP TIME: ABOUT 30 MIN | COOK TIME: ABOUT 25 MIN | YIELD: 4 SERVINGS

INGREDIENTS

3 tablespoons olive oil

2 large leeks, white and light green parts only, washed and cut into ½-inch pieces

2 large cloves garlic, chopped

1 red bell pepper, cored, seeded, and diced

¾ teaspoon ground cumin

¼ to ½ teaspoon red pepper flakes, or to taste

3 ripe plum tomatoes, cored and diced

1 cup dry white wine

1 cup water

Salt and black pepper

1 pound medium shrimp, shelled and deveined

¾ pound sea scallops, cut in half

¼ cup coarsely chopped cilantro or parsley

DIRECTIONS

1 Heat the oil in a large, deep sauté pan or skillet over medium heat. Add the leeks and cook, stirring occasionally, about 4 minutes, or until they wilt.

2 Add the garlic and cook, stirring often, for another 1 to 2 minutes, until just golden.

3 Add the red bell pepper, cumin, and red pepper flakes. Cook over low heat about 8 minutes, or until the peppers are tender, stirring occasionally.

4 Add the tomatoes, wine, water, and salt and black pepper to taste. Cover and bring the mixture to a boil. Reduce the heat to medium and cook, partially covered, for 6 to 8 minutes.

5 Add the shrimp and scallops and cook, partially covered, about 5 minutes more, or just until the shrimp is evenly pink and the scallops are opaque.

6 Remove from the heat, stir in the cilantro or parsley, and serve.

PER SERVING: *Calories 318 (From Fat 111); Fat 12g (Saturated 2g); Cholesterol 210mg; Sodium 551mg; Carbohydrate 13g (Dietary Fiber 2g); Protein 36g.*

TIP: You can prepare this stew several hours ahead of serving time. Complete the recipe through Step 4, and 5 minutes before you want to serve the stew, add the seafood and finish cooking.

VARY IT! Can't find leeks? Substitute one medium white onion, chopped, for the leeks in this recipe.

Pot Roast with Vegetables

| PREP TIME: 20 MIN | COOK TIME: ABOUT 3 HR | YIELD: 8 SERVINGS |

INGREDIENTS

2 tablespoons vegetable oil

4 pounds first-cut beef brisket

2 large yellow onions, chopped

3 large cloves garlic, chopped

½ cup dry white wine

½ cup water

1 bay leaf

¼ teaspoon dried thyme

Salt and black pepper

4 large Idaho potatoes, peeled and cut into bite-size chunks

3 large carrots, peeled and sliced crosswise into 2-inch pieces

3 tablespoons chopped fresh parsley

DIRECTIONS

1 Heat the oil in a large (preferably cast-iron) Dutch oven over high heat. Add the brisket and sear on both sides, about 7 to 8 minutes, until golden brown. Remove the brisket to a large plate.

2 Reduce the heat to medium-high. Add the onions and garlic, and sauté until the onions are lightly browned, stirring frequently. (Don't let the garlic brown.)

3 Return the brisket to the pot. Add the wine, water, bay leaf, thyme, and salt and black pepper to taste.

4 Cover, bring to a boil, lower the heat, and simmer for 2¾ to 3 hours, turning the meat several times and adding ½ to 1 cup more water if the liquid evaporates.

5 About 10 minutes before the end of the cooking time, add the potatoes and carrots.

6 When the meat is tender (easily pierced with a fork), remove it to a carving board with a long-handled fork. Cover it with foil and let it rest for 10 to 15 minutes.

7 Continue cooking the potatoes and carrots in the covered pot until tender, about 10 to 15 minutes more.

8 Slice the brisket across the grain and arrange the slices on a serving platter.

9 Remove the potatoes and carrots from the gravy and spoon them around the meat.

10 Skim the fat from the surface of the remaining juices, remove the bay leaf and discard, heat the juices through, and spoon over the meat and vegetables. Sprinkle with the chopped parsley. Serve the extra gravy in a gravy boat.

PER SERVING: Calories 546 (From Fat 199); Fat 22g (Saturated 7g); Cholesterol 133mg; Sodium 199mg; Carbohydrate 38g (Dietary Fiber 5g); Protein 47g.

SOLVING COOKING WOES

What do you do if a stew or a braised dish is . . .

- **Flat-tasting?** Add salt and black pepper. Or try a little sherry or Madeira.

- **Tough?** Cook it longer in a liquid of some sort. Additional cooking breaks down the sinew in muscular cuts of meat. Make sure there's enough braising liquid; if not, add water. You may want to remove the vegetables in the dish with a slotted spoon to prevent them from overcooking.

- **Burned on the bottom?** It may be too late to salvage. Try carefully scooping out the unburned portion of the stew into a separate pot. Add water or stock to stretch it if necessary, and add sherry and a chopped onion. (The sweetness in an onion can mask many mistakes.)

- **Too thin?** Blend 1 tablespoon flour with 1 tablespoon water. Combine this mixture with 1 cup stew liquid and return to the pot with the rest of the stew. Stir well. Heat slowly until thickened.

Chicken Tagine with Tomatoes, Olives, and Preserved Lemons

PREP TIME: ABOUT 25 MIN	COOK TIME: ABOUT 40 MIN	YIELD: 4 SERVINGS

INGREDIENTS

5 bone-in, skin-on chicken thighs (about 2 pounds)

2 chicken breast halves, bone-in (about 1½ pounds)

Salt and black pepper to taste

1 tablespoon extra-virgin olive oil

1 large onion, finely chopped (about 1½ cups)

3 cloves garlic, thinly sliced

1¼ teaspoons cinnamon

¾ teaspoon ground ginger

½ teaspoon paprika

2 dashes cayenne red pepper (optional)

1½ cups water

2 large ripe plum tomatoes, peeled, seeded, and chopped, or 1½ cups canned diced tomatoes

½ teaspoon crushed saffron threads or powdered saffron

Half a preserved lemon rind, rinsed well and cut into small pieces

12 pitted green olives, halved

Couscous or loaf of crusty bread for serving

DIRECTIONS

1 Trim the chicken of excess fat, and if the breast halves are very large, cut them in half crosswise. Season the chicken pieces lightly with salt and black pepper. (Salt lightly because the preserved lemon and olives add salt).

2 Heat the oil in a large heavy-bottomed saucepan or Dutch oven over medium-high. Add the chicken thighs, skin-side down, and cook for about 5 minutes or until the skin is lightly browned. Turn and cook about 3 to 4 minutes to brown the other side. Remove the thighs to a plate, and repeat with the breast pieces.

3 Pour off all but about 1 tablespoon of fat in the pan. (Keep the browned bits in the pan; remove any bits that are burned.) Heat the fat over medium heat. Add the onion and cook 4 to 5 minutes or until softened and lightly browned, stirring often. Add the garlic, cinnamon, ginger, paprika, and cayenne red pepper (if desired); cook, stirring about 30 seconds or just until the garlic and spices are fragrant.

4 Return the chicken to the pan with any juices that accumulated on the plate. Add 1½ cups water, the tomatoes, and saffron. Nestle the chicken into the liquid so the pieces are nearly covered in the sauce. Cover the pan and bring to a boil over high heat; reduce the heat and simmer about 20 minutes, turning the chicken pieces over in the sauce halfway through cooking. (The chicken is cooked when an instant-read thermometer inserted into the thickest part of a thigh registers 165 degrees.)

5 Add half of the chopped preserved lemon peel and the olives, nestling them into the sauce, and cook uncovered 5 minutes. Remove the chicken to a serving platter and cover to keep warm. Simmer the sauce about 3 to 4 minutes to reduce and concentrate it slightly. Pour the sauce over the chicken on the platter. Serve with couscous or crusty bread, and the remaining preserved lemon as a condiment.

PER SERVING: *Calories 964 (From Fat 450); Fat 50g (Saturated 13g); Cholesterol 368mg; Sodium 797mg; Carbohydrate 44g (Dietary Fiber 5g); Protein 89g.*

TIP: Use poultry shears to cut large and meaty chicken breast halves crosswise into two pieces. If you don't have poultry shears, you can use a chef's knife or a Chinese cleaver.

TIP: If you want to make your own preserved lemons, flip to the recipe in Chapter 18. If you don't have any lemons that you preserved yourself, you can purchase them at many fine specialty markets.

THE SCOOP ON TAGINES

The word *tagine* refers to the distinctive clay pot Moroccans use to cook traditional savory stews slowly over a wood fire. But in present-day Morocco, the tagine isn't used much anymore. A large wide stainless-steel pan or Dutch oven does the job. Tagines are noble stews with big bold flavor that can be served either for a casual dinner or a special occasion. Some combine lamb shoulder with dried fruits, such as apricots or prunes, and add seasonings like honey, cinnamon, and ginger to sweeten the meat. Others, like our Chicken Tagine with Tomatoes, Olives, and Preserved Lemons recipe, are more savory and rely on the salty-tartness of preserved lemons and green olives.

Sautéed and Braised Kale with Rosemary and Garlic

PREP TIME: ABOUT 5 MIN	COOK TIME: ABOUT 15 MIN	YIELD: 4 SERVINGS

INGREDIENTS

10 to 12 ounces trimmed kale

3 tablespoons extra-virgin olive oil

4 large cloves garlic, halved and lightly crushed

2 to 3 sprigs fresh rosemary

Juice of half a lemon

⅔ cup chicken broth

Salt and black pepper to taste

DIRECTIONS

1 Rinse the kale leaves, and then stack a few of them on top of each other and slice crosswise into 1- to 2-inch-wide pieces. Repeat with the remaining kale leaves.

2 Heat 2 tablespoons of the olive oil in a wide, shallow 3- to 4-quart saucepan over medium until it shimmers. Reduce the heat to very low; add the garlic and cook until pale golden, about 3 to 4 minutes. Use tongs to turn the garlic in the oil every 1 to 2 minutes so the garlic doesn't burn or brown too quickly.

3 Add the rosemary and cook until fragrant, about 1 minute, turning a few times in the oil. Remove and discard any burnt or overly browned garlic from the pot.

4 Increase the heat to medium; add the kale and turn it over in the oil, coating it well. Cook about 1 minute more or until the kale starts to wilt.

5 Add the lemon juice and chicken broth. Cover the pot and cook over medium-low heat about 10 minutes, or until the kale is tender.

6 Use tongs to remove the kale and garlic to a serving bowl. Remove and discard the rosemary stalks, leaving any rosemary leaves. Drizzle the kale with the remaining olive oil. Taste and season with salt and black pepper. Mix well and serve.

PER SERVING: *Calories 186 (From Fat 108); Fat 12g (Saturated 1.5g); Cholesterol 0mg; Sodium 189mg; Carbohydrate 17g (Dietary Fiber 4g); Protein 8g.*

Braised Cabbage with Apples and Caraway

PREP TIME: ABOUT 25 MIN	COOK TIME: ABOUT 25 MIN	YIELD: 4 SERVINGS

INGREDIENTS

3 tablespoons vegetable oil

1 medium yellow onion, coarsely chopped

1 large clove garlic, minced

1 small head green cabbage (about 1½ pounds)

1 medium apple

½ cup chicken or vegetable stock

1 tablespoon white vinegar

1 teaspoon caraway seeds

Salt and black pepper

DIRECTIONS

1 Heat the oil in a large skillet or sauté pan over medium heat. Add the onion and garlic and cook, stirring often, until the onion is wilted, about 2 to 3 minutes. (Don't brown the garlic.) Remove from the heat.

2 Cut the cabbage in half, remove its core, and coarsely shred it. Peel, core, and cut the apple into thin slices.

3 Add the cabbage, apple, stock, vinegar, caraway seeds, and salt and black pepper to taste to the skillet and return it to the stove.

4 On high heat, bring the mixture to a boil. Cover, reduce the heat to low, and simmer for 15 to 20 minutes, or until the cabbage is crisp-tender, stirring occasionally.

5 Uncover. If a lot of liquid is still in the pan, raise the heat to high and cook, stirring, for about 1 to 2 minutes or until most of the liquid is evaporated.

PER SERVING: *Calories 163 (From Fat 97); Fat 11g (Saturated 1g); Cholesterol 0mg; Sodium 254mg; Carbohydrate 16g (Dietary Fiber 5g); Protein 3g.*

Chapter **8**

Roasting Poultry, Meats, and Veggies

A chicken, ham, or pot roast in your oven perfumes your home like nothing else can. Some people are intimidated by roasting, but we're here to show you that it's truly simple. Add in the facts that you don't have to stand over a stove for hours and the results taste fabulous, and you can see why we think roasting is the way to go, whether you're preparing a holiday feast or a small family meal.

Roasting the Right Way

Roasting is easy, but knowing a few techniques can help you make the most of your roasted dishes. How do you season meats, fish, and vegetables for roasting? Do you need to sear a cut of meat before roasting it? When and how do you baste? And why do some meat roasts need to rest before they're served? We answer all these questions in this section.

Seasoning your roasts

Have you ever eaten a superb beef roast or pork loin that lingers on the palate like an aged wine? Part of its appeal comes from being seasoned before cooking. You can season meat, poultry, fish, and vegetables with salt, black pepper, herbs, and spices, but the trick is to know how much of which seasonings to use.

Salt is a flavor enhancer that brings out the best in many foods. However, it's easy to overdo it. We advise using no more than a teaspoon of salt per two pounds of meat roast, and many people would choose to use much less. Fresh herbs, dried herbs, and ground spices can all enhance a roast. It's all about balance and harmony, and this is something you can learn at home.

TIP

Until you're more accomplished, limit yourself to no more than two or three seasonings in any roasted dish. For instance, you may combine oregano, thyme, and parsley to season a pot roast. You may enhance a roasted chicken with tarragon and lemon pepper or rosemary and white pepper. Cumin or chili powder can add punch to a roasted turkey. The possibilities are endless. (See Chapter 3 for more on seasonings.)

Brining to retain moisture

Brining is an alternative way to prepare your meat for roasting. Soaking lean meats in a brine solution — just salt and water — is a great way to minimize moisture loss and enhance flavor. It also curtails shrinking. Meat can lose about 30 percent of its weight during cooking. Brining it can cut that to as little as 15 percent. The salt water also breaks down some of the proteins in tough muscle fibers, turning them from solid to liquid. Some cooks add sugar to the brine solution to import a hint of sweetness.

Table 8-1 gives salt quantities and brining time for various foods. Concentrations listed are for kosher salt. For table salt, cut salt amounts by half.

Searing meat before you roast

Searing refers to the technique of heating oil in a very hot pan and then browning meat or poultry on all sides. But why on earth would you cook your food twice: first in a hot pan and again in the oven?

TABLE 8-1

Brining Chart for Various Meats

Meat	Salt-to-Water Ratio*	Time
Whole turkey	2 cups salt to 1 gallon water	12 to 24 hours
Turkey breast	½ cup salt to 1 gallon water	4 to 6 hours
Pork chops	½ cup salt to 1 quart water	4 hours
Large whole chicken	1 cup salt to 2 quarts water	2 hours
Cornish hens	1 cup salt to 2 quarts water	1 hour

Salt amounts given for kosher salt. Use half the salt amount for table salt.

The advantage of searing a meat roast or chicken before roasting it is this: Searing creates a nice texture and boosts the flavors of seasonings. Here's something searing does *not* do (contrary to what you've probably heard on many TV shows): Searing does *not* seal in meat juices. It merely creates a savory crust.

With all that said, just know that searing is an option; it isn't required prior to roasting. If you don't sear, your poultry or roast will likely be lighter in color and flavor, but you can always boost your seasonings if necessary.

Basting during cooking

Many recipes call for *basting* a roast or poultry, which means brushing or drizzling pan juices over it during cooking. Basting is a good way to add flavor to the surface of the meat or poultry, but contrary to popular belief, it doesn't create a crisp crust. In fact, just the opposite is true: Moistening poultry skin by basting prevents the skin from getting crispy.

To baste, use a large spoon, bulb baster, or basting brush to coat the roast's surface with the pan juices or oil. Baste the meat every 15 to 30 minutes throughout the roasting process.

WARNING

Be careful when basting, however, because you'll be reaching into a hot oven. You can pull out the oven rack to minimize the chances of burning your hands on the oven coils, but remember, you're still handling sizzling-hot juices, and a spill or a too-vigorous squeeze of the bulb baster could result in spattering juices and burns. Baste with care!

Taking a rest

REMEMBER

If you're like us, by the time a pot roast emerges from the oven, the intoxicating aroma has you so hungry that you could tear at it like a dog. Instead, take a deep breath, have some brie and crackers, and let the roast sit out, covered with aluminum foil, for 15 to 20 minutes to allow internal juices to redistribute. Even a roast chicken or duck should sit for 10 minutes. Resting helps you keep more of the juice inside the meat or poultry when you cut into it. (It also makes carving easier because the food isn't quite so hot!)

Roasting Times and Temperatures for Poultry and Meat

Tables 8-2 through 8-5 give approximate cooking times and temperatures for roasting beef, poultry, pork, and lamb. You want to remove a meat roast when its internal temperature is 5 to 10 degrees *less* than final internal temperature, and then let it rest for about 15 minutes. During the resting time, the roast cooks 5 to 10 degrees more. None of this is an exact science, though; you have to use a meat thermometer to get the results you like. See Figure 8-1 for illustrated instructions for using a meat thermometer.

TIP

When inserting a meat thermometer into a roast, don't let the metal touch the bone — the bone is hotter than the meat and registers a falsely higher temperature.

Where to put a Dial (or Oven-proof) Meat Thermometer

Boneless Roast

Insert to core

Poultry

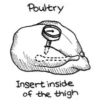

Insert inside of the thigh

Meat with bone

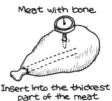

Insert into the thickest part of the meat

* For an accurate reading, do NOT touch the bone, fat, or bottom of the pan with the thermometer.

FIGURE 8-1:
How to insert a meat thermometer in various roasts.

Illustration by Elizabeth Kurtzman

TABLE 8-2

Beef Roasting Chart

Beef Roast	Preheated Oven Temperature (°F)	Weight	Approximate Total Cooking Time	Remove from Oven at This Meat Temperature
Boneless rib eye roast (small end)	350°	3 to 4 pounds	Medium rare: 1½ to 1¾ hours	135°
			Medium: 1¾ to 2 hours	150°
		4 to 6 pounds	Medium rare: 1¾ to 2 hours	135°
			Medium: 2 to 2½ hours	150°
		6 to 8 pounds	Medium rare: 2 to 2¼ hours	135°
			Medium: 2½ to 2¾ hours	150°
Bone-in rib roast (chine bone removed)	350°	4 to 6 pounds (2 ribs)	Medium rare: 1¾ to 2¼ hours	135°
			Medium: 2¼ to 2½ hours	150°
		6 to 8 pounds (2 to 4 ribs)	Medium rare: 2¼ to 2½ hours	135°
			Medium: 2¾ to 3 hours	150°
		8 to 10 pounds (4 to 5 ribs)	Medium rare: 2½ to 3 hours	135°
			Medium: 3 to 3½ hours	150°
Round tip roast (sirloin tip)	325°	3 to 4 pounds	Medium rare: 1¾ to 2 hours	140°
			Medium: 2¼ to 2½ hours	155°
		4 to 6 pounds	Medium rare: 2 to 2½ hours	140°
			Medium: 2½ to 3 hours	155°
		6 to 8 pounds	Medium rare: 2½ to 3 hours	140°

(continued)

TABLE 8-2 *(continued)*

Beef Roast	Preheated Oven Temperature (°F)	Weight	Approximate Total Cooking Time	Remove from Oven at This Meat Temperature
			Medium: 3 to 3½ hours	155°
Tenderloin roast	425°	2 to 3 pounds	Medium rare: 35 to 40 minutes	135°
			Medium: 45 to 50 minutes	150°
		4 to 5 pounds	Medium rare: 50 to 60 minutes	135°
			Medium: 60 to 70 minutes	150°

Medium rare doneness: 140° to 145° final meat temperature after 10 to 15 minutes standing time

Medium doneness: 155° to 160° final meat temperature after 10 to 15 minutes standing time

Allow ¼ to ⅓ pound of uncooked boneless beef per serving and ½ to 1 pound of bone-in meat per serving, depending on the cut.

Source: National Cattlemen's Beef Associaion

TABLE 8-3   ## Poultry Roasting Chart

Bird	Weight	Preheated Oven Temperature	Cooking Time
Chicken, broiler/fryer (unstuffed)	3 to 4 pounds	350°	1¼ to 1½ hours
Chicken, roaster (unstuffed)	5 to 7 pounds	350°	2 to 2¼ hours
Whole turkey (thawed and unstuffed)	8 to 12 pounds	325°	2¾ to 3 hours
Whole turkey (thawed and unstuffed)	12 to 14 pounds	325°	3 to 3¾ hours
	14 to 18 pounds	325°	3¾ to 4¼ hours
	18 to 20 pounds	325°	4¼ to 4½ hours
Duck (whole, unstuffed)	4 to 5½ pounds	325°	2½ to 3 hours

Depending on the size of the bird, allow 15 to 20 minutes additional cooking time if stuffed.

Internal temperature for stuffing should be 165°.

Internal temperature for meat should be minimum 165° in the thigh.

Allow about ¾ to 1 pound of uncooked chicken or turkey on the bone per serving.

Source: National Chicken Council

TABLE 8-4   Pork Roasting Chart

Cut	Thickness/Weight	Remove from Oven at This Meat Temperature	Cooking Time
Loin roast (bone-in)	3 to 5 pounds	145°	20 minutes per pound
Boneless pork roast	2 to 4 pounds	145°	20 minutes per pound
Tenderloin (roast at 425° to 450°)	½ to 1½ pounds	145°	20 to 30 minutes
Crown roast	6 to 10 pounds	145°	20 minutes per pound
Boneless loin chops	1 inch thick	145°	12 to 16 minutes
Ribs		Tender	1½ to 2 hours

Roast in a shallow pan, uncovered, at 350°.

Internal temperature should be minimum 145°.

Allow about ¼ to ⅓ pound of uncooked boneless meat per serving and about ½ to 1 pound of bone-in meat per serving, depending on the cut.

Source: National Pork Producers Council

TABLE 8-5   Lamb Roasting Chart

Roast	Weight	Final Internal Temperature	Approximate Cooking Time Per Pound
Leg (bone-in)	5 to 7 pounds	Medium rare: 145° to 150°	15 minutes
		Medium: 150° to 155°	20 minutes
Boneless (rolled and tied)	4 to 7 pounds	Medium rare: 145° to 150°	20 minutes
		Medium: 150° to 155°	25 minutes
Sirloin roast (boneless)	about 2 pounds	Medium rare: 145° to 150°	25 minutes
		Medium: 150° to 155°	30 minutes
Top round roast	about 2 pounds	Medium rare: 145° to 150°	45 minutes
		Medium: 150° to 155°	55 minutes

Preheat oven to 325° and remove from oven about 10° below desired temperature.

Internal temperature should be minimum 145°.

Allow ¼ to ⅓ pound of boneless lamb per serving and ⅓ to ½ pound of bone-in lamb per serving.

Source: American Lamb Council

Keep in mind that every oven is different. Some ovens are off by as much as 50 degrees, which can be like trying to make gourmet coffee with hot tap water. Roasting can be a disaster without precision. Investing in an oven thermometer is worthwhile.

TIP

The associations and companies that produce and market poultry use these roasting tables only as a rough guideline. For actual cooking times, they recommend always using a meat thermometer to ensure that poultry of any kind reaches a safe minimal internal temperature of 165 degrees.

WARNING

We understand that it can be irresistible, but don't keep opening the oven door to see whether your roasted dish is done. Your kitchen will get hot, you'll get hotter, and the meat or vegetables will take longer to cook.

Putting Poultry in the Oven

Contrary to what some people think, roasting a chicken involves more than just tossing the bird into the oven and mixing a gin and tonic. Sometimes what seems to be the simplest of endeavors requires the most attention (like poker).

Starting at the very beginning, after you open the package, you have to remove that mysterious paper packet inside the bird that contains the "giblets" (the neck, heart, gizzard, and liver). Set it aside while you're preparing the chicken, but don't throw it out — you can use it later to make delicious gravy.

WARNING

A commonly held belief is that you should rinse raw chicken under cold water to eliminate harmful bacteria like salmonella. More than 75 percent of poultry carries some amount of salmonella, a result of mass processing. In fact, rinsing poultry can make matters worse, so don't do it! While handling and carrying raw poultry, you can contaminate not only your hands but also your clothing, the floor, the sink, faucet, and countertops. The only way to kill salmonella bacteria is by roasting and sautéing the chicken to the proper temperature.

Pat the skin dry with paper towels, wash your hands thoroughly before touching anything else, and season with salt and black pepper.

If you want your bird to hold its shape perfectly while roasting, you can *truss* it (tie it with string). See Figure 8-2 for illustrated instructions, or check out www.dummies.com/go/trussingpoultry. You then place your poultry in a large metal roasting pan.

TRUSSING A CHICKEN

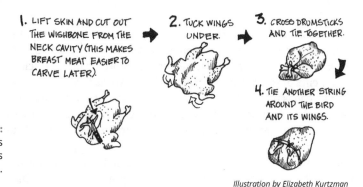

1. LIFT SKIN AND CUT OUT THE WISHBONE FROM THE NECK CAVITY (THIS MAKES BREAST MEAT EASIER TO CARVE LATER).

2. TUCK WINGS UNDER.

3. CROSS DRUMSTICKS AND TIE TOGETHER.

4. TIE ANOTHER STRING AROUND THE BIRD AND ITS WINGS.

FIGURE 8-2: Trussing helps poultry keep its shape.

Illustration by Elizabeth Kurtzman

The most common mistake home cooks make when roasting chicken is using an insufficiently hot oven. The Roasted Chicken recipe in this chapter calls for a 425-degree oven, which yields a crispy, golden-brown skin.

TIP

As you cook the bird, use a meat thermometer. As we explain in Chapter 2, you can choose between an *instant-read* type, which you stick in the meat when you suspect it's nearing doneness to get an immediate temperature reading, and an *oven-proof* version — the kind you insert in the meat when you first put it in the oven. Either way, insert your thermometer deep into the flesh between the bird's thigh and breast.

If you don't have a thermometer, insert a knife into the thick part of the thigh; if the juices run clear, the bird is thoroughly cooked. If they run pink, let the meat cook for another 15 minutes or so before testing for doneness. Then go buy a thermometer.

RECIPE ALERT

So what do you do with the packet of giblets? You can add them — all but the liver — to homemade soups and stocks or to canned stocks to enrich their flavors. The Roasted Chicken recipe we provide later in this chapter uses the giblets to make a delicious pan gravy.

Here's a tip for using your roasted chicken leftovers: Roasted chicken, either hot or cold, goes well with a mildly spicy mustard mayonnaise. Blend Dijon mustard to taste into ½ cup of mayonnaise. (Start with about a teaspoon and work your way up if it isn't zippy enough for you.) Season with salt and black pepper and freshly chopped herbs, such as tarragon, basil, chervil, parsley, or oregano. This spicy mayo is also good with cold pork, fish, and grilled meats.

Mastering Roasted Meats

Americans have two immutable love affairs: automobiles and meat. If you want proof of our carnivorous cravings, just look at the steakhouse explosion from coast to coast. Sure, people have become more health-conscious, and many seek leaner cuts of meat. The beef and pork industries have responded, making considerable strides in breeding leaner animals without sacrificing too much tenderness. Add to that America's continuing interest in low-carb protein diets, and (no offense to vegetarians) meat seems to be an integral part of American life.

TIP

Concerning pork and other meats, good butchers are frequently knowledgeable cooks. They can offer recipes, tips, and information on preparing your piece of meat so that it's "oven-ready." For example, an oven-ready roast is trimmed of excess fat and sometimes tied with butcher's string to make it as uniform as possible for cooking. A leg of lamb should have its fat and shank bone removed. The skin and rind of a smoked ham are trimmed away, leaving just a thin layer of fat that you can score to make a decorative diamond pattern. (Don't worry — we show you how!)

Beef

RECIPE ALERT

Roast beef is a traditional Anglo favorite. You simply *must* check out the Roasted Fillet of Beef recipe later in this chapter. This savory dish, although on the pricey side, is fast, simple, and always delicious — a real last-minute party saver. Serve it with simple dishes like garlic-flavored mashed potatoes and Steamed Broccoli with Lemon Butter (see Chapter 5).

The roast referred to as *fillet* is also called *tenderloin,* so you can use these terms interchangeably. But the fillet roast is different than the cut called *filet mignon,* which is defined as the extremely tender cut from the small end of the tenderloin.

Looking for a roast that's a bit more economical? A *round tip roast,* also referred to as a *sirloin tip roast,* is leaner and less tender than a more expensive roast such as prime rib. If cooked the right way, a round tip roast makes a great family dinner. To serve a round tip roast for six people, follow these steps:

1. **Purchase a 3- to 4-pound sirloin tip roast.**

2. **Rub it with fresh chopped garlic, a little olive oil, salt, black pepper, and your favorite herbs.**

3. **Place it on a rack in a shallow roasting pan in a preheated 325-degree oven and cook until a meat thermometer inserted into the center of the roast registers 140 degrees for medium-rare, or 145 degrees for medium.**

   Remember that a resting roast continues cooking, adding about 5 degrees on a meat thermometer. A 3- to 4-pound roast will cook to medium-rare in 1¾ to 2 hours and to medium in 2¼ to 2½ hours.

4. **Remove the roast from the oven and let stand, loosely covered with foil, for 15 minutes before carving.**

TIP

What happens if you overcook a roast beef? Unfortunately, ovens don't have reverse gears. But you can salvage overcooked roast beef in many tasty ways. Make roast beef hash or beef pot pie, various soups, or beef stroganoff. Any recipe that calls for liquid or a cream-based sauce is good, too, for making delicious use of overcooked beef.

Pork

RECIPE
ALERT

Compared to some types of roasts, pork remains a relative bargain. Pork is lighter and leaner than ever before, and if you know how to cook it properly, it will be moist and tender. Our recipe for Roast Loin of Pork later in this chapter is a perfect example.

People used to believe that if you ate pork that was cooked below 185 degrees, you could contract a disease called trichinosis. The average person didn't know what that was, but it sure sounded unpleasant. Thus, for years, everyone ate overcooked pork. About a decade ago, scientists discovered that harmful trichinae parasites are killed at 135 degrees. Cooking pork to 145 degrees is considered plenty safe and yields a much juicier result.

Ribs

Whether done over a grill or in an oven, ribs need long, slow cooking. Some recipes call for *parboiling* (partially boiling) ribs before roasting or grilling, but we've found that a lot of the flavor winds up in the cooking water. The best alternative we've found is roasting spareribs in a 300-degree oven for 2 hours, which leaves them succulent and flavorful.

RECIPE
ALERT

Ribs are delicious when rubbed with spices before cooking. The recipe later in this chapter for Roasted Pork Ribs with Country Barbecue Sauce calls for brown sugar, salt, and black pepper. A sweet element always gives the ribs a seductive flavor; the other ingredients can vary according to your taste. If you like them spicy, add a little cayenne pepper to the mix (about ¼ teaspoon or more if you like it extra hot). Other seasonings you could experiment with include sweet paprika, onion powder, garlic powder, ground cumin, ground coriander, cinnamon, dried thyme, and dried basil. However you choose to prepare ribs, they're great for casual entertaining. Just be sure to have lots of moist towels around. Ribs get messy! (But that's half the fun.)

Keep in mind that our Country Barbecue Sauce also works exceptionally well with barbecued chicken and beef. It may be prepared a day or two in advance, refrigerated, and reheated before using.

Ham

Hams have more identities than a secret agent. Sorting them out isn't terribly complicated, however. Remember that all hams are *cured* (which means seasoned and aged), and some are also smoked. The two most common methods of preparing a ham are *dry curing* and *wet curing.* In the dry method, a ham is rubbed with salt and seasonings and hung in a cool, dry place to age, anywhere from a few weeks to a year or more. Wet cured hams are soaked in *brine* (salt water), or injected with brine, to give them more flavor.

Here is a primer on some other terms for hams:

>> **Aged ham:** Heavily cured and smoked hams that have been dry-aged at least one year.

>> **Bayonne ham:** A dry-cured ham from the Basque country of France, specifically the city of Bayonne.

>> **Canned ham:** Cured but not always smoked, and ready to eat. A little cooking, though, improves the flavor.

>> **Country ham:** A dry cured ham that is smoked, salted, and then aged for at least six months.

>> **Half ham:** Comes from the shank bone, butt, or ham end. The shank portion is best and easiest to deal with.

>> **Fully cooked ham:** The same as a "ready-to-eat" ham. You can eat it without cooking.

>> **Prosciutto:** Strictly speaking, a ham from Parma, Italy, that is seasoned, salt cured, air dried, and pressed to make the meat very firm. It is usually eaten in very thin slices over bread.

- » **Smithfield ham:** The pride of Smithfield, Virginia; a salty, wonderfully flavorful ham seasoned, smoked, and hung for at least a year.

- » **Sugar-cured ham:** Rubbed with salt and brown sugar or molasses before aging.

- » **Virginia ham:** Another salty, dry-cured ham. It's made from hogs that eat peanuts, acorns, and other high-protein foods.

- » **Westphalian ham:** A rosy, sweetish, German ham made from hogs that are fed sugar beet mash. It's usually eaten like prosciutto.

RECIPE ALERT

Later in this chapter, we give you a recipe for Smoked Ham with Apricot Glaze. In this recipe, you brush the ham with an apricot-and-mustard glaze and then serve it with a pan sauce made from the luscious drippings. Ham and fruit make a natural pairing, and you can use this combination to good effect not only in the glaze but also in the garnish. Decorate your platter with pieces of fruit, such as pineapple slices, apricot halves nestled in pear halves, or slices of oranges. You can also brush the fruits with the glaze for a beautiful presentation.

If you're used to buying your ham precooked, you may wonder why some hams have a pretty little diamond pattern all over them. That pattern is created by *scoring* the ham with a sharp knife. To do so, you first remove the thick skin, or *rind*, of the ham by cutting it away to expose a thin layer of fat. Then you make small cuts in the fat all over the surface, as shown in Figure 8-3. Doing so helps a glaze penetrate the meat. (If you want to add a decorative effect, you can also insert a clove into the center of each diamond cut.)

FIGURE 8-3: How to score a ham.

Illustration by Elizabeth Kurtzman

SWEET LITTLE PIGGIES

Baked hams — more accurately called "roasted hams" — are often brushed with a sweet marmalade or other glaze that counterbalances the saltiness of the meat. The glaze is applied during the last 30 minutes of baking, or when the ham has reached an internal temperature of 120 degrees; if applied sooner, the glaze could burn. Glazes can be mixtures of all sorts of flavors: jams, brown sugar, molasses, corn syrup, mustard, cinnamon, cloves, ginger, whiskey, rum, orange juice, Port, or white wine. Some producers douse the ham with Coca-Cola to produce a syrupy coating — no kidding.

Because ham is a fatty meat, if you want to use the juices that accumulate during roasting (to help create a glaze, for example), you likely need to skim the fat before using them. To do so, after roasting the ham, pour its juices into a bowl. Tilt the bowl, and with a spoon, skim the surface fat. Or you can use a fat skimmer such as the one shown in Figure 8-4.

FIGURE 8-4:
A fat skimmer.

Illustration by Elizabeth Kurtzman

TIP

In the recipe for smoked ham in this chapter, we show you how to use the ham's pan juices when serving the ham slices. You can flavor a ham's pan juices in many ways. Try adding 2 to 3 tablespoons of dark raisins, 2 tablespoons of dark rum, or some dry white wine or apple cider. Grated orange zest and freshly squeezed orange juice give the pan juices a clean, citric edge.

Lamb

RECIPE ALERT

Hankering for some lamb instead? We offer a delicious, easy-to-make recipe for Glazed Leg of Lamb with Pan Gravy and Red Currant Glaze later in this chapter. This dish is excellent with some root vegetables like carrots and potatoes scattered around the roasting pan.

If you enjoy lamb cooked medium, roast it until the internal temperature reaches 145 degrees — it will continue to cook for about 15 minutes after being removed from the oven. But keep in mind that a roasted leg of lamb yields meat of varying degrees of doneness. The meat at the thin, shank end is browned and well done, and the meat at the thicker end ideally is quite pink and medium rare. The drier meat is great for hash.

A whole leg of lamb can leave you with delicious leftovers. Prepare cold lamb sandwiches or Shepherd's Pie (see Chapter 16).

Remembering (to Roast) Your Veggies!

Some vegetables, such as broccoli, onions, potatoes, carrots, and other heart vegetables, are delicious roasted because the technique brings out their natural sugars. Simply cut up the vegetable into chunks, toss them in olive oil, and generously season with salt and black pepper. Roast in a 375-degree oven for about half an hour, or until the vegetable begins to brown. Cooking at high heat beautifully caramelizes the sugars.

**RECIPE
ALERT**

Virtually all kinds of vegetables can be roasted by using the simple techniques explained in the two great recipes later in this chapter: Crispy Roasted Root Vegetables (for winter root veggies) and Roasted Summer Vegetables.

The Crispy Roasted Root Vegetables are a great companion for many entrees. If you're roasting a side of beef or a chicken, for example, just scatter a variety of root vegetables (such as cut-up carrots, onions, and peeled potatoes) in the roasting pan. Turn them every so often in the pan drippings. This makes for a great presentation at the table — that is, if you don't eat them all in the kitchen.

Keep in mind that summer vegetables release quite a bit of water when roasted. To get them browned and crisp, place them on the lowest oven rack, close to the heating element. You may also sprinkle a little brown sugar over the vegetables to bring out their natural sweetness and counterbalance the tastes of fresh ginger, garlic, and hot pepper.

If you have leftover roasted vegetables, use them the next day in a salad, rolled in a tortilla with hot sauce, or even in an omelet. If you want to make them crisp again, place them in a 400-degree oven for about 5 minutes.

TIP

If you combine different vegetables on the same roasting pan, be sure to choose those that will cook in about the same amount of time. Tomatoes cook much faster than carrots, so you wouldn't combine those two, for example. Another way to achieve even cooking is to cut the hardest vegetables (carrots, parsnips, potatoes, and so on) into smaller pieces than the soft vegetables (celery, bell peppers, eggplant, and so on). Or *blanch* the hard vegetables before roasting: Plunge them into boiling water for a few seconds and then into cold water to stop the cooking process.

Hard-shelled winter squashes include acorn, butternut, and delicata, and they're cooked until well done to bring out their natural sweetness. With their nearly impervious skins and odd shapes, a winter squash is difficult to cut open. See Chapter 4 for the best way to cut squash open for roasting.

RECIPE ALERT

Acorn squash is slightly easier to cut in half than butternut or other hard-shelled squash, and it doesn't require you to peel it. The two halves created, after cutting and removing the seeds and fibers, make lovely individual serving vessels that can be filled with assorted sweet or savory seasonings before they're roasted tender. When planning your next dinner party, consider serving them with a roast of any kind. Or serve alongside a turkey burger (see recipe in Chapter 6) for a delicious casual dinner. The recipe for Roasted Acorn Squash with dark brown sugar later in this chapter makes a slightly sweetened squash, but you can skip the sugar and use your own combination of butter and savory herbs, like thyme or tarragon.

Roasted Fillet of Beef

PREP TIME: ABOUT 10 MIN | COOK TIME: ABOUT 45 MIN | YIELD: 8 SERVINGS

INGREDIENTS

One 4-pound beef fillet (tenderloin) roast, oven-ready

Salt and black pepper

2 tablespoons vegetable oil

Herb butter (optional)

DIRECTIONS

1 Preheat the oven to 425 degrees.

2 Sprinkle the fillet of beef with salt and black pepper to taste.

3 Place the meat on a rack in a heavy roasting pan and brush or rub it with the oil. Roast for about 45 minutes for medium rare (135 to 140 degrees) or until desired doneness. Halfway through the roasting time, invert the meat and baste once with the pan juices.

4 Transfer the meat to a carving board, cover with aluminum foil, and let stand for 10 minutes.

5 Carve the fillet into approximately ½-inch-thick slices and serve immediately, topped with a pat of butter and a sprinkle of herbs, such as fresh chopped or dried basil (if desired).

PER SERVING: *Calories 528 (From Fat 356); Fat 40g (Saturated 15g); Cholesterol 135mg; Sodium 176mg; Carbohydrate 0g (Dietary Fiber 0g); Protein 40g.*

Roasted Chicken

PREP TIME: ABOUT 15 MIN	COOK TIME: ABOUT 1 HR 15 MIN	YIELD: 4 SERVINGS

INGREDIENTS

One 4- to 4½-pound chicken with giblets

Salt and black pepper

1 lemon, pricked several times with a fork

2 sprigs fresh thyme, or ½ teaspoon dried

1 whole clove garlic, peeled

2 tablespoons olive oil

Trussing string (optional)

1 medium yellow onion, quartered

½ cup chicken stock

½ cup water, plus more as necessary

2 tablespoons butter

Parsley, rosemary, tarragon, or other fresh herbs to taste (optional)

DIRECTIONS

1 Preheat the oven to 425 degrees. Remove the giblets from the chicken's cavity; rinse and reserve. Pat the chicken dry with paper towels.

2 Sprinkle the chicken inside and out with salt and black pepper to taste. Insert the lemon, thyme, and garlic into the cavity of the chicken. Rub the outside of the chicken all over with the olive oil.

3 Truss the chicken with string (if desired).

4 Place the chicken, breast-side up, on a rack in a shallow metal roasting pan. Scatter the giblets and onions on the bottom of the pan. Roast for 45 minutes.

5 Remove the roasting pan from the oven. Using a large spoon, skim fat from the pan juices. Add the chicken stock, water, and butter to the pan. Roast for another 20 to 30 minutes or until an instant-read thermometer inserted into the thickest part of the thigh registers 165 degrees.

6 Lift the chicken to let the cavity juices flow into the pan. Transfer chicken to a carving board or serving platter, cover with aluminum foil, and let rest for 10 to 15 minutes.

7 Place the roasting pan on top of the stove. Using a slotted spoon, remove and discard any pieces of giblets or onion. Add water or stock if necessary to make about 1 cup liquid.

8　Bring the liquid to a boil and reduce for 1 to 2 minutes to let the sauce condense while you stir and scrape the bottom of the pan. Add fresh herbs to taste (if desired).

9　Turn off the heat when the sauce is reduced to about ¾ cup. Strain the sauce into a gravy boat or small bowl just before serving.

10　If you trussed the chicken, cut the string off. Remove and discard the lemon and thyme sprigs.

11　Carve the chicken into serving pieces and serve with the hot pan juices. (See Chapter 4 for how to carve a whole chicken.)

PER SERVING: *Calories 636 (From Fat 395); Fat 44g (Saturated 13g); Cholesterol 194mg; Sodium 395mg; Carbohydrate 0g (Dietary Fiber 0g); Protein 57g.*

Roast Loin of Pork

PREP TIME: ABOUT 25 MIN	COOK TIME: ABOUT 1 HR 5 MIN	YIELD: 6 SERVINGS

INGREDIENTS

One 3-pound center-cut boneless loin of pork

4 tablespoons olive oil

2 tablespoons chopped fresh thyme, or 1 teaspoon dried

Salt and black pepper

6 medium red potatoes, peeled and halved lengthwise

3 medium yellow onions, peeled and quartered

4 carrots, peeled and cut into 2-inch pieces

1 bay leaf

2 large cloves garlic, finely chopped

½ cup water

¼ cup chopped fresh parsley

2 cups applesauce (optional)

DIRECTIONS

1 Preheat the oven to 400 degrees.

2 Place the pork in a large roasting pan (without a rack) and brush or rub the meat all over with 3 tablespoons of the oil. Season with the thyme and salt and black pepper to taste. Roast, fat-side up, for 15 minutes.

3 Remove the pan from the oven and reduce the oven temperature to 350 degrees.

4 Scatter the potatoes, onions, carrots, and bay leaf around the roast and drizzle the remaining 1 tablespoon of oil over the vegetables. Using a large spoon, turn the vegetables in the cooking juices.

5 Sprinkle the garlic over the vegetables and season them with salt and black pepper to taste. Add the water to the pan.

6 Roast for 45 to 50 minutes or until a meat thermometer registers 145 degrees in the thickest part of the roast.

7 Transfer the roast to a cutting board. Cover with aluminum foil and let rest for 15 minutes.

8 Reduce the oven temperature to 300 degrees and place the pan with the vegetables in the oven to keep warm.

9 Carve the meat and transfer it and the vegetables to a large platter. Pour any juices that have collected around the meat into the roasting pan. Remove the bay leaf from the pan, and place the pan over two burners on high.

10 Bring the juices to a boil, stirring and scraping the bottom and sides of the pan with a wooden spoon. Cook about 1 to 2 minutes or until the sauce is reduced and slightly thickened. Pour the juices over everything, sprinkle with the chopped parsley, and serve with applesauce (if desired).

PER SERVING: *Calories 574 (From Fat 175); Fat 20g (Saturated 5g); Cholesterol 150mg; Sodium 244mg; Carbohydrate 43g (Dietary Fiber 5g); Protein 54g.*

Roasted Pork Ribs with Country Barbecue Sauce

PREP TIME: ABOUT 20 MIN PLUS CHILL TIME	COOK TIME: ABOUT 2 HR 30 MIN	YIELD: 4 SERVINGS

INGREDIENTS

1 tablespoon packed brown sugar

1½ teaspoons salt, or to taste

1 teaspoon black pepper, or to taste

3 to 4 pounds pork spareribs

Country Barbecue Sauce (see the following recipe)

DIRECTIONS

1 Preheat the oven to 300 degrees.

2 Make a spice rub by combining the brown sugar, salt, and black pepper in a small bowl. Stir well.

3 Trim excess fat from the ribs. Place the ribs on a cutting board. Cut the slabs into pieces of one to two ribs each.

4 Arrange the spareribs in one layer on a roasting pan. Sprinkle the ribs with the spice rub, pressing the seasonings firmly onto the meat all around. Cover loosely and refrigerate about 30 minutes.

5 Roast in the oven for 1½ hours, turning them over after 45 minutes. While the ribs cook, make the Country Barbecue Sauce.

6 Increase the oven temperature to 350 degrees. Remove the roasting pan from the oven; carefully pour off all the fat (or transfer ribs to a clean roasting pan).

7 Brush the ribs generously on all sides with the barbecue sauce and roast another 25 to 30 minutes, or until the meat easily pulls away from the bone. Serve with extra sauce on the side.

Country Barbecue Sauce

2 tablespoons vegetable oil

1 small yellow onion, minced

2 cloves garlic, minced

¾ cup water

⅔ cup ketchup

½ cup packed dark brown sugar

6 tablespoons cider vinegar

1 tablespoon Worcestershire sauce

1 tablespoon molasses

1 teaspoon ground cumin

Salt and black pepper

DIRECTIONS

1 Heat the oil in a saucepan over medium heat. Add the onion and cook, stirring often, until it starts to soften; add the garlic and continue cooking and stirring for about 1 minute.

2 Add the water, ketchup, brown sugar, vinegar, Worcestershire sauce, molasses, cumin, and salt and black pepper to taste and stir well. Increase the heat to high and bring to a boil.

3 Reduce the heat and simmer 25 to 30 minutes, or until thickened, stirring occasionally.

PER SERVING: *Calories 875 (From Fat 495); Fat 55g (Saturated 19g); Cholesterol 191mg; Sodium 1,699mg; Carbohydrate 47g (Dietary Fiber 1g); Protein 47g.*

Smoked Ham with Apricot Glaze

PREP TIME: 20 MIN	COOK TIME: ABOUT 2 HR 15 MIN	YIELD: 14 SERVINGS

INGREDIENTS

7- to 9-pound smoked, bone-in, cooked ham

About 30 whole cloves (optional)

About 1 cup water

Apricot Glaze (see the following recipe)

1 cup chicken stock

Mustard (optional)

DIRECTIONS

1　Preheat the oven to 325 degrees.

2　Remove the rind from the ham with a sharp knife and discard. With a sharp knife, score the thin layer of fat remaining. If using the cloves, insert them into the ham, placing them all over and about 2 inches apart.

3　Place the ham in a heavy roasting pan; add ½ cup of the water to the pan and put it in the oven. While the ham roasts, prepare the Apricot Glaze.

4　If the roasting pan gets dry, add ½ cup more water to it. When a meat thermometer inserted into the center of the ham reads 120 degrees (after about 1½ to 2 hours), remove the ham from the oven and increase the oven temperature to 400 degrees.

5　Brush or spoon the glaze all over the ham and return it to the oven. Bake for 20 to 25 minutes, or until a thermometer inserted in the center registers 140 degrees (be careful not to burn the glaze).

6　Place the ham on a large carving board; cover with foil and let rest 15 minutes.

7　Pour the juices from the roasting pan into a small shallow bowl. Skim the fat that accumulates on the surface, and return the skimmed juices to the pan. Place it over a burner on high heat, and add the chicken stock.

8　Cook the juices, stirring and scraping up browned bits on the bottom of the pan, until the liquid is reduced and slightly thickened. Pass the sauce through a fine strainer.

9　Thinly slice the ham (remove and discard any cloves); serve with pan juices and a good mustard (if desired).

Apricot Glaze

INGREDIENTS

½ cup apricot preserves or orange marmalade

2 tablespoons Dijon-style mustard

1 tablespoon dark rum (optional)

Black pepper to taste

DIRECTIONS

1 In a small pan, heat the apricot preserves over low heat; mash any large pieces of fruit with a fork. Stir in the mustard and the rum (if desired). Season with black pepper to taste.

2 Boil, stirring occasionally, until the mixture thickens enough to coat a spoon, about 3 minutes.

PER SERVING: *Calories 435 (From Fat 253); Fat 28g (Saturated 10g); Cholesterol 103mg; Sodium 2,076mg; Carbohydrate 8g (Dietary Fiber 0g); Protein 36g.*

Glazed Leg of Lamb with Pan Gravy and Red Currant Glaze

PREP TIME: ABOUT 20 MIN	COOK TIME: ABOUT 1 HR 40 MIN	YIELD: 10 SERVINGS

INGREDIENTS

One 6- to 7-pound leg of lamb, well trimmed

3 cloves garlic, thinly sliced

1 tablespoon vegetable oil

½ teaspoon ground ginger

Salt and black pepper

Red Currant Glaze (see the following recipe)

DIRECTIONS

1 Preheat the oven to 425 degrees.

2 With a paring knife, make small incisions along the leg. Insert the garlic slivers into the incisions.

3 Rub the lamb with the oil and place it on a rack in a shallow roasting pan, fat-side up. Sprinkle the meat with the ginger and salt and black pepper to taste.

4 Roast for 20 minutes; reduce the heat to 350 degrees and roast for an additional 1 hour and 20 minutes (until a meat thermometer registers 145 degrees in the thickest part of the leg for medium).

5 During the last 30 minutes of roasting (starting when the meat thermometer reads 115 degrees), brush the top and sides of the lamb every 10 minutes with Red Currant Glaze and pan juices.

6 Remove from the oven, cover with foil, and let rest for 20 minutes. Carve and serve with some of the pan juices spooned over the slices.

Red Currant Glaze

INGREDIENTS

½ cup red currant jelly

Juice and grated peel of ½ lemon

1½ teaspoons Dijon-style mustard

DIRECTIONS

Combine all the ingredients in a small saucepan and heat until the jelly is melted (about 1 minute). Use as a basting sauce for the leg of lamb.

PER SERVING: *Calories 287 (From Fat 105); Fat 12g (Saturated 4g); Cholesterol 117mg; Sodium 168mg; Carbohydrate 6g (Dietary Fiber 0g); Protein 37g.*

Crispy Roasted Root Vegetables

PREP TIME: ABOUT 10 MIN	COOK TIME: ABOUT 30 MIN	YIELD: 4 SERVINGS

INGREDIENTS

4 medium carrots, washed (skins on), halved, and chopped crosswise into about 4 pieces

2 red or yellow bell peppers, cored, seeded, and sliced into ½-inch strips

3 medium red potatoes, quartered

3 small turnips, peeled and quartered

2 medium yellow onions, quartered

2 small bulbs fennel, trimmed and quartered

1 tablespoon minced fresh rosemary, or ½ tablespoon dried

¼ cup olive oil

Salt and black pepper

DIRECTIONS

1 Preheat the oven to 400 degrees.

2 Place the vegetables, fennel, and rosemary in a large mixing bowl. Pour the olive oil over them and season generously with salt and black pepper. Toss well to blend.

3 Transfer vegetables to a roasting pan that can hold them in one layer. Place the pan in the oven and roast for 25 to 30 minutes, turning the vegetables several times.

PER SERVING: *Calories 334 (From Fat 127); Fat 14g (Saturated 2g); Cholesterol 0mg; Sodium 252mg; Carbohydrate 48g (Dietary Fiber 9g); Protein 6g.*

TIP: If after 25 minutes the vegetables are tender but not browned, place them under the broiler for a minute or two — but don't let them burn.

Roasted Summer Vegetables

PREP TIME: ABOUT 15 MIN | COOK TIME: ABOUT 35 MIN | YIELD: 4 SERVINGS

INGREDIENTS

3 medium carrots, peeled and cut into ¼-inch slices

2 to 3 tablespoons olive oil

1 red or yellow bell pepper, cored, seeded, and cut into ½-inch cubes

1 small zucchini, halved lengthwise and cut into ½-inch-thick slices

1 small yellow squash, halved lengthwise and cut into ½-inch-thick slices

½ pound asparagus, trimmed of thick stems and cut diagonally into 1-inch pieces

1 small red onion, chopped into ⅛-inch cubes

1 large clove garlic, chopped

½ to 1 jalapeño pepper or small red chile pepper (according to taste), seeded and minced

1 tablespoon chopped fresh basil, marjoram, or thyme, or 1 teaspoon dried

2 teaspoons peeled and minced fresh ginger

1 teaspoon brown sugar (optional)

Salt and black pepper

DIRECTIONS

1 Preheat the oven to 425 degrees.

2 Scatter the carrots over a large roasting pan. Drizzle them with 1 tablespoon of the olive oil; toss to coat. Place the pan on the oven rack closest to the heating element, and roast for 10 minutes.

3 Take the pan from the oven and add the bell pepper, zucchini, yellow squash, asparagus, onion, garlic, and jalapeño. Sprinkle with the basil (or marjoram or thyme), ginger, brown sugar (if desired), and salt and black pepper to taste.

4 Drizzle the remaining 1 to 2 tablespoons of olive oil over the vegetables, using only enough to lightly coat them. Toss well, spreading the vegetables out in a single layer.

5 Return the roasting pan to the oven and roast about 20 to 25 minutes, or until tender, turning once with a spatula or wooden spoon after 15 minutes so the vegetables brown evenly.

PER SERVING: *Calories 123 (From Fat 63); Fat 7g (Saturated 1g); Cholesterol 0mg; Sodium 181mg; Carbohydrate 14g (Dietary Fiber 4g); Protein 3g.*

TIP: If after 25 minutes the vegetables are tender but not browned, place them under the broiler for a minute or two — but don't let them burn.

Roasted Acorn Squash

PREP TIME: ABOUT 5 MIN	COOK TIME: 35–45 MIN	YIELD: 2 SERVINGS

INGREDIENTS

1 acorn squash, halved lengthwise and seeded

1 tablespoon butter

4 teaspoons packed dark brown sugar or maple syrup

2 teaspoons minced or grated peeled fresh ginger

Salt and black pepper to taste

About ¼ cup water

DIRECTIONS

1 Place an oven rack in the middle position and preheat the oven to 375 degrees.

2 Place the squash halves, cut-side up, in a small baking pan or oven casserole. Place the butter, brown sugar, and ginger into each half, dividing it equally. Season with salt and black pepper to taste. Add about ¼ cup water to the pan to keep the squash skin from overbrowning while roasting.

3 Roast about 35 to 45 minutes or until a skewer or the tip of a sharp knife inserted into the flesh goes in and out easily. (Cooking time will depend on the weight and size of the squash.)

4 Remove from the oven; spoon some of the brown-sugar butter sauce over the top areas and serve.

PER SERVING: *Calories 176 (From Fat 54); Fat 6g (Saturated 4g); Cholesterol 15mg; Sodium 62mg; Carbohydrate 32g (Dietary Fiber 3g); Protein 2g.*

VARY IT! Coarsely chop one slice thick-cut bacon and sprinkle pieces, dividing them evenly, into the bowl of each squash half, and then roast as directed. Or fill squash halves with a mixture of sausage meat, chopped onions, and savory herbs, and then bake as directed.

Chapter 9

Coals and Coils: Grilling and Broiling

oosely speaking, the terms *grilling* and *broiling* are almost interchangeable. In grilling, which is done on a barbecue grill, the heat source is below; in oven broiling, it's above. Because both methods involve intense heat, they're best reserved for relatively thin pieces of meat, poultry, and vegetables — thick cuts of meat can burn on the outside before cooking sufficiently in the middle. The advantage of grilling and broiling is that the surface of the food develops that characteristic browned, crispy, flavorful "grilled" quality.

TIP

Broiling is usually done 4 to 6 inches from the heating coil. It's always best to put the food on a broiler pan with sides and a grated top that allows juices to fall into the pan. And watch out for flare-ups, either in the oven or on the grill. Flare-ups not only pose a fire danger, but they also can burn meat and give it an acrid flavor. Use the oven door or grill's cover to extinguish flames, and keep a spray bottle of water on hand.

The grilled recipes in this chapter work for broiling as well. Because you can't see food that's broiling as readily as food on a grill, check it more often until you get used to the timing. Keep in mind that broilers are typically hotter than charcoal, so food usually cooks faster.

Watch the video at www.dummies.com/go/grilling for visual tips on grilling and broiling.

Mastering Your Grill

If you're in the market for a grill, your choices range from a small hibachi to a "grilling unit" that's roughly the size of a Fiat and sports everything from gas burners and cutting boards to rotisseries and satellite TV (just kidding . . . we think). High-end grills can run into the thousands of dollars. Are the pricey models worth it? Or are you good to go with the hibachi? Look more closely at your grill options before you shell out the big bucks.

Obviously, the grill you choose is a matter of personal preference. But after you make your decision, you need to know how to master your heat source. This section covers the fundamentals you need to know if you're using a charcoal or gas grill.

Charcoal grilling

Many hard-core barbecue experts prefer charcoal grilling over any other type because of the flavor it imparts to meat and vegetables. Charcoal grills can be short or tall, large or small, but they all have one thing in common: Instead of turning a switch or lighting a gas flame, you actually light briquettes or wood and cook your food over this sometimes temperamental heat source.

Charcoal grilling does produce a unique flavor you can't get from a gas or electric grill, and charcoal grills are usually much less expensive. Moreover, you don't have to worry about buying and/or refilling a propane tank; for charcoal grilling, you can use charcoal briquettes or real wood briquettes (which are dense chunks of wood). Some briquettes are pretreated with lighter fluid so they're easy to light; we prefer real wood briquettes and/or special woods like mesquite, hickory, apple, and others.

INDIRECT GRILLING

At least once, you've probably cooked chicken over too hot a fire, burning its skin but finding it nearly raw in the center. With indirect grilling, which is comparable to oven roasting, the food cooks slowly off to one side of the heat, allowing the heat to circulate. You don't need to monitor the food closely or turn it over very often, and there's little chance of it burning. Another advantage of indirect grilling is that it creates two levels of heat in one grill. You have a direct fire for quickly searing foods and an indirect fire to finish cooking food more slowly. Finally, because indirect grilling cooks food in a covered grill, the food is infused with smoky barbecue flavor. See our recipe later in this chapter for Lemony Chicken, which cooks chicken thighs indirectly.

The key to successful charcoal grilling is an even source of heat. Probably the most common failing of amateur cooks is cooking with a charcoal fire that's too hot, either from having too many briquettes or positioning the grate too close to the fire. Here are more tips for having the perfect charcoal grilling experience:

>> As a rule, 30 charcoal briquettes can cook about 1 pound of meat. If you're cooking 2 pounds of meat, you need around 45 briquettes. Don't overload your grill with charcoal — too hot a fire will char food before it's fully cooked.

>> Spread the coals in a solid layer about 4 to 6 inches below the food grate.

WARNING

>> Never light cooking fires with kerosene, gasoline, or other chemicals unless you have a terrific home insurance plan.

TIP

Perhaps the best lighting technique is using a *stovepipe starter,* which looks like a piece of stovepipe with a handle. All you do is crumple some newspaper in the center of the empty grill and place the pipe over it. Then fill the top with briquettes. When you ignite the paper, the heat intensifies and shoots straight up, quickly lighting the coals. When the coals are mostly white, reverse the pipe and spread them over the bottom of the grill. (If you need extra briquettes, just place them over the hot ones.)

>> Allow 30 to 35 minutes for the coals to burn to medium (they should be about 75 percent white). To gauge the temperature, place the palm of your hand just above the grill's grid. If you can hold your hand in that position for 2 seconds, the coals are hot; a 3-second hold tells you the coals are medium-hot; 4 seconds is medium; and 5 indicates it's time to think about the microwave.

>> If you're cooking a large quantity of food and the fire begins to fade before you finish, add a small amount of fresh charcoal.

Gas grilling

Gas grills can get pretty fancy . . . and pretty expensive! But they look impressive on the patio. Thankfully gas-powered grills have become increasingly popular and more affordable in recent years. And they have several advantages over charcoal grills:

>> They heat up quickly.

>> The heat is adjustable and consistent.

>> They are easy to clean and maintain.

Some gas grills use lava rocks to simulate charcoal, which works exceedingly well. The cooking technique is the same as for charcoal grills, but the flavor isn't as pronounced.

One major difference between a gas and a charcoal grill is that gas grills run off a propane tank. That means you need to buy propane, attach it to your grill, and refill it when it runs out — usually when the steak is barely seared. Some people shy away from propane, but if you follow the directions for your grill, propane is safe.

Grilling with wood chips

Home cooks don't need a professional barbecue pit or a smoker when working with wood chips. All you need is a kettle charcoal grill with a cover or a standard gas grill with a wood chip-smoking box. (Charcoal yields the best results.)

Hard woods that are low in resin, such as cherry, apple, mesquite, and hickory, make the best smoking chips. But not all smoking chips are the same. Hickory and mesquite are relatively strong; apple, peach, cherry, and other fruit chips are relatively mild and sweet. Experiment with different types to discover what you like most and how much smoke you want in your food.

To use chips in a charcoal grill, simply cover two to three large handfuls with water in a bowl or other container and soak them for about 30 minutes. The soaking keeps the chips from burning when you throw them directly on the charcoal. Open the grill vents in the lid halfway. Ideally, you want the food enveloped in smoke, but you also want to keep the smoke circulating and moving. Depending on how long it takes to cook the food, you may need to add more chips to the coals. So keep the container of soaking chips close, just in case you need to throw on another handful.

BARBECUING DOESN'T EQUAL GRILLING

The terms *barbecuing* and *grilling* are often incorrectly interchanged. Grilling, like broiling, is a quick technique that cooks relatively small, tender pieces of food (such as chicken breasts, pork kebabs, or skewered shrimp) directly over a heat source. Barbecuing is more like oven roasting. With barbecuing, larger cuts of meat (such as spare ribs, pork butts, or whole turkeys) are slowly roasted over an indirect fire, in a covered grill, sometimes for hours, until the food is very tender and succulent. To make an indirect fire, the coals are moved to one side of the grill in the fire box. (On a gas grill, only one side of the grill is heated.) The food is cooked opposite the fire and covered, to trap the heat and smoke. This chapter focuses on grilling only. For both grilling and barbecuing information, tips, and recipes, check out *Grilling For Dummies,* by Marie Rama and John Mariani (Wiley).

For gas grills, put the soaked chips in a smoker box or wrap them in aluminum foil poked with lots of holes. Place them on the grill as close to the heat source as possible so they can smolder.

A low, slow cooking fire extends the cooking time and gives the smoke time to impart its flavor into the food. Fish, burgers, vegetables, and other relatively soft, quick-cooking foods absorb the smoke more quickly than thick cuts of meat like briskets, pork shoulders, and whole chickens or turkeys.

Marinating for Flavor

A common misperception is that marinades tenderize meat. They don't. A marinade barely penetrates the outer ⅛ inch of the surface of meat, poultry, or game. What a marinade can do is add flavor to the surface.

Most marinades involve an acidic ingredient (vinegar, lemon, or some kinds of wine), oil, herbs, and perhaps a base flavor ingredient (beef or chicken stock, for example). You want to end up with a marinade that's well balanced and flavorful.

Consider this example: You have a chuck shoulder steak. Ask yourself whether you want to add a hot, medium, or sweet flavor. Your answer depends largely on the main ingredient. You may not want a sweet flavor on fish, for example. With pork, though, you may.

Say for now that you want a hot marinade for the steak. Start with red chile flakes (carefully!). Then what? You need a liquid that goes with beef as well as chiles. You can use beef stock (homemade or canned beef broth) or red wine. To that, think of what goes well with hot things. Minced garlic and black peppercorns maybe. Chopped cilantro adds flavor, too. (As you begin to cook, you'll discover more about ingredients in the supermarket and how to blend them.) Depending on your taste, you may want to add a little dried cumin or coriander seed. Then, at the end, add 2 to 3 tablespoons of good olive oil, salt, and black pepper.

So there you have your basic hot marinade for steak, which you can vary as you go along to make it hotter, milder, or whatever. Now you try!

Put your meat into a Ziploc bag or shallow pan and cover it with the marinade. Turn it once to coat the meat, and let it soak up the flavor for at least one hour — or even overnight in the refrigerator. Remove it from the marinade, pat it dry, and grill as you like.

WARNING

Be sure to marinate meats, fish, poultry, and vegetables in the refrigerator. Bacteria forms on the surface of room-temperature food very quickly.

A marinade can be turned into a good finishing sauce but only if it's been kept constantly refrigerated. Bring it to a full boil to destroy any harmful bacteria from raw poultry, fish, or meat juices before you pour it over cooked food.

Perfecting Your Grilling Technique

Before you fire up the grill, keep the following tips in mind:

» Clean the grill grate well with a wire brush between uses. A dirty grate can affect the taste of your food — and it looks gross.

» Before igniting the fire, brush some vegetable oil over the grates to prevent sticking.

» Get yourself organized. Set up a small table next to the grill with all your ingredients, utensils, serving platters, and so on. What utensils do you need? It depends on what you're making. Common examples include a long-handled metal spatula, fork, and tongs.

» Trim meat of excess fat to avoid grease flare-ups that blacken the meat and give it a burned flavor.

After you place your meat, chicken, or veggies on the grill, take these tips to heart:

>> Cooking times for outdoor grill recipes are approximate, so don't throw the meat on and jump in the pool for 15 minutes. Many variables affect cooking time: wind, intensity of coals, thickness of meat, and your fondness for dancing every time a Justin Bieber song comes on.

>> Use the grill lid. Many barbecue grills come with lids, which, when secured, create an oven that can exceed 450 degrees. Certain foods that take a relatively long time to cook — chicken legs, thicker slices of steak, and so on — grill faster and better with the lid on. Essentially, you're grilling and roasting at the same time. A lid traps much of the heat, directing it into the food rather than allowing it to blow away. The lid also can create a smoky effect that infuses the food with delicious aromas and flavors (especially if you grill over woods like apple, hickory, and mesquite). But be sure to lift the lid frequently to check on the food.

WARNING

>> Don't apply sweet barbecue sauces to meat until the last 10 minutes of cooking or the sugar in them may burn.

Be sure to shut off the valve of your gas grill when finished. On a charcoal grill, close the lid to extinguish the hot coals.

Making Each Dish Delicious

In this section, we offer a few words of advice for how to create some outdoor masterpieces.

Burgers

If you want the perfect hamburger — juicy and meaty, moist and not fatty — you have to start with the right meat. The best all-around meat for hamburgers is ground chuck, which has about 15 to 20 percent fat, just enough to keep it moist. (Supermarkets usually list the percentage of fat on the label.) Also look for coarsely ground meat, which yields a looser patty. Many people think that if they buy the "best" meat, like ground sirloin or ground round, they'll have a superior burger. The flavor may be good, but those cuts are so lean that they tend to be dry.

Hamburgers for the grill should be plump and well seasoned. The ingredients and flavors you can add are limitless. Consider minced onions, minced garlic, minced basil, and chopped thyme or rosemary; soy sauce, seasoned breadcrumbs, and a beaten egg; Worcestershire sauce; minced bell peppers; or Tabasco sauce if you like it hot. And you don't even have to stick to beef: Lamb and turkey burgers, or blends of all three, are super, too.

REMEMBER

You may enjoy getting your hands (washed, please!) into a mound of rosy ground meat and playing sculptor. But if you get too aggressive when forming your hamburger patties and mold them too firmly, they'll tighten up on the grill. And nobody wants a tight hamburger! To get the most tender burger, keep it loose and don't overwork the meat.

Chicken

Barbecued chicken has a smoky, sweet, tangy flavor that can come from a broiler but that we think tastes even better off the grill. Just be sure the chicken is cooked all the way. Prick the chicken with a fork. If the juices run clear, the chicken is done, but to be really accurate, use a meat thermo-meter. The internal temperature of chicken parts on the bone should be 165 degrees. (Be sure the thermometer isn't touching a bone, which can give a false high reading.)

Remember, grill times in recipes are approximate, depending on the heat of your grill and the size of the chicken pieces. To shorten cooking time, you can microwave chicken pieces for about 3 minutes per pound before grilling.

RECIPE ALERT

If the mere thought of chicken hot off the grill makes you salivate, you'll love the Barbecued Chicken recipe we offer later in the chapter. We suggest that you use our Chapter 8 recipe for Country Barbeque Sauce when making it, but you can take a shortcut and use store-bought sauce if you want.

Vegetables

Charcoal imparts a pleasing texture and a smoky essence to vegetables. Moreover, preparation is easy and quick. Here are some examples:

>> **Corn:** Pull back the husks to remove the silk, but leave the husks attached to the base of the ear. Wrap the husks back around the corn and tie at the top with string or a strip of husk. Grill 20 minutes or until tender, turning frequently. Serve with melted butter flavored with herbs and fresh lemon juice.

>> **Eggplant and zucchini:** Cut them lengthwise into 1-inch-thick slices. Brush with oil, season to taste, and grill, turning occasionally, for 5 to 8 minutes or until golden brown and tender. For additional flavor, marinate in a 3-to-1 oil-vinegar mixture with salt and black pepper and maybe Dijon-style mustard for about 15 minutes before grilling.

>> **Potatoes, carrots, onions, and turnips:** Peel and slice into uniform pieces and precook in boiling water until almost tender. Rinse in cold water to stop the cooking and drain well. Wrap in aluminum foil with seasonings such as olive oil, lemon juice, fresh herbs, and salt and black pepper to taste. Grill for 10 to 15 minutes or until tender. (You can also thread them onto skewers before grilling.)

>> **Tomatoes:** Slice firm, ripe tomatoes into 1-inch-thick pieces. Brush with olive oil; sprinkle with dried basil or parsley and salt and black pepper. Grill until heated through, about 5 minutes total, turning once.

RECIPE ALERT

Porous vegetables, such as mushrooms and sliced eggplant, need not be marinated before grilling. You simply brush them with a flavorful liquid, as in the recipe for Garlic-Grilled Portobello Mushrooms later in this chapter.

If you're going to grill mushrooms, you need to know how to clean, trim, and slice them. Rinse or brush raw mushrooms with a damp paper towel or a vegetable brush. If you do rinse them, drain them well in a colander or dab off any excess moisture before sautéeing. Then, just cut off the stem and slice the cap into pieces.

Steak and pork

RECIPE ALERT

Steak on the grill may be one of summer's nicest luxuries, as long as you cook the steak the right way! A dry, tough steak is disappointing, so don't overcook. Medium or medium rare yields a more tender steak than well-done. You can also add flavor with a good marinade. Check out our recipe for The Perfect Steak later in this chapter.

RECIPE ALERT

Grilling a pork tenderloin couldn't be easier, and the results are simply delicious. Our recipe for Grilled Pork Tenderloin later in this chapter shows you how to brine the pork prior to cooking it so it retains maximum moisture and flavor.

Seafood

Shrimp require minimal cooking time. It takes only a few minutes before they turn pink and succulent. Be sure not to overcook them, or they could become rubbery.

To prepare shrimp for grilling, you may want to remove the bitter black vein that runs along the outside. Some cooks do, some don't. In grilling, the vein likely burns off, but see the illustration in Chapter 7 if you want to devein. You can leave the tails on, or pull them off. You want to double-thread the shrimp onto skewers so that the skewer pierces both ends of the shrimp (which prevents them from sliding off). If you use wooden skewers, soak them for 30 minutes in cold water and cover the tips with foil to prevent burning. (*Note:* Don't pack the shrimp too tightly on the skewers; allow a little space between each piece so the heat can circulate and to ensure even cooking.)

**RECIPE
ALERT**

Get creative with our Grilled Shrimp Skewers recipe by alternating each shrimp with veggies, or even fruit. Try chunks of onion and cherry tomatoes, or cubes of pineapple. You can also serve shrimp skewers with a dipping sauce, such as melted butter with a squeeze of fresh lemon juice, barbecue sauce (store-bought or the Country Barbecue Sauce recipe in Chapter 8), or Asian chili sauce (available in the Asian food section of your grocery store).

**RECIPE
ALERT**

Our Grilled Tuna with Niçoise Dressing recipe is a variation on the classic French dish and makes a delicious light lunch. If you don't want to fire up the grill, you can also make it under the broiler. (Keep in mind that some people prefer grilled tuna very rare, and others medium, so don't overcook it.) Other types of fish and shellfish work with this recipe as well. Choose those that can hold up to grilling, such as firm-fleshed salmon, halibut, swordfish, mako shark, and monkfish. Avoid delicate fish such as sole, which tends to flake and fall apart on the grill.

The Perfect Hamburger

PREP TIME: ABOUT 10 MIN	COOK TIME: 10–14 MIN	YIELD: 4 SERVINGS

INGREDIENTS

Oil for the grill rack

1½ pounds ground chuck

¼ teaspoon salt, or to taste

¼ teaspoon black pepper, or to taste

4 hamburger buns

DIRECTIONS

1 Oil the grill and prepare a medium fire in a charcoal or gas grill.

2 While the grill is heating, combine in a bowl the ground chuck, salt, and black pepper. Mix lightly but thoroughly, using your hands. Shape the mixture into 4 patties, each about ¾ inch thick.

3 Place the patties on the grill grid. Grill directly over the heat for 5 to 7 minutes per side for medium, or less for rare or medium rare.

4 Just before the burgers are finished, toast the buns on the edges of the grill. Serve.

PER SERVING: Calories 344 (From Fat 105); Fat 12g (Saturated 4g); Cholesterol 97mg; Sodium 450mg; Carbohydrate 22g (Dietary Fiber 1g); Protein 35g.

TIP: The USDA recommends cooking ground meat patties made from beef, veal, lamb, or pork to a minimum internal temperature of 160 degrees.

GO-WITH: In our opinion, nothing goes better with a great burger than French Potato Salad (see recipe in Chapter 12).

TIP: Quick and tasty burger toppings include thinly sliced red or yellow onions, tomato slices marinated in a basil vinaigrette dressing, flavored mustards, mango or tomato chutney, tomato-based salsa, grilled peppers, and garlic-grilled mushrooms.

TIP: Though you may be tempted to do it, don't press down on the patties as they cook. Pressing releases the hamburger's tasty juices into the fire.

Barbecued Chicken

PREP TIME: ABOUT 10 MIN	COOK TIME: ABOUT 50 MIN	YIELD: 4 SERVINGS

INGREDIENTS

Oil for the grill rack

1 chicken, cut into 4 pieces, or 4 chicken breasts with ribs (about 3 pounds total)

Salt and black pepper

1 cup Country Barbecue Sauce (see recipe in Chapter 8) or store-bought barbecue sauce

DIRECTIONS

1 Oil the grill grid and prepare a medium-hot fire in a charcoal or gas grill.

2 Season each piece of chicken with salt and black pepper on both sides.

3 Put the chicken pieces, bone-side up, on the grill. Cook for 30 minutes. Flip chicken pieces with tongs. Cook for an additional 20 minutes or more, as needed.

4 During the last 10 minutes of cooking, brush the chicken pieces with barbecue sauce. The chicken is done when it's no longer pink inside or when an instant-read thermometer inserted into the thickest part of the thigh registers 165 degrees.

PER SERVING: *Calories 514 (From Fat 253); Fat 28g (Saturated 7g); Cholesterol 134mg; Sodium 452mg; Carbohydrate 21g (Dietary Fiber 0g); Protein 43g.*

GO-WITH: The assertive flavor of the barbecue sauce marries well with side dishes like French Potato Salad or Bell Pepper Rice Salad (find both recipes in Chapter 12), or Grilled Corn on the Cob and All-American Coleslaw (see Chapter 20).

Indirectly Grilled Lemony Chicken

PREP TIME: 20 MIN PLUS MARINATING TIME	COOK TIME: 35–40 MIN	YIELD: 4 SERVINGS

INGREDIENTS

4 bone-in chicken legs and thighs (about 2½ to 3 pounds total)

¼ cup extra-virgin olive oil

¼ cup honey

¼ cup chopped fresh mint

Juice of 2 lemons

2 teaspoons grated lemon peel

4 large cloves garlic, peeled and minced

1 tablespoon peeled and grated fresh ginger

1 teaspoon ground cumin

⅛ teaspoon cayenne red pepper

Salt and black pepper to taste

DIRECTIONS

1 If necessary, separate the chicken legs from the thighs by cutting through the thigh-leg joint with a sharp knife. Place the pieces in a large, resealable plastic bag or a large, shallow nonreactive baking dish.

2 Combine all the remaining ingredients to make the marinade in a mixing bowl or liquid measuring cup. Pour the marinade over the chicken, turning the pieces over to coat all sides. Seal the bag or cover the dish; refrigerate for 4 to 6 hours, turning occasionally.

3 Prepare an indirect, medium-hot fire in a covered charcoal or gas grill. Place a drip pan under the side of the grill without heat.

4 Remove the chicken from the marinade, reserving the remaining marinade. Place the chicken pieces, skin-side down, on the lightly oiled grill grid, directly over the heat. Grill until browned on both sides, turning every 2 to 3 minutes to prevent the skin from charring.

5 Move the chicken to the side of the grill without heat; baste both sides with some of the remaining marinade. Cover the grill and cook 30 to 35 minutes, or until an instant-read thermometer inserted into the thickest part of the thigh registers 165 degrees.

PER SERVING: *Calories 742 (From Fat 468); Fat 52g (Saturated 12g); Cholesterol 283mg; Sodium 318mg; Carbohydrate 20g (Dietary Fiber 0g); Protein 51g.*

Garlic-Grilled Portobello Mushrooms

PREP TIME: ABOUT 10 MIN	COOK TIME: ABOUT 6 MIN	YIELD: 4 SERVINGS

INGREDIENTS

Oil for the grill rack

1 pound portobello mushrooms

⅓ cup extra-virgin olive oil

3 tablespoons lemon juice

2 large cloves garlic, minced (about 2 teaspoons)

Salt and black pepper

2 tablespoons minced fresh parsley (optional)

DIRECTIONS

1 Oil the grill grid and prepare a medium-hot fire in a charcoal or gas grill.

2 Clean the mushrooms and remove the stems.

3 In a small bowl, combine the oil, lemon juice, and garlic. Brush the mushroom caps with the flavored oil and season to taste with salt and black pepper.

4 Place the mushroom caps on the grill, top-side down, for about 3 minutes. (Don't let them burn.) Turn the mushroom caps over and grill for another 3 to 4 minutes, or until you can easily pierce the caps with a knife and the mushrooms are nicely browned.

5 Remove the mushrooms to a platter, garnish with the parsley (if desired), and serve.

PER SERVING: *Calories 213 (From Fat 171); Fat 19g (Saturated 3g); Cholesterol 0mg; Sodium 152mg; Carbohydrate 6g (Dietary Fiber 1g); Protein 2g.*

GO-WITH: Steak — such as the Broiled Skirt Steak, Cajun-Style (see the recipe later in this chapter) — is the natural accompaniment to these savory mushrooms.

The Perfect Steak

PREP TIME: 5 MIN PLUS MARINATING TIME	COOK TIME: 8–20 MIN	YIELD: 4 SERVINGS

INGREDIENTS

2 T-bone, porterhouse, or top loin steaks, about 1 inch thick

½ cup dry red wine (try Merlot or Shiraz)

1 tablespoon Worcestershire sauce

1 large clove garlic, minced (about 1 teaspoon)

1 teaspoon ground cumin

¼ teaspoon black pepper

Oil for the grill rack

1 teaspoon salt

DIRECTIONS

1 Place the steaks in a large resealable plastic bag. Add the wine, Worcestershire sauce, garlic, cumin, and black pepper to the bag, seal, and marinate in the refrigerator for about 30 minutes, turning once after about 15 minutes.

2 Oil the grill grid and prepare a medium fire in a charcoal or gas grill.

3 Remove the steaks from the bag and discard the marinade. Put the steaks on the grill.

4 Grill for about 8 minutes for rare, 15 minutes for medium, or 20 minutes for well-done, turning the meat once with the tongs halfway through cooking. Season with the salt and serve immediately.

PER SERVING: *Calories 273 (From Fat 137); Fat 15g (Saturated 5g); Cholesterol 77mg; Sodium 675mg; Carbohydrate 0g (Dietary Fiber 0g); Protein 30g.*

GO-WITH: This steak tastes great with side dishes that are a step above standard picnic fare. Try Penne with Parmesan Cheese and Basil (see recipe in Chapter 13), Risotto (Chapter 13), or a Grilled Vegetable Platter with Fresh Pesto (Chapter 12).

Grilled Pork Tenderloin

PREP TIME: 5 MIN PLUS BRINING TIME	COOK TIME: ABOUT 1 HR	YIELD: 6–8 SERVINGS

INGREDIENTS

3 tablespoons kosher salt

½ cup granulated sugar

2 cups hot tap water

2 cups cold water

1½ to 2 pounds pork tenderloin (1 or 2 pieces)

Salt and black pepper to taste

DIRECTIONS

1   In a large container, dissolve the salt and sugar in the hot water, stirring. Add the cold water and stir again. Let the brine cool.

2   Add the tenderloin, cover, and refrigerate for 1 to 3 hours. The pork should be submerged in the brine; if necessary, add more cold tap water to cover.

3   Remove pork from the brine, rinse well, and dry thoroughly with paper towels.

4   Heat the grill, turning gas burners to high or letting charcoals get white. Season the tenderloin generously with salt and black pepper.

5   Cook the pork with the grill lid closed. Turn it every few minutes so all sides get well browned. Cook for 8 to 10 minutes, until an instant-read thermometer inserted into the thickest part registers 145 degrees.

6   Transfer pork to a cutting board, cover loosely with foil, and let rest 5 minutes. To serve, slice crosswise into 1-inch-thick pieces.

PER SERVING: *Calories 173 (From Fat 60); Fat 7g (Saturated 2g); Cholesterol 78mg; Sodium 318mg; Carbohydrate 2g (Dietary Fiber 0g); Protein 25g.*

Grilled Shrimp Skewers

PREP TIME: ABOUT 10 MIN	COOK TIME: ABOUT 15 MIN	YIELD: 4 SERVINGS

INGREDIENTS

Oil for the grill rack

¼ cup butter, melted

2 teaspoons lemon juice

1 clove garlic, minced

1 pound medium shrimp
(the size that equals about
20 per pound)

DIRECTIONS

1   Oil the grill grid and prepare a medium fire in a charcoal or gas grill.

2   Combine the butter, lemon juice, and garlic in a small bowl. Reserve half of the mixture.

3   Peel and devein the shrimp, and double-thread them onto four skewers.

4   Brush the shrimp on both sides with half of the lemon-butter mixture.

5   Place skewers on the grate and grill for about 8 minutes, or until golden, turning the skewers once halfway through the cooking time.

6   Remove to a platter and drizzle with the remaining lemon-butter mixture. Serve immediately.

PER SERVING: *Calories 188 (From Fat 111); Fat 12g (Saturated 7g); Cholesterol 199mg; Sodium 195mg; Carbohydrate 1g (Dietary Fiber 0g); Protein 18g.*

GO-WITH: Try this dish with a light accompaniment like Sautéed Spinach Leaves (see recipe in Chapter 5) or Roasted Summer Vegetables (in Chapter 8).

Grilled Tuna with Niçoise Dressing

PREP TIME: 10 MIN PLUS MARINATING TIME	COOK TIME: 6–7 MIN	YIELD: 4 SERVINGS

INGREDIENTS

1 green onion, trimmed and minced

1 tablespoon finely chopped black olives

1 tablespoon finely chopped capers

2 tablespoons balsamic vinegar

¼ teaspoon black pepper

1 teaspoon finely chopped anchovy fillets or anchovy paste (optional)

2 tablespoons chopped parsley

½ cup plus 3 tablespoons olive oil

4 tuna steaks, about 1-inch thick (1½ pounds total)

1 teaspoon minced fresh thyme, or ½ teaspoon dried

Salt and black pepper

Oil for the grill rack

DIRECTIONS

1 Make the dressing by combining in a bowl the green onion, olives, and capers. Stir in the vinegar and black pepper. Beat in the anchovy fillets or paste (if desired) and parsley and then ½ cup of the oil. Set aside.

2 Put the tuna on a roasting pan and season with the remaining 3 tablespoons of oil, thyme, and salt and black pepper to taste. Turn the steaks to coat well. Let sit, refrigerated, for about 15 minutes.

3 Brush the grill grid with oil and heat a gas or charcoal grill to medium-high.

4 Place the tuna on the grill and cook for about 3 minutes. Using a spatula, turn the fillets and grill for 3 minutes on the other side. Remove one of the steaks and test for doneness by making a small incision in the center. Medium-rare tuna appears opaque on the outside and reddish-pink in the center; an instant-read thermometer will register 125 degrees.

5 When the tuna steaks have cooked, transfer them to warm serving dishes. Spoon half of the dressing over the steaks. Serve the remaining dressing on the side.

PER SERVING: *Calories 454 (From Fat 288); Fat 32g (Saturated 4g); Cholesterol 74mg; Sodium 200mg; Carbohydrate 2g (Dietary Fiber 0g); Protein 38g.*

GO-WITH: This entrée goes nicely with a soup, such as the Carrot Soup with Dill, or a salad, such as Bell Pepper-Rice Salad or Cucumber-Dill Salad (see recipes in Chapter 12).

Broiled Skirt Steak, Cajun-Style

PREP TIME: ABOUT 5 MIN PLUS MARINATING TIME	COOK TIME: ABOUT 6 MIN	YIELD: 4 SERVINGS

INGREDIENTS

4 skirt steaks, ½ pound each

Salt

2 tablespoons olive oil

1 teaspoon chili powder

½ teaspoon ground cumin

½ teaspoon dried thyme

¼ teaspoon cayenne pepper

¼ teaspoon black pepper

2 tablespoons butter

2 tablespoons finely chopped fresh parsley

DIRECTIONS

1 A half hour before broiling or grilling, sprinkle the steaks with salt to taste. In a small bowl, combine the oil, chili powder, cumin, thyme, cayenne, and black pepper and stir well to mix. Brush this mixture all over the steaks. Cover the steaks with plastic wrap but don't refrigerate.

2 Preheat the broiler or set a charcoal or gas grill to medium-high.

3 Remove steaks from plastic wrap. If broiling, arrange the steaks on a rack and place under the broiler about 6 inches from the heat source. Broil for 3 minutes with the door partly open. Turn the steaks and continue broiling with the door partly open. Broil about 3 minutes more for medium rare, or to the desired degree of doneness.

If grilling, put the steaks on a medium-hot oiled grill and cover. Cook for 3 minutes. Turn the steaks, cover, and cook about 3 minutes more for medium rare, or to the desired degree of doneness.

4 Transfer the steaks to a hot platter and dot with butter. Let them stand in a warm place for 5 minutes to redistribute the internal juices, which accumulate as the steaks stand.

5 Sprinkle with parsley and serve with the accumulated butter sauce.

PER SERVING: *Calories 487 (From Fat 278); Fat 31g (Saturated 12g); Cholesterol 122mg; Sodium 292mg; Carbohydrate 1g (Dietary Fiber 1g); Protein 49g.*

TIP: To check for doneness, make a small incision with a sharp knife into the center or thickest part of the steak.

Chapter **10**

Baking Basics

For some reason, people find baking intimidating. But why? Sure, baking may seem a little mystical. Get flour wet and put it in a hot oven, and it turns into something entirely different: bread, cake, cookies, cupcakes, pie, pastry. What kind of magic could be more fun than that?

Baking *is* fun, if you know the basics. However, it also requires a more scientific approach than other kinds of cooking. You can't just throw in a little of this, a little of that, and hope for the best. Baking is more a science than an art. Throw off the proportion of dry ingredients (like flour, baking powder, and salt) to wet ingredients (like milk, eggs, and vanilla extract), for example, or fail to mix, whip, or knead the batter or dough as directed, and your results won't be the same as the recipe intended. In fact, the recipe may not turn out at all, with cookies running all over the tray, cakes falling in the center, or breads refusing to rise.

But that fact, viewed from a different perspective, should actually make baking *less* intimidating: All you have to do is follow the recipe — exactly — and your baked goods will fill the house with their heavenly scent. And you'll find that people will begin to do you little favors . . . *just in case you make another one of those batches of cupcakes.*

Don't Wing It: Measuring with Care

Baking's number-one rule is to measure accurately. Recipes for baked goods, if they're good recipes, are carefully formulated so that all the elements result in the perfect texture and flavor. In baking, different kinds of ingredients must be measured in different ways for accuracy. The following sections give you what you need to know.

WARNING

Don't measure liquid or dry ingredients over your working bowl, especially if it's filled with other ingredients. You may accidentally add too much of an ingredient.

WHY YOU SHOULD OWN A KITCHEN SCALE

In the United States, most recipes for home cooks are measured in cups and spoons, but it's a good idea to have a kitchen scale for when they're given by weight, particularly when it comes to baking. Additionally, measuring cups and spoons aren't always precisely accurate. This is especially true with ingredients like flour that can settle after being weighed.

There are several types of home scales:

- **Mechanical devices, also known as spring scales:** These are inexpensive and functional. Many come with measuring bowls and can hold 5 pounds or more.
- **Digital scales:** Digital scales are easy to use, and you can find a perfectly good one for less than $20. Make sure it has an easy-to-read LCD display and wide, sturdy platform and measures in ounces, grams, pounds, and kilograms. Some feature what's called a *tare function,* which means it can automatically subtract the weight of food containers.

Illustration by Elizabeth Kurtzman

Measuring dry ingredients

Baking generally begins with dry ingredients like flour and sugar, and these must be measured in a particular way. Use a dry measuring cup — not the kind with a spout, but the kind with a flat top.

TIP

Flour and sugar are measured the same way, but let's focus on flour. First, stir up your flour (in the bag or canister) to fluff it up, and then dip in your measuring cup — whatever size the recipe calls for (1 cup, ½ cup, and so on) — so the flour is mounded higher than the rim of the measuring cup. Using the flat side of a knife, skim it over the top of the cup — this is called *leveling* — so you push the excess flour back into the bag or canister. When you're done, the flour should come *exactly* to the top of the measuring cup — no higher, no lower. Now you can add the flour to your recipe.

If the recipe calls for *sifted flour,* you must sift it *before measuring.* Sifting changes the volume of the flour, and because measuring is so important, sifting is, too. Using a dry measuring cup, scoop out the approximate amount of flour called for in the recipe and place it in the top of the sifter. Sift the flour into a large mixing bowl or over a piece of wax paper. After sifting, so as not to lose the flour's new "lightness," gently spoon the flour into the appropriate measuring cup, fill to overflowing, and then level it off with the straight edge of a knife.

Recipes often call for smaller amounts of other dry ingredients, such as baking powder, baking soda, active dry yeast, and salt. You can also level dry ingredients in a tablespoon, teaspoon, or smaller measure. Don't use your table silverware to measure dry ingredients — use measuring spoons. As with a measuring cup, scoop the measuring spoon into your dry ingredient so you have a heaping spoonful, and then run the flat side of a knife over the top to level the ingredients. Some baking ingredients, like baking powder cans and baking soda boxes, come with a built-in leveling surface so you can dip in your spoon and level as you pull it out of the can or box by running the top of the spoon along the flat surface.

Measuring wet ingredients

Wet or liquid ingredients, such as milk, water, and oil, require different kinds of measuring cups than dry ingredients — namely *liquid* measuring cups. These cups typically have spouts for easy pouring and rims that are higher than the highest measuring mark. For example, a 2-cup liquid measuring cup will hold more than 2 cups if you fill it to the brim. To measure liquid ingredients, pour them into the measuring cup exactly to the line indicated for the amount you need. Make sure the cup is sitting on a flat surface. Be exact for best results.

When you need to measure smaller quantities of liquid ingredients, such as vanilla or almond extract, use the same measuring spoons that you use for dry ingredients.

Measuring other types of ingredients

Certain ingredients require other measuring techniques. When a recipe calls for brown sugar, for example, you don't measure it the same way you do regular sugar. Instead, you pack the brown sugar tightly into your measuring cup, pressing it down with the back of a spoon. The same is true when you're working with shortening or peanut butter.

TIP

To easily remove sticky foods like shortening, peanut butter, honey, or molasses from a measuring cup or spoon, coat the cup or spoon first with a small amount of vegetable oil or spray.

When a recipe calls for butter or margarine, your best bet is to use the kind that's packaged in stick form. Use the measure marks on the wrapper to slice off a specific amount.

Working with Eggs

Many baking recipes call for eggs, and you can probably surmise that they don't mean for you to include the shell. Eggs are technically a liquid ingredient, but you don't have to measure them the way you do water, milk, and oil. Instead, you have to be able to break them so you get all the good stuff into your bowl and the crunchy stuff into the garbage can or compost pile. In this section, we help you do just that — and we walk you through the process of separating the yolk from the egg white.

Breaking with care

To get the good stuff out of that mysterious ovoid, follow these instructions:

1. **Hold the egg in one hand.**

2. **Tap the egg on the side of a small bowl or glass measuring cup to gently break the shell.**

    Don't tap too hard, or you'll shatter the egg and your egg will be full of shell pieces.

3. **Put your two thumbs inside the crack and gently open the egg so the yolk and white fall into the bowl or measuring cup.**

   If a piece of shell falls in the egg, use the edge of one of the egg shell halves to nudge it up the side of the bowl and out. Egg shell pieces tend to stick to other egg shell pieces.

TIP Always break eggs into a separate bowl or cup before adding them to a recipe. That way, you can remove any stray shell pieces before they get lost in, say, the birthday cake batter.

Separating an egg

Many recipes require separated egg whites and yolks. Separating eggs isn't difficult; it just takes a little practice. Follow these steps, as illustrated in Figure 10-1, to separate an egg without breaking the yolk. (If a recipe calls for just egg whites, you don't want any yolk in them or the recipe likely won't turn out as expected.)

1. **Hold the egg in one hand above two small bowls.**

2. **Crack the shell on the side of one bowl — just enough to break through the shell and the membrane without piercing the yolk or shattering the shell.**

   This step may take a little practice. Repeat on the other side if necessary.

3. **Pry open the eggshell with both thumbs and gently let the bulk of the white fall into one of the bowls.**

How to Separate an Egg

1. Hold the egg in one hand over two small bowls.

2. Crack the shell on the side of one bowl.

3. Let the white fall into one of the bowls.

4. Pass the yolk back & forth, each time releasing more white.

5. When all the white is in the bowl, drop the yolk in the other bowl.

FIGURE 10-1: Separating an egg.

Illustration by Elizabeth Kurtzman

4. Carefully pass the yolk back and forth from one shell cavity to the other, each time releasing more white.

5. When all the white is in the bowl, carefully transfer the yolk to the other bowl (it doesn't matter if the yolk breaks at this point). Cover and refrigerate the yolk if you're not using it right away.

TIP

If you're more of a visual learner, be sure to check out the video at www.dummies.com/go/separatingegg.

Folding, Whipping, Kneading, and More: Getting the Techniques Right

You've got your flour, your baking powder, your milk, your eggs. It's all measured and ready to go. Now what? Next, you have to mix it all together, but not willy-nilly. Remember, *follow the directions*, which will include some techniques for mixing that you need to know if you want light cakes, chewy cookies, tender cupcakes, and bread that actually rises. When you work the batter or dough the right way, you get good results, so consider this your official guide to (literally) whipping that batter or dough into shape. Here's what the various baking techniques mean:

>> **Stirring:** Moving ingredients around with a spoon until they're combined.

>> **Beating:** Mixing ingredients together vigorously (more vigorously than stirring), in a circular motion, by hand or with an electric mixer, until they become smooth. If you're the sort who likes to keep track of such things, 100 brisk hand-beaten strokes generally equal one minute with an electric mixer.

>> **Whipping:** Similar to beating, but whipping incorporates more air into ingredients, such as egg whites or cream, by using a whisk or electric beater with a whisk attachment rather than a spoon or standard beater attachment.

TIP

Many recipes call for egg whites whipped into soft or stiff peaks, to lighten batters or make meringues or soufflés. Before whipping egg whites, make sure your mixing bowl and beaters are clean and dry. Even a speck of dirt, oil, or egg yolk can prevent the whites from beating stiff. To get your bowl really clean, wipe it with a cloth dipped in vinegar, which will remove any fat or grease. Then rinse and dry the bowl. Avoid using plastic bowls when beating whites; fat and grease adhere to plastic, which can diminish the volume of the beaten whites.

If any of the yolk breaks and falls into the separated whites before you beat them stiff, remove the yolk by dabbing with a piece of paper towel. Beat the whites slowly until they're foamy; then increase the beating speed to incorporate as much air as possible until the whites form smooth, shiny peaks. If you overbeat the egg whites so they lose their shine and start to look dry and grainy, add another egg white and beat briefly.

>> **Whisking:** Whipping briefly and lightly by hand using a wire whisk, to combine ingredients (such as eggs and milk) and incorporate air.

>> **Creaming:** Beating butter, margarine, or shortening with sugar by hand or with an electric mixer until it's completely combined and turns light and fluffy.

>> **Kneading:** Working yeast bread dough by hand or with dough hook attachments on an electric mixer. The pushing, folding, and pressing action develops the gluten in the dough and gives it a smooth, elastic texture so it will rise.

>> **Folding:** Combing a light mixture, such as beaten egg whites or whipped cream, into a heavier mixture, such as cake batter. For example, to fold egg whites into cake batter, begin by stirring about one-quarter of the beaten whites into the yolk mixture. (This step lightens the batter somewhat.) Then pile the remaining egg whites on top. Use a large rubber spatula to cut down through the center of the mixture, going all the way to the bottom of the bowl. Pull the spatula toward you to the edge of the bowl, turning it to bring some of the batter up over the whites. Give the bowl a quarter-turn and repeat this plunging, scooping motion about 10 to 15 times (depending on the amount of batter) until the whites and batter are combined. Be careful not to overblend, or the beaten whites will deflate. See Figure 10-2 for illustrated instructions of this technique.

THE COPPER CONNECTION

We won't go into the scientific details of why copper bowls are best for whipping egg whites — just believe us. As far back as the mid-18th century, this was common knowledge. Just remember that if you're making a meringue or other dish that requires whipped whites, whipping the whites in a copper bowl with a balloon whisk yields a fluffier and more stable foam.

A 10-inch copper bowl for whisking costs about $60. If you don't have a copper bowl, a pinch of cream of tartar added to the egg white can also stabilize the foam.

How to Fold Egg Whites into a Cake Batter

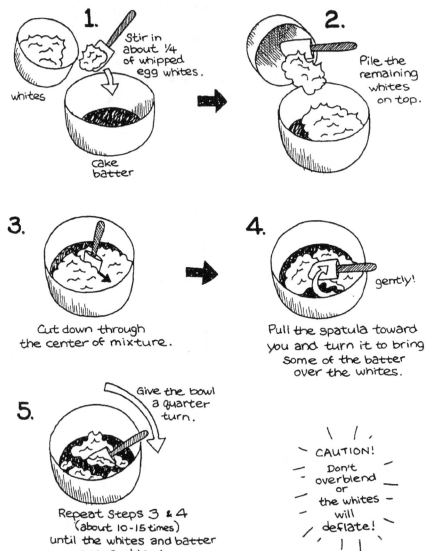

1. Stir in about ¼ of whipped egg whites.

whites

cake batter

2. Pile the remaining whites on top.

3. Cut down through the center of mixture.

4. Pull the spatula toward you and turn it to bring some of the batter over the whites. gently!

5. Give the bowl a quarter turn. Repeat Steps 3 & 4 (about 10-15 times) until the whites and batter are combined.

CAUTION! Don't overblend or the whites will deflate!

FIGURE 10-2: Folding egg whites into a cake batter involves a plunging, scooping motion.

Illustration by Elizabeth Kurtzman

Perfecting Your Pie Crust

Everybody loves pie, or so the saying goes. But everybody can love *your* pie the most if you master homemade pie dough (easier than it sounds) and the art of a thick, rich, fruity, creamy, or chocolaty pie filling. The two keys to pie are a light flaky crust and a proper filling that doesn't run all over the pie plate when you cut the pie.

TIP

Your food processor is a helpful ally in your quest for the perfect pie dough. Pie dough is a delicate blend of flour, butter, and shortening, and the less it's handled, the flakier it will be. The goal is to mix cold butter into flour and keep it from melting, which would make your pie crust tougher and greasier. A food processor blends the butter and flour *fast*, with no warm hands touching the delicate dough. However, you can make pie the old-fashioned way, too, with a pastry blender (see Figure 10-3).

You want to chill the dough at every stage, to keep those flaky butter layers intact. Roll out the chilled disks quickly, and transfer them to your pie plate. If your effort falls apart, try again. Practice makes perfect pie crust.

TIP

When your pie crust is nicely in the pan, let it rest for 30 minutes in the refrigerator before trimming off the edges. The crust shrinks a bit during this resting period, so this trick keeps your pie crust in the proper shape.

Not sure how to roll out the dough or get it safely tucked into the pie plate? Figure 10-4 shows the steps involved, including how to deal with dough when you're making a pie with both a top and bottom crust.

When you make a pie with a single crust, the recipe often calls for you to prebake the crust before adding the pie filling. In that case, you want to prevent the crust from bubbling up during baking. Figure 10-5 shows that by covering the pie shell with foil and pouring in dried beans, your crust will stay flat in the pan. To bake a single crust, put it in a 400-degree oven for 15 minutes; then, lower the heat to 350 degrees and bake another 10 minutes. Check the crust during the final few minutes of baking to make sure it isn't getting too brown.

RECIPE
ALERT

We recommend making pie as often as possible — you know, just so you can refine your technique. Of course, then your family and friends will just have to consume the happy byproducts of your homework assignment. Why not start practicing now? Look for our All-Butter Pie Crust recipe later in the chapter, and then use it to make the Apple Pie recipe that follows.

For the Apple Pie recipe, you need to peel and core apples for the filling. Flip back to Chapter 4 for hints on how to do this.

Making Pie Dough by Hand

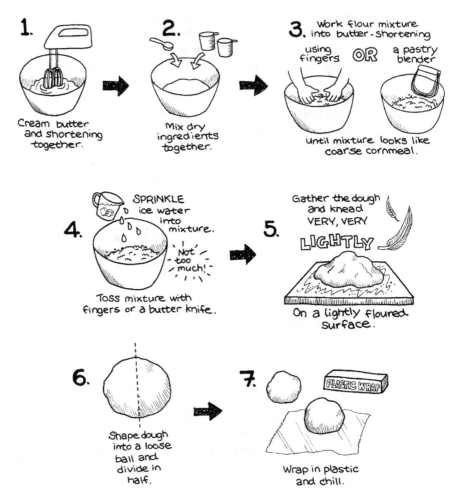

1. Cream butter and shortening together.

2. Mix dry ingredients together.

3. Work flour mixture into butter-shortening using fingers **OR** a pastry blender until mixture looks like coarse cornmeal.

4. SPRINKLE ice water into mixture. *Not too much!* Toss mixture with fingers or a butter knife.

5. Gather the dough and knead VERY, VERY **LIGHTLY** On a lightly floured surface.

6. Shape dough into a loose ball and divide in half.

7. PLASTIC WRAP Wrap in plastic and chill.

Illustration by Elizabeth Kurtzman

FIGURE 10-3: How to make pie dough by hand.

How to Roll Dough

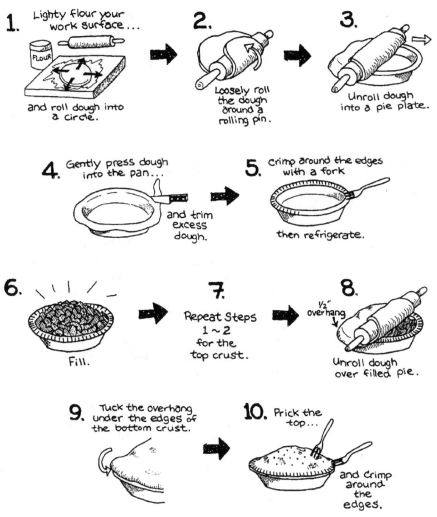

1. Lightly flour your work surface... and roll dough into a circle.

2. Loosely roll the dough around a rolling pin.

3. Unroll dough into a pie plate.

4. Gently press dough into the pan... and trim excess dough.

5. Crimp around the edges with a fork then refrigerate.

6. Fill.

7. Repeat Steps 1~2 for the top crust.

8. ½" overhang. Unroll dough over filled pie.

9. Tuck the overhang under the edges of the bottom crust.

10. Prick the top... and crimp around the edges.

FIGURE 10-4:
The technique for rolling pie pastry dough.

Illustration by Elizabeth Kurtzman

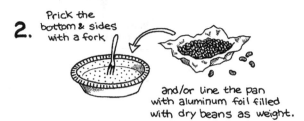

For a Single Crust

1.

Follow
"How to Roll Dough,"
Steps 1 ~ 5.

2. Prick the
bottom & sides
with a fork

and/or line the pan
with aluminum foil filled
with dry beans as weight.

FIGURE 10-5:
Preparing dough
for a single crust.

Illustration by Elizabeth Kurtzman

Making Cakes and Quick Breads for a Sweet Treat

Cake = heaven. At least, we think so. The fairy queen of baked goods, cake should be tender, moist, rich, light, and full of melt-in-your-mouth flavorful sweet goodness. And cupcakes? The fairy princesses! Shall we go on? Okay, we'll stop waxing poetic about cake if you promise to try baking one without the crutch that is a box of prepackaged cake mix. Those boxes may be easy to prepare, but actual from-scratch cake takes just a tiny bit more effort and isn't laden with artificial ingredients. Get used to home-baked cake, and the boxed stuff won't ever be quite as satisfying again. Top a home-baked cake with homemade frosting, and you've got the stuff of sweet dreams.

The secret to great cake is to follow directions precisely, mix ingredients thoroughly, have all ingredients at *room temperature* before you start mixing, and be sure your baking powder has not expired.

RECIPE ALERT

Try your hand at cake with two recipes at the end of this chapter. The first is a dense, fudgy Perfect Chocolate Cake, which is bliss for chocoholics. (When you're shopping for the bittersweet chocolate called for in the recipe, keep in mind that Lindt, Valrhona, and Callebaut are excellent brands.) The second may be a bit trendy, but we don't care. Rosy Red Velvet Cupcakes are simply a delight, and we find them delicious *and* charming.

Quick bread is fast and easy to make, and it's tough to find a good reason *not* to make it if you crave sweet banana bread, zucchini bread, pumpkin bread, cranberry bread, or any other favorite. Quick breads are called "quick" because they don't use yeast. Instead, they rise via the action of baking powder. Mix them up as you would a cake, pour into a loaf pan, bake, and enjoy the sweet results. (Some quick breads, such as Irish soda bread or Boston brown bread, aren't sweet but are quick nevertheless.)

RECIPE ALERT

Be sure to make the practically effortless and delectable Chocolate Chip Banana Bread that you really can't pass up if you don't want to waste those three overripe bananas that we just know are sitting on your countertop right now.

PICK A FLOUR

Will a flour by any other name bake the same? Absolutely not! Different kinds of flours are made from either high-protein hard wheat, low-protein soft wheat, or a combination, and each kind of flour has a different gluten content. (*Gluten* is a protein in wheat and some other grains that gets stretchy with beating or kneading and helps baked goods rise.)

Choosing the right kind of flour for your recipe can have a big impact on the results, so choose wisely:

- *All-purpose flour* is made from a mixture of hard and soft wheat, with a midrange gluten content, making it appropriate for many baked goods and adequate for most baked goods. Use it for cookies, biscuits, quick bread, and cake — unless you want a very light, delicate cake, in which case you should use cake flour.

- *Cake flour* is made mostly from soft wheat and has a finer texture, lower gluten content, and higher starch content than all-purpose flour. Similarly, *pastry flour* is made primarily from soft wheat, although it has a slightly higher protein content than cake flour, so it's better for pastries that need a flakier structure, such as puff pastry, pie crust, and biscuits.

- *Bread flour* is made primarily from hard wheat. Its high protein/gluten content makes it best for yeast breads that need to rise.

- *Gluten-free flour* (which could contain rice, garbanzo, amaranth, quinoa, corn, sorghum, tapioca, or any number of other flours) is more difficult to use in baking precisely because it lacks gluten, which is largely responsible for the characteristic texture of many baked goods. However, when other ingredients are added to compensate for the lack of gluten, gluten-free flour can stand in for regular flour. For best results, follow a recipe designed for gluten-free flour.

- *Self-rising flour* is essentially all-purpose flour that has baking powder and salt added to it. Intended as a convenience, it falls short of the mark. The primary problem is that there's no way to control how much baking powder it contains. Moreover, when stored in your pantry, the baking powder in the flour will quickly lose its effectiveness, leaving it unpredictable at best. There is little reason to buy this.

- *Potato flour* is a handy item in the baker's arsenal, having relatively high gluten content. This aids the elasticity needed to hold together buttery layers of croissants, puff pastries, and some pie crusts.

Be wary of "bargain" flours that appear in some supermarkets. They may not meet commercial specifications and lead to disappointment. Stick with recognized brands.

All–Butter Pie Crust

PREP TIME: ABOUT 30 MIN PLUS CHILL TIME

YIELD: ENOUGH FOR A 9-INCH DOUBLE-CRUST PIE

INGREDIENTS

2¼ cups all-purpose flour, plus more for rolling out the dough

¾ teaspoon salt

1 tablespoon sugar

Grated peel of half a lemon (optional)

16 tablespoons (2 sticks) very cold butter, cut into ¼-inch pieces

6 to 8 tablespoons ice water

DIRECTIONS

1 Add the flour, salt, sugar, and grated lemon peel (if desired) to the bowl of a food processor and pulse two or three times just to combine.

2 Add the butter and pulse about 8 to 10 times or just until the butter and flour are barely blended and the mixture resembles cornmeal.

3 Turn the mixture into a large bowl and sprinkle with 6 table-spoons of the ice water.

4 Using your hands, mix the dough just until it forms into a ball, adding another tablespoon or two of ice water if necessary to hold the dough together.

5 Divide the dough in half; gently flatten and shape each half into a flat disk. Wrap each disk in plastic and refrigerate at least 30 minutes and up to 2 days before rolling out.

6 When ready to make your pie, lightly flour a large, clean countertop area or pastry board. You want just enough flour to keep the dough from sticking. Too much will cause the dough to dry out. Also lightly flour your rolling pin.

7 Remove one disk from the refrigerator and roll on the floured surface into an 11- to 12-inch circle; transfer to a 9-inch pie plate, gently press it into the sides and rim. Trim the excess dough to about ½ inch all around the plate. Refrigerate the pie shell while making the filling.

8 Fill the chilled pie shell, roll out the second disk to an 11- to 12-inch round and place it over the filling. Trim to leave an overhang of about ½ inch. Tuck the overhang under the lower crust; crimp firmly by pressing the tines of a fork around the edge or by pinching the dough together at 1-inch intervals. Prick the top crust a few times with a fork before baking.

PER SERVING: Calories 322 (From Fat 207); Fat 23g (Saturated 15g); Cholesterol 61mg; Sodium 221mg; Carbohydrate 26g (Dietary Fiber 1g); Protein 4g.

TIP: You want the butter to be very cold when you add it to the dry ingredients. Place it in the freezer for 10 minutes after cutting. Also, be sure to use actual ice water in Step 3, not just cold water from the tap. Ice water helps keep the butter cold, which is important for making a tender, flaky crust.

NOTE: If the dough sticks to the counter as you roll it out, gently slip a long thin spatula underneath it to loosen from the surface.

Apple Pie

PREP TIME: ABOUT 30 MIN   COOK TIME: ABOUT 1 HR   YIELD: 8 SERVINGS

INGREDIENTS

7 large tart-style apples, peeled, cored, and sliced about ½-inch thick

¾ cup sugar

2 tablespoons all-purpose flour

1 tablespoon fresh lemon juice

¾ teaspoon cinnamon

½ teaspoon grated lemon zest

⅛ teaspoon nutmeg

Prepared pastry for double-crust pie (see the preceding recipe)

1 tablespoon butter

About 2 tablespoons milk or water (optional)

About 1 teaspoon sugar (optional)

DIRECTIONS

1 Preheat the oven to 450 degrees.

2 Combine the apples, sugar, flour, lemon juice, cinnamon, lemon zest, and nutmeg in a large bowl. Toss gently to evenly coat the apples with sugar and seasonings.

3 Fill the uncooked 9-inch pie shell with the apple mixture. Dot with the butter. Fit the top crust over the apples, trim off excess, and crimp the edges firmly.

4 Prick the top crust several times with a fork. For an attractive crust, use a pastry brush to brush the crust lightly with milk or water and then sprinkle sugar (if desired) over it.

5 Bake for 15 minutes. Reduce the heat to 350 degrees and bake another 45 minutes, or until the pie crust is golden brown. Cool the pie on a wire rack for at least 20 minutes before serving.

PER SERVING: *Calories 430 (From Fat 189); Fat 21g (Saturated 9g); Cholesterol 28mg; Sodium 220mg; Carbohydrate 59g (Dietary Fiber 3g); Protein 4g.*

VARY IT! You can substitute fruits such as peaches, strawberries, apricots, and berries, varying the spices as desired. For example, toss peaches with sugar, cinnamon, and rum extract. For pears, try sugar, nutmeg, and vanilla extract. A tablespoon of rum or brandy adds sophistication. Substituting brown or raw sugar for white gives the filling a slightly caramelized flavor. Also, try this classic taste pairing: Melt slices of cheddar cheese on top of apple pie servings.

TIP: You also can use the basic pie crust for individual ramekins (single-serving, porcelain baking dishes) and fill them with fruits. Reduce the baking time by half.

Perfect Chocolate Cake

PREP TIME: ABOUT 15 MIN	COOK TIME: ABOUT 30 MIN	YIELD: 8–10 SERVINGS

INGREDIENTS

6 ounces bittersweet chocolate, chopped into small pieces

½ cup butter (1 stick)

5 eggs, separated

½ cup sugar

½ teaspoon cream of tartar

¼ cup sifted cake flour

½ cup chopped walnuts (optional)

1 teaspoon ground cinnamon (optional)

2 tablespoons unsweetened cocoa powder or confectioner's sugar (optional)

DIRECTIONS

1 Preheat the oven to 350 degrees. Line the bottom of a 9-inch springform cake pan with a circular piece of greased parchment paper. Grease the sides of the pan.

2 Fill the bottom of a double boiler halfway with water and bring to a boil. Place the chocolate and butter in the top of the double boiler. Turn off the heat, leaving the double boiler on the stove. Stir until the chocolate and butter are melted and combined.

3 Using an electric mixer on high with beater or whisk attachment, beat the egg whites, 1 teaspoon of the sugar, and the cream of tartar until the mixture gets fluffy. Drizzle in the remaining sugar as you continue to beat the mixture until it forms stiff peaks.

4 Beat the egg yolks in a medium bowl, and whisk them into the cooled chocolate mixture. Add the flour, and the walnuts and/or cinnamon (if desired). Stir to combine.

5 Gently fold the egg-white mixture into the chocolate with a rubber spatula. Immediately pour the mixture into the prepared cake pan. Smooth the top with the spatula.

6 Bake for 25 minutes, or until a knife or toothpick inserted into the middle comes out clean. Let the cake cool in its pan.

7 When the cake is cool enough to handle, run a sharp knife along the edge and remove the side of the pan. If desired, decorate the cake with the cocoa powder or confectioner's sugar. Shake either topping through a sieve, dusting the surface of the cake evenly.

PER SERVING: *Calories 254 (From Fat 170); Fat 19g (Saturated 10g); Cholesterol 131mg; Sodium 33mg; Carbohydrate 22g (Dietary Fiber 1g); Protein 5g based on 10 servings.*

Rosy Red Velvet Cupcakes

PREP TIME: ABOUT 20 MIN | COOK TIME: ABOUT 20 MIN | YIELD: 24 SERVINGS

INGREDIENTS

3 cups sifted cake flour

1 teaspoon baking powder

1 tablespoon unsweetened cocoa powder

¾ teaspoon salt

1½ cups sugar

1 cup butter (2 sticks), softened

1 cup buttermilk

2 eggs

2 tablespoons red food coloring

1 tablespoon white vinegar

1 teaspoon vanilla extract

Cream Cheese Frosting (see the following recipe)

DIRECTIONS

1 Preheat the oven to 350 degrees. Line two 12-cup muffin pans with cupcake liners.

2 In a mixing bowl, combine flour, baking powder, cocoa powder, and salt. Stir to mix everything together.

3 In a separate bowl, use an electric mixer to cream the sugar and butter until light and fluffy (about 2 minutes). Add buttermilk, eggs, food coloring, vinegar, and vanilla extract and beat until well combined, about 2 minutes.

4 Add the dry ingredients to the wet ingredients and beat until smooth and combined, about 1 minute.

5 Divide the batter among the cupcake tins, filling each well about ⅔ full. Bake for 15 minutes or until a toothpick inserted into a cupcake comes out clean. Cool completely, and then frost with a small spatula or butter knife.

Cream Cheese Frosting

1 pound (two 8-ounce packages) cream cheese, softened

1 cup butter (2 sticks), softened

1 teaspoon vanilla extract

4 cups sifted confectioner's sugar

1 In a mixing bowl, combine cream cheese, butter, and vanilla extract. Beat with an electric mixer until smooth.

2 Add the confectioner's sugar, ½ cup at a time, beating after each addition until smooth. If the frosting is too stiff, add milk, 1 teaspoon at a time, until it's spreadable.

PER SERVING: *Calories 383 (From Fat 201); Fat 22g (Saturated 14g); Cholesterol 79mg; Sodium 152mg; Carbohydrate 44g (Dietary Fiber 0g); Protein 3g.*

TIP: All the ingredients in this recipe should be brought to room temperature before beginning. If you don't have buttermilk, add 1 tablespoon of white vinegar to a liquid measuring cup. Fill the cup to the 1-cup mark with milk. Let it sit for 10 minutes, and use it in place of 1 cup buttermilk.

Chocolate Chip Banana Bread

PREP TIME: ABOUT 15 MIN	COOK TIME: 45–50 MIN	YIELD: 12 SERVINGS

INGREDIENTS

2 cups all-purpose flour

1 cup granulated sugar

½ teaspoon baking powder

1 teaspoon baking soda

¾ teaspoon salt

1½ cups mashed bananas

1 cup brown sugar

2 eggs, lightly whisked together

½ cup plain or vanilla yogurt

⅓ cup canola oil

1 teaspoon vanilla extract

1 cup chocolate chips

½ cup chopped nuts (optional)

DIRECTIONS

1 Preheat the oven to 350 degrees. Spray two loaf pans (8 x 5 or 9 x 5) with cooking spray.

2 Into a sifter set over a mixing bowl, add flour, granulated sugar, baking powder, baking soda, and salt. Sift into the bowl.

3 In a separate bowl, combine mashed bananas, brown sugar, eggs, yogurt, oil, and vanilla extract.

4 Pour liquid ingredients into flour mixture and stir with a wooden spoon until just combined.

5 Add chocolate chips and nuts (if desired) and stir to distribute them evenly through the batter.

6 Pour the batter evenly in the two loaf pans. Bake for 50 minutes or until the top is deep golden brown and a toothpick inserted near the center comes out mostly clean. Cool completely (about an hour) before slicing.

PER SERVING: Calories 376 (From Fat 105); Fat 12g (Saturated 3g); Cholesterol 36mg; Sodium 293mg; Carbohydrate 67g (Dietary Fiber 2g); Protein 5g.

THE (CLEAN) TOOTHPICK TEST

Cake and quick bread recipes frequently call for the "toothpick test." To check that a cake or quick bread is done, pull it carefully out of the oven and insert a wooden toothpick most of the way into the bread or cake, and then pull it back out. If batter clings to the toothpick, your bread or cake isn't done yet. Try again every 5 minutes. If a few moist crumbs cling to the toothpick, the bread or cake is probably done or mostly done. If the toothpick comes out clean, your recipe has definitely cooked for long enough.

3

Expand Your Repertoire

Start your day with easy and nutritious breakfast recipes that will fuel you all day long.

Mix up your midday meal with all sorts of soups and salads that are a change from the typical sandwich or combo meal.

Discover how you can use grains and pastas as side dishes or the basis for your main meal.

Get saucy with recipes that can add a whole new flavor to meats, vegetables, and desserts.

Impress dinner guests with irresistible desserts that will have everyone begging for seconds.

Chapter **11**

Conquering Breakfast

We love breakfast. What a perfect way to start the day! We think few things are more fun than rolling out of bed and grabbing the nearest skillet, but even if you feel more bleary-eyed than bright-eyed in the morning, you can still cook breakfast without too much effort, as long as you have some basic know-how under your bathrobe sash and a little inspiration to give you a spring in your fuzzy bunny slippers. In this chapter, we walk you through the basics of a good breakfast and then set you free to go further.

Starting the Day with the Incredible, Edible Egg

They just may be the quintessential breakfast food, and they're one of nature's most perfect protein sources. We're talking about eggs, a great way to start the morning, especially if you're one of those savory breakfast people more tempted by a bacon omelet than a gooey cinnamon roll. But you can't just put a raw egg on your plate and dig in. (Well, you could, but we're guessing that's not the way you prefer your eggs.) So let's talk about egg cookery. You'll be frying, poaching, boiling, and folding faster than you can hit the snooze button.

Understanding the grade, size, and color of eggs

So what's up with eggs — aren't they all the same? Actually, they aren't. Eggs are distinguished by grade, size, and color.

In the supermarket, you generally see two grades of eggs: AA and A. Grade AA is the highest quality, but A is also a high-quality egg, and the differences between the grades are hardly noticeable to the average home cook. Purchase either grade; it doesn't matter one bit to us. Grade B eggs wouldn't normally be available in the supermarket — they're used mostly for making commercial products that contain eggs.

Egg size is based on a minimum weight per dozen: 30 ounces per dozen for jumbo eggs, 27 ounces for extra large, 24 ounces for large, and 21 ounces for medium. Most recipes (and all of them in this book) call for large eggs, and this is important for baking, when slight changes in ingredient amounts can actually alter the finished product. If you're making breakfast, however, we can honestly say that size doesn't matter.

Shell color isn't related to quality and is simply a function of the breed of hen. Cooking beside a stoneware crock filled with brown eggs may help you feel like you're invoking your grandma's farm kitchen, but we'd bet money that you couldn't tell the difference between white and brown eggs in a blind taste test.

Deciding whether to splurge on specialty eggs

You may have noticed some additional choices in your supermarket beyond the standard range of size and color. What's with those specialty eggs available today?

You know, the ones that say "free-range" or "organic" or "added omega-3s for better health." They may imply a promise of improved nutrition or environmental responsibility, but look at that price tag! If you shell out all that extra money for these so-called superior eggs, are you going to end up with egg on your face? The following info may help you decide whether that highfalutin carton is worth the highfalutin price:

>> **Free-range eggs:** These eggs come from hens that have the opportunity to leave the dark shelter of the hen house for sunnier spots, but that doesn't mean they do. Often, they just stay inside and aren't out pecking in dirt, as you may have imagined. Similarly, cage-free eggs mean the hens are likely confined inside a dark, windowless building, milling around in a sort of poultry mosh pit (but less fun). On the other hand, hens in tiny cages are probably not particularly enjoying life, either. "Free range" versus conventional eggs may be six of one, half-a-dozen of the other. If you really want to know how the hens who produced your eggs live, buy from a small local farm and pay it a visit to see for yourself.

>> **Organic eggs:** These eggs come from chickens that weren't fed any drugs, hormones, antibiotics, or animal byproducts (something chickens really aren't meant to eat). Proponents believe that this type of diet makes the eggs safer, more pure, and (some say) more nutritious, although little if any evidence of this exists. There are also standards for humane treatment of animals whose products are labeled "organic," so if cruelty is your issue, consider organic eggs.

>> **Eggs with added omega-3s:** These eggs have more of those fatty acids purported to benefit heart health, and they typically have a higher vitamin E content than regular eggs. These benefits result when hens are fed a diet high in omega-3s, typically including flax seed. They're probably a good source of these healthy fats. Only you can decide whether you want to pay for your omega-3s that way or just eat more fish or take a supplement.

Some brands of eggs have all of these qualities: free-range hens on organic diets producing eggs with extra essential fatty acids. Many people buy these eggs not only because they want the extra dose of nutrition and they want to support farmers who treat their hens more humanely but also because they think (and we generally concur) that the eggs taste better.

TIP

Eggs from local farmers tend to be fresher because they're likely to be recently collected. Keep in mind that some locally produced eggs will be organic, even if the farmer can't afford to pay for official certification. If you get the chance to visit the farm or meet the farmer at the market, just ask.

ARE EGG BEATERS REALLY BETTER FOR YOU?

Egg beaters are essentially egg whites that have been flavored and infused with vitamins and minerals. This trademarked egg substitute was developed in the 1970s as an alternative to whole eggs. At the time, fresh whole eggs were being demonized as heart attacks in a shell, a notion that since has been largely debunked. (For most people, consuming eggs several times a week is perfectly healthful and doesn't trigger a skyrocketing cholesterol count.) Egg beaters are considerably lower in calories than fresh eggs, have a similar amount of protein, and contain virtually no cholesterol.

Do egg beaters taste like real eggs? In a word, no. And if you wonder why, just read the label, which resembles something you'd find in a pharmacy rather than a supermarket.

WHAT'S THAT SPOT?

Contrary to what most people believe, blood spots inside a raw egg are not a sign that the egg was fertilized. They are usually the result of a blood vessel rupturing on the surface of the yolk. The spot doesn't affect flavor, and the egg is perfectly safe to eat. You can remove the blood spot with the tip of a knife, but you don't need to do so. It's not going to hurt you.

Cooking Perfect Eggs

Eggs can become so many delectable dishes. From simple scrambled eggs to complex meringues and soufflés, eggs have it all, but in our opinion, the incredible, edible egg reigns supreme at breakfast. Here's the scoop on the breakfasty egg dishes we all know and love (and please feel free to have them for *any* meal).

Simply scrambled

Scrambled eggs are one of the easiest things in the world to cook, which is why we include a recipe for them in Chapter 1. Mix eggs in a bowl, add a splash of water or milk (or not), and cook in a hot, buttered skillet for just a few minutes, stirring all the while. You can whip up scrambled eggs in minutes, and they will keep you satisfied for hours.

Frankly fried

For the classic sunny-side-up fried egg, break an egg into a hot, buttered skillet and wait until it looks done: The whites turn white rather than clear, and the yolk is cooked to your preferred consistency. It takes just a few minutes for a soft yolk and a few more minutes if you like the yolk firm, not runny. To speed up the process, place a lid over the skillet to trap the heat.

TIP

If you like your eggs sunny-side-up but you prefer a firmer yolk, get your skillet lid ready. Pour a tablespoon of water into the skillet and quickly cover it. Steam the egg for one or two minutes.

To make fried eggs "over," begin the same way as with a sunny-side-up egg. When the whites are set (they're not runny), carefully coax a spatula under the egg and gently flip it over. Sometimes the yolk will break; sometimes it won't. The more you practice, the better you'll get at flipping the egg without breaking the yolk. Plenty of butter (or cooking spray) will make flipping easier. Cook for just a minute on the flip side, and then serve. Practice with a few eggs to see how long it takes to cook one to your desired degree of doneness.

Perfectly poached

A poached egg is cooked in boiling water — not a drop of butter. Although you can poach eggs in an egg poacher, isn't that so, well . . . 1950s? We think so. Who has an egg poacher anymore? (No offense to those who do.) All you need is a saucepan and a slotted spoon. Fill the saucepan a little over half full of water, cover it, and bring the water to a heavy simmer: The water should have frequent gentle bubbles but not be boiling vigorously because that will break up the egg white too much. When the water is simmering, remove the cover and add a tablespoon of white vinegar to the water.

Break an egg carefully into a small cup or bowl. Using your slotted spoon, stir the boiling water in a circle until you get a little whirlpool of water (be careful not to splash). Then with your other hand, gently and slowly pour the egg from the cup into the middle of your whirlpool. Let it cook for 3 minutes (or up to 5 minutes if you like a firmer yolk). Remove the egg with your slotted spoon and enjoy it immediately.

Poached eggs aren't usually symmetrical or even very smooth. Some of the egg white will break away from the egg and form long thin strands as it's cooking. That's fine; everything is just the way it's supposed to be. Just leave those parts in the water. Even if your poached egg isn't going to win any beauty contests, it will still taste delicious on toast or an English muffin.

TIP

The key to losing as little egg white as possible is to use the vinegar and to ease the egg *very gently* into the center of the whirlpool you create with your spoon.

Beautifully boiled

Hard-cooked eggs make great snacks and a much more nutritious grab-and-go breakfast than a doughnut. Soft-cooked eggs are nice in a cup or a bowl while still warm, with a good thick slab of crispy toast to mop up the runny yolk. Boiling eggs is even easier than scrambling, although it takes a little bit longer.

Because boiled eggs are great for any meal — not just breakfast — we include the cooking instructions in Chapter 5. With our step-by-step guidance, you'll never over- or undercook a boiled egg again.

Craftily folded omelets

A classic French omelet is a simple dish of beaten eggs cooked until set and folded over themselves, with or without a filling. Omelets are quick and easy in their basic form. Some people prefer to make a fancier version called a *soufflé omelet*, which is thicker and puffier, lightened with whipped egg whites and beaten yolks and finished in the oven, or in a special soufflé omelet pan. We don't usually go to those lengths because the basic French-style omelet literally takes about 1 minute to make.

If you cook an omelet properly, the outside will be smooth and the center a little moist. Omelets can be simplicity itself or a party in your mouth — try adding any kind of cheese, cooked vegetables, chopped meat, pesto, salsa, or whatever else you have in your refrigerator.

The only potentially intimidating aspect to cooking an omelet is that it all happens very fast. You have to have all your senses firing so your omelet doesn't end up brown or rubbery or burned. Although making an omelet is a bit of a "ready, set, go!" proposition, when you know how to do it, you can whip them out one after the other. Beat your eggs, melt your butter, pour the eggs in the pan, shake the pan, and voilà! Your omelet is served.

Afraid that you won't be able to properly fold an omelet? It does take a bit of practice, but it isn't too tough. Figure 11-1 can help.

RECIPE
ALERT

Are you ready to practice making an omelet? Of course you are! Try the recipe for Omelet with Herbs later in this chapter.

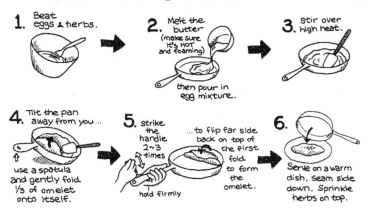

Folding an Omelet

1. Beat eggs & herbs.

2. Melt the butter (make sure it's HOT and foaming) then pour in egg mixture.

3. Stir over high heat.

4. Tilt the pan away from you... use a spatula and gently fold 1/3 of omelet onto itself.

5. strike the handle 2~3 times ...to flip far side back on top of the first fold to form the omelet. hold firmly

6. Serve on a warm dish, seam side down. Sprinkle herbs on top.

Illustration by Elizabeth Kurtzman

FIGURE 11-1:
Folding an omelet isn't as hard as you may think.

Oven-worthy frittatas and stratas

Frittata rhymes with strata, but the two dishes are completely different. They have only the oven, and eggs, in common. Frittatas are basically omelets made in the oven without the folding and flipping part (read: *easier!*). And they feel *so* Italian.

Stratas are casseroles made with torn-up bread, omelet-style fillings, and eggs as a custard poured over the whole thing and baked until puffy. You can have your eggs, bacon, cheese, and toast, all in one dish. You can prepare a strata the night before and then pop it in the oven whenever you desire. We think of stratas as a bit "Junior League," so you may want to serve yours with crustless cucumber sandwiches or a Waldorf salad for lunch in the garden (don't forget your floppy hat). But we also think they are just dandy with orange juice or fruit and coffee, particularly when you've invited company for brunch.

Both dishes are delicious and can get time-pressed cooks out of a jam. Either dish is great for breakfast, but it can also make a wonderful lunch main course or light supper, accompanied by a salad.

RECIPE ALERT

To give frittatas and stratas a try, see the recipes later in this chapter for Mushroom-Swiss Frittata and Bacon and Cheese Strata.

Making Mouth-Watering Breakfast Meats

Many delicious and savory meats can play leading roles at the breakfast table, flirting with the eggs, ravishing the waffles, and pushing the pancakes straight over the edge of ecstasy. Hot, crispy, salty bacon dripping with real maple syrup? Still our beating hearts!

Breakfast meats are also relatively easy to cook, making them practically irresistible. Although you may not want to start every day with bacon, sausage, or a nice breakfast steak, after this section, you'll know just what to do come Sunday morning when you have a little extra time and a hankering for something above and beyond your usual bowl of cereal.

Breaking the fast with bacon

What is it about bacon? Luscious, luscious bacon? We aren't naming any names, but we know a few fellows who would do just about anything for the crispy, smoky stuff.

Bacon is cured side pork meat. (*Curing* is a process of preserving meat, typically involving salting and smoking.) It's usually sold sliced and packaged, but you may also be able to find slab bacon, which you slice yourself. You can buy it in the supermarket cut thick or thin, peppered or sugared, maple-flavored or spicy. If you live in farm country, you can probably also buy bacon from local farmers. Some enterprising souls even buy side pork or pork belly and cure it and smoke it themselves.

For starters, however, a regular old package of good-quality bacon from the supermarket is all you need to practice makin' the bacon. And these days, there's more than one way to prepare your bacon. Read on for the traditional method and some alternatives.

Fryin' up the bacon

Bacon is easy to cook on the stove, if you can remember two things: (1) Keep the heat low to prevent grease spatters, and (2) watch it carefully so it doesn't burn.

Unwrap the package and lay out the desired number of bacon strips neatly in a cold skillet or on a griddle. Don't overlap the strips. Turn the heat to medium-low. (You can also cook bacon on medium heat, but if the fat gets too hot, it can spatter and pop, so be careful.) When the bacon begins to sizzle, lift up the edge of a slice with a pair of tongs. When the underside looks like it's beginning to get crispy, flip the slice over and cook the other side.

Watch your bacon like a hawk! One long glance at your phone or tablet to read and reply to a text, and all could be lost, so don't allow yourself to get distracted.

Cook the strips just until they're golden and crisp. You can flip them over several times if you like. When they're done, use your tongs to transfer them to a double layer of paper towels (to drain off some of the fat), and then serve. If you like, pour the flavorful bacon fat remaining in the pan into a jar and use it in place of butter in other savory recipes (just keep in mind that bacon grease tends to be salty). When it cools, the fat will turn white and look like lard. It will keep in the refrigerator for a couple weeks.

Bakin' your bacon

If you don't want to stand at the stove to monitor your bacon while it cooks, you can pop it in the oven. Start by positioning a rack in the center of the oven and preheating the oven to 400 degrees. Next, line a large broiler pan or sturdy rimmed baking sheet with aluminum foil (to make cleaning the pan easier). Place a rack into the broiler pan or baking sheet; arrange 6 to 8 slices of bacon in a single layer on the rack. Bake in the preheated oven 10 to 14 minutes until the bacon is crisp. (The actual cooking time will depend on the thickness of the bacon slices.) After about 6 minutes, rotate the pan 180 degrees so the back faces the front of the oven.

Remove the pan from the oven and cool the bacon on the rack about 2 minutes. Use tongs to transfer the slices to a paper towel–lined plate to absorb any remaining grease.

To make delicious strips of sweetened bacon, simply sprinkle a mixture of 1 teaspoon brown sugar, and cinnamon and black pepper to taste onto each bacon slice before baking.

Microwavin' the bacon

On those days when you just can't wait for your bacon, you can microwave it. Simply place 4 to 5 raw bacon slices in a single layer between two pieces of paper towel on a microwave-safe plate (the paper towels will absorb most of the grease). Microwave on high power for 45 seconds to 1 minute per slice. (Cooking times will vary depending on the power of your microwave and the thickness of the bacon.) The bacon should appear slightly crisp with the fat almost fully rendered. For more crispness, cook further, 15 to 30 seconds at a time, until done as desired. Wear an oven mitt to remove the very hot plate from the microwave, and use metal tongs to transfer the bacon to a serving dish.

Spicing it up with savory sausage

Links, patties, crumbles — sausage can make the difference between a ho-hum and an oh-yum breakfast. Sausage is meat ground up with fat and mixed with salt and spices. Typically made with pork in its breakfast incarnations, it can also be made with other meats, from lamb to chicken to venison.

Fry links and patties in a skillet over medium heat, turning every few minutes until the surface is golden brown and the center is hot and no longer pink. (Some sausage links and patties available in the supermarket are pre-cooked, and although these heat up more quickly and can even be cooked in the microwave, we think they don't taste quite as fresh and delicious.) If you're cooking crumbled sausage, fry it in a skillet while stirring and breaking chunks apart with your spatula until it's no longer pink.

Steak-ing your claim (to breakfast!)

If you're a rancher and you've been up since sunrise wrangling your wayward herds (can you tell that we're not ranchers?), you're going to need a heartier breakfast than most folks. Or maybe you just love a good hunka beef for breakfast. Breakfast steaks are small steaks, pan-fried and served with eggs. For directions on how to pan-fry a steak, see Chapter 6.

Taking a Tour of Breakfast Breads

Some people can imagine no sweeter breakfast than a crispy piece of toast and a cup of hot coffee or tea, but breakfast bread doesn't have to be quite so literal. Bread can come in many forms; English muffins, bagels, biscuits, and croissants come to mind. So do French toast and pancakes, which we feature in this section.

French toast

RECIPE ALERT

French toast takes toast to the next level. Stale bread, dipped in an egg-and-milk mixture, is fried in a skillet and then topped with butter and syrup — *ooh la la*. French toast is an easy and satisfying dish to make and a great way to use up bread that has gone slightly stale. To give it a try in your own kitchen, look for the recipe for Fabulous French Toast later in this chapter.

You can have a healthy breakfast any day of the week. Enjoy the Tex-Mex Breakfast Burrito or the Strawberry-Mango Fruit Smoothie on your way out the door. Prepare the Blueberry Buttermilk Pancakes with Hot Buttery Syrup on a weekend morning. Find the recipes in Chapter 11.

When you cook at home, you can feed your family healthy, great-tasting food, even on a tight budget. Make a meal out of our Barbecued Chicken (Chapter 9) with Country Barbecue Sauce (Chapter 8) and a side of Roasted Summer Vegetables (Chapter 8).

Weekend lunches don't have to be boring affairs. The Sweet Potato Pancakes (Chapter 19), Panini with Sun-Dried Tomatoes and Ham (Chapter 19), and Pizza Pizazz (Chapter 17) can be easy, midday meals that keep you fueled for afternoon activities.

Add a spicy kick to your meal to turn up the flavor. Pair some simple Steamed Broccoli with Lemon Butter (Chapter 5) and Basic Rice Pilaf (Chapter 13) with our Tuna Steaks with Ginger-Chili Glaze (Chapter 6) for a healthy meal with just a touch of heat.

You don't always need to splurge on the most expensive ingredients to create a meal that wins rave reviews. Our Broiled Skirt Steak, Cajun-Style (Chapter 9) uses a very affordable cut of meat that pairs nicely with Red Pepper Purée (Chapter 4) and Sautéed Skillet Potatoes (Chapter 6).

Your taste buds will dance with delight when you try some Mediterranean dishes. Chicken Tagine with Tomatoes, Olives, and Preserved Lemons (Chapter 7), Spanish Lentils with Vegetables (Chapter 18), and Preserved Lemons (Chapter 18) will transport you halfway around the world without leaving home.

Many dishes that look restaurant-fancy are surprisingly simple to make. Need proof? Try our recipes for savory Mediterranean Seafood Stew (Chapter 7) and creamy Carrot Soup with Dill (Chapter 12).

You can brighten your dessert table and indulge your sweet tooth at the same time. Try our recipes for Rosy Red Velvet Cupcakes (Chapter 10), Strawberry Lemonade (Chapter 20), and Red, White, and Blue Berry Shortcake (Chapter 20).

Pancakes and waffles

Cake, without all the baking? With syrup? What's not to like? Pancakes are an essential part of a classic American breakfast. They also make a perfect canvas for fanciful additions: blueberries, chocolate chips, walnuts, sliced almonds, peanut butter, bananas, coconut — pancake adornment need know no limits!

RECIPE ALERT

For the very best pancakes that are light and fluffy, not tough and tasteless, buttermilk is a must-use ingredient. If a recipe calls for buttermilk, you can make your own in no time. Simply pour 1 tablespoon of lemon juice or white vinegar into a liquid measuring cup. Add whole or low-fat milk to reach the 1-cup mark. Allow the mixture to sit at room temperature for 5 to 10 minutes. Try the recipe for Blueberry Buttermilk Pancakes later in this chapter.

Blending Your Way to a Healthy Breakfast

They say that breakfast is the most important meal of the day, but sometimes you just don't have time to whip up something on the stove, and on some days, even pouring a bowl of cereal and milk feels too time-consuming. Yet you want to eat something healthier than a doughnut.

You may be tempted to reach for a container of fruited yogurt for breakfast, but be warned; many of them are loaded with sugar. Instead, try a fruit smoothie. Fruit smoothies combine fresh fruit and unsweetened yogurt. They require no cooking, are nutritious, and are kid-friendly. You can vary the ingredients for different results, adding just the amount of sugar that you desire — or none at all. Sprinkle a little wheat germ on the finished smoothie if you want, and you'll start your day off with fiber, protein, and antioxidants — all in one glass.

RECIPE ALERT

On mornings when you have little time for breakfast, use your blender to make a nutritious fruit smoothie. Check out the upcoming recipe for a Strawberry-Mango Fruit Smoothie. Keep seasonal fresh fruit and yogurt on hand for preteens and teens to make their own.

Omelet with Herbs

PREP TIME: ABOUT 10 MIN | COOK TIME: ABOUT 1 MIN | YIELD: 1 SERVING

INGREDIENTS

1 teaspoon chopped fresh tarragon, or ¼ teaspoon dried

2 teaspoons chopped fresh parsley, or ½ teaspoon dried

1 tablespoon chopped chives (fresh or dried)

3 eggs

Salt and black pepper

2 teaspoons butter

DIRECTIONS

1 Combine the tarragon, parsley, and chives in a medium mixing bowl. Remove and set aside 1 teaspoon of the fresh herb mixture for garnish. (If you're using dried herbs, chop extra chives for garnish.)

2 Add the eggs and a few dashes each of salt and black pepper to a mixing bowl and beat with a fork for about 20 seconds, combining the whites and yolks without overbeating.

3 Heat an 8- or 10-inch omelet pan or skillet over medium-low heat. Let it heat up for at least 5 minutes, and then add the butter and melt it, turning the pan to coat evenly. The butter should be hot and foaming, but not browned, before you add the eggs.

4 Pour in the egg mixture. It should begin to set at the edges immediately.

5 Using a spatula, stir the eggs just a few times to fluff them up, then gently pull the cooked edges up a bit so the runny mixture in the middle can flow around the edge.

6 When the mixture solidifies but the center is still a bit moist, shake the pan sharply a few times to loosen the omelet from the bottom. Remove the pan from the heat and let it rest for a few seconds. (Add any fillings at this point.)

7 Fold the omelet and use a spatula to press the omelet closed at the seam.

8 Roll the omelet onto a warm dish, seam-side down. Sprinkle the remaining herbs on top.

PER SERVING: *Calories 294 (From Fat 204); Fat 22g (Saturated 9g); Cholesterol 658mg; Sodium 773mg; Carbohydrate 2g (Dietary Fiber 0g); Protein 19g.*

GO-WITH: For lunch or a light dinner, serve this omelet with a tossed green salad and Sautéed Skillet Potatoes (see Chapter 6) or the French Potato Salad in Chapter 12.

TIP: Another way to fold an omelet is to slide half the omelet onto a serving plate and turn the pan over to flip the omelet into a half-moon shape. This technique helps if the omelet gets stuck in the pan.

OMELET VARIATIONS

The great thing about omelets is that they can contain just about any savory filling. To alter the Omelet with Herbs recipe, omit the herbs and chives and use ½ cup of any of the following ingredients. Have your filling ready to go before you start cooking the eggs. For a cheese omelet, add grated hard cheese, such as cheddar, Swiss, or Gruyère, or soft and semisoft cheese, such as mozzarella, goat, or Brie, to the egg mixture before pouring it in the pan.

To make the following types of omelets, place the fillings on the omelet just before folding:

- **Spanish:** Fried onions, fried potatoes, and olive oil instead of butter
- **Vegetarian:** Any combination of cooked, chopped vegetables, such as asparagus, artichoke hearts, mushrooms, spinach, broccoli, or cauliflower — a great way to use leftover cooked vegetables
- **Western, also known as Denver:** Chopped ham, onions, and green bell peppers
- **Mediterranean:** Feta cheese, tomatoes, chopped olives, onions, and spinach
- **Seafood:** Smoked salmon or trout, crab meat, or cooked shrimp
- **Meat:** Cooked, crumbled bacon or sausage; diced cooked ham; or salami
- **Mixed greens:** Watercress, arugula, or spinach, with a dollop of sour cream
- **Mushroom:** Sautéed button, portobello, cremini, or oyster mushrooms, with or without a sprinkling of cheese

Mushroom-Swiss Frittata

PREP TIME: ABOUT 20 MIN	COOK TIME: ABOUT 25 MIN	YIELD: 4 SERVINGS

INGREDIENTS

8 eggs

2 tablespoons water

2 tablespoons finely chopped basil or parsley, or 2 teaspoons dried

Salt and black pepper

¼ pound Swiss cheese, cut into small cubes

2 tablespoons butter

2 cups sliced white mushrooms

1 small yellow onion, chopped

1 tablespoon olive oil

DIRECTIONS

1   Preheat the oven to 400 degrees. Beat the eggs and water in a medium mixing bowl with the basil or parsley and the salt and black pepper to taste. Add the cheese and set aside.

2   Heat the butter in an omelet pan or 10-inch cast-iron skillet over medium-high heat. Add the mushrooms and onions and sauté for about 7 minutes, until the onions get soft and translucent (but not brown) and the mushrooms begin to shrink.

3   Scoop out the mushrooms and onions with a slotted spoon and put them on a plate.

4   Add the olive oil and the egg-cheese mixture to the skillet and cook for about 1 minute. Don't stir, but run a rubber spatula around the edges to make sure it doesn't stick.

5   Spread the mushroom-onion mixture over the top of the eggs. Cover and reduce the heat to medium. Cook for 4 to 5 minutes, or until the bottom is set and golden brown. The top should still be wet.

6   Uncover the skillet and place it in the oven on a middle rack. Bake for an additional 10 minutes, or until the top is cooked solid and golden.

7   Run a rubber spatula around the outside of the frittata to loosen it. Coaxing with your spatula, slide the frittata onto a plate and cut into wedges (like a pizza) to serve.

PER SERVING: Calories 349 (From Fat 243); Fat 27g (Saturated 12g); Cholesterol 466mg; Sodium 348mg; Carbohydrate 5g (Dietary Fiber 1g); Protein 22g.

TIP: For this recipe, you need a skillet that can go into the oven. That means no plastic handle (unless it's ovenproof). An all-metal skillet is ovenproof.

Bacon and Cheese Strata

PREP TIME: ABOUT 25 MIN PLUS STANDING TIME	COOK TIME: ABOUT 40 MIN	YIELD: 6 SERVINGS

INGREDIENTS

Butter to grease the baking dish

8-ounce loaf seedless Italian bread (or about 8 ounces of any slightly stale bread)

5 slices bacon

1½ cups grated Gouda, Gruyère, Italian fontina, or other favorite cheese

½ cup rinsed, chopped, packed fresh spinach or sorrel leaves

5 eggs

2 cups milk

2 tablespoons tomato-based salsa (optional)

Salt and black pepper

DIRECTIONS

1 Butter the bottom and sides of a 2½- to 3-quart shallow baking dish. (Use a rectangular dish that allows bread slices to fit snugly in one layer.)

2 Trim and discard about 1 inch off each end of the loaf of bread and cut it into about 16 slices. If the bread is fresh, dry the slices in a 175-degree oven for about 15 minutes. Arrange the slices in the baking dish, overlapping the edges so they fit.

3 Sauté the bacon in a large skillet over medium-high heat, about 5 minutes or until crisp. Drain on paper towels. When it's cool enough to handle, crumble it into small pieces.

4 Sprinkle the crumbled bacon over the bread slices and top with cheese and spinach or sorrel.

5 In a medium bowl, beat together the eggs, milk, salsa (if desired), and a few dashes each of salt and black pepper. Pour the mixture evenly over the bread, bacon, cheese, and spinach.

6 Using a fork, press the bread slices down to soak them in the egg mixture. Let it set for about 15 minutes.

7 Meanwhile, preheat the oven to 350 degrees.

8 Bake the strata about 35 minutes, or just until the custard mixture is firm and lightly browned. Remove from the oven and serve immediately, cutting into squares.

PER SERVING: *Calories 363 (From Fat 185); Fat 21g (Saturated 10g); Cholesterol 230mg; Sodium 729mg; Carbohydrate 24g (Dietary Fiber 1g); Protein 20g.*

TIP: You can prepare this strata through Step 6 and let it sit overnight, covered, in the refrigerator.

Tex-Mex Breakfast Burrito

PREP TIME: ABOUT 15 MIN	COOK TIME: ABOUT 5 MIN	YIELD: 4 SERVINGS

INGREDIENTS

Four 10-inch whole-wheat tortillas (burrito size)

1 tablespoon vegetable or olive oil

3 scallions, both white and green parts, chopped

1½ cups canned black beans, rinsed and drained

6 large eggs

3 tablespoons bottled salsa, plus more for serving

Salt and black pepper to taste

2 tablespoons butter

2 tablespoons chopped fresh cilantro leaves (optional)

1 cup coarsely grated Monterrey Jack cheese (about 4 ounces)

Sour cream (optional)

DIRECTIONS

1 Preheat the oven to 325 degrees.

2 Cut two 12-x-8-inch sheets of foil. Wrap 2 tortillas tightly in each sheet and warm in oven 10 to 15 minutes, or until heated through.

3 Meanwhile, heat the oil in a large skillet over medium. Add the scallions and sauté 1 to 2 minutes or until softened, stirring occasionally; stir in the black beans and cook 1 to 2 minutes more or until the mixture is warmed through. Transfer to a small bowl and cover with foil to keep warm.

4 Crack the eggs into a medium bowl; add the salsa, salt, and black pepper to taste, and whisk to combine.

5 Set a large nonstick skillet over medium heat; add the butter and, as it melts, tilt the pan to coat the bottom.

6 Pour the egg-and-salsa mixture into the pan. Let the mixture set for about 30 seconds, and then stir the eggs, pulling them gently across the bottom and side of the pan with a rubber spatula or wooden spoon to help them cook evenly for about 2 to 3 minutes (the eggs should still be a little moist). Remove from the heat; sprinkle with the cilantro leaves (if desired) and the grated cheese. Cover the skillet to keep warm.

7 Divide the eggs and the scallion-bean mixture between the 4 tortillas, placing them in vertical rows across the center and leaving room to fold over bottom and sides. Fold the left and right sides of the tortilla into the center, overlapping them slightly, and then roll the bottom edge toward the top to completely enclose the filling. Repeat with the remaining tortillas and serve while still warm with sour cream (if desired) and extra salsa.

PER SERVING: *Calories 565 (From Fat 270); Fat 30g (Saturated 13g); Cholesterol 319mg; Sodium 1,355mg; Carbohydrate 44g (Dietary Fiber 26g); Protein 29g.*

Blueberry Buttermilk Pancakes with Hot Buttery Syrup

PREP TIME: 15 MIN	COOK TIME: 10 MIN	YIELD: 4–6 SERVINGS

INGREDIENTS

2 cups all-purpose flour

1 tablespoon sugar

2 teaspoons baking powder

½ teaspoon baking soda

½ teaspoon salt

2 cups well-shaken buttermilk

1 egg

2 tablespoons melted and cooled butter

1 to 2 tablespoons vegetable oil

1 cup blueberries, rinsed and well drained

DIRECTIONS

1 Preheat the oven to 200 degrees.

2 Combine the flour, sugar, baking powder, baking soda, and salt in a large bowl.

3 Add the buttermilk to a large liquid measuring cup; beat in the egg and the melted and cooled butter.

4 Make a well in the center of the dry ingredients and pour the buttermilk mixture into the center of the well. Stir gently, mixing only to moisten the flour. Avoid overmixing, which can cause the pancakes to toughen. Leave a few lumps in the batter.

5 Add 1 teaspoon vegetable oil to a large nonstick skillet or griddle and tilt the pan to spread the oil and coat the bottom of the pan. Heat until the oil shimmers.

6 Add the batter to the skillet using a ¼ cup dry measuring cup. Don't crowd the pan. You want to be able to turn the pancakes over easily, without them running together.

7 Cook the pancakes about 2 minutes or until large bubbles appear in the batter and the side facing the skillet is lightly browned. Sprinkle each pancake with 4 to 5 blueberries and then flip using a wide, nonstick spatula. Cook 1 to 2 minutes more or until browned on second side.

8 Transfer the pancakes to an ovenproof plate and place in the oven to keep warm. Repeat with additional oil, remaining batter, and blueberries.

(continued)

Hot Buttery Syrup

1 cup maple syrup

3 tablespoons butter

1 cup fresh blueberries, rinsed and drained

1 Combine the syrup and butter in a small saucepan over medium heat and cook about 1 minute or until the butter melts, stirring occasionally.

2 Reduce the heat to low, add the blueberries, and cook about 2 minutes or just until the blueberries soften. Reduce the heat to very low to keep the syrup warm while making the pancakes.

PER SERVING: *Calories 575 (From Fat 171); Fat 19g (Saturated 9g); Cholesterol 76mg; Sodium 730mg; Carbohydrate 94g (Dietary Fiber 2g); Protein 11g.*

VARY IT! Instead of blueberries, place thin banana slices into each pancake before turning and cooking through.

TIP: For best results whenever making any pancakes or waffles, let all ingredients come to room temperature before mixing the batter.

TIP: If the skillet isn't sufficiently hot when you add the batter, the pancakes won't brown properly. So make one small pancake to test the skillet's heat. If the bottom of the test pancake browns in about 2 minutes without burning, the skillet is hot enough.

TIP: Wrap leftover pancakes individually in plastic and freeze. To reheat, unwrap and microwave for about 30 seconds or pop them in the toaster.

SLEUTHING OUT THE DIFFERENCE BETWEEN REAL AND ARTIFICIAL MAPLE SYRUP

Real maple syrup is to artificial syrups what a Bentley is to a Beetle. And like Bentleys, there's a limited supply of real maple syrup, which is one reason it's relatively expensive (around $15 to $20 a quart). Harvesting it is also labor-intensive.

Sugar maple trees grow mainly in New England as well as in the Canadian Maritime Provinces. Real maple syrup is made by boiling down 50 gallon batches of sap from trees to make one gallon of syrup. The sap is collected in the early spring when it's above freezing during the day and below freezing at night.

Artificial maple syrup is little more than sugar water given a caramel color. When it comes to nutrition, honey and maple syrup are more or less the same — about 50 to 60 calories per tablespoon. Artificial syrups are slightly more.

Fabulous French Toast

PREP TIME: ABOUT 5 MIN	COOK TIME: ABOUT 5 MIN	YIELD: 4 SERVINGS

INGREDIENTS

8 slices French or 4 slices (larger) Italian or sourdough bread, preferably stale

4 eggs

¼ cup milk or cream

½ teaspoon vanilla extract

¼ teaspoon cinnamon

¼ teaspoon salt

1 tablespoon butter, or cooking spray

Syrup, butter, or fresh fruit for garnishing

DIRECTIONS

1 Heat a skillet or griddle over medium heat.

2 Break the eggs into a shallow pan and beat them with a fork or whisk until yolks and whites are combined, about 20 seconds. Add milk or cream, vanilla extract, cinnamon, and salt. Whisk a few more seconds.

3 Place bread slices into egg mixture. Turn them over to coat both sides and let them sit for about 1 minute.

4 Put butter into the skillet or griddle, or spray with cooking spray.

5 Pick up each bread slice, dip both sides again in egg mixture, and place it on the skillet or griddle. Slices can be touching but shouldn't overlap. (Cook in batches if needed.)

6 Cook for 2 minutes, and then use a hard spatula to lift up one slice to check for doneness. If it's golden brown, flip it over and repeat on the other side.

7 Remove the French toast to individual plates with the spatula and serve immediately with butter and syrup or fresh fruit.

PER SERVING: *Calories 462 (From Fat 110); Fat 12g (Saturated 5g); Cholesterol 222mg; Sodium 996mg; Carbohydrate 68g (Dietary Fiber 4g); Protein 18g.*

Strawberry-Mango Fruit Smoothie

| PREP TIME: 5 MIN | YIELD: 2 SERVINGS |

INGREDIENTS

1½ cups strawberries, rinsed, hulled, and sliced

1 medium ripe mango, peeled, pitted and sliced (about 2 cups)

½ cup plain low-fat yogurt

⅓ cup fresh orange juice

1 teaspoon honey or agave, or to taste

4 to 6 ice cubes, lightly crushed

DIRECTIONS

Add all the ingredients, except the ice, to a blender container. Cover, start the motor on slow speed, and then increase speed to blend smooth. Add 4 of the ice cubes and blend again a few seconds to incorporate them somewhat, without crushing them completely, into the smoothie. If desired, add the remaining ice to thin the smoothie a little more. Pour into glasses and serve.

PER SERVING: *Calories 161 (From Fat 14); Fat 1.5g (Saturated 0.5g); Cholesterol 4mg; Sodium 34mg; Carbohydrate 36g (Dietary Fiber 4g); Protein 4g.*

Chapter **12**

Super Soups and Savory Salads

Homemade soups and salads are easy to make, are impressive to serve, and create a soul-satisfying meal. They're also nutritious and taste so good that you'll wonder why you ever ate any other kind. Whether you serve them as the centerpieces of a meal or as the first two courses on the road to something even greater, soups and salads are a home cook's best friends.

Mastering Essential Soup Skills

Making soup is a great way to clean out your vegetable crisper. No, it doesn't have magical powers and can't transform moldy ingredients into something edible. But if you aren't sure how to use up that bag of carrots or that whole bunch of celery, soup is the answer! Carrots, celery, an onion, a clove of garlic, some pepper . . . sounds like a tasty vegetable soup to us. Strain out the vegetables after boiling them for an hour, and you have vegetable stock for use in your next super soup.

Soup can get pretty fancy and complicated, but here we stick to the basics: simple puréed soups and easy chunky soups in classic flavors you'll want to make again and again. (For even more soup recipes, check out *Cooking Soups For Dummies*, by Jenna Holst, published by Wiley.)

Sautéing meat and vegetables first

Chapter 6 shows you how to sauté both meat and vegetables, but essentially, sautéing means cooking something quickly in fat, such as butter or olive oil, until it gets golden brown and extra tasty.

When you sauté your soup ingredients before adding them to the pot, you add an extra level of complexity to the flavor. Just about any soup can benefit from the addition of sautéed onions and garlic as well as other ingredients like meat, poultry, fish, and vegetables — from tomatoes to turnips.

We like to use our soup pot as a sauté pan. Heat up the soup pot (a high-sided pot, such as a Dutch oven), add a little oil or butter, throw your soup ingredients in, toss them around for a few minutes, and then add your broth. If you're making up your own soup recipes, give this a try. Many soup recipes you'll see (including the ones at the end of this chapter) have a similar process involving cooking the soup ingredients in oil before adding the broth or water.

Thickening your soup

It's easy to thin a soup: Just add water or more broth. However, sometimes you want to thicken your soup so it looks more luxurious and tastes richer. Try this classic thickening technique:

1. **Work 1 tablespoon of slightly softened butter together with 1 tablespoon of all-purpose flour.** Mash them together in a small bowl with the back of a spoon or a fork until they form a smooth, buttery paste.

2. **Scoop a cup or so of soup liquid into a small bowl and mix in the flour-butter mixture until it has fully melted and been incorporated into the soup liquid.**

3. **Stir this mixture back into the soup pot and cook over medium heat for about 5 minutes, until you notice the soup has slightly thickened.**

WHAT AM I EATING? SOUPS DEFINED

Soups come in several different categories. Here are some types of soup you've proba-bly heard about:

- **Bisque:** A thick, rich, puréed soup with added cream, traditionally made from shell-fish (such as crab or lobster) but now often made from other ingredients, such as tomatoes.

- **Broth:** A clear, flavored liquid made from simmering vegetables, herbs, meat, poul-try, or fish bones in water. Strain the solids and refrigerate or freeze to use as a base for your next great soup.

- **Chili:** A thick, stew-like concoction of beef or other meat in a tomato base with chili powder and typically onions, peppers, and kidney or pinto beans.

- **Chowder:** A typically thick and chunky fish soup, usually with vegetables, such as potatoes.

- **Consommé:** The "consummate" broth, made by simmering egg whites, and some-times finely chopped meat and vegetables, in stock. As the egg whites solidify, they trap any impurities. After simmering an hour or more, the stock is strained through layers of cheesecloth, resulting in a very clear, pure soup.

- **Court bouillon:** A broth, usually strained, that simmers for only a short time — no more than 30 minutes — but long enough to draw out the flavor of the vegetables added to the broth. It's used as a poaching liquid for fish, seafood, and vegetables.

- **Fumet:** A strained stock of fish bones, water, vegetables, and herbs. Fumet (French for "fish stock") cooks for about 30 minutes and is used as a flavoring base for soups and sauces.

- **Gumbo:** A soup that typically combines assorted shellfish, poultry, vegetables, a long-cooked dark brown roux of flour and oil, okra, and *filé powder* (a seasoning made from ground sassafras leaves), which thicken and flavor the soup as it cooks. *Gumbo* is the African word for okra.

- **Puréed soup:** A creamy textured soup in which solid ingredients are whirled in a blender or food processor or forced through a food mill until smooth.

- **Stew:** Thicker than your basic soup but thinner than, say, a casserole, stew consists of meat and vegetables simmered in a small amount of broth, or in their own juices.

- **Stock:** The foundation of countless soups and sauces, stock is essentially a richly flavored broth. White stock involves poultry or veal bones or carcasses boiled with vegetables and strained. Brown stock requires that bones be browned first by roasting and then added to the water, boiled, and strained. Vegetable stock is essentially the same as vegetable broth.

Here's another thickening method that's even easier:

1. **Using a fork or a small wire whisk, blend 1 tablespoon all-purpose flour, cornstarch, potato starch, arrowroot powder, or other starch with 2 tablespoons soup broth.**

2. **Stir, add about 1 cup more broth, stir again, and add to the soup.**

3. **Cook over medium heat for 5 to 10 more minutes, or until the soup has slightly thickened.**

TIP

Dare we admit it? Instant potato flakes make a great and almost instantaneous thickener! Add a tablespoonful and stir until the soup thickens. You can also add leftover mashed potatoes, cooked rice, stale corn tortilla pieces, or vegetable purée to any soup to make it thicker.

You can always simmer or even boil down a soup to get it to thicken because the longer a soup cooks, the more moisture evaporates (and flavors concentrate). However, don't boil soups containing milk or cream unless the recipe calls for it. Cream soups burn easily, which ruins the taste. Typically, milk or cream is stirred in toward the very end of cooking so it gets only gently warmed.

Skimming soups and stocks

When making soup, especially one that contains dried beans or lentils, meat, or poultry, you may need to skim the scum from the surface as the soup cooks. To do so, use a spoon with a long handle.

Sometimes, fat rises to the surface, especially if your soup contains high-fat meat, such as sausage. As the soup cooks, skim off any fat floating on the surface with a large spoon. Or, to make the job even easier, if you're making the soup the day before, refrigerate it and, when the fat congeals on the top, just scoop it off and throw it away before reheating the soup.

Enriching store-bought stocks

Most commercial chicken and beef stocks, which are sold in cans and cartons, are relatively bland. To enrich them, pour them into a pot and add some chopped celery, carrots, onions, garlic, and seasonings of choice. Dried rosemary and thyme are particularly nice, giving the stocks a fresh, aromatic flavor. When finished, simply strain through a mesh strainer.

RECIPE
ALERT

Scores of recipes call for chicken stock in lieu of water. By learning to make this building block of cuisine, which calls for a simple simmering technique, you can vastly enhance many dishes. To make your own Chicken Stock, flip to the recipe section at the end of this chapter.

Peeling and seeding a tomato

For many soup recipes, tomatoes are a staple, but you don't want their peels or seeds — just the meat. To peel and seed a fresh tomato, bring a covered pot of water to a rolling boil over high heat, and then follow these steps (shown in Figure 12-1):

1. **Cut the core out of the tomato at the stem end with a paring knife.**

   Run your knife around the stem at an angle pointing inward, and then lift out the core.

2. **Cut a shallow X in the bottom of the tomato, just slicing through the skin.**

3. **Put the tomato in a sieve with a handle, remove the lid from the pot, and lower the tomato into the boiling water for 10 to 30 seconds.**

   If you don't have a sieve, you can use a slotted spoon or even a pair of kitchen tongs for this step.

TIP

4. **Remove the tomato from the pot and immerse it in cold water until it's cool enough to handle.**

5. **Peel off the skin, starting from the X you cut in the bottom.**

   The skin should come off easily, but if it doesn't, return the tomato to the boiling water for another 30 seconds.

6. **Cut the peeled tomato in half.**

7. **Squeeze out the seeds and discard them.**

8. **Chop the remaining tomato flesh.**

Showing garlic, onions, and herbs some respect

In Chapter 4, we show you exactly how to chop an onion and mince cloves of garlic. You may want to check out that chapter because so many soup recipes call for one or both of these ingredients.

How to Peel, Seed, and Chop Tomatoes

1. Insert paring knife diagonally. Cut out stem.

2. Cut a shallow "x" on the bottom.

3. Drop into boiling water for about 10 seconds or so.

4. Remove with a long-handled fork. Immerse in cold water.

5. Starting at the "x," peel off the skin. Easy! (Peel peaches and apricots the same way.)

6. cut in half.

7. Squeeze! Seeds ooze out

8. chop into desired size.

FIGURE 12-1:
Dropping tomatoes in boiling water makes peeling them much easier.

Illustration by Elizabeth Kurtzman

TIP

Herbs are another soup mainstay, and here's a crucial how-to: Always add fresh herbs to soups (or sauces) at the last minute before serving. That way, the herbs remain vibrant and alive with flavor. If you use dried herbs, add them earlier in the cooking process to help release their flavors. See Chapter 3 for lots of info about herbs and spices.

Trying Your Hand at Puréed Soups

To make puréed soups, you use a blender or food processor to whirl the ingredients into a smooth texture. After you understand the puréeing technique, the variations you can make on this cooking theme are limitless. Asparagus, broccoli, corn, cucumbers, mushrooms, parsnips, spinach, rutabaga, tomatoes, winter squash, pumpkin, turnips, and watercress are among the vegetables that purée to a rich and smooth consistency.

RECIPE ALERT

In this chapter, we present recipes for three puréed soups:

>> Carrot Soup with Dill uses low-fat ricotta cheese instead of cream, making this a delicious and health-conscious recipe. Dill is a natural sidekick to carrots. *Port* (a Portuguese dessert wine) adds a touch of sweetness, but it's optional.

» Cream of Potato Soup is simple, quick, and easy. It isn't particularly low in calories or fat, but it sure tastes good! It's also good if you don't purée it and instead prefer a soup with chunks of potato. Your call.

» What child (or adult!) doesn't love tomato soup with a grilled cheese sandwich? It's comfort food supreme. Our Tomato Soup recipe is almost as easy as opening a can, and it tastes fantastic. It's a great way to use up overflow from a tomato garden in the summer, but canned tomatoes work, too.

WARNING

If you're going to purée a soup in a blender, let it cool slightly first. Otherwise, the trapped steam could explode and redecorate your ceiling (not to mention burn you!).

Stimulating Your Palate with Fresh Salads and Dressings

A salad can be many things to a meal: a stimulating first course, a fresh and crisp accompaniment to a main dish, or the centerpiece of the meal itself.

The key to really great salads is twofold: Use only the freshest ingredients, and chop everything into bite-sized portions for easy eating. Who wants to try to fold unwieldy pieces of lettuce dripping with oily vinaigrette onto a fork? If everything is neatly chopped into small pieces, lightly dressed with a delicious creamy dressing or tangy vinaigrette, and arranged to present a colorful and attractive plate, you have a truly spectacular dish without ever turning on the stove.

In this section, we show you how to select your greens and whip up your own salad dressings. (Sorry, salad dressing companies, but we're tired of all the high-fructose corn syrup.) Plus, we offer ten quick salad ideas that show you how simple it is to jazz up some greens with yummy ingredients to make your salads seem truly gourmet.

The soul of the salad: Crisp, fresh greens

A salad demands the freshest greens and herbs and the tastiest vegetables you can find. If at all possible, buy produce in season the day (hour?) you plan to eat it, and then speed home with your lights flashing. Better yet, grow some in your yard, if you can.

Getting your greens squeaky-clean

Did you ever fall asleep at the beach with your mouth open and the wind blowing sand in your direction? That's just what unwashed salad can taste like. To make sure you get all the grit out of lettuce, remove the leaves from the stem and soak them briefly in cold water, shaking occasionally. Then run them under the tap, being careful to rinse the root ends thoroughly.

REMEMBER

Drying lettuce completely is critical, or else the dressing slides right off. Layering greens between paper towels works, but it's a nuisance — and not "green" in the environmentally friendly sense. The easiest method is to use a salad spinner that dries with centrifugal force.

Buying and storing greens

When buying greens, avoid those that are wilted or limp. A fresh head of romaine should look like a bouquet of green leaves, clumped tightly together without any rust-colored edges or signs of decay. Pass up the watercress if its leaves are yellowing. Brown spots on iceberg lettuce indicate rot. Greens sold in bunches, such as arugula and dandelion, are especially delicate and prone to quick decay; consume them within a day or two of purchase. And don't believe (just because you watched your mother do it) that wilted greens revive when plunged into cold water.

PACKAGED GREENS — WORTH THE PRICE?

Okay, fess up; packaged greens can be irresistible. You race into the supermarket to find ingredients for a quick family dinner. As you whiz through the produce section, there they are, staring at you with smug expressions: pre-cut "baby" carrots, packaged salad greens, pre-washed spinach, Caesar salad assortment. Isn't it silly to pay up to a third or more to have someone (or some machine) trim, wash, and dry produce for you? Well, it depends how much your time is worth. If you want to spend the extra cash for the convenience of dumping your greens, preplucked and washed, from bag to salad bowl, that's your call. If you already know that's the only way you're going to eat your greens, then we say go for it.

Should you wash packaged greens even if the label says that they have been "triple washed"? There is no scientific consensus on this. Just because greens are sealed in antiseptic packaging doesn't mean they're bacteria-free. But nor are greens after you wash them yourself. Always read labels closely for those that call for washing.

Store rinsed and dried greens in the extra-cold crisper drawer of the refrigerator, wrapped in damp paper towels.

A glossary of greens

Greens range in taste from mild to pungent and even bitter. Don't limit yourself to bland iceberg lettuce, which lacks the higher flavor and nutritional content of more deeply colored greens. The more variety of greens in the bowl, the better. Our favorite salad greens, some of which are pictured in Figure 12-2, include those listed in the following sections.

MILD GREENS

Typically crunchy and slightly sweet, these greens are easy to eat and go well with a highly flavored vinaigrette:

>> **Bibb (or limestone) lettuce:** Tender, rippled leaves form a small, compact head. Bibb has the mildness of Boston lettuce but more crunch. It tends to be expensive, but a little makes a big impression.

>> **Boston lettuce:** Buttery textured, this lettuce looks like a green rose. It mixes well with all varieties and stands well alone topped with sliced, ripe summer tomatoes.

>> **Iceberg lettuce:** The white bread of the salad world, iceberg is common to salad bars and political banquets. Iceberg has more texture than flavor, and, if wrapped, can be used for foul-shot practice.

TIP

To remove the core of iceberg lettuce, smash the head (core side down) on a cutting board or countertop. The hard core should then twist out easily.

>> **Loose-leaf lettuce:** This green is also called *red leaf* or *green leaf* lettuce, depending on its color. Its long, curly leaves are buttery and almost sweet. Add the red leaf variety to green salad for an elegant contrast, or mix red and green leaf together in one bowl.

>> **Red oak leaf lettuce:** Named for the oak tree leaves it resembles, this green is sweet and colorful. It's good mixed with Boston or Bibb lettuce and makes a pretty plate garnish.

>> **Romaine lettuce:** The emperor green of Caesar salad, romaine has dark green exterior leaves with a pale yellow core. It mixes well with other greens. One advantage of romaine is that it keeps well for up to a week in the refrigerator. Like other dark, leafy greens, romaine is a good source of vitamin A.

FIGURE 12-2: Our favorite salad greens.

Illustration by Elizabeth Kurtzman

PUNGENT GREENS

Composing a salad of tart radicchio with a sharp vinaigrette is like catching base-balls without a glove — ouch! These more pungent greens have a bite. Use them to add interest to milder greens, or serve them with a mild creamy dressing, such as the Homemade Ranch Dressing in this chapter.

>> **Arugula:** You can practically taste the iron in arugula's dark green leaves. The peppery flavor mixes well with any mild lettuce, or you can toss it with grilled portobello mushrooms, red onions, and a lemon vinaigrette.

>> **Belgian endive:** Its pale yellow and white leaves are packed tightly together in a cigar-like shape. This green has lots of crunch and a slightly bitter taste. Pull the leaves away from the base and tear them into pieces in green salads, or use an entire leaf as a serving base for various cheese and vegetable spreads and fillings.

>> **Cabbage:** Red or green, cabbage is a great salad addition and amazingly inexpensive. Tear or shred leaves with a knife and toss with other greens to add color and texture. Cabbage is a long-storage vegetable and a good source of vitamin C.

>> **Curly endive (sometimes called chicory):** Similar to escarole in flavor, this green has very curly leaves.

>> **Dandelion:** A green that you can probably harvest off your front lawn (if you don't have dogs and don't spray your yard with chemicals), dandelion leaves arrive on the market in the spring. Italians cherish its bitter, crunchy qualities. Choose young, tender leaves; the older ones are too bitter and tough. Toss in a mixed green salad with chopped, hard-cooked eggs and a vinaigrette dressing. Dandelion greens are a good source of vitamin A, vitamin C, and calcium.

>> **Escarole:** You can consume this green raw in salad or sauté it in olive oil and garlic. A member of the endive family, escarole is rather tart and stands up to strong-flavored dressings.

>> **Frisee:** Mildly bitter, this pale yellow green has lacy leaves. Mix it sparingly with other greens for contrasting texture and taste. It's similar to curly endive in appearance but with a more delicate taste.

>> **Kale:** Faintly bitter with large thick leaves, this is the green of the moment. It's great braised in chicken stock, chopped in a salad, or even deep-fried. Remove the thick tough center rib.

>> **Mesclun** (pronounced mess-*clan*): This type of green is a salad mix that usually contains frisee, arugula, radicchio, red leaf lettuces, mustard greens, and other delicate greens. Mesclun is very expensive, so purchase it only if it appears very fresh, or the greens will wilt before you get home. It's best to buy a small amount to mix with other less expensive salad greens.

>> **Radicchio:** A small, tightly wound head with deep magenta leaves that can add brilliant splashes of color to a bowl of greens, radicchio is extremely pungent and comparatively expensive. Use it sparingly. It keeps well in the refrigerator (up to two weeks), especially if wrapped in moist paper towels. Like cabbage, radicchio also may be grilled, baked, or sautéed.

>> **Spinach:** These deep green, slightly crumpled leaves are full of iron. Discard the thick stems. The leaves of baby spinach are smaller, oval shaped, smooth, and buttery. Rinse all spinach thoroughly to rid the leaves of sand. Dry well. Mix with milder greens like Boston, Bibb, or loose-leaf.

>> **Watercress:** Its clover-shaped leaves lend peppery crunch to any salad. Snap off and discard the tough stems and be sure to rinse well. Watercress makes a pretty soup or plate garnish.

RECIPE ALERT

Kale is a strong winter green that's increasingly finding its way to the summer table. Although it's traditionally sautéed, baked, or simmered in stews and soups, inventive cooks have found that treating it to a massage turns this tough cookie of a green into one that's soft and silky. You'll find two kinds of kale at your market: curly and lacinato, also known as Tuscan or dinosaur kale ("dino" for short). Lacinato is less fibrous and grassy tasting than curly kale, and we recommend it over curly kale for making salads, such as the Kale Salad with Bacon and Eggs recipe in this chapter.

TIP

To massage kale, place the kale in a large bowl. Pick up a bunch of trimmed leaves with both hands and simply rub them together. You'll notice that two minutes of massaging creates soft and silky kale leaves and also extracts some of the kale's bitterness. After two minutes, taste a leaf. If the kale is still bitter, massage a bit more. Then mix other vegetables or fruits into the bowl and toss with a dressing of choice.

To trim kale, lay a kale leaf on a cutting surface, fold the leaf in half over the kale's stem, and, using a sharp knife, cut from tip of the leaf to the base of the stem. Then remove the stem from leaf. Save the stems to add to soup pots when making stock.

RECIPE ALERT

After you've trimmed the stems from the greens, you need to cut them into ribbons. The French term for herbs or leafy green vegetables cut into thin strips is *chiffonade*. Stack two or three leaves on a cutting surface and roll them up into a cigar-like shape (see Figure 12-3). Using a sharp knife, cut through the rolled leaves, making thin ribbon slices (which are perfect for raw salads; see the recipe for Kale Salad with Bacon and Eggs later in this chapter).

Skipping the greens but keeping the salad

RECIPE ALERT

Sometimes, a great salad doesn't require any greens at all. Other vegetables such as green beans, peas, tomatoes, and cauliflower may serve as the salad's centerpiece, not to mention beans, potatoes, and pasta. If you're curious to try a green-less salad, be sure to check out our recipes for Broccoli Salad with Warm Bacon Dressing and French Potato Salad later in this chapter. Also check out the upcoming section

"Ten easy salad ideas" where you discover that several of them don't involve greens at all.

How to Chiffonade!

To chiffonade, roll several leaves together. TIGHTLY!

Slice narrow, ⅛" strips crossways, across stems.

This action makes ribbons of the leaves, called chiffonades.

FIGURE 12-3:
Cut rolled leaves into thin strips.

Illustration by Elizabeth Kurtzman

So many dressings, so little time

A good dressing is a lot like a good outfit. It decorates in a pleasing way, adding style to the basic substance. If you go to the supermarket and look at the dressing section, you find many kinds and brands of dressing. You probably tend to reach for the same thing every time: the Italian dressing perhaps, or the creamy ranch dressing. Store-bought dressing can be quite good if you choose a quality brand with quality ingredients, but a store-bought dressing can't possibly be fresh. A homemade dressing is something extra special — it has fresh ingredients and a personal touch. Why not try making yours at home?

When you break them down, dressings are essentially of two kinds: those based on oil and vinegar (vinaigrette) and those based on a creamy mayonnaise (like ranch or Thousand Island). Both types are simple to prepare.

Puckering up for tangy vinaigrettes

Vinaigrette is among the most versatile of dressings. It goes with all sorts of salad greens and grilled vegetables, but it can also work with meat, poultry, and fish, as a marinade or as a light and tasty sauce. The advantage of vinaigrette-based dressing is that you can make a large quantity and store it, sealed, in an old wine bottle or Mason jar. It lasts for weeks in the refrigerator. Homemade vinaigrette in a fancy bottle makes a great gift, too.

Vinaigrette has two essential ingredients: vinegar (or another acid, like lemon juice or lime juice) and oil. Add herbs, spices, and other flavorings, and you can give your vinaigrette its unique character.

THE SKINNY ON OLIVE AND OTHER SALAD OILS

Some people say that a salad dressing is only as good as the oil it contains, and few oils make a more delicious, complex, and interesting salad dressing than olive oil. But buying olive oil in the supermarket has become as confusing as ordering coffee, what with all the nationalities and fancy labels and terminology in baffling languages. Do you get Italian or Spanish or a blend, or maybe something artisanal from California? What color and what brand do you buy? Should it be green or yellow or as light as possible?

DON'T GET SCAMMED WHEN BUYING OLIVE OIL

As much as 70 percent of the virgin and extra-virgin olive oil you purchase in supermarkets and gourmet stores is fake — that is, adulterated with other oils, watered down, colored with dyes, or misrepresented for place of origin. And because this country has scant resources to uncover fraud, it's largely up to the consumer to figure it out.

Virgin olive oil is generally defined as being oil from olives that haven't been grown with chemicals or additives of any kind and obtained from only the first pressing of the fruit (not by subsequent pressings of the leftover residue). Extra-virgin is the highest grade, produced from olives pressed within 24 hours of harvest. It can range in color from yellow to green, must be free from defects and fatty acids. The oil must be obtained by physically milling or pressing the fruit, not by heating it. Additives aren't permitted.

So what can you do to avoid buying fake olive oil? Here are a few tips:

- Be suspicious of inexpensive "extra-virgin" olive oil, say anything less than $10 a liter.

- Look for a harvesting date on the label. Olive oil deteriorates with age. Don't purchase oil more than two years old.

- Look for a seal from the International Olive Oil Council (OIC) or PDO, the European Union's stamp of approval.

- Anything light or pure is likely a blend and not extra-virgin.

- A USDA organic certification, clearly displayed on the bottle, means that at least 95 percent of the oil is pesticide-free.

- Good olive oil should be sold in dark bottles because they protect them from oxidation.

- If an oil is labeled "product of Italy," that means only that it was packed and shipped in Italy. The olives could be from Greece, Spain, Tunisia, or any number of places.

TIP

Don't worry about all that. The most important thing to look for in olive oil is its *grade*, which is usually printed right on the front of the bottle. In ascending order of quality, you'll find *pure*, *virgin*, and *extra-virgin.*

The grade has to do with the oleic acid content of the oil, with the finest oils having the least acidity. All three varieties of olive oil come from the olive's first *pressing* (the crushing process that releases the oil from the olives), but extra-virgin is the highest quality. Extra-virgin olive oil usually has the richest aroma and strongest flavor. Pure olive oil can come from both the first and second pressing of the tree-ripened olives and may be blended with 5 to 10 percent virgin olive oil to enrich its flavor.

TIP

Don't be misled by olive oil sold as "light." The "light" has nothing to do with its fat content; instead, it refers to its pale color and extremely bland flavor, a result of the way it's processed. One tablespoon of any olive oil contains the same 120 calories.

Other salad oils include base oils like canola, corn, safflower, and other neutral-tasting vegetable oils; more intensely flavored oils, such as walnut, hazelnut, and sesame; and oils flavored with garlic, herbs, citrus, or hot chilis. Each has its place. The neutral oils can be mixed with equal amounts of olive oil to lighten the taste (and the cost), or you can add smaller dashes of nut oils or flavored oils for drama.

TIP

The shelf life of oil depends on its variety. Olive oils should keep for up to a year if tightly capped and stored out of the sun in a cool, dark place. Nut oils last only a few months, so purchase them in small quantities.

WHAT PUTS THE VINEGAR IN VINAIGRETTE?

Oil in a salad dressing needs an acidic counterpoint — a tart ingredient that stimulates the palate and cuts through the oil's richness. In most cases, vinegar is the choice, but fresh citrus juice can also add a pleasing tartness.

Vinegar comes in many different forms. Red or white wine is the most common liquid base, but anything that ferments can be used to make vinegar:

>> **Cider vinegar:** Made from apples, this strong, clear, brownish vinegar holds up well with pungent greens and is especially good sprinkled on meat, fish, or fruit salads. It's also excellent with ginger or curry dressings.

>> **Red or white wine vinegar:** Made from any number of red or white wines, this vinegar is full bodied and perfect for dressing pungent, dark greens.

- **Rice vinegar:** Common to Japan and China, rice vinegars are less tart than white vinegars and combine well with sesame oil for an Asian-inspired flavor. They're also good in seafood salads.

- **White vinegar:** Colorless and sharp, white vinegar is distilled from assorted grains, and it's terrific in cold rice or pasta salads.

Experiment with different vinegars to find ones with flavors you enjoy. Your unique choices will make your homemade vinaigrette dressing all yours.

RECIPE ALERT

MAKING YOUR OWN VINAIGRETTE

We offer a basic recipe for Vinaigrette Dressing later in this chapter, but the proportions in the recipe are only approximations. You must taste it as you go along to balance the vinegar and olive oil flavors.

Keep in mind that vinaigrette is a basic formula to which you can add many different ingredients for color, flavor, texture, and taste. Following are some variations on the basic Vinaigrette Dressing recipe in this chapter:

- Replace 2 tablespoons of the olive oil with 2 tablespoons of walnut or hazelnut oil to give the vinaigrette a distinctive, nutty flavor. Serve with mixed green salads or salads with grilled poultry.

BALSAMIC: THE WORLD'S MOST EXPENSIVE VINEGAR

Traditional balsamic vinegar is a dark, sweet, syrupy, aged liquid that is worth its weight in gold. The real thing is made in the area around Modena, Italy, and nowhere else (the word *Modena* should be on the label). Virtually all those large bottles of balsamic vinegar you see in supermarkets are imitations — some aged, some not — made to look like the real thing. This "fake" balsamic vinegar isn't necessarily bad, just different. And way less expensive.

Recognizing real balsamic vinegar is easy: You start to hyperventilate upon seeing the price. Real balsamic vinegar is sold only in little bulb-shaped bottles — they look like perfume. It's usually more than 25 years old and costs $100 and up for a tiny portion. Such rarefied vinegar isn't to be tossed around in salads. Italians use it to jazz up soups, drizzle over fresh fruit (with ripe strawberries, it's sublime), add to a braised dish just before serving, reduce and dribble over vanilla ice cream, or add a touch to a marinade.

>> Add 1 teaspoon drained capers and 1 tablespoon chopped fresh chervil, tarragon, basil, or lemon thyme. This herby vinaigrette really enlivens a cold pasta salad.

>> Place one small ripe tomato in a blender or food processor container with the rest of the dressing and blend well.

>> To thicken the vinaigrette, combine it in a blender with 1 to 2 tablespoons of ricotta cheese. Low-fat ricotta enriches just like cream, with far fewer calories.

RECIPE ALERT

After you create your perfect vinaigrette, be sure to check out our recipe for French Potato Salad later in this chapter. A delicious European-style potato salad hinges on a good vinaigrette. It's not your grandmother's potato salad (unless your grandmother is French).

Concocting creamy dressings

A creamy dressing can enhance various greens, complementing bitter or pungent flavors with the mellow flavor of mayonnaise. Creamy dressings also go well with cold shellfish, meat, and poultry. One downside to creamy dressings is that they spoil more quickly than vinaigrettes, so be sure to keep them refrigerated and use them within a week or so.

RECIPE ALERT

Later in this chapter, we provide a recipe for Homemade Ranch Dressing. We suggest using both sour cream and mayonnaise in this dressing because the combination adds a nice, sharp edge, but you can use all mayo if you prefer. You can drizzle this dressing on your salad, or add 1 teaspoon horseradish (or to taste) and use it as a sandwich spread.

Ten easy salad ideas

Salads are easy to improvise. Simply follow the advice of your taste buds to create your own salads. Need some inspiration to get you started? Try a few of these simple combinations, but don't be afraid to substitute, experiment, or add different vegetables or dressings according to your taste:

>> **Tomato, Red Onion, and Basil Salad:** Slice ripe, red tomatoes ¼-inch thick and layer on a platter with diced red onion and 4 or 5 large chopped fresh basil leaves. Drizzle with oil and vinegar and season with salt and black pepper. This salad tastes great with fresh mozzarella cheese, too.

>> **Bell Pepper–Rice Salad:** Combine about 3 cups cooked white rice with 1 cup cooked green peas and 2 cups seeded, cored, and chopped red, green, or yellow bell peppers (or any combination of colors). Toss with enough herb

vinaigrette dressing to moisten the ingredients sufficiently, add salt and black pepper to taste, and chill before serving.

» **Cucumber-Dill Salad:** Toss peeled, sliced, and seeded cucumbers in a dill-flavored vinaigrette.

» **Cherry Tomato and Feta Cheese Salad:** Toss 1 pint cherry tomatoes, rinsed and sliced in half, with 4 ounces crumbled feta cheese and ½ cup sliced, pitted black olives. Season with vinaigrette dressing to taste.

» **Pasta Medley Salad:** Combine about 2 cups of your favorite pasta, cooked, with ½ cup chopped, sun-dried tomatoes. Season lightly with oil, vinegar, and black pepper to taste.

» **Garbanzo Bean Toss:** Combine one 15.5- to 16-ounce can drained garbanzo beans, ½ cup chopped red onion, 1 or 2 cloves crushed garlic, and the grated zest of 1 lemon. Toss with lemon vinaigrette dressing.

» **Layered Cheese and Vegetable Salad:** Arrange alternating thin slices of ripe tomatoes and mozzarella cheese on a round platter. Fill the center with slices of avocado sprinkled with fresh lemon juice to prevent discoloration. Drizzle with olive oil and lemon juice; garnish with fresh basil.

» **Grilled Vegetable Platter with Fresh Pesto:** Arrange any assortment of grilled vegetables (see Chapter 9) on a platter. Serve with spoonfuls of fresh pesto (see Chapter 14).

» **Fruit Salsa:** Combine 1 ripe, peeled, pitted, and chopped avocado; 2 ripe, peeled, seeded, and chopped mangoes; ½ cup chopped red onion; and 1 teaspoon seeded, chopped jalapeño pepper with a dressing of 1 tablespoon honey and the grated zest and juice of 1 lemon. Serve as a side salad with broiled hamburgers, chicken, or fish.

» **Three-Berry Dessert Salad:** Combine 2 pints rinsed and hulled strawberries, 1 pint rinsed blueberries, and 1 pint rinsed raspberries in a bowl. Toss with a dressing of ½ cup heavy cream sweetened with confectioner's sugar to taste.

Chicken Stock

PREP TIME: ABOUT 10 MIN	COOK TIME: 2 HR	YIELD: ABOUT 8 CUPS

INGREDIENTS

1 whole chicken (about 4 pounds)

2 stalks celery, rinsed and halved crosswise

2 carrots, trimmed and halved crosswise

1 large onion, peeled and halved

Small bunch parsley

2 bay leaves

10 black peppercorns

Water to cover

DIRECTIONS

1 Place everything in a large, deep pot, and bring to a boil. Reduce the heat and simmer partially covered for about 2 hours, skimming foam off the surface with a slotted spoon as necessary.

2 Let the stock cool, and then strain through a large colander set over a large pot or bowl to separate the broth from the chicken and vegetable parts. Set aside solids and refrigerate the strained stock. After the stock is completely cooled, scrape off any fat that has risen to the surface and solidified. If desired, freeze the stock in small containers or in ice cube trays for later use.

PER CUP: *Calories 86 (From Fat 27); Fat 3g (Saturated 1g); Cholesterol 7mg; Sodium 343mg; Carbohydrate 8g (Dietary Fiber 0g); Protein 6g.*

TIP: You can literally clean out your refrigerator of old vegetables that you'd otherwise discard (as long as they're not moldy!) by adding them to the stock pot. This includes herbs that have lost their freshness, potatoes, turnips, leeks, garlic, and tough cooking greens like kale and collard and mustard greens.

TIP: Don't discard the cooked chicken! Instead, use it to make a chicken salad, to fill tortillas or tacos, or to add into mixed greens with a dressing of choice for a quick meal. Or you can use it to make our Chicken and Biscuit Pot Pie recipe in Chapter 16.

Carrot Soup with Dill

INGREDIENTS

2 tablespoons butter

1 medium yellow onion, finely chopped

1½ pounds carrots, peeled and cut into 1-inch-thick pieces

4 cups homemade or canned chicken or vegetable stock

2 cups water

Salt and black pepper

½ cup low-fat ricotta cheese

2 to 3 tablespoons Port (optional)

2 tablespoons chopped fresh dill, or 2 teaspoons dried

DIRECTIONS

1 In a large, deep saucepan or soup pot over medium heat, melt the butter. Add the onion and cook, stirring often, until it softens, about 5 minutes.

2 Add the carrots, stock, water, and salt and black pepper to taste. Cover and bring to a boil.

3 Reduce the heat and simmer, uncovered, for 30 minutes, skimming off any foam that rises to the surface. Cool for 15 minutes.

4 Set a colander over a big bowl or another pot. Carefully pour the soup into the colander. Save the liquid.

5 Put the drained carrot-onion mixture into a blender or food processor. Add the ricotta cheese and about a cup of the saved liquid. Purée until smooth.

6 Add the purée to the pot holding the remaining cooking liquid and turn the heat to medium-high. Stir well with a wooden spoon until the soup just comes to a boil, about 10 minutes.

7 Remove from the heat, stir in the Port (if desired), garnish with the dill, and serve.

PER SERVING: *Calories 120 (From Fat 42); Fat 5g (Saturated 3g); Cholesterol 15mg; Sodium 588mg; Carbohydrate 15g (Dietary Fiber 3g); Protein 5g.*

VARY IT! If you prefer, omit the dill and add ½ to ¾ teaspoon ground ginger.

Cream of Potato Soup

PREP TIME: ABOUT 15 MIN PLUS COOLING TIME	COOK TIME: ABOUT 50 MIN	YIELD: 6 SERVINGS

INGREDIENTS

4 tablespoons butter

6 medium red potatoes, peeled and quartered

4 cloves garlic, peeled

4 cups chicken broth

1 cup heavy cream

1½ teaspoons salt (optional)

½ teaspoon black pepper

6 slices bacon, cooked until crispy, crumbled

1 tablespoon chopped chives, fresh or dried

DIRECTIONS

1 In a large saucepan or pot, melt the butter.

2 Add the potatoes and garlic and stir to coat. Cook for about 5 minutes.

3 Add the chicken broth, and bring the soup to a simmer. Cook until the potatoes are tender and easy to mash against the side of the pan, about 30 minutes.

4 Remove the soup from the heat and cool for 15 minutes. Spoon the mixture into a blender and purée well.

5 Return the soup to the pot and turn the heat to medium-low. Add the cream and stir constantly until the soup is hot and just barely simmering (showing tiny bubbles), about 10 minutes.

6 Add the salt (if desired) and black pepper, and garnish each soup bowl with the bacon and chives.

PER SERVING: *Calories 425 (From Fat 255); Fat 28g (Saturated 16g); Cholesterol 84mg; Sodium 798mg; Carbohydrate 36g (Dietary Fiber 3g); Protein 8g.*

TIP: If you don't want to purée this soup, cut the potatoes into bite-sized pieces, mince the garlic, and skip Step 4.

Tomato Soup

PREP TIME: ABOUT 15 MIN | COOK TIME: ABOUT 15 MIN | YIELD: 6 SERVINGS

INGREDIENTS

2 tablespoons butter

1 small yellow onion, peeled and chopped

1 clove garlic, minced

3 cups canned chicken or vegetable stock

6 large ripe tomatoes, peeled, seeded, and coarsely chopped, or two 14-ounce cans tomatoes, undrained and coarsely chopped

2 tablespoons fresh lemon juice

2 teaspoons sugar

Salt and black pepper

1 tablespoon chopped fresh cilantro, basil, or tarragon (optional)

DIRECTIONS

1 In a medium saucepan, melt the butter over medium-high heat. Add the onions and garlic and sauté until soft, about 10 minutes.

2 Add the stock and tomatoes to the onion-garlic mixture. Bring to a boil.

3 Remove from the heat and allow to cool 5 minutes.

4 Pour carefully into a blender or food processor. Purée until smooth.

5 Return the mixture to the saucepan; add the lemon juice, sugar, and salt and black pepper to taste; and heat over medium until hot again, about 5 minutes, stirring with a wooden spoon. Garnish with the cilantro, basil, or tarragon (if desired).

PER SERVING: Calories 102 (From Fat 58); Fat 6g (Saturated 3g); Cholesterol 13mg; Sodium 614mg; Carbohydrate 11g (Dietary Fiber 2g); Protein 2g.

French Onion Soup

PREP TIME: ABOUT 20 MIN | COOK TIME: ABOUT 1 HR | YIELD: 6 SERVINGS

INGREDIENTS

4 tablespoons butter

4 large sweet onions, like Vidalia, peeled and thinly sliced

7 cups beef broth

1 bay leaf

6 slices French bread, toasted

1 cup grated Swiss cheese

DIRECTIONS

1 Melt the butter over medium heat in a large soup pot. Add the onions. Toss to coat the onions with the butter and cook until they become transparent, about 10 minutes.

2 Add 1 cup of the beef broth and continue stirring until the broth almost completely cooks away, scraping the pan to keep the caramelized parts moving, about 35 minutes.

3 Add the remaining 6 cups broth and the bay leaf. Cover and bring to a boil. Reduce the heat and simmer for 15 minutes, stirring occasionally.

4 Remove the bay leaf from the soup and discard. Ladle the soup into 6 ovenproof crocks or bowls. Put a slice of French bread in each bowl and sprinkle each with one-sixth of the cheese. Put the crocks on a sturdy baking sheet.

5 Turn on the broiler of your oven and carefully put the baking sheet under the broiler on the top rack, about 4 inches from the heat source. When the cheese turns golden brown (in 1 or 2 minutes), carefully remove the baking sheet and serve.

PER SERVING: *Calories 364 (From Fat 131); Fat 15g (Saturated 8g); Cholesterol 37mg; Sodium 1,606mg; Carbohydrate 41g (Dietary Fiber 3g); Protein 16g.*

TIP: When simmering thick soups like this one, occasionally stir and scrape the bottom of the pot with a wooden spoon to prevent the mixture from sticking and burning. Add more broth (or water) if necessary.

Easy Mixed Green Salad

PREP TIME: ABOUT 20 MIN | YIELD: 6 SERVINGS

INGREDIENTS

6 cups mixed lettuces, such as romaine, red leaf, Boston, or mixed spring greens

⅓ cup coarsely chopped red onion

2 carrots, grated

1 rib celery, minced

½ cup grated red or green cabbage (optional)

1½ tablespoons red or white wine vinegar

½ teaspoon dried basil or oregano

Salt and black pepper

¼ cup olive oil

DIRECTIONS

1 Rinse the lettuce leaves in cold water. Remove tough stems, and spin the greens in a salad spinner to dry.

2 Tear the greens into bite-sized pieces and put them in a salad bowl. Add the onion, carrots, celery, and cabbage (if desired).

3 Put the vinegar in a small bowl and add the basil or oregano and the salt and black pepper to taste. Start beating while gradually adding the oil.

4 Pour the dressing over the salad and toss to evenly coat.

PER SERVING: *Calories 107 (From Fat 82); Fat 9g (Saturated 1g); Cholesterol 0mg; Sodium 133mg; Carbohydrate 6g (Dietary Fiber 2g); Protein 1g.*

VARY IT! For variety, substitute freshly squeezed lemon juice for the vinegar; add 2 teaspoons mayonnaise, yogurt, or sour cream for a creamy vinaigrette; or whisk 2 teaspoons Dijon-style mustard into the vinaigrette. Add minced herbs, such as tarragon, thyme, chervil, sage, or savory, to taste. Crumble goat cheese or blue cheese over the greens.

Broccoli Salad with Warm Bacon Dressing

PREP TIME: ABOUT 25 MIN	COOK TIME: ABOUT 10 MIN	YIELD: 4 SERVINGS

INGREDIENTS

1 large head broccoli, cut into bite-sized pieces (include part of the stalk)

1 medium red onion, cut into quarters and thinly sliced

2 stalks celery, minced

½ cup raisins

¼ cup chopped walnuts

1 pound bacon, cut into small pieces

½ cup red wine vinegar

¼ cup mayonnaise

2 teaspoons Dijon mustard

DIRECTIONS

1   In a mixing bowl, toss together broccoli, onion, celery, raisins, and walnuts. Set aside.

2   In a skillet over medium heat, fry the bacon pieces until crispy. Drain off bacon fat, reserving 2 tablespoons.

3   In a small mixing bowl, combine reserved bacon fat, vinegar, mayonnaise, and mustard. Whisk to combine. Stir in bacon pieces.

4   Drizzle the bacon mixture over the broccoli mixture and stir to coat all the vegetables with the dressing. Serve immediately.

PER SERVING: *Calories 460 (From Fat 314); Fat 35g (Saturated 9g); Cholesterol 40mg; Sodium 790mg; Carbohydrate 25g (Dietary Fiber 5g); Protein 16g.*

DON'T OVERDRESS

A common mistake with salads is overdressing them, which is like overdressing for dinner — *so* tacky, just when you were trying to be *so* cool. Drizzle just enough dressing over the greens to lightly coat them when tossed well. And when you toss, really toss. Using salad tongs or a large fork and spoon, mix those leaves up really well. The dressing should be evenly distributed on every piece of greenery. Now that's class.

Kale Salad with Bacon and Eggs

PREP TIME: 20 MIN	COOK TIME: ABOUT 30 MIN	YIELD: 4 SERVINGS

INGREDIENTS

2 bunches Lacinato kale, rinsed, trimmed, and sliced into thin ribbons (about 16 ounces total)

½ teaspoon salt

6 tablespoons extra-virgin olive oil

5 slices thick cut bacon, cut into 2- to 3-inch pieces

1 large clove garlic, crushed

¼ cup balsamic vinegar

1 tablespoon apple cider vinegar

½ teaspoon Dijon-style mustard

1 red pepper, cored, seeded, and chopped

Black pepper to taste

3 hard-cooked eggs, peeled and quartered

DIRECTIONS

1 Place the kale in a large bowl; sprinkle with the salt and 2 tablespoons of the olive oil. Using your hands, massage the kale for 2 minutes. Pour off and discard any liquid in the bottom of the bowl and set the kale aside.

2 Add the bacon to a medium skillet and cook over medium heat, about 5 to 7 minutes or until lightly browned and most of the fat is rendered. Transfer the bacon to a paper towel–lined plate to drain. Pour off and discard all but 1 tablespoon of the bacon fat in the skillet. Add the garlic and cook over medium heat about 30 seconds, or just until the garlic is fragrant. Remove and discard the garlic.

3 Add 2 tablespoons of the balsamic vinegar to the skillet and cook over medium heat, stirring to scrape up any browned bits in the bottom of the pan. Pour the pan sauce into a large serving bowl and whisk in the remaining 2 tablespoons balsamic vinegar, the apple cider vinegar, the remaining 4 tablespoons of olive oil, and the mustard.

4 Add the kale, bacon, and red pepper to the dressing, and toss well to combine. Taste and adjust seasoning with black pepper. Add the eggs and toss gently.

PER SERVING: *Calories 375 (From Fat 270); Fat 30g (Saturated 5g); Cholesterol 150mg; Sodium 581mg; Carbohydrate 16g (Dietary Fiber 3g); Protein 12g.*

TIP: Massaging kale reduces its volume by about half. Unlike other more tender salad greens, kale is so hearty that you can dress it a day before serving and put it in the refrigerator to let the flavors blend; the leaves won't wilt further.

Vinaigrette Dressing

PREP TIME: 5 MIN | **YIELD: 6 SERVINGS**

INGREDIENTS

2 tablespoons red or white wine vinegar

1 teaspoon Dijon-style mustard

⅓ cup olive oil

Salt and black pepper

DIRECTIONS

1 Place the vinegar and mustard in a bowl. Whisk to blend well.

2 Add the olive oil in a stream while whisking. Season with salt and black pepper to taste.

PER SERVING: *Calories 107 (From Fat 106); Fat 12g (Saturated 2g); Cholesterol 0mg; Sodium 119mg; Carbohydrate 0g (Dietary Fiber 0g); Protein 0g.*

VARY IT! Try a flavored vinegar or substitute fresh lemon juice for the vinegar.

Homemade Ranch Dressing

PREP TIME: 5 MIN | YIELD: 6 SERVINGS

INGREDIENTS

½ cup mayonnaise

⅓ cup sour cream

¼ cup buttermilk or regular milk

¼ cup minced yellow onion

1 teaspoon garlic powder

2 tablespoons minced fresh or dried parsley

2 teaspoons dried dill

1 teaspoon salt

¼ teaspoon black pepper

DIRECTIONS

Combine all ingredients in a bowl and whisk well. Adjust seasonings to taste.

PER SERVING: *Calories 169 (From Fat 157); Fat 17g (Saturated 4g); Cholesterol 17mg; Sodium 221mg; Carbohydrate 3g (Dietary Fiber 0g); Protein 1g.*

VARY IT! For a seafood salad, add 1 tablespoon drained capers and 1 tablespoon minced fresh tarragon, or 1 teaspoon dried. For a cold meat dish or for a chicken or shrimp salad, make a curry dressing by adding 1 teaspoon curry powder (or to taste) to this dressing. For cold vegetable salad, crumble ½ cup or more blue cheese or Roquefort and mix it into the dressing.

French Potato Salad

PREP TIME: ABOUT 15 MIN PLUS STANDING TIME	COOK TIME: ABOUT 30 MIN	YIELD: 4 SERVINGS

INGREDIENTS

2 pounds red potatoes, well scrubbed

6 tablespoons olive oil

1 tablespoon white vinegar

½ cup red onion, chopped

¼ cup finely chopped parsley

1 large clove garlic, finely chopped

Salt and black pepper

¼ cup dry white wine at room temperature

DIRECTIONS

1 In a medium saucepan, cover the potatoes with lightly salted cold water and bring to a boil.

2 Boil for 20 minutes or until the potatoes are tender when pierced with a knife. Drain and let stand until cool enough to handle.

3 As the potatoes cook, make the dressing. Whisk together the oil and vinegar in a small bowl. Add the red onion, parsley, garlic, and salt and black pepper to taste.

4 Peel the cooked potatoes and cut them into ¼-inch slices. Layer the slices in a shallow serving bowl, sprinkling the wine between the layers.

5 Pour the dressing over the potatoes and gently toss to blend well.

6 Let the salad stand about 30 minutes to blend the flavors. Stir from the bottom before serving, either chilled or at room temperature.

PER SERVING: *Calories 401 (From Fat 186); Fat 21g (Saturated 3g); Cholesterol 0mg; Sodium 167mg; Carbohydrate 47g (Dietary Fiber 5g); Protein 6g.*

VARY IT! Instead of white wine, use ¼ cup white grape juice or 2 tablespoons cider vinegar. Add ¼ cup minced green onions; 2 tablespoons chopped herbs like rosemary, chervil, or basil; or 1 cup diced, roasted bell peppers.

Chapter **13**

From Sides to Mains: Great Grains and Pastas

Throughout history, many people all over the planet have survived almost solely on grains and grain-like foods: rice, wheat, barley, oats, cornmeal, wheat berries, quinoa, amaranth, buckwheat, and more. Grains make bread, pasta, even beer. They're the staff of life, and despite what the low-carb lovers say, we love them. Chewy, tender, moist — they make a meal filling.

Most grains are prepared by boiling or steaming, which you can read about in Chapter 5. In this chapter, we celebrate the great diversity of grains with recipes for rice and other grains as well as all the fantastical things you can do with pasta.

Sprucing Up Standard Rice

Rice is one of the most versatile foods on the planet. Quite literally, it feeds most of the world. It's not all that glamorous on its own, but because of its mild taste, pleasing texture, and affinity with about a billion and seven other flavors, rice is one of the best things a home cook can have in the cupboard.

So many different cultures use rice, and preparing a variety of rice dishes can feel like taking a trip around the globe. India alone has more than 1,100 rice varieties. To give your rice international flair, you don't even really need a recipe. Channel your inner traveler by picking a country and then adding the listed components to plain white rice:

>> **France:** Garlic, tomatoes, fresh herbs (thyme, tarragon, basil)

>> **India:** Curry and spices like cumin, coriander, cardamom, and fennel

>> **Mexico:** Garlic, hot peppers, onions, pinto or black beans

>> **Middle East:** Onions, raisins, cinnamon, allspice, turmeric, cardamom

>> **Spain:** Saffron, nuts, bell peppers and other vegetables, garlic

>> **United States (Louisiana):** Spicy sausage, onions, garlic, cayenne, okra, bell peppers

Here are the most common types of rice used in the United States:

>> **Converted or parboiled rice:** No, your rice hasn't suddenly found religion. The term *converted* refers to a process by which whole grains of rice are soaked in water, steamed, and then dried. This precooking, also called *parboiling,* makes milling easier and also conserves nutrients that are otherwise lost. Steaming also removes some of the rice's sticky starch, leaving each grain smoother in texture, and it shortens cooking time.

RECIPE ALERT

If you can't wait to try your hand at rice, see the simple recipe for Converted Rice that appears later in this chapter.

>> **Long-grain rice:** This basic form of white or brown rice has (obviously) a longer grain. This category includes the fragrant Indian basmati rice essential for Indian cuisine.

RECIPE ALERT

The term *pilaf* refers to a dish in which the grain (rice or another whole grain) is browned slightly in butter or oil and then cooked in a flavored liquid, like chicken or beef stock. After you get the technique down, you can add any flavors you like. We offer a recipe for Basic Rice Pilaf later in the chapter.

» **Short-grain rice:** This rice also comes in white or brown and has a shorter, stubbier shape. It's used to make *risotto* (the creamy, long-stirred specialty of northern Italy) as well as sushi.

The technique for cooking long-grain rice and short-grain rice is essentially the same, except when making risotto, which frequently uses the short-grained rice called *Arborio rice* (available in gourmet markets).

**RECIPE
ALERT**

When making risotto (as you can do with the help of our recipe later in this chapter), you want the rice to slowly absorb enough of the hot broth to form a creamy blend of tender yet still firm grains. It's difficult to give exact proportions for making risotto because absorption rates can vary. The key is to keep stirring the rice over low heat, adding only enough liquid (a little at a time) so the rice is surrounded by, but never swimming in, broth.

» **Instant rice:** Precooked and dehydrated, it's fast, we must admit — but it's not nearly as good as rice you cook for the *first* time. It doesn't have the same texture and toothsomeness as other forms of rice.

» **Brown rice:** This healthful, unrefined rice hasn't been "polished" — that is, nothing but the tough, outer husk has been removed. With its bran layer intact, brown rice is superior in nutrition to polished (white) rice and is also a little more expensive. Brown rice has a faintly nutty flavor and a shorter shelf life than white rice. You can store white rice almost indefinitely, but brown rice should be consumed within 6 months of purchase.

» **Wild rice:** Not really rice at all, *wild rice* is a remote relative of white rice — it's actually a long-grain, aquatic grass. The wild version (it's now cultivated) grows almost exclusively in the Great Lakes region of the United States and has become quite expensive because of its scarcity. You can save money by combining it with brown rice.

Checking Out Other Grains

Rice is nice, but other grains are great, too. Most grains cook quickly in boiling water or flavored boiling liquid, like beef stock or chicken stock. They usually don't need to be soaked before cooking, but they should be rinsed to remove any surface grit. Here are some of the more common whole grains, other than rice:

» **Barley:** A great substitute for rice in soups and side dishes, barley is commonly sold as "pearl" barley, with its outer hull and bran removed. It cooks relatively quickly — about 25 minutes in boiling water or stock. You season it with butter, salt, and black pepper.

>> **Buckwheat:** Although buckwheat isn't really a grain, we treat it like one. Buckwheat is really a grass and a cousin of the rhubarb plant. It has an earthy, almost nutlike flavor and tastes more like brown rice than other grains. Kasha, also called *buckwheat groats,* is simply buckwheat that's been roasted.

>> **Couscous:** Associated with the cuisines of North Africa, couscous is a very fine golden semolina grain that's perfectly suited for soaking the lusty braising liquids and sauce. It also mixes beautifully into salads and can be flavored with herbs like basil, coriander, and mint. It's also good tossed with dried fruits, like raisins or apricots. Couscous is a very neutral — and nutritious — base for all sorts of dishes. Widely available, it comes in regular and the instant variety.

>> **Farro:** This is an ancient wheat grain that goes back to the period of the Fertile Crescent (unfortunately, archeologists have failed to dig up any recipes). It has a chewy texture and mellow nuttiness (packing tons of fiber) and has become quite fashionable in recent years. Most farro has been pearled or semi-pearled, which makes it faster and easier to cook. Pearled farro cooks in about 20 to 30 minutes; whole farro takes closer to an hour. Because it's a kind of wheat, it shouldn't be served to anyone who has celiac disease or is gluten intolerant.

Whole-grained is the most nutritious and has the most fiber, but it requires soaking and takes about twice as long to cook as semi-pearled or pearled. Purchase the semi-pearled farro, which can be boiled in about 15 to 20 minutes so, just like al dente pasta, it's tender with a firm bite when done.

>> **Wheat berries and bulgur:** *Wheat berries* are unprocessed grains of wheat. *Bulgur wheat,* used to make tabbouleh, is a wheat berry that has been steamed and then hulled, dried, and cracked. Bulgur cooks very quickly. (Note that a much more processed form of wheat berries is *cream of wheat* hot cereal, a breakfast porridge.)

**RECIPE
ALERT**

In the Tabbouleh Salad recipe in this chapter, you use bulgur wheat that's rehydrated with boiling water and mixed with some simple ingredients. The result is a fresh grain salad with a Middle Eastern flair.

>> **Cornmeal:** Basic cornmeal is often called by its Italian name, *polenta.* Although it's a less common grain-based side dish in the United States than rice and pasta, it tastes delicious. *Grits,* that southern specialty often served with breakfast, is also made of cornmeal. (See Chapter 9 for a terrific Southern Fried Grits recipe.)

Cornmeal comes finely or coarsely ground. The finely ground type cooks much faster than the coarsely ground meal. The latter has a nuttier texture and takes longer to cook. Try both to see which you prefer.

For a change of pace, try polenta with your meal. If you don't have time to make polenta from scratch, you can buy it ready-made, wrapped in a tube of plastic that looks like a fat sausage; it's available in most supermarkets. Ready-made polenta is good sliced, brushed with a little butter or olive oil, and grilled on both sides until lightly browned. Use polenta in any form — homemade or store-bought — as a base for grilled chops, chicken, sausages, and vegetables.

RECIPE ALERT

Making polenta from scratch doesn't actually take much time at all. To prove it, we've included a Polenta with Herbs recipe later in the chapter for you to try. It makes a great side dish that's a delightful change from pasta or rice, or it's a quick and tasty light meal in itself when covered with a good tomato-meat sauce.

>> **Oats:** Most popular as a breakfast cereal, oats boiled with water make a creamy porridge that tastes great with milk or cream and a little sugar, maple syrup, or honey.

>> **Quinoa:** A small grain that's power-packed with nutrients, quinoa (pronounced *keen*-wah) is available in most health food stores, Middle Eastern shops, and quality supermarkets. You must rinse quinoa a few times before cooking. It takes about two parts liquid to one part quinoa and cooks in about 15 minutes.

RECIPE ALERT

You can make a protein-rich pilaf out of quinoa, for a change of pace from rice. Try the Quinoa Pilaf recipe later in this chapter.

Canoodling with Everyone's Favorite: Pasta

Ah, the unassuming noodle — so simple, yet so delectable. Pasta can be transformed into so many different kinds of meals, from side dish to main course, from modest macaroni and cheese to multi-layered lasagna to exotic Thai-spiced rice noodles in coconut milk.

Americans learned to love pasta when Italian immigrants brought classic dishes from Italy to the United States, and Italian-American cuisine is among the most beloved cuisines in this country today, but you don't have to know Italian cooking to make great pasta. All you really have to do is follow the simple preparation instructions on any package of dried or fresh pasta.

You can eat pasta hot or cold or anywhere in between, dressed in a little butter and freshly grated Parmesan cheese, tossed with a handful of chopped fresh tomatoes and garlic, or drenched in a long-simmered meaty meatball marinara. Try rice noodles with a drizzle of sesame oil, soy sauce, a pinch of ginger, and some chopped scallions for an Asian-inspired side dish or, with the addition of sautéed meat or tofu, as a main course.

Most pasta is made out of *semolina*, a coarsely ground grain (usually durum wheat). However, most grocery stores now stock a variety of gluten-free pastas (such as rice, quinoa, and buckwheat) for those who avoid wheat. If you stick to moderate portions, pasta is low in calories and fat. (One big ladleful of Alfredo sauce can easily destroy all that, but don't blame us!) No matter how you love your pasta, find out how to cook it perfectly at home, and the next time you crave noodles in any shape, you won't have to go out to a restaurant to get them.

RECIPE ALERT

When you start cooking your own pasta, you'll be hooked. To get you going, we provide two great recipes later in the chapter: Spaghetti with Quick Fresh Tomato Sauce, and Penne with Parmesan Cheese and Basil.

Don't sweat the fresh stuff: Dried versus fresh pasta

Fresh pasta isn't inherently better than dried, as some folks would have you believe; it's just different. Many fine dried pastas are available, and the choice between fresh and dried is really a matter of personal taste. Fresh homemade pasta — that is, well-made homemade pasta — is definitely lighter and more delicate, in part because it's usually made from all-purpose flour rather than semolina.

TIP

Specialty food markets and many supermarkets sell fresh pasta in the refrigerator section, so if you want to try fresh pasta, you don't need to make your own. Fresh pasta is good, but you pay a premium. For purposes of this chapter, we concentrate on dried pasta because it's widely available, lasts longer in the pantry, and is more economical. In any case, the sauce is what really elevates pasta from ordinary to sublime.

Pasta tips and tricks

Cooking pasta isn't difficult, but a few pieces of select pasta knowledge make the job easier and ensure perfectly cooked pasta every time:

>> *Al dente* isn't the name of an Italian orthodontist. It's a sacred term in Italy that means "to the tooth" or "to the bite." In cooking, *al dente* means "slightly firm to the bite." Cook pasta to this point — not until it's soft all the way through. When pasta cooks too long, it absorbs more water and becomes mushy. Here are three ways to test for doneness:

  • The time-tested method for checking pasta for doneness is still the best: Scoop out a strand or two with a fork, take the pasta in hand, jump around and toss the scorching pasta in the air, and then taste it. (You don't really have to toss it in the air, but it makes the process more fun.)

- Some people swear by the old method of throwing a piece of pasta against the wall. If it sticks, it's done. If it slides down onto the floor and the dog eats it, it isn't ready yet.

- Pull the ends of a piece of cooked pasta until it snaps. You can actually hear the snap. Look at the broken end and, if it's cooked correctly, it will have a very small dot of uncooked pasta running through the center.

>> Use a lot of water (5 to 6 quarts per pound of pasta) and an 8-quart pot. Pasta, like a tango dancer, needs room to move. If you don't have a pot large enough to hold that much water and still be three-fourths full or less, splitting pasta into two pots of boiling water is better than overloading one pot. An overloaded pot will splash boiling water all over the stovetop.

WARNING

A large pot of boiling water is one of the most dangerous elements in any kitchen. Use a pot with short handles that can't be tipped easily and set it to boil on a back burner, away from small and curious hands or clumsy kitchen helpers.

>> Salt the water to add flavor and to help the pasta absorb the sauce. As a general guideline, 5 quarts of water take about 2 teaspoons of salt, and 6 quarts of water call for 1 tablespoon of salt.

>> Oil is for salads, not pasta water. You don't need to add oil to the water if you use enough water and stir occasionally to prevent sticking.

REMEMBER

Stir the pasta immediately and thoroughly after adding it to the water, to prevent it from sticking together.

>> Cover the pot to hasten heat recovery. After you add pasta to the water, the water ceases to boil. When the water begins boiling again, remove the lid and finish cooking. Stay with the pot and pay attention so you catch it before it boils over.

>> Save a cup of the cooking liquid when the pasta is done. You can use some of the liquid to add moisture to the sauce. The starch in the water binds the sauce, helping it adhere to the pasta.

>> Do not rinse pasta. When the pasta is al dente (tender but firm), pour it gradually into a colander. *Do not rinse!* You want starch on the pasta to help the sauce adhere to it. The only exceptions are if you're making a cold pasta salad or a casserole such as lasagna where the ingredients are layered.

>> After draining it, you may want to place the pasta in the pan in which the sauce is cooking and stir well. This method coats the pasta better than spooning the sauce on top. Serve from the saucepan.

>> Never combine two types or sizes of pasta in the same pot of water. Fishing out the type that is done first is a real nuisance.

>> Always have the sauce ready and waiting before the pasta is cooked. Cooked pasta needs to be sauced immediately after it's drained, or it becomes stiff and gluey. In many recipes, you work on the sauce as the water for the pasta boils or the pasta cooks. This way, you can ensure that your pasta and sauce will be ready at about the same time.

>> In general, figure about 2 ounces of dried pasta per person. If the pasta is the main course, or you have a lot of big eaters at the table, you may need to figure up to 4 ounces per person. In other words, on average, when served as a side dish, a pound of pasta will feed about eight people (or one teenaged boy). The pasta box or bag tells you how many servings it includes.

>> Don't try to speak broken Italian when you serve your pasta. "Bonissimo! Perfect-amente mia amigas, Mangia, Mangia!" You'll sound silly and irritate your guests.

Name that pasta: Pasta types and cooking times

If your supermarket were to carry all of the pastas produced in the world, they'd spill out onto the parking lot. Twenty years ago, there were maybe 20 types of pasta sold in the United States; today, there are a hundred or more, both fresh and dried.

The size and contours of pasta don't come randomly. Each is well suited to certain kinds of sauces and ingredients. Here's a glossary of the most common varieties:

>> *Macaroni* has distinctive shapes, hollows, and curves. Also known as *tubular pasta,* macaroni is served with thick, rich sauces.

>> *Spaghetti,* which means "little strings," is pasta cut into delicate strands. Strand pasta is best served with thin, flavorful sauces that are rich in oil, which keeps the very thin pasta from sticking together.

>> Sometimes *linguine* and *fettuccine* noodles are identified apart from spaghetti because their strands are flattened. *Flat ribbon pasta* is excellent with rich, creamy sauces such as Alfredo or with simple butter sauces with fresh sautéed vegetables.

>> Filled with meat, cheese, fish, or vegetables, *stuffed pastas* are best coated with simple tomato or light, cream-based sauces. The dough is often flavored and tinted with spinach, tomato, mushrooms, or *saffron,* a fragrant spice. Typically, stuffed pastas are fresh or frozen. Frozen stuffed pasta takes longer to cook than fresh. If buying fresh, just follow the directions on the package.

>> *Asian pasta* is usually in spaghetti-like form. The most common types are soba noodles made from buckwheat flour, udon noodles made from wheat flour, and rice noodles.

Figure 13-1 depicts some common Italian pasta shapes.

Illustration by Elizabeth Kurtzman

FIGURE 13-1:
Various shapes
of pasta.

Topping Your Pasta with the Perfect Sauce

Pasta sauce comes in many forms and flavors, from light to rich, creamy to tangy, and everything in between.

TIP

Before you serve up a sauce, check out these tips for making foolproof sauces:

>> Figure about ½ cup of sauce per person.

>> Stir sauces often to prevent sticking.

>> A tablespoon of olive oil adds flavor and a rich texture to tomato-based sauces.

>> Sauces are a great place to hide puréed vegetables. The kids will never know!

>> For added sweetness, try a grated carrot instead of sugar.

>> To jazz up a canned pasta sauce, add one or two of the following: sliced green or black olives, sautéed chopped shallots, a drained can of tuna, 1 cup of white beans, 4 slices of crumbled bacon, sliced smoked sausage, ½ pound of small cooked shrimp, or ¼ cup freshly grated Parmesan cheese.

Italian pasta sauces are as inventive and varied as pasta shapes. We briefly describe a few of the classic ones, so the next time you dine at an expensive trattoria where the puttanesca is $24 a plate, you'll know what you're paying for.

>> **Alfredo:** A rich sauce of cream, butter, Parmesan cheese, and white or black pepper (which is usually tossed over fettuccine).

>> **Carbonara:** Crisply cooked bacon (usually Italian pancetta) combined with a sauce of eggs, cream, garlic, and Parmesan cheese, served over strand pasta.

>> **Marinara:** The basic Italian tomato sauce, slow cooked and infused with garlic and Italian herbs like oregano and basil. Marinara is easy to adapt to different recipes by adding mushrooms, ground meat, meatballs, and vegetables like onions and sweet peppers.

>> **Pesto:** Fresh basil leaves, pine nuts, garlic, Parmesan cheese, and olive oil blended to a fine paste and tossed with any hot pasta.

>> **Primavera:** A mixture of sautéed spring vegetables (such as sweet red pepper, tomatoes, asparagus, and snow peas) and fresh herbs, which is tossed into pasta.

>> **Puttanesca:** A pungent sauce of anchovies, garlic, tomatoes, capers, and black olives, typically served with strand pasta.

>> **Ragù alla Bolognese:** A long-simmered sauce of meat (usually ground beef, veal, pork, or a combination) and tomatoes, named for the city of Bologna, where it was invented. For a true Bolognese, you brown the meat lightly and then cook it in a small amount of milk and wine before adding tomatoes.

Converted Rice

| PREP TIME: 5 MIN | COOK TIME: ABOUT 25 MIN | YIELD: 4 SERVINGS |

INGREDIENTS

2¼ cups water

1 cup converted rice

1 tablespoon butter

½ teaspoon salt, or to taste

DIRECTIONS

1 Bring the water to a boil in a medium saucepan. Add the rice, butter, and salt. Stir and cover.

2 Reduce the heat to low and simmer for 20 minutes.

3 Remove from the heat and let stand, covered, until all the water is absorbed, about 5 minutes. (If you have excess water, strain it off. If the rice is too dry, add a little boiling water and stir; let sit for 3 to 5 minutes.)

4 Fluff the rice with a fork and check the seasoning, adding more salt (or black pepper) to taste.

PER SERVING: *Calories 195 (From Fat 26); Fat 3g (Saturated 2g); Cholesterol 8mg; Sodium 291mg; Carbohydrate 38g (Dietary Fiber 0g); Protein 4g.*

VARY IT! To boost the flavor of your rice, cook it in chicken, beef, or vegetable broth. You can also add seasoned herbs, a dash of saffron, lemon zest or juice, or any combination of herbs and spices you like to flavor the cooking liquid. If adding fresh herbs, do so in the last 10 minutes of cooking.

Basic Rice Pilaf

PREP TIME: 5 MIN	COOK TIME: ABOUT 25 MIN	YIELD: 4 SERVINGS

INGREDIENTS

1 tablespoon olive oil

½ medium yellow onion, minced

½ red bell pepper, minced

1 teaspoon cumin powder

½ teaspoon salt, or to taste

1 cup converted rice

2¼ cups chicken broth

½ cup chopped almonds (optional)

¼ cup currants or raisins (optional)

Black pepper

DIRECTIONS

1 In a medium saucepan, heat the olive oil over medium-high heat. Add the onion, bell pepper, cumin powder, and salt. Sauté until the onion begins to soften, about 5 minutes.

2 Add the rice and cook, stirring until the rice is coated, about 3 minutes.

3 Pour the chicken broth into the sauté pan and bring to a boil. Stir and cover.

4 Reduce the heat to low and simmer for 20 minutes.

5 Remove from the heat and let stand, covered, until all the chicken broth is absorbed, about 5 minutes. (If the rice is too dry, add a little boiling water and stir; let sit for 3 to 5 minutes.)

6 Fluff the rice with a fork. Stir in the almonds, currants, or raisins (if desired). Add black pepper to taste.

PER SERVING: Calories 311 (From Fat 114); Fat 13g (Saturated 2g); Cholesterol 3mg; Sodium 854mg; Carbohydrate 43g (Dietary Fiber 2g); Protein 8g.

GO-WITH: This slightly sweet, starchy side dish is delicious with Osso Buco (see Chapter 18) or Roasted Pork Ribs with Country Barbecue Sauce (see Chapter 8).

Risotto

PREP TIME: ABOUT 15 MIN | COOK TIME: ABOUT 35 MIN | YIELD: 4 SERVINGS

INGREDIENTS

1 teaspoon olive oil

3 strips lean bacon, cut into 1-inch pieces

½ cup chopped shallots or yellow onions

About 5 cups chicken or vegetable stock

1½ cups Arborio rice

Salt and black pepper to taste

DIRECTIONS

1 Place the olive oil and bacon in a large skillet or sauté pan and cook over medium heat, stirring occasionally until the bacon is brown, about 2 to 3 minutes.

2 Add the chopped shallots (or onions) and lower the heat to medium-low. Cook the shallots until golden but not browned, stirring occasionally.

3 While the shallots are cooking, bring the stock to a boil in a small, covered saucepan. Reduce the heat to a simmer.

4 When the shallots are golden, add the rice to the skillet. Raise the heat to medium and cook 1 to 2 minutes, stirring constantly, until the rice is well coated with the oil.

5 Add ½ cup hot stock to the rice and stir it in with a wooden spoon. When most of the liquid is absorbed, add another ½ cup stock to the rice, stirring constantly. Loosen the rice from the bottom and sides of the pan to keep it from sticking.

6 Continue cooking for 25 to 30 minutes, stirring and adding the remaining stock in increments after most of the broth is absorbed.

7 Remove from the heat. Taste for seasoning and add salt and black pepper. Serve immediately.

PER SERVING: *Calories 406 (From Fat 92); Fat 10g (Saturated 3g); Cholesterol 10mg; Sodium 1,477mg; Carbohydrate 68g (Dietary Fiber 1g); Protein 12g.*

TIP: When you add the liquid in this recipe, the rice should be surrounded by liquid but never swim in the stock.

VARY IT! A few minutes before the risotto is done, try stirring in 1 cup fresh or frozen peas or ½ cup chopped parsley. Or add chopped fresh kale, spinach leaves, sliced mushrooms, or broccoli rabe to the pan after browning the shallots. Small shrimp or bits of crab can make risotto into a special main course.

Tabbouleh Salad

PREP TIME: 5 MIN PLUS ABSORPTION AND CHILL TIME | YIELD: 4 SERVINGS

INGREDIENTS

½ cup bulgur wheat

1 cup boiling water

2 tomatoes, coarsely chopped

3 scallions, chopped, including green parts

½ medium cucumber, peeled and chopped

1 cup fresh parsley or cilantro leaves, or a combination of both, minced

½ teaspoon dried mint leaves or 1 tablespoon minced fresh mint leaves

¼ cup lemon juice (fresh or bottled)

¼ cup extra-virgin olive oil

2 cloves garlic, minced

½ teaspoon salt

Few dashes black pepper

DIRECTIONS

1 Put the bulgur wheat in a large bowl. Add the boiling water. Let sit until all the water is absorbed, about 25 minutes.

2 Fluff the bulgur with a fork. Stir in the tomatoes, scallions, cucumber, parsley, mint, lemon juice, olive oil, garlic, salt, and black pepper.

3 Cover and chill for at least 30 minutes. Serve cold or at room temperature.

PER SERVING: *Calories 213 (From Fat 128); Fat 14g (Saturated 2g); Cholesterol 0mg; Sodium 312mg; Carbohydrate 21g (Dietary Fiber 5g); Protein 4g.*

TIP: If possible, make this salad the night before you eat it so the flavors have time to meld.

Farro Salad

PREP TIME: ABOUT 15 MIN | COOK TIME: ABOUT 15 MIN | YIELD: 4-6 SERVINGS

INGREDIENTS

1 cup semi-pearled farro, rinsed and drained

2 teaspoons salt, plus more to taste

10 cherry tomatoes, halved

1 small cucumber, peeled, seeded and cut into ½-inch pieces (about 1 cup)

1 cup canned chickpeas, rinsed and drained

½ cup red onion, diced

½ cup chopped fresh flat-leaf parsley

2 teaspoons minced, seeded jalapeño pepper

¼ cup plus 1 to 2 tablespoons extra-virgin olive oil

Juice of 1 lemon (about 2 tablespoons)

1 large clove garlic, minced

Black pepper to taste

DIRECTIONS

1 Bring 4 to 5 cups of water to boil in a medium pot or saucepan. Stir in the farro and salt. Cover the pan, bring to a boil, and then reduce the heat and simmer, partially covered, about 15 minutes or until just tender. (You want the farro to have a little bite with a softened center, so be careful not to overcook it.) Drain and set the farro aside to cool.

2 Place the tomatoes, cucumber, chickpeas, red onion, parsley, and jalapeño pepper in a large mixing or salad bowl.

3 Combine ¼ cup of the olive oil and the lemon juice in a small mixing bowl or glass measuring cup; whisk to mix well. Stir the garlic into the dressing.

4 Stir the cooled farro into the tomato-cucumber mixture. Add the lemon dressing and toss to combine. Add a little more olive oil, 1 tablespoon at a time, if the salad appears dry. Adjust seasoning with salt and black pepper to taste.

PER SERVING: *Calories 328 (From Fat 144); Fat 16g (Saturated 2g); Cholesterol 0mg; Sodium 1,094mg; Carbohydrate 37g (Dietary Fiber 5g); Protein 9g.*

VARY IT! Substitute either corn kernels or shelled edamame for the canned chickpeas.

Polenta with Herbs

PREP TIME: 5 MIN	COOK TIME: 3–5 MIN	YIELD: 4 SERVINGS

INGREDIENTS

3¼ cups chicken stock or water

1 cup precooked polenta

⅓ cup freshly grated Parmesan cheese (optional)

1 tablespoon butter

1 tablespoon fresh, chopped tarragon, marjoram, or thyme, or 1 teaspoon dried

Salt and black pepper

DIRECTIONS

1 In a heavy, deep pot, bring the stock or water to a boil.

2 Slowly stir in the polenta. Reduce the heat to low and continue stirring until the mixture thickens to a porridge consistency, about 3 to 5 minutes.

3 Stir in the cheese (if desired) and then the butter, tarragon (or marjoram or thyme), and salt and black pepper to taste. Serve hot.

PER SERVING: *Calories 219 (From Fat 55); Fat 6g (Saturated 3g); Cholesterol 12mg; Sodium 958mg; Carbohydrate 36g (Dietary Fiber 4g); Protein 5g.*

TIP: Continuous stirring helps prevent polenta from getting lumpy. If lumps form, stir with a wire whisk to break them up. Also, polenta hardens very quickly after it's cooked, so be sure to bring it to the table steaming.

VARY IT! Add sautéed onion and garlic along with the butter and herbs. You can also blend in cooked carrots, celery, turnips, broccoli rabe, or even hot Italian sausages. After the polenta is cooked, spread it over a greased baking pan, brush it with melted butter or olive oil (flavored, if you like), and place it under a broiler to brown. Then cut it into squares and serve like bread.

Quinoa Pilaf

PREP TIME: 5 MIN	COOK TIME: ABOUT 30 MIN	YIELD: 4 SERVINGS

INGREDIENTS

1 cup quinoa

1 tablespoon olive oil

½ medium yellow onion, minced

1 clove garlic, minced

2 cups vegetable broth

1 bay leaf

Juice and grated rind from 1 fresh lemon

Salt and black pepper

DIRECTIONS

1 Rinse the quinoa with cold water in a fine-mesh strainer.

2 In a medium saucepan, heat the olive oil over medium-high heat. Add the onion. Sauté until the onion begins to soften, about 5 minutes. Add the garlic and sauté for 1 minute longer.

3 Add the quinoa, stir until it's coated with the oil mixture, and cook about 2 minutes.

4 Pour the vegetable broth into the saucepan. Add the bay leaf, lemon juice, and grated lemon rind. Bring to a boil. Stir once and cover the pan.

5 Reduce the heat to low and simmer for 15 to 20 minutes, or until all the liquid is absorbed.

6 Remove from the heat and let stand, covered, until all the vegetable broth is absorbed, about 5 minutes. Remove and discard bay leaf. Season with salt and black pepper. Serve warm.

PER SERVING: *Calories 208 (From Fat 57); Fat 6g (Saturated 1g); Cholesterol 0mg; Sodium 656mg; Carbohydrate 33g (Dietary Fiber 3g); Protein 7g.*

Spaghetti with Quick Fresh Tomato Sauce

PREP TIME: ABOUT 15 MIN	COOK TIME: ABOUT 10 MIN	YIELD: 4 SERVINGS

INGREDIENTS

5 to 6 ripe plum tomatoes, about 1½ pounds

Salt and black pepper

¾ pound spaghetti (or other pasta)

3 tablespoons olive oil

2 teaspoons peeled and minced garlic (about 2 large cloves), or 1 teaspoon garlic powder

2 tablespoons coarsely chopped fresh basil leaves, or 2 teaspoons dried

3 tablespoons grated Parmesan cheese

DIRECTIONS

1 Core, peel, and chop the tomatoes.

2 Bring 4 to 5 quarts lightly salted water to a boil over high heat in a large, covered pot. Add the spaghetti, stir thoroughly with a long fork to separate the strands, and cook, uncovered, for about 8 minutes (just until al dente).

3 While the spaghetti cooks, heat the oil in a saucepan or skillet over medium heat. Add the garlic. Cook and stir about 30 seconds with a wooden spoon.

4 Add the cubed tomatoes to the saucepan or skillet, and add salt and black pepper to taste. Cook, crushing the tomatoes with a fork and stirring often, for about 3 minutes.

5 When the pasta is ready, drain it and put the pasta in a serving bowl or on individual plates. Ladle the sauce over it. Garnish with basil and Parmesan. Serve immediately.

PER SERVING: *Calories 418 (From Fat 116); Fat 13g (Saturated 2g); Cholesterol 3mg; Sodium 430mg; Carbohydrate 63g (Dietary Fiber 5g); Protein 12g.*

VARY IT! You can omit the Parmesan cheese and add a small can of drained, flaked tuna. Or keep the cheese and toss in some sliced black olives and cooked artichoke hearts. A few sautéed shrimp and asparagus spears, or even sautéed chicken livers, also work with this classic sauce.

Penne with Parmesan Cheese and Basil

| PREP TIME: ABOUT 5 MIN | COOK TIME: ABOUT 12 MIN | YIELD: 4 SERVINGS |

INGREDIENTS

Salt

½ pound penne pasta

2 tablespoons olive oil

1 tablespoon butter

¼ cup grated Parmesan or Romano cheese

¼ cup chopped fresh basil or Italian parsley

⅛ teaspoon freshly grated or ground nutmeg

Black pepper to taste

DIRECTIONS

1 Bring 3 to 4 quarts lightly salted water to a boil in a large, covered pot over high heat. Add the penne, stir thoroughly to separate the macaroni, and return to a boil. Cook, uncovered, for about 10 minutes or until the pasta is al dente.

2 Just before the penne is done, carefully scoop out ¼ cup of the cooking liquid.

3 When the penne is ready, drain it and return it to the pot. Add the olive oil and butter and toss to coat. Add the cheese, basil, nutmeg, black pepper to taste, and the reserved cooking liquid.

4 Toss together over medium–high heat for 30 seconds. If necessary, add salt to taste. Serve immediately.

PER SERVING: *Calories 315 (From Fat 107); Fat 12g (Saturated 4g); Cholesterol 12mg; Sodium 156mg; Carbohydrate 43g (Dietary Fiber 2g); Protein 10g.*

VARY IT! To transform this recipe into Pasta Primavera, add 1 to 2 cups fresh, lightly steamed summer vegetables to the pasta in Step 3, before adding the olive oil and butter. Some good choices are broccoli and/or cauliflower florets, sliced carrots, sliced summer squash, and sliced zucchini. One-half cup each marinated artichoke hearts and pitted olives would also be good.

Pasta with Escarole, Beans, and Sausage

PREP TIME: 20 MIN	COOK TIME: ABOUT 20 MIN	YIELD: 4 SERVINGS

INGREDIENTS

Salt

12 ounces multi-grain, gluten-free, or semolina flour penne or gemelli pasta

2 tablespoons olive oil

12 ounces sweet Italian sausage, cut into 1-inch pieces

1 medium onion, chopped (about 1½ cups)

10 ounces escarole or Swiss chard (tough stems removed) leaves cut into 2-inch pieces

⅔ cup chicken broth or dry white wine

One 15-ounce can cannelloni beans, rinsed and drained

½ teaspoon crushed red pepper, or to taste

½ cup grated Pecorino Romano or Parmesan cheese for serving

DIRECTIONS

1 Fill a large pasta pot with 4 to 5 quarts of water; cover and bring it to a boil over high heat. Add salt to taste. Add the pasta to the water and boil according to package directions until al dente or just tender. Remove and reserve about ½ cup of the cooking water. Drain the pasta and return it to the pot.

2 While waiting for the pasta to cook, heat the oil in a large nonstick skillet over medium heat. Add the sausage and sauté until nearly cooked with just a trace of pink, about 8 minutes, turning the pieces over to brown on all sides. Using a slotted spoon, transfer the sausage to a bowl, leaving any fat and drippings from cooking the sausage in the skillet.

3 Add the onion to the skillet and cook over medium heat about 5 minutes or until softened and lightly browned, stirring occasionally. Add the escarole and chicken broth, stir to combine; cover and cook until the escarole is wilted, about 2 to 3 minutes. Add the beans, reserved sausage, including any juices that accumulated in the bowl, and the crushed red pepper. Stir to combine; partially cover and cook about 3 minutes to heat through and blend flavors. Season with salt to taste.

4 Add the sausage-bean mixture to the cooked pasta; stir well to combine, add a little of the reserved pasta cooking water to moisten, if necessary. Serve immediately with the cheese on the side.

PER SERVING: *Calories 839 (From Fat 189); Fat 21g (Saturated 5g); Cholesterol 38mg; Sodium 1,124mg; Carbohydrate 126g (Dietary Fiber 17g); Protein 38g.*

TIP: Ideally, you want to prepare the sauce and pasta so they finish cooking at about the same time. Pasta that sits around after it's drained without being sauced gets dreadfully sticky. If you prefer, you can make the sauce first, set it aside covered, and then make the pasta, assuring that the sauce will be ready when the pasta is drained.

Indian Rice with Ginger, Walnuts,and Raisins

PREP TIME: ABOUT 15 MIN	COOK TIME: ABOUT 25 MIN	YIELD: 4 SERVINGS

INGREDIENTS

1¾ cups homemade or canned chicken or vegetable stock

2 tablespoons butter

¼ cup finely chopped yellow onion

1 cup chopped walnuts

1 teaspoon grated fresh ginger root

½ teaspoon cinnamon

¼ teaspoon red pepper flakes, or to taste

1 cup raw converted rice

2 tablespoons brandy or orange juice

½ cup raisins

3 tablespoons finely chopped cilantro or parsley

Salt (optional)

DIRECTIONS

1 Heat the stock to just below boiling. Keep it hot.

2 Melt the butter in a saucepan over medium heat. Add the onion and cook, stirring often, until the onion is wilted, about 2 to 3 minutes.

3 Add the walnuts, ginger root, cinnamon, and pepper flakes to the onion. Cook, stirring constantly, for about 30 seconds.

4 Stir the rice into the onion mixture, coating the grains in the melted butter, and cook for 1 more minute, stirring constantly.

5 Carefully add the hot stock to the rice mixture. Cover and simmer over low heat for 20 minutes, or until the rice is tender and all the liquid is absorbed.

6 While the rice is cooking, pour the brandy or orange juice over the raisins and let them soak.

7 When the rice is done, stir in the raisins, any remaining brandy or orange juice, and cilantro or parsley. Add salt if necessary, and serve.

PER SERVING: *Calories 492 (From Fat 229); Fat 26g (Saturated 5g); Cholesterol 15mg; Sodium 279mg; Carbohydrate 60g (Dietary Fiber 4g); Protein 11g.*

Pasta and Bean Soup

PREP TIME: 10 MIN	COOK TIME: 45 MIN	YIELD: 8 SERVINGS

INGREDIENTS

¼ cup olive oil

1 medium yellow onion, peeled and chopped

2 carrots, peeled and diced

1 stalk celery, diced

1 large clove garlic, peeled and chopped

One 14.5-ounce can diced tomatoes

7 to 8 cups chicken broth

1 tablespoon chopped fresh basil, or 1 teaspoon dried

1 teaspoon chopped fresh thyme, or ½ teaspoon dried

One 15-ounce can cannellini or red kidney beans, rinsed and drained

1 bay leaf

1 cup small dried pasta, such as elbow macaroni

Salt and black pepper

Grated Parmesan cheese for garnish

DIRECTIONS

1 In a large, heavy-bottomed soup pot or saucepan, heat the oil over medium heat. Add the onion and cook, stirring occasionally, until wilted, about 5 minutes. Stir in the carrots, celery, and garlic and cook over medium-high heat another 5 minutes, or until the vegetables are softened, stirring often.

2 Add the tomatoes with their juice, 7 cups of the broth, the basil, and thyme. Cover the pot, bring to a boil, and then reduce the heat and simmer gently for 20 minutes.

3 Carefully ladle 1½ to 2 cups of the soup into a blender container; pulse for just a few seconds. Stir the mixture back into the soup.

4 Add the beans and the bay leaf; cover the pot and simmer another 5 minutes.

5 Add the pasta and cook, partially covered, until al dente — about 10 minutes; stir occasionally.

6 If too much of the liquid evaporates and the soup seems too thick, add enough remaining broth to thin to a desired consistency.

7 Remove the bay leaf. Adjust seasoning with salt and black pepper to taste. Ladle the soup into bowls; sprinkle each with the grated cheese.

PER SERVING: *Calories 195 (From Fat 73); Fat 8g (Saturated 1g); Cholesterol 0mg; Sodium 515mg; Carbohydrate 23g (Dietary Fiber 4g); Protein 23g.*

Chapter **14**

Making Sensational Sauces: Fear No More

Probably no aspect of cooking sends a kitchen novice running for a restaurant like sauce making. All the reducing and whisking and straining can seem as mysterious as DNA testing. In fact, sauce making is within the reach of the cooking rookie. Some sauces require nothing more than cooking several ingredients in a pan (or not cooking them at all) and tossing them in the blender.

The image of sauces as loaded with cream and butter is somewhat outdated. Many sauces served in restaurants today are Mediterranean-, Californian-, and Asian-inspired. They're made with olive oil, sesame oil, flavored vinegars, vegetable purées, aromatic herbs, wine, yogurt, and other healthy ingredients.

In this chapter, we show you how to master a variety of savory sauces as well as a few dessert sauces, which can be a sweet fruit purée spiked with a flavored liqueur, a simple custard, or a luscious chocolate creation.

Starting with the ABCs of Sauces

Think of a sauce as a primary liquid (chicken stock, beef stock, fish stock, vegetable stock, or wine) flavored with ingredients (sautéed shallots, garlic, tomatoes, and so on) and seasoned with salt and black pepper and herbs of choice.

Before it's served, a sauce is often reduced. *Reduced* simply means that the sauce is cooked and evaporated on the stove so it thickens and intensifies in flavor. Sometimes, you strain a sauce through a sieve to eliminate all the solids, such as parsley sprigs or chunks of onion. Other times, you purée everything in a blender.

The best way to understand sauces is to become familiar with their foundations:

>> *Brown sauces* are based on dark stocks like lamb or beef.

>> *White sauces* usually contain milk or cream.

>> *White butter sauces* are based on a reduction of butter, vinegar, and shallots.

>> *Vegetable sauces* are made from cooked puréed vegetables, such as tomatoes.

>> *Vinaigrettes* are made up of oil, vinegar, mustard, and seasonings.

>> *Hollandaise* and its variations, like béarnaise sauce, are based on cooked egg yolks and butter.

>> *Mayonnaise* is based on uncooked or slightly cooked egg yolks and oil.

>> *Dessert sauces* are typically made with fruits or chocolate with sugar; they may also have a caramel, butterscotch, or nut base.

RECIPE ALERT

The French call browned butter *hazelnut butter* because the browning causes it to taste pleasantly nutty. It's simple to make and is perfect as a finishing sauce for sautéed white fish, scallops, shrimp, and roasted and steamed vegetables, such as asparagus, cauliflower, carrots, or grilled corn on the cob. You can try your hand at browned butter by making the Browned Butter, Lemon, and Herb Sauce recipe later in this chapter.

CAJUN ROUX: GAUR-RON-TEED DELICIOUS

If you love the Cajun gumbos and jambalayas, you may want to try your hand at making a Cajun-style roux. A *roux* is little more than fat (vegetable oil, shortening, or animal fat) in a hot pan stirred with flour until it forms a thick, browned toasty paste. To this, you add chopped onions, bell peppers, celery, seasonings, and then some form of liquid, like chicken stock. A roux is the foundation upon which all kinds of Louisiana dishes are built.

Deglazing for Delicious Pan Sauces

Today's "dark" sauces are typically made by using the deglazing technique. When you sauté meat or vegetables in a hot pan, it leaves behind little particles that stick to the surface. These bits, called *fond*, are packed with flavor, and you want to incorporate them into any sauce you make by adding liquid and scraping up the fond into the sauce.

For example, when you remove a steak from the pan, you may deglaze with red wine (you generally deglaze with wine or stock of some sort). As the wine (or stock) sizzles in the pan, you scrape the pan's bottom (preferably with a wooden spatula or spoon) to release those tasty little particles. That process is called deglazing. After you do that, you finish the sauce with seasonings of your choice and serve. Sometimes you swirl in a little butter at the end to create a smooth finish. (Flip to Chapter 6 for more on deglazing as it relates to sautéing. Chapter 6 also includes an illustration that shows you how to make a good pan sauce.)

RECIPE ALERT

If you don't have a pan filled with fond, you can still make the sauce in a clean pan. Simply begin by adding 2 to 3 teaspoons of oil to the pan, and then continue with the recipe. It won't be as good, but it'll do just fine. See the Mushroom and Madeira Pan Sauce recipe later in this chapter for a deliciously simple pan sauce.

TIP

Food doesn't cling to nonstick cookware (or at least not much), so it's handy to have a stainless steel sauté pan when you want to deglaze. Cast iron also works well.

COOKING WITH WINE

Although cooking with reduced stocks is delicious, adding wine to pan sauces adds a whole new dimension. Deglazing with white wines adds a distinctive grassy or buttery sensation, while red wine is more concentrated. Red wine sauces go particularly well with red meat. White wine sauce is suitable for shellfish and fish.

Some chefs like to sweeten sauces with *fortified wines* — wines that have alcohol added during fermentation. The result is a wine roughly 17 to 20 percent alcohol (versus around 11 percent for regular wine). The most common fortified wines are Madeira, Sherry, Port, and Marsala. All are sweet and potent, so you'll have to experiment. These wines are often added to stews and braised meats. (See Mushroom and Madeira Pan Sauce for a delicious recipe using a fortified wine.)

Will you get tipsy eating dishes that include alcohol? It's unlikely. About half of the alcohol cooks off, leaving hardly enough to notice.

DRIED VERSUS FRESH HERBS

Unless you live in the southern or western regions of the United States — areas where fresh herbs are available year-round — you may need to substitute dried herbs in the off-season. Keep in mind that dried herbs are twice as concentrated as fresh. So if a recipe calls for 1 tablespoon of fresh thyme, add ½ tablespoon and taste. See Chapter 3 for much more information about using herbs and spices.

Whirling Light Blender Sauces in Minutes

For cooks in a hurry, the blender is an invaluable tool. You can make blender sauces literally in minutes. And they can be healthful, too, especially if bound with vegetables, low-fat cheeses (like ricotta), yogurt, and the like.

Although food processors are unsurpassed for chopping, slicing, and grating, blenders have an edge when it comes to liquefying and sauce making. Their blades rotate faster, *binding* (or pulling together) liquids better. The two-level slicing blade on a food processor cuts through liquids instead of blending them, and its wide, flat work bowl is too large for mixing small quantities of sauce.

Certain fruit sauces for desserts also work better in a blender, whether it's a purée of raspberries spiked with framboise (French raspberry brandy) or of mango with lime and rum.

RECIPE ALERT

Here are some ideas for everyday blender sauces:

>> **Blender Dill Sauce:** Place about ½ cup chopped dill and an equal amount of finely chopped scallions in a blender. Add ½ cup vegetable oil and blend thoroughly. In a mixing bowl, combine ½ cup sour cream and 1 tablespoon Dijon mustard. Whisk. Add 2 teaspoons red wine vinegar. Mix the blender ingredients into the bowl and season to taste. The recipe makes about 1½ cups and is good with just about any cold summer entrée.

   Variation: Use basil or fresh coriander in place of the dill.

>> **Blender Salsa Verde:** Combine in a blender a finely chopped medium bunch of scallions, a clove of garlic, ½ small white onion coarsely chopped, 2 stalks celery coarsely chopped, and a medium peeled and chopped cucumber (seeded). Add 3 tablespoons olive oil, 3 tablespoons Dijon mustard, and 2 tablespoons red wine vinegar. Blend until smooth. Taste for seasonings. The recipe yields 1½ cups and is superb with grilled or broiled meat and fish.

   Variation: For a thicker sauce, add one boiled potato.

» **Sour Cream and Watercress Sauce:** Place 1 cup sour cream and 4 tablespoons watercress in a blender and mix at slow speed until the sour cream liquefies and begins to incorporate the watercress. Turn the blender on high for several seconds. Add just enough salt to bring out the flavor of the watercress. The recipe makes about 1 cup. This sauce is terrific with smoked fish, cold poultry and meats, and cold shellfish.

Variations: Add grated fresh horseradish or well-drained store-bought horseradish. You can also add fresh dill, basil, or thyme.

» **Mint Mango Sauce:** Scoop about 3 cups of flesh from one or two ripe mangoes and combine in a blender with 6 tablespoons water and 4 tablespoons sugar (more if the mango isn't very sweet). Blend until slightly smooth. Stir in 2 to 3 tablespoons chopped mint. The recipe yields about 2 cups and is wonderful with desserts.

Variation: Substitute papaya for mango.

RECIPE ALERT

Traditional pesto with fresh basil and pine nuts (see the Fresh Summer Pesto Sauce recipe later in this chapter) makes a quick sauce and is easily assembled in the blender. You can make pesto blender sauces using other herbs and nuts, too. Try the Nutty Sage Pesto recipe (also in this chapter), where fresh sage and almonds, blended with olive oil and garlic, take center stage.

You can transform simple poached fish into something special by combining some of the poaching liquid with wine, fresh watercress, seasonings, and just a dab of cream or ricotta cheese in a blender. You can create all kinds of great vinaigrette-based sauces by using fresh herbs of your choice.

Sweetening Things Up with Delectable Dessert Sauces

Dessert sauces come in two basic types: cream based and fruit based. Cream-based recipes usually require cooking, but you can often make the fruit sauces in a blender.

RECIPE ALERT

Later in the chapter, you find recipes for the following popular dessert sauces and ways to modify them:

» Our smooth and creamy Vanilla Custard Sauce dresses up ice cream, fresh strawberries, pound cake, poached pears, soufflés, cold mousses, and more. Keep in mind that when you're making this sauce, as well as custards, you *scald* milk primarily to shorten the cooking time. To scald milk, heat it in a saucepan over a medium-low setting until it foams. Don't bring it to a boil.

Also, be careful not to cook the vanilla sauce too long, to prevent scorching it. Maintain a low to medium-low heat setting to prevent the sauce from *curdling* — separating into coagulated solids (curds) and liquids (whey). A curdled sauce isn't a pretty sight. If the sauce curdles, whisk it quickly or whirl it in a blender container to cool it rapidly.

TIP

Many recipes for ice cream, custards, puddings, cakes, cookies, and chocolate desserts are flavored with vanilla. You can use either the whole vanilla bean or pure vanilla extract. Although the whole beans are somewhat preferable because they have much more of an intense flavor than the extract, they're also more expensive and less convenient. Never purchase "artificial" or "imitation" extracts.

>> Our Cracklin' Hot Fudge Sauce is a twist on regular chocolate sauce and is ideal for ice cream. Because it has butter in it, the sauce turns hard when poured over ice cream and forms a thin, cracklin' crust. You can buy this kind of sauce in the grocery store, but it's laden with hydrogenated fat. Our version, while hardly diet food, is free from trans fats.

One great thing about this recipe is that you can prepare it up to a week ahead of time and keep it covered and refrigerated. Rewarm it in a double boiler or in the microwave.

>> You have no excuse for serving chemical-tasting, aerosol whipped cream. The real thing is so easy and so good that everyone should know how to make it. We show you how in our Whipped Cream recipe. Spoon sweetened, flavored whipped cream over pies, pudding, cakes, mousses, poached fruit, your cat's nose — anything!

TIP

When making a recipe that requires homemade whipped cream, be careful not to overbeat it or it can turn to butter. Be sure to start with very cold cream, cold beaters, and a cold bowl (cold hands can't hurt, either). Whether using a hand-held beater or a stand-up kitchen mixer, start beating slowly, and gradually increase the speed. Don't strive for stiff cream but rather soft, floppy peaks. Always refrigerate whipped cream, covered, unless you're serving it right away.

>> Quick sauces made with fresh, seasonal fruit couldn't be easier. The technique we illustrate in our Fresh Strawberry Sauce recipe also works for blueberries and raspberries. (When making raspberry sauces, strain the sauce through a fine sieve before serving to remove the seeds.) Fresh strawberry sauce is wonderful as a topping for ice cream, custards, and puddings.

Béchamel

INGREDIENTS

1¼ cups milk

2 tablespoons butter

2 tablespoons flour

¼ teaspoon ground nutmeg, or to taste

Salt and black pepper

DIRECTIONS

1 Heat the milk over medium heat in a small saucepan until almost boiling. Remove from the heat.

2 Meanwhile, in a medium saucepan, melt the butter over medium heat (don't let it darken or burn). Add the flour and whisk constantly for 2 minutes. The mixture should reach a thick paste consistency.

3 Gradually add the hot milk while continuing to whisk the mixture vigorously. When the sauce is blended smooth, reduce heat and simmer for 3 to 4 minutes, whisking frequently. The sauce should be very thick.

4 Remove from heat, add the nutmeg and the salt and black pepper to taste, and whisk well.

PER SERVING: *Calories 56 (From Fat 37); Fat 4g (Saturated 3g); Cholesterol 13mg; Sodium 92mg; Carbohydrate 3g (Dietary Fiber 0g); Protein 2g.*

TIP: If the butter burns or even gets brown, you should probably start over, or your white sauce will have a brown tint.

VARY IT! Whip up some creamed spinach by adding béchamel to cooked spinach. Or do the same thing with other cooked vegetables, such as corn, peas, or sliced carrots.

Browned Butter, Lemon, and Herb Sauce

PREP TIME: 5 MINUTES	COOK TIME: ABOUT 5 MIN	YIELD: 2–4 SERVINGS

INGREDIENTS

6 tablespoons unsalted butter, cut into ½-inch pieces

1 large clove garlic, minced

2 to 3 teaspoons minced fresh thyme, parsley, or sage, according to taste

2 teaspoons fresh lemon juice

Salt and black pepper

DIRECTIONS

1 Place the butter in a small saucepan or skillet with a light interior (not a nonstick) over medium–high heat and, holding the pan by the handle, swirl the butter in the pan constantly over the heat until it turns a dark hazelnut color, 2 to 3 minutes. (Watch carefully! The butter can quickly turn from brown to burned.)

2 Remove from the heat; add the garlic and thyme or sage, and let set about 30 seconds or just until the garlic is fragrant.

3 Stir in the lemon juice; taste and adjust seasoning with salt and black pepper. Cover to keep warm.

PER SERVING: *Calories 206 (From Fat 206); Fat 23g (Saturated 15g); Cholesterol 61mg; Sodium 198mg; Carbohydrate 0g (Dietary Fiber 0g); Protein 0g.*

TIP: For best results, use a heavy-bottom skillet with a light-colored interior. If you use a dark nonstick pan, you won't be able to gauge when the butter is properly browned, and it may burn.

VARY IT! This recipe makes enough butter for 2 to 3 servings of fish and 3 to 4 servings of vegetables. If you need more sauce, simply increase the amount of butter, use the same browning technique, and add the garlic, lemon juice, and herbs according to taste. For a note of heat, add hot sauce or cayenne pepper to taste. For more saltiness, add 1 to 2 tablespoons of drained capers.

Mushroom and Madeira Pan Sauce

PREP TIME: ABOUT 15 MIN	COOK TIME: ABOUT 10 MIN	YIELD: 4 SERVINGS

INGREDIENTS

1 tablespoon extra-virgin olive oil

10 ounces cremini or baby portobello mushrooms, stems trimmed, wiped clean, and sliced about ¼ inch thick

½ cup chicken stock

1 large ripe plum tomato, seeded and chopped

2 medium cloves garlic, thinly sliced

1½ teaspoons fresh minced sage or thyme

⅔ cup Madeira or Marsala

1½ tablespoons butter

Salt and black pepper to taste

⅓ cup chopped parsley (optional)

DIRECTIONS

1 Heat the olive oil in the skillet over medium heat. Add the mushrooms and ¼ cup of the chicken stock. Increase the heat to medium-high and cook the mushrooms until most of the liquid in the pan evaporates, about 5 minutes.

2 Add the tomato, garlic, 1 teaspoon of the sage or thyme, and cook, stirring often, until the tomato softens, about 1 minute.

3 Add the Madeira or Marsala and the remaining ¼ cup chicken stock. Increase the heat to high and bring the sauce to a simmer. Adjust the heat and simmer 3 to 5 minutes to reduce and concentrate slightly.

4 Remove from the heat and whisk in the butter and remaining sage or thyme. Taste and season with salt and black pepper. Sprinkle with parsley (if desired).

PER SERVING: *Calories 107 (From Fat 72); Fat 8g (Saturated 3g); Cholesterol 12mg; Sodium 195mg; Carbohydrate 6g (Dietary Fiber 1g); Protein 3g.*

TIP: You can make this pan sauce in a clean pan, but it is even better when you start with a pan filled with browned bits left in the bottom of the pan from sautéing pieces of poultry, pork, or fish.

Red Pepper Purée

PREP TIME: 10 MIN | COOK TIME: ABOUT 20 MIN | YIELD: 6 SERVINGS

INGREDIENTS

1 tablespoon olive oil

3 medium red bell peppers, cored, seeded, and chopped

¼ cup chopped red onion

2 garlic cloves, peeled and minced or put through a garlic press

1 teaspoon paprika

1 tablespoon fresh chopped cilantro, or 1 teaspoon dried

Juice of ½ lemon

½ teaspoon salt

Few dashes black pepper

DIRECTIONS

1 Heat the olive oil in a skillet over medium–high heat until you begin to smell the oil, about 3 minutes.

2 Add the peppers, onion, and garlic. Sauté until they're soft but not browned, about 15 minutes.

3 Put the vegetables in a food processor with the paprika, cilantro, and lemon juice. Process until smooth, about 15 seconds.

4 Stir in the salt and black pepper, and serve warm.

PER SERVING: Calories 42 (From Fat 22); Fat 2g (Saturated 0g); Cholesterol 0mg; Sodium 196mg; Carbohydrate 5g (Dietary Fiber 1g); Protein 1g.

TIP: If you make this dish in advance, you can warm it up for 15 to 30 seconds in the microwave or for about 5 minutes in a saucepan over low heat on the stove.

VARY IT! Try mixing this purée with a little cream or half-and-half and serve over pasta.

GO-WITH: This purée brightens up any mild meat or fish, or try it on baked potatoes or steamed asparagus.

Fresh Summer Pesto Sauce

INGREDIENTS

2 cups lightly packed fresh basil leaves, stems removed, about 2 ounces

½ cup extra-virgin olive oil

3 tablespoons pine nuts or walnuts

3 large cloves garlic, coarsely chopped

Salt and black pepper

½ cup grated Parmesan cheese

1 tablespoon hot water

DIRECTIONS

1 Rinse and pat dry the trimmed basil leaves.

2 Put the basil leaves in the container of a food processor or blender. Add the oil, pine nuts or walnuts, garlic, and salt and black pepper to taste.

3 Blend mixture to a fine texture but not a smooth purée, stopping the motor once to scrape down the sides of the container and force the ingredients down to the blades.

4 Add the Parmesan cheese and water and blend just a few seconds more. Chill until served.

PER SERVING: *Calories 158 (From Fat 146); Fat 16g (Saturated 3g); Cholesterol 3mg; Sodium 139mg; Carbohydrate 1g (Dietary Fiber 1g); Protein 3g.*

Nutty Sage Pesto

PREP TIME: ABOUT 10 MIN	COOK TIME: ABOUT 1 MIN	YIELD: 4 SERVINGS

INGREDIENTS

¼ cup extra-virgin olive oil, plus more if needed

¼ cup loosely packed chopped fresh sage

2 large cloves garlic, peeled and smashed

⅓ cup almonds or hazelnuts, toasted

DIRECTIONS

1 Add the olive oil, sage, and garlic to a small saucepan; cook over low heat just until the oil bubbles. Remove and discard one of the garlic cloves.

2 Add the oil-sage mixture with the garlic clove to the bowl of a mini food processor or blender container. Add the toasted almonds or hazelnuts and process into a fine crumble, adding a little more olive oil if the pesto is very stiff or difficult to process. (You want a pesto that's more nutty and less oily than a traditional one.) Spoon over roasted butternut or acorn squash or grilled fish or chicken.

PER SERVING: *Calories 216 (From Fat 180); Fat 20g (Saturated 2g); Cholesterol 0mg; Sodium 3mg; Carbohydrate 7g (Dietary Fiber 0g); Protein 3g.*

TIP: Toast almonds, hazelnuts, or other nuts in a small dry skillet over very low heat until their ends are lightly browned, stirring occasionally and watching carefully to prevent them from burning. Depending on the pan and the heat of your range, this should take about 5 to 8 minutes.

Vanilla Custard Sauce

PREP TIME: ABOUT 15 MIN PLUS COOLING TIME	COOK TIME: ABOUT 25 MIN	YIELD: 8 SERVINGS

INGREDIENTS

1 cup heavy cream

1 cup milk

1 vanilla bean, split lengthwise

4 egg yolks

¼ cup sugar

DIRECTIONS

1 Place the cream, milk, and vanilla bean in a heavy medium saucepan. *Scald* (bring to a foam but don't boil) the mixture over medium-low heat. Remove from the heat and let sit for 15 to 20 minutes.

2 Using a handheld or stand mixer, beat the egg yolks and sugar in a bowl for several minutes. The mixture should be pale yellow and thick.

3 Remove the vanilla bean from the cream mixture and split it open lengthwise with the tips of a paring knife to expose the tiny black seeds. Scrape the seeds out with the knife and add them to the cream mixture.

4 Return the cream mixture to the heat and scald it again.

5 Pour about one-quarter of the hot cream mixture into the egg yolks and whisk vigorously.

6 Pour the egg mixture into the saucepan with the rest of the cream mixture. Cook over low heat, stirring with a wooden spoon, about 4 to 5 minutes or until it thickens enough to coat the back of the spoon.

7 Strain the sauce through a sieve into a bowl, cover, and chill.

PER SERVING: *Calories 175 (From Fat 131); Fat 15g (Saturated 8g); Cholesterol 151mg; Sodium 30mg; Carbohydrate 9g (Dietary Fiber 0g); Protein 3g.*

TIP: Look for vanilla beans in the spice section of your supermarket.

VARY IT! Add 3 or 4 tablespoons of Grand Marnier, kirsch, or brandy to the sauce.

Cracklin' Hot Fudge Sauce

PREP TIME: ABOUT 15 MIN | COOK TIME: ABOUT 5 MIN | YIELD: 8 SERVINGS

INGREDIENTS

1 cup confectioners' sugar, sifted

½ cup (1 stick) butter

½ cup heavy cream

8 ounces (8 squares) bittersweet chocolate, finely chopped

2 teaspoons vanilla extract

DIRECTIONS

1 In a heavy medium saucepan over medium-low heat, combine the confectioners' sugar, butter, and cream. Stir with a wooden spoon until the butter is melted and the mixture is smooth.

2 Remove the pan from the heat and add the chocolate, stirring until smooth. Add the vanilla and stir to blend.

PER SERVING: *Calories 354 (From Fat 261); Fat 29g (Saturated 17g); Cholesterol 51mg; Sodium 7mg; Carbohydrate 30g (Dietary Fiber 2g); Protein 2g.*

VARY IT! If you can't find bittersweet chocolate, substitute semisweet chocolate and reduce the powdered sugar by 2 tablespoons.

TIP: Chop chocolate into pieces on a cutting board with a sharp knife or whirl the chocolate in the container of a blender or food processor for a few seconds.

Fresh Strawberry Sauce

PREP TIME: ABOUT 10 MIN	YIELD: 8 SERVINGS

INGREDIENTS

1 quart fresh strawberries, hulled (stems removed) and washed

2 tablespoons confectioners' sugar, or to taste

1 tablespoon fresh lemon juice

DIRECTIONS

1 Place all the ingredients in the container of a blender or food processor; purée until smooth. Taste for sweetness and add more sugar if desired.

PER SERVING: *Calories 29 (From Fat 0); Fat 0g (Saturated 0g); Cholesterol 0mg; Sodium 1mg; Carbohydrate 7g (Dietary Fiber 2g); Protein 0g.*

VARY IT! For extra flavor, add rum, kirsch, flavored vodka, or other liquor of choice. You also can make this sauce with frozen strawberries; just thaw them first.

Whipped Cream

PREP TIME: ABOUT 5 MIN | YIELD: 8 SERVINGS

INGREDIENTS

1 cup well-chilled heavy cream

1 tablespoon sugar, or to taste

1 teaspoon vanilla extract, or to taste

DIRECTIONS

1 In a chilled bowl, combine the cream, sugar, and vanilla. Beat with a whisk or electric mixer on medium speed until the cream thickens and forms peaks. (Don't overbeat, or the cream will become lumpy.)

PER SERVING: Calories 110 (From Fat 99); Fat 11g (Saturated 7g); Cholesterol 41mg; Sodium 11mg; Carbohydrate 2g (Dietary Fiber 0g); Protein 1g.

VARY IT! Before mixing, add 1 tablespoon unsweetened cocoa powder; 1 tablespoon instant coffee; or 1 or 2 tablespoons Grand Marnier, Kahlúa, Cointreau, crème de menthe, or other liqueur.

Chapter **15**

Delectable Desserts

For most of us, desserts are hard to resist. Even if you're counting calories, a sweet indulgence every now and then lifts the spirit, and it can serve as a reward for your hard-earned efforts. That's what this chapter is all about. Here, you find everything from old-fashioned cobblers to luscious baked fruits and ever-popular chocolate creations.

Many home cooks — and even some professionals — shy away from making desserts and pastries because they're so precise and unforgiving. That may be true, but the recipes in this chapter are as doable as they are delicious.

Creating Creamy Chocolate Sweets

RECIPE
ALERT

Pudding is a satisfying finish to any meal. We offer the following recipes later in the chapter:

» **Double Chocolate Pudding:** Put away your packaged pudding mixes forever. This pudding is so rich and delicious that it will be everyone's favorite, and it's a snap to make, too! You can dress it up by spooning it into a tall wine or parfait glass and topping it with sweetened whipped cream and chocolate shavings.

>> **Chocolate Mousse:** You can assemble this popular dessert in just minutes, and it doesn't require the skills of a pastry chef. Mousse is lighter, airier, and less rich than pudding. Because it has less sugar than some other desserts, chocolate mousse is a good lower-carb option for folks who are watching their weight. And you can make this simple yet festive dessert days in advance.

Several of our recipes in this chapter are wonderful if served with homemade whipped cream. We provide the recipe in Chapter 14.

Finding the Indulgent Side of Fruit, Fresh from the Oven

RECIPE ALERT

Later in this chapter, we serve up three fruit-based recipes: Peach-Blueberry Cobbler, Free-Form Fresh Fruit Tart, and Apple-Pear Crisp. Here's how they differ:

>> *Cobblers* are deep-dish fruit desserts in which sweetened fruits (fresh berries or apples are the traditional choices) are topped with biscuit dough before baking. Almost any type or combination of fruits can be used, and just about any kind of baking dish — round, square, oval, or rectangular.

>> A *tart* features a pastry crust topped with artfully arranged slices of fruit. The crust in our recipe combines the richness of an egg yolk with the sweetness of a little sugar to make a rich cookie-like dough that's easy to roll out. The open-faced tart is baked until the fruit is soft (but not mushy) and the pastry golden brown.

>> In a *crisp,* the fruit is baked under a crumbly topping, usually made with flour, butter, and sugar and sometimes oats, nuts, and spices.

Baked fruit recipes aren't difficult, but a few simple tips will help you to make them great:

>> Baked fruit recipes often contain spices like cinnamon, ginger, nutmeg, and cloves. Before cooking, smell the spices that have been sitting on your shelf for months or years. If they've lost their potency, replace them. (See Chapter 3 for the scoop on spices and their shelf life.)

>> Throughout this book, we often call for unsalted butter, and with good reason: Margarine doesn't taste as good as butter, and if you use salted butter, the salt can affect the delicate sweetness of many baked goods. Sometimes,

however, you can use margarine or shortening in combination with butter to add a light and flaky quality to pastry crusts.

>> Baked fruit recipes often include lemon juice to keep the fruit from turning brown. The acid in lemon juice slows the oxidation of fruit when it's exposed to air. When a recipe calls for fresh lemon juice, never use the bottled reconstituted kind; it tastes more like furniture polish than lemon juice.

RECIPE ALERT

For the best results with our Peach-Blueberry Cobbler recipe, be sure the fruit is ripe. Taste the sweetened fruit mixture before covering it with the biscuit dough. If the fruit isn't quite ripe (or if it's tart), you may need to sprinkle on a little more sugar. Some recipes call for removing the skins of the peaches by blanching them in boiling water for 1 minute and then peeling them off. However, we don't think it's necessary. And note that nectarine skins, which are thinner than peach skins, don't need to be removed.

RECIPE ALERT

When you try the Free-Form Fresh Fruit Tart, have Figure 15-1 on hand to help you roll out the pastry, place it on the baking sheet, and arrange the fruit beautifully on the pastry crust.

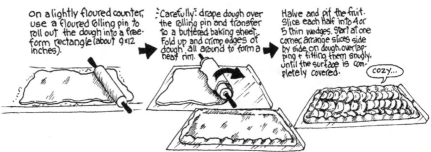

FIGURE 15-1: Making a gorgeous fruit tart.

Illustration by Elizabeth Kurtzman

Collecting Cookies: All You Need Is a Glass of Milk

Cookies make a delicious, fun, informal dessert for kids and adults alike. You can "drop" cookie dough by the spoonful onto a greased cookie sheet and pat into cookie shapes or roll into a log and slice. You can also shape the dough with cookie cutters or roll it by hand into balls and dust with sugar and cinnamon. From there, you may want to add chocolate chips, nuts, or slivers of raw garlic (kidding).

TIP

Here are a few important cookie-baking tips:

>> **Timing:** Every oven is different, and some can be alarmingly imprecise (especially gas ovens; electric ovens are more consistent). Always check the cookies a few minutes before they're supposed to be done. Buy an oven thermometer to determine whether your oven temperature setting is accurate; if it's not, adjust the temperature dial as necessary each time you bake. Or better yet, call your range service person or gas company to have your oven properly calibrated.

The same rule about timing applies to bar cookies, which should be moist (but not raw) in the center.

>> **Baking sheets:** Traditional aluminum sheets can produce cookies with burnt bottoms and pale tops. We prefer these two options:

- *Insulated baking sheets,* which have two layers of aluminum with air space between them. They're less likely to burn the cookies.

- *Stone cookie sheets,* which are similar to pizza stones but are rectangular. They produce an evenly baked cookie.

For bar cookies, glass or aluminum baking pans both work, but dark aluminum cooks faster than lighter, silver-colored aluminum, and both cook faster than glass, so keep an eye on those cookies!

Nonstick baking equipment makes removing things like cookies, breads, cakes, and other baked desserts much easier.

>> **Greasing the sheets:** For recipes that call for a greased cookie sheet, you don't need to degrease baking sheets after you've removed one batch of baked cookies. If you use a nonstick sheet, you don't need to grease the cookie sheet at all — doing so can make your cookies spread out too much and turn out too thin.

For recipes containing butter, just use the wrapper from the stick of butter to rub on the cookie sheet. Or use cooking spray for a lower-fat nonstick option (as long as your type of bakeware doesn't specifically warn against using cooking spray).

RECIPE
ALERT

If you never want your cookie jar to be empty, you can find lots of recipes in *Cookies For Dummies* by Carole Bloom (Wiley). Or try some of ours that we provide later in this chapter:

» **Old-Fashioned Chocolate Chip Cookies:** A chocolate chip cookie manufacturer once told us that the secret to his famous cookie dough was a little bit of grated lemon peel. It makes sense. Lemon zest, loaded with rich, lemony oil and without a trace of sourness, is frequently used by bakers to heighten the flavors of cookies and other sweet desserts. When grating citrus peel, be sure to remove only the colored portion of the skin. The white portion underneath, called the *pith,* is bitter.

In our recipe, the grated lemon zest punches up the flavor of the chocolate chips, and a little heavy cream in the dough gives the cookie a pleasant, melt-in-your-mouth softness. These cookies freeze very well in covered, plastic containers; they also keep for a week at room temperature in an airtight tin, provided you place it where the kids can't reach it.

» **Divine Brownies:** Many cooks, even good ones, don't consider making brownies from scratch, because so many great commercial mixes are available. But we believe that homemade is almost always better than the mix. So we give you this classic brownie recipe that's easy, rich, moist, and better (we guarantee it!) than any boxed mix you can buy. Plus, the brownies freeze well, so you can bake them ahead of time and save them for an upcoming event.

» **Lemon Bars:** This recipe is a Sunkist Growers classic that we've altered just a bit by decreasing the sugar and adding flaked coconut. The results are perfectly chewy bars with intense lemon flavor. You can serve these bars as is or sift powdered sugar over the top for a prettier finish.

TIP

For our Lemon Bars recipe, you need to line a 13-x-9-inch pan with foil. Figure 15-2 shows you how.

FIGURE 15-2:
Lining a baking pan with aluminum foil.

Illustration by Elizabeth Kurtzman

Taking on Tiramisu

RECIPE ALERT

In Chapter 10, we feature a recipe for the Perfect Chocolate Cake — a surefire favorite. When you're feeling more adventurous in the cake department, try our recipe for the oh-so-trendy Tiramisu, which you find later in this chapter. This coffee-flavored confection is arguably one of the most beloved desserts in U.S. restaurants. Over the years, what originally was a simple little treat has been altered so that the one often served in the United States is more like a cream-drenched, coffee-flavored chocolate cake.

Tiramisu comes from Italy where, as the story goes, older ladies used to play cards in the afternoon, and, after their card games were finished, they made a sweet treat called tiramisu, which means "pick me up." They would take out some biscuits or cookies, drench them with espresso, and then slather some mascarpone cheese on top. And tiramisu was born.

This terrific recipe comes from our friend Bill Yosses, who was a pastry chef at the White House (yes, that one!). It calls for a combination of sweetened whipped cream, sour cream, and mascarpone cheese. (If you can't find mascarpone, use softened cream cheese or increase the amount of whipped cream and sour cream.) The hallmark of a good tiramisu is a strong coffee flavor. You don't need to make espresso; instant coffee does the trick just fine.

Double Chocolate Pudding

INGREDIENTS

¼ cup water

2½ tablespoons cornstarch

½ cup sugar

⅓ cup unsweetened cocoa powder

Pinch of salt

⅓ cup milk, heated just to warm

2 ounces (2 squares) semisweet chocolate, coarsely chopped

2 cups heavy cream

1¼ teaspoons vanilla extract

Sweetened whipped cream (optional)

Chopped pecans or almonds, lightly toasted (optional)

DIRECTIONS

1 In a small bowl, stir together the water and the cornstarch thoroughly until the cornstarch is dissolved and the mixture is smooth. Set the mixture aside.

2 In a heavy, medium saucepan, mix together the sugar, cocoa, and salt. Using a wooden spoon, stir in the warm milk to make a smooth paste.

3 Place the saucepan over medium heat and bring the mixture to a boil while stirring constantly, about 2 to 3 minutes. Add the chopped chocolate and stir until it completely melts.

4 Gradually stir in the heavy cream. Add the cornstarch mixture and stir it into the chocolate mixture.

5 Continue stirring over medium heat for about 5 minutes, or until the pudding begins to thicken and boil. (Sweep the spoon along the bottom and sides of the pan to prevent the pudding from getting lumpy or burning.)

6 Reduce the heat to low and cook for about 1 minute more while stirring constantly.

7 Remove the saucepan from the heat and stir in the vanilla.

8 Pour the pudding into a serving bowl or individual serving cups. To prevent a skin from forming, lay a piece of plastic wrap or wax paper directly on the surface of the pudding.

9 Refrigerate before serving. Garnish with sweetened whipped cream and/or chopped nuts (if desired).

PER SERVING: Calories 626 (From Fat 462); Fat 51g (Saturated 32g); Cholesterol 166mg; Sodium 93mg; Carbohydrate 44g (Dietary Fiber 3g); Protein 6g.

Chocolate Mousse

PREP TIME: ABOUT 10 MIN PLUS CHILL TIME	COOK TIME: ABOUT 10 MIN	YIELD: 12 SERVINGS

INGREDIENTS

8 ounces bittersweet chocolate

6 eggs, separated

3 tablespoons water

2 cups heavy cream, well chilled

6 tablespoons sugar

Whipped cream or grated bittersweet chocolate for garnish

DIRECTIONS

1 Chop the chocolate coarsely with a chef's knife. Place the chocolate pieces in a saucepan or pot and set the pot over a larger pot holding barely simmering water. Cover the pot containing the chocolate.

2 Meanwhile, put the egg yolks in a saucepan and add the water. Place the saucepan over very low heat while whisking vigorously. When the yolks thicken slightly, remove the saucepan from the heat.

3 Check the chocolate. When it's melted, stir well with a whisk. Add the melted chocolate to the egg mixture and blend thoroughly. Scrape the mixture into a large mixing bowl.

4 With a hand-held electric mixer, beat the cream in a chilled bowl until it forms soft peaks, adding 2 tablespoons of the sugar toward the end and fold into the chocolate mixture.

5 Wash and dry both the bowl and the mixer thoroughly to remove the cream before proceeding.

6 Using the mixer, beat the egg whites in the clean bowl until they form soft peaks. Beat in the remaining 4 tablespoons of the sugar and continue beating until the egg whites form stiff peaks. Then fold this into the chocolate mixture.

7 Spoon the mousse into a serving bowl and chill thoroughly before serving. Garnish with whipped cream or grated bittersweet chocolate.

PER SERVING: *Calories 293 (From Fat 228); Fat 25g (Saturated 14g); Cholesterol 161mg; Sodium 47mg; Carbohydrate 17g (Dietary Fiber 1g); Protein 5g.*

WARNING: Some raw egg whites may contain salmonella bacteria, which could compromise the health of certain individuals. If you're worried about this risk, use commercially prepared pasteurized egg white product or egg white powder.

Apple-Pear Crisp

PREP TIME: ABOUT 20 MIN | COOK TIME: 40–45 MIN | YIELD: 6 SERVINGS

INGREDIENTS

3 large Granny Smith apples

2 large firm, ripe pears

2 to 3 tablespoons brandy or dark rum (optional)

¾ cup flour

⅔ cup granulated sugar

2 tablespoons brown sugar, packed

Grated zest of ½ lemon

¼ teaspoon salt

½ teaspoon ground cinnamon

¼ teaspoon ground nutmeg

½ cup (1 stick) cold butter, cut into small pieces

½ cup toasted chopped almonds or pecans

Vanilla ice cream or whipped cream (optional)

DIRECTIONS

1 Position a rack in the lower third of the oven. Preheat the oven to 375 degrees.

2 Peel and core the apples and cut them into 1-inch chunks. Core the pears and cut them into 1-inch chunks. (You don't have to peel them.)

3 Spread the fruit evenly over the bottom of an unbuttered, shallow, 2-quart baking dish. If desired, sprinkle the fruit with the brandy or rum.

4 In a medium mixing bowl, combine the flour, granulated sugar, brown sugar, lemon zest, salt, cinnamon, and nutmeg. Using a pastry blender or two knives, cut the butter into the dry ingredients until the mixture resembles coarse breadcrumbs. Mix in the chopped nuts.

5 Spread the topping evenly over the fruit. Bake for 40 to 45 minutes, or until the fruit is tender and the crust is lightly browned. Serve warm with vanilla ice cream or whipped cream (if desired).

PER SERVING: *Calories 445 (From Fat 184); Fat 21g (Saturated 10g); Cholesterol 41mg; Sodium 101mg; Carbohydrate 66g (Dietary Fiber 5g); Protein 4g.*

VARY IT! Add ½ cup of fresh, rinsed cranberries to the apple-pear mixture before spreading on the sugar topping. Or, for a summer crisp, substitute peaches and nectarines for the apples and pears.

Peach-Blueberry Cobbler

| PREP TIME: 35–40 MIN | COOK TIME: 45 MIN | YIELD: 8 SERVINGS |

INGREDIENTS

2 pounds firm, ripe nectarines or peaches (or a combination of both)

1 cup blueberries or black-berries, rinsed and stemmed

⅓ cup plus 2 tablespoons granulated sugar, or more to taste

2 tablespoons light brown sugar, packed

1½ cups plus 2 tablespoons all-purpose flour

½ teaspoon cinnamon

Grated zest and juice of ½ lemon

7 tablespoons cold butter, cut into small pieces

2 teaspoons baking powder

½ teaspoon salt

1 teaspoon fresh lemon juice

8 to 10 tablespoons heavy cream or half-and-half

¾ cup heavy cream, well chilled

Confectioners' sugar to taste

½ teaspoon vanilla extract

DIRECTIONS

1 Preheat the oven to 375 degrees.

2 Cut the nectarines or peaches in half and remove the pits. Cut each half into 4 to 5 wedges and place in a large mixing bowl.

3 Add the berries, 1/3 cup of the granulated sugar, the light brown sugar, 2 tablespoons of the flour, cinnamon, and the grated lemon zest and juice. Toss to mix well. Taste the fruit and see whether it's sweet enough. If necessary, add more sugar.

4 Place the fruit mixture in a 2-quart baking dish that's 2 inches deep. Dot the top of the fruit with 1 tablespoon of the butter and bake for 10 minutes.

5 As the fruit bakes, prepare the dough. In a medium mixing bowl, mix the remaining 1½ cups flour, the remaining 2 tablespoons sugar, baking powder, and salt.

6 Add the remaining 6 tablespoons butter and, using a pastry blender or two knives, cut the butter into the dry ingredients until the mixture resembles coarse breadcrumbs. Sprinkle the mixture with the lemon juice.

7 Using a fork, wooden spoon, or rubber spatula, gradually stir in just enough of the heavy cream or half-and-half to moisten the dough so it holds together and can be rolled or patted.

8 Gather the dough into a ball and place it on a lightly floured work surface. Roll out or pat the dough with your hands so it is about ½-inch thick and roughly matches the shape of the top of the baking dish.

9 Using a biscuit cutter, round cookie cutter, or knife, cut the dough into 2½-inch circles. (You should have 9 to 10 circles.)

10 After 10 minutes, remove the fruit from the oven. Place the dough on top of the fruit.

11 Return the cobbler to the oven and bake 30 to 35 minutes more, until the topping is golden brown and the fruit is bubbling around the edges.

12 As the cobbler bakes, make the sweetened whipped cream. Pour the heavy cream into a medium mixing bowl. Using an electric mixer, beat the cream just until it starts to thicken. Add the confectioners' sugar to taste and the vanilla and continue beating until soft peaks form. Refrigerate until ready to use.

13 To serve, put the warm cobbler into shallow bowls. Spoon some of the cream over each serving; drizzle some of the fruit juices over the cobbler and serve.

PER SERVING: *Calories 355 (From Fat 146); Fat 16g (Saturated 10g); Cholesterol 47mg; Sodium 251mg; Carbohydrate 51g (Dietary Fiber 3g); Protein 4g.*

VARY IT! Substitute other summer fruits for the peaches and blueberries, such as plums, raspberries, or apricots. Add other spices, such as allspice, ginger, or nutmeg, or sprinkle the fruit with a fruit liqueur. Substitute vanilla or lemon ice cream for the sweetened whipped cream.

Free-Form Fresh Fruit Tart

PREP TIME: ABOUT 30 MIN PLUS CHILL TIME	COOK TIME: 30–35 MIN	YIELD: 6 SERVINGS

INGREDIENTS

7 tablespoons butter, softened

¼ cup plus 1½ tablespoons sugar, or more to taste

1 egg yolk

Grated zest of ½ lemon

¼ teaspoon vanilla extract

1 cup all-purpose flour

Pinch of salt

Butter for the baking sheet

4 to 6 ripe, medium peaches or nectarines, or a combination of both

3 tablespoons apricot or peach jam

1 tablespoon Cointreau or other fruit liqueur (optional)

2 tablespoons finely chopped almonds

¼ cup blueberries or raspberries, rinsed, drained, and stemmed

Vanilla ice cream or whipped cream (optional)

DIRECTIONS

1 To make the pastry, in a medium mixing bowl, use a wooden spoon to blend 6 tablespoons of the butter, ¼ cup of the sugar, egg yolk, lemon zest, and vanilla extract. Add the flour and salt.

2 Use your fingers or a pastry blender to lightly work the butter-egg mixture into the dry ingredients until it forms a smooth dough. Press the dough into a ball; enclose in plastic wrap and chill for about 30 minutes.

3 Preheat the oven to 425 degrees. Butter a large, flat baking sheet, preferably nonstick.

4 On a lightly floured counter, use a floured rolling pin to roll out the dough into a free-form rectangle, about 9 by 12 inches.

5 Carefully drape the dough over the rolling pin and transfer it to the buttered baking sheet. Fold up and lightly crimp the edges of the dough all around to form a neat rim. Set aside.

6 Halve and pit the fruit; slice each half into 4 to 5 thin wedges.

7 Starting at one corner, arrange the fruit slices side by side on the dough, overlapping and fitting them snugly, until the surface of the pastry is completely covered.

8 In a small saucepan over low heat, combine the jam and the remaining 1 tablespoon butter. Cook a few minutes, stirring constantly, until the butter is melted and the jam is runny. Remove the saucepan from the heat and stir in the Cointreau (if desired).

9 Using a pastry brush, coat the fruit slices with the jam-butter mixture.

10 In another small mixing bowl, combine the remaining 1½ tablespoons of the sugar and almonds.

11 Sprinkle the berries over the top of the fruit slices and then sprinkle the sugar–almond mixture evenly over the fruit. Taste and add more sugar if desired.

12 Bake the tart for about 25 to 30 minutes until the dough is crisp and golden and the fruit is tender.

13 Cut the tart into 6 pieces. Using a metal spatula, transfer each piece to an individual serving plate. Serve warm or cold, with a little whipped cream or vanilla ice cream (if desired).

PER SERVING: *Calories 316 (From Fat 140); Fat 16g (Saturated 9g); Cholesterol 71mg; Sodium 31mg; Carbohydrate 42g (Dietary Fiber 2g); Protein 4g.*

TIP: If baked ahead, the tart can be reheated in a 375-degree oven for 10 to 15 minutes.

VARY IT! Try substituting ripe plum slices for some of the peaches and/or nectarines.

Old-Fashioned Chocolate Chip Cookies

PREP TIME: ABOUT 20 MIN	COOK TIME: 8–10 MIN PER BATCH	YIELD: ABOUT 36 COOKIES

INGREDIENTS

1 cup plus 2 tablespoons all-purpose flour

½ teaspoon baking powder

½ teaspoon grated lemon zest

¼ teaspoon salt

½ cup (1 stick) butter, softened

⅓ cup plus 2 tablespoons light brown sugar, packed

⅓ cup plus 2 tablespoons granulated sugar

1 egg

2 tablespoons heavy cream or half-and-half

½ teaspoon vanilla extract

1 cup (6-ounce package) semisweet chocolate chips

⅓ cup coarsely chopped walnuts or pecans (optional)

DIRECTIONS

1 Preheat the oven to 375 degrees.

2 In a medium mixing bowl, stir together the flour, baking powder, lemon zest, and salt.

3 Using an electric mixer at medium speed, cream the butter with the brown and granulated sugars, about 3 minutes. Beat in the egg, heavy cream, and vanilla until well blended.

4 Using a wooden spoon or a rubber spatula, stir the flour mixture into the butter mixture until well blended. Stir in the chocolate chips and the nuts (if desired).

5 Drop heaping teaspoons of the batter onto a greased baking sheet, about 1 to 2 inches apart.

6 Bake one sheet at a time, until the cookies are lightly golden on the top with slightly browned edges, about 8 to 10 minutes. Rotate the sheet 180 degrees halfway through baking to ensure even browning.

7 Remove the baking sheet to a wire rack and let the cookies cool for about 2 minutes. Using a metal spatula, carefully remove the cookies from the baking sheet and slide them onto a wire rack to cool completely.

PER COOKIE: *Calories 84 (From Fat 40); Fat 4g (Saturated 3g); Cholesterol 14mg; Sodium 26mg; Carbohydrate 11g (Dietary Fiber 0g); Protein 1g.*

Divine Brownies

| PREP TIME: 25 MIN | COOK TIME: 20–25 MIN | YIELD: 24 BROWNIES |

INGREDIENTS

Butter and flour to prepare the baking pan

1 cup (2 sticks) butter

1 ounce (1 square) unsweetened chocolate, coarsely chopped

2 cups sugar

¾ cup unsweetened cocoa powder

4 eggs

2 teaspoons vanilla extract

1⅓ cups flour

½ cup chopped walnuts or pecans (optional)

DIRECTIONS

1 Preheat the oven to 375 degrees. Grease and flour a 9-x-13-inch baking pan.

2 In a small, heavy saucepan, over very low heat, melt the butter and unsweetened chocolate, stirring occasionally until the mixture is smooth. Set the mixture aside to cool slightly.

3 In a large mixing bowl, combine the sugar and the cocoa powder; add the melted chocolate-butter mixture and stir well to combine.

4 Add the eggs, one at a time, stirring with a wooden spoon or rubber spatula, only until well blended. Stir in the vanilla.

5 Add the flour, in three batches, stirring after each addition, just until the ingredients are blended. Stir in the walnuts (if desired). Don't overmix.

6 Scrape the batter into the prepared pan, spreading it evenly and to the edges. Bake in the top half of the preheated oven for 20 to 25 minutes, until the center is firm to the touch when lightly pressed.

7 Remove the pan to a rack and let stand until completely cool before cutting into squares.

PER BROWNIE: *Calories 182 (From Fat 86); Fat 10g (Saturated 6g); Cholesterol 56mg; Sodium 13mg; Carbohydrate 24g (Dietary Fiber 1g); Protein 3g.*

Tiramisu

PREP TIME: ABOUT 20 MIN PLUS CHILL TIME | YIELD: 8 SERVINGS

INGREDIENTS

3 heaping tablespoons instant coffee crystals or granules

3 tablespoons granulated sugar

1 cup water

Two 6-ounce packages ladyfingers

1 pint heavy cream, well chilled

¼ cup confectioners' sugar

2 teaspoons vanilla extract

⅓ cup mascarpone cheese

2 heaping tablespoons sour cream

1 tablespoon unsweetened cocoa powder

DIRECTIONS

1 In a small bowl, combine the instant coffee and granulated sugar.

2 Bring the water to a boil and pour it over the coffee mixture, stirring. Set aside and let cool to room temperature.

3 Place about half of the ladyfingers on the bottom of a 9- or 10-inch square or round serving dish.

4 Using a tablespoon, drizzle half of the coffee mixture evenly over the ladyfingers in the serving dish. Set aside.

5 In a bowl, combine the cream, confectioners' sugar, and vanilla. With a whisk or an electric mixer, whip the mixture until it forms soft peaks. Refrigerate for at least 1 hour.

6 In another bowl, combine the mascarpone and sour cream. Using a wooden spoon, stir the mixture until smooth.

7 Fold half of the whipped-cream mixture into the cheese-and-sour-cream mixture until well blended. Then fold in the rest, being sure not to overmix.

8 Using a metal spatula or spoon, spread half of the mixture over the ladyfingers, and place another layer of ladyfingers, curved side down, over it.

9 Drizzle the ladyfingers with the remaining coffee and cover them with the other half of the cream mixture. Using a sieve, sprinkle the cocoa powder evenly over the top.

10 Refrigerate for 2 hours before cutting into pieces to serve.

PER SERVING: *Calories 450 (From Fat 281); Fat 31g (Saturated 18g); Cholesterol 251mg; Sodium 93mg; Carbohydrate 37g (Dietary Fiber 1g); Protein 7g.*

Lemon Bars

PREP TIME: 15 MIN	COOK TIME: ABOUT 35 MIN	YIELD: 24 BARS

INGREDIENTS

Butter for the foil lining

½ cup butter, softened

1½ cups plus 6 tablespoons sugar

Grated zest of 1 lemon

1½ cups plus 3 tablespoons all-purpose flour

4 eggs

¼ teaspoon baking powder

¾ cup sweetened flaked coconut

6 tablespoons freshly squeezed lemon juice (about 2 lemons)

1 teaspoon vanilla extract

DIRECTIONS

1 Preheat the oven to 350 degrees.

2 Line a 13-x-9-inch baking pan (nonstick is best) with aluminum foil. Butter the foil.

3 In a medium mixing bowl, cream together the ½ cup butter, 6 tablespoons of the sugar, and half of the lemon zest, using an electric mixer. Gradually stir in 1½ cups of the flour to form a soft, crumbly dough.

4 Turn the dough into the foil-lined pan and press it evenly into the bottom. Bake for 12 to 15 minutes or until the crust is firm and lightly browned.

5 Prepare the filling as the crust bakes. In a large mixing bowl, use an electric mixer or a wire whisk to beat the eggs well. Add the remaining 1½ cups sugar, 3 tablespoons flour, and the baking powder, and beat well to combine. Stir or whisk in the coconut, the lemon juice, the remaining half of the lemon zest, and the vanilla, just until blended.

6 Using a rubber spatula, spread the filling over the hot, baked crust, being sure to evenly distribute the coconut throughout the filling.

7 Return the pan to the oven and bake for about 20 minutes, or until the top is lightly golden and the filling is set.

8 Set the pan on a wire rack to cool completely. Lift the foil by the ends to lift out the bar cookie, and then set it on a cutting board. Gently loosen the foil along all the sides. With a long, sharp, wet knife, cut into squares. Refrigerate the squares until ready to serve.

PER BAR: *Calories 151 (From Fat 49); Fat 5g (Saturated 3g); Cholesterol 46mg; Sodium 21mg; Carbohydrate 24g (Dietary Fiber 0g); Protein 2g.*

4

Now You're Cooking! Real Menus for Real Life

Save time and effort by cooking an entire meal in one pot.

Discover how to feed your family healthy meals without breaking the grocery budget.

Add some international flair to your dinner table by trying some Asian and Mediterranean dishes.

Keep your meal simple by preparing recipes that require a minimum of ingredients (many of which you likely have on hand).

Plan the perfect summer party with no-fuss recipes that take you from drinks to dessert.

Host a successful holiday gathering by preparing our variations on many of the traditional winter dishes.

Chapter **16**

Taking It Easy with One-Pot Meals

Archeological digs in the Middle East's Fertile Crescent have discovered that ancient Sumarians favored one-pot cooking (they pulled out their second pot for feasts). Just toss some lamb in a cast-iron receptacle over a low fire (slaves stoked it periodically), add some veggies, and head out to work over at the Nile. This technique has changed little over the centuries — okay, we no longer have slaves, and electricity simplifies things — although now we refer to it as slow cooking or braising.

Aside from its simplicity, one-pot slow cooking is the best way to tenderize tougher cuts of meat and infuse them with flavor. We like to make large batches of stews and casseroles and freeze the leftovers.

Not every one-pot meal actually uses only one pot. Sometimes, you need a few other dishes to prepare individual ingredients to go into the final pot, such as a skillet to brown the ground beef or a pasta pot to pre-boil noodles.

Whether you want to save time or just love the comfort-food appeal of one-pot meals, this chapter shows you how to become an expert at this delicious form of culinary minimalism.

Slow Cookers: Small Input, Big Output

The most common home slow cookers, which consist of a ceramic crock with a lid that fits into an electric holder, simmer food for about 6 to 12 hours. A major plus is that you don't have to keep watching the food to save it from burning — but you do have to make certain there's enough liquid in the pot. Then you can do something else — even leave the house — while the slow cooker does all the labor.

Slow cookers can do many things besides prepare dinner: They can bake, make hot apple cider or cheese dip for a party, and even make gravy while your Thanksgiving turkey is resting.

Although you can cook a lot of things in a slow cooker, they can't do everything (we're sorry to say). Here are a few rules to remember:

>> **Slow cookers can't brown ground meat.** Slow cookers don't get hot enough to cook ground meat safely. For dishes like chili or spaghetti sauce, brown ground meat in a skillet before putting it into the slow cooker. You can put steak, roasts, poultry, and fish into the slow cooker without cooking them first — you can even put them in frozen solid —but ground meat is the exception.

>> **Slow cookers can't cook pasta.** They don't boil water, so the pasta won't cook properly. If a slow cooker recipe calls for pasta, cook it first according to package directions (in boiling water), and then add it to the slow cooker toward the end of cooking so it doesn't get mushy.

TIP

Treat beans the same way as pasta: If your dish calls for canned beans (such as for chili or bean soup), add them toward the end of cooking so they don't turn to mush.

>> **Slow cookers cook everything at the same pace.** For best results, cut vegetables into bite-sized pieces for even cooking. Vegetables that take longer to cook, like potatoes, should be in smaller pieces than vegetables that cook quickly, like tomatoes.

>> **You should always follow the manufacturer's directions for your individual slow cooker.** Cookers vary, some running hotter or cooler than others.

Most slow cookers come with a recipe book to get you started, and you can also find some great recipes and general slow cooking tips in *Slow Cookers For Dummies*, by Tom Lacalamita and Glenna Vance (published by Wiley). Also check out the video at www.dummies.com/go/slowcooking.

RECICE
ALERT

Slow Cooker Pulled Pork is the perfect dish when you want to feed a crowd. You can throw everything into the ceramic cooking pot, and then run off to do other things while the pork cooks in 6 to 8 hours.

From Oven to Table: Simplicity in a Casserole Dish

Another great way to make a one-pot meal is with the good old-fashioned casserole dish. Load up the dish with ingredients, from chicken with potatoes to a layered lasagna, and let the oven do most of the work. There's just something homey and comforting about dinner out of the oven. If you have kids who don't like their foods to touch each other, they may not appreciate the charm of the casserole, but for the rest of us, it's love in a dish.

RECIPE
ALERT

Casserole dishes can contain everything from an old-style casserole to a piece of meat surrounded by potatoes and other vegetables to homey dessert like fruit baked with a crumbly topping, all in one dish. Later in the chapter, we offer some tasty recipes to bake in your oven:

>> **Chicken and Biscuit Pot Pie:** You may remember those frozen chicken pot pies from childhood, but our version is made from scratch and oh-so-much tastier. The recipe takes a little time, but the end result is worth every warm, comforting bite. We hope you'll try it.

>> **Shepherd's Pie:** In Ireland, the classic Shepherd's Pie is made with beef, not lamb. We prefer the more distinctive flavor of lamb, so that's what our recipe uses. If you want to try it with beef, simply substitute the same amount of meat.

>> **Hungry Family Lasagna:** An easy way to make your family happy, this layered meat-and-noodle dish is even easier if you use the lasagna noodles that don't need to be pre-boiled. Look for them in your store.

TIP

You can make lasagna unique by adding a variety of ingredients to the essential layers of noodles, cheese, and sauce. For example, combine ¼ to ⅓ cup cooked, chopped, drained, fresh or frozen spinach or broccoli with the cheese mixture. Or sprinkle the layers with ⅓ to ½ pound cooked ground beef or cooked shredded chicken or turkey. Or sprinkle the layers with 1 cup cooked chopped vegetables, such as mushrooms, zucchini, or carrots.

>> **Homestyle Macaroni and Cheese:** You *could* make the stuff out of the box, but why do that when this easy recipe is so much creamier, cheesier, and more delicious? This is comfort food at its ultimate.

Slow Cooker Ratatouille

PREP TIME: ABOUT 20 MIN | COOK TIME: 6–8 HR | YIELD: 6 SERVINGS

INGREDIENTS

3 tablespoons olive oil

1 medium eggplant, peeled and cut into 1-inch cubes

1 medium zucchini, cut into 1-inch cubes

1 medium red onion, chopped

1 large red bell pepper, cored, seeded, and chopped

1 large green bell pepper, cored, seeded, and chopped

2 cloves garlic, minced

Two 14-ounce cans whole tomatoes

1 teaspoon salt

2 teaspoons dried basil

1 teaspoon dried thyme

½ teaspoon black pepper

1 bay leaf

Hot cooked rice

6 tablespoons grated Parmesan cheese

DIRECTIONS

1 Heat the olive oil in a skillet over medium-high heat. Sauté the eggplant, zucchini, onion, red and green bell peppers, and garlic until the vegetables look golden but not dark brown, about 15 minutes.

2 Put the cooked vegetable mixture, tomatoes, salt, basil, thyme, black pepper, and bay leaf in the slow cooker. Turn on low and cook for 6 to 8 hours.

3 Remove the bay leaf and serve over rice. Garnish each serving with 1 tablespoon Parmesan cheese.

PER SERVING: Calories 156 (From Fat 79); Fat 9g (Saturated 2g); Cholesterol 4mg; Sodium 682mg; Carbohydrate 17g (Dietary Fiber 5g); Protein 5g.

Spanish Paella

PREP TIME: ABOUT 15 MIN	COOK TIME: ABOUT 1 HR 10 MIN	YIELD: 8 SERVINGS

INGREDIENTS

¼ cup olive oil

1 chicken, cut into pieces (about 2 pounds)

8 ounces kielbasa or other smoked sausage, sliced

1 large yellow onion, chopped

3 cloves garlic, peeled and minced

2 stalks celery, minced, including some of the leaves

5 cups chicken broth

2 cups raw white rice

1 pinch of saffron threads

1 cup frozen peas

1 pound medium shrimp, shelled and deveined

DIRECTIONS

1 In a Dutch oven or large saucepan, heat the olive oil over medium-high heat.

2 Add the chicken pieces and sauté, turning the chicken to cook all sides, for about 10 minutes.

3 Add the sausage, onion, garlic, and celery and continue to sauté until the chicken is golden brown and the vegetables are soft, about 10 additional minutes.

4 Add the chicken broth, rice, and saffron. Stir to combine. Bring to a boil and then reduce the heat.

5 Add the peas and stir. Cover and simmer over medium-low until the rice is cooked through and has absorbed all the liquid and the chicken is no longer pink inside, about 45 minutes. (Check after the first 25 minutes of simmering; if the rice looks dry, add more broth.)

6 Stir in the shrimp and cook for an additional 3 to 4 minutes, or until the shrimp turns pink. Serve immediately.

PER SERVING: *Calories 543 (From Fat 241); Fat 27g (Saturated 7g); Cholesterol 151mg; Sodium 1,104mg; Carbohydrate 41g (Dietary Fiber 4g); Protein 33g.*

TIP: You can find saffron threads with the herbs and spices at the grocery store.

Slow Cooker Pulled Pork

| PREP TIME: 20 MIN | COOK TIME: 6–8 HR | YIELD: 10–12 SERVINGS |

INGREDIENTS

1 large yellow onion, thinly sliced

1 cup chicken broth or stock

1½ teaspoons chili powder

1½ teaspoons ground cumin

1 tablespoon packed dark brown sugar

1 teaspoon cinnamon

2 teaspoons kosher salt

¼ teaspoon black pepper

⅛ teaspoon cayenne pepper, or to taste (optional)

4 to 4½ pounds boneless pork shoulder (also known as pork butt)

1⅔ to 2 cups homemade or store-bought barbecue sauce

10 to 12 potato buns

Coleslaw for serving (optional)

DIRECTIONS

1 Place the onion in the slow cooker and add the chicken broth or stock.

2 Combine the chili powder, cumin, brown sugar, cinnamon, salt, black pepper, and cayenne pepper (if desired) in a small bowl. Pat pork dry with paper towels, and then massage spice mix all over and into the meat.

3 Place the meat into the slow cooker on top of the onions. Cover and cook until the pork is fork-tender, about 6 to 8 hours on high or 8 to 10 hours on low.

4 Turn off the slow cooker and use a long-handled fork to remove the pork to a large bowl. Strain the cooking liquid into a mesh strainer set over a medium bowl. Return the solids to the slow cooker.

5 Heat the barbecue sauce in a small saucepan over medium.

6 As the barbecue sauce heats, use a large spoon to skim off and discard the fat from the top of the strained cooking liquid. Add 1 cup of the skimmed cooking liquid and 1½ cups of the heated barbecue sauce to the slow cooker.

7 Use two forks to shred the meat into bite-sized pieces, removing and discarding any bone or large pieces of fat. Place the shredded pork back into the slow cooker and mix into the sauce until well combined, adding a little more of the barbecue sauce, if necessary, until the pork mixture is moistened as desired.

8   Set the temperature to high and cook about 20 minutes, or until the pork is warmed through. Taste and season with salt to taste. Serve directly from the slow cooker ceramic pot with the buns and coleslaw on the side (if desired).

PER SERVING: *Calories 685 (From Fat 243); Fat 27g (Saturated 9g); Cholesterol 175mg; Sodium 1,464mg; Carbohydrate 54g (Dietary Fiber 2g); Protein 54g.*

VARY IT! Feel free to adjust the rub and make it your own. Not a cumin fan? Leave it out and add some garlic powder, a little dry mustard, or maybe some paprika. You can also skip the barbecue sauce and simply moisten the pork with some of the strained and skimmed cooking juices.

Chicken and Biscuit Pot Pie

PREP TIME: ABOUT 15 MIN	COOK TIME: ABOUT 1 HR 10 MIN	YIELD: 8 SERVINGS

INGREDIENTS

2 pounds skinless, boneless chicken breasts

3 cups chicken broth

1 medium yellow onion, chopped

2 celery stalks, trimmed of leaves and diced

2 cloves garlic, minced or put through a garlic press

3 carrots, trimmed, scraped, and sliced

1 medium boiling potato, peeled and diced

3 tablespoons butter

1 tablespoon all-purpose flour

¼ cup heavy cream

¼ teaspoon ground nutmeg

Salt and black pepper

1 cup fresh or frozen peas

1 tablespoon sherry (optional)

One 10- to 12-ounce can refrigerated biscuit dough (about 8 to 10 biscuits)

DIRECTIONS

1 Combine the chicken breasts, broth, onion, celery, and garlic in a 4-quart pot. Add water to just cover the chicken and vegetables. Cover the pot and bring to a boil.

2 Uncover, reduce the heat, and simmer for 15 minutes. Remove the chicken, cut into bite-sized pieces, and return the pieces and any juice to the pot.

3 Add the carrots and potato to the pot. Bring the broth back to a boil and then lower the heat and simmer 15 minutes more, or until the chicken and vegetables are just tender. Let cool for about 5 minutes in the liquid.

4 Carefully pour the broth with the chicken and vegetables into a large colander set over a larger pot (such as a Dutch oven) to catch and reserve the liquid. Put the pot with the liquid back on the stove over medium heat.

5 Melt the butter in a pot or large saucepan over medium heat. (You can use the same pot that you used to make the stock.) Add the flour and cook, whisking constantly, for about 1 minute. Stir in the hot broth, whisking occasionally and cooking about 2 to 3 minutes until the sauce comes to a boil and thickens. Add the cream and nutmeg. Season with salt and black pepper to taste.

6 Preheat the oven to 425 degrees.

7 Stir the chicken, vegetables, peas, and sherry (if desired) into the sauce. Spoon the mixture into a 3-quart or 9-x-13-inch shallow baking dish.

8 Arrange the refrigerated biscuits on top of the chicken mixture and bake for about 25 minutes, or until the biscuits are lightly browned. Serve immediately.

PER SERVING: *Calories 371 (From Fat 146); Fat 16g (Saturated 7g); Cholesterol 86mg; Sodium 940mg; Carbohydrate 28g (Dietary Fiber 3g); Protein 28g.*

Hungry Family Lasagna

PREP TIME: ABOUT 20 MIN	COOK TIME: ABOUT 1 HR	YIELD: 8 SERVINGS

INGREDIENTS

12 lasagna noodles

1 pound mozzarella cheese (reduced-fat variety, if desired)

2 cups ricotta cheese (reduced-fat variety, if desired; about one 15-ounce container)

⅓ cup plus 2 tablespoons grated Parmesan or Romano cheese

Salt and black pepper

5 cups (approx.) tomato sauce or jarred red pasta sauce (two 26-ounce jars)

DIRECTIONS

1 Bring an 8-quart pot filled with about 6 quarts of lightly salted water to a boil over high heat.

2 Add the lasagna noodles a few at a time. Cover the pot to bring the water back to a boil and then cook uncovered, according to package directions, until barely tender, not soft.

3 As the noodles cook, preheat the oven to 375 degrees.

4 Cut the mozzarella cheese into ½-inch cubes.

5 In a small bowl, combine the ricotta, ⅓ cup of the Parmesan cheese, and 1 tablespoon of water taken from the boiling pasta pot. Season the mixture with salt and black pepper to taste and set aside.

6 When the noodles are cooked, drain them in a colander and run cold water over them.

7 To assemble the lasagna, spread a heaping cup of the tomato sauce on the bottom of a 13-x-9-x-3-inch ovenproof pan. Place three noodles over the sauce so they completely cover the bottom of the pan (they should touch but not overlap). Spread one-third of the ricotta mixture evenly over the noodles. Sprinkle one-third of the mozzarella cheese cubes over the ricotta. Spread a heaping cup of the sauce over this layer. Season with salt and black pepper to taste.

8 Continue making layers, following the same order as Step 7 and ending with a thin layer of sauce. Sprinkle the top layer with the remaining 2 tablespoons Parmesan cheese.

(continued)

9 Bake in the preheated oven, checking after 30 minutes. If the top layer appears to be dry, cover with foil. Bake for another 20 to 25 minutes, or until the lasagna is bubbly. Let stand, covered, for 15 minutes before cutting into squares and serving.

PER SERVING: *Calories 464 (From Fat 216); Fat 24g (Saturated 13g); Cholesterol 73mg; Sodium 1,116mg; Carbohydrate 36g (Dietary Fiber 3g); Protein 27g.*

Homestyle Macaroni and Cheese

PREP TIME: ABOUT 20 MIN	COOK TIME: ABOUT 35 MIN	YIELD: 4 SERVINGS

INGREDIENTS

2 cups elbow macaroni

2½ cups milk

5 tablespoons butter

3 tablespoons all-purpose flour

½ teaspoon paprika

Generous dash of Tabasco sauce to taste

2 cups grated sharp cheddar cheese

Salt and black pepper

½ cup cubed Italian Fontina cheese

1 cup fresh white breadcrumbs

DIRECTIONS

1 Preheat the oven to 350 degrees.

2 Bring a 4- or 5-quart pot of lightly salted water to a boil. Add the macaroni and cook for about 6 to 8 minutes, or until just tender.

3 As the macaroni cooks, make the cheese sauce. Heat the milk almost to the boiling point in a small saucepan over medium-low heat.

4 Melt 3 tablespoons of the butter in a large saucepan over medium heat. Add the flour and whisk constantly over low heat for 1 to 2 minutes. Don't let it brown.

5 Gradually whisk in the hot milk and then add the paprika and Tabasco. Cook over medium heat for 2 to 3 minutes or until the sauce thickens, whisking occasionally. Whisk in the grated cheddar cheese and remove from the heat. Season with salt and black pepper.

6 Drain the macaroni as soon as it's done, return it to the pot, and add the cheese sauce and the cubes of Fontina cheese, stirring well to blend.

7 Use 1 tablespoon of butter to grease a deep, 2- to 3-quart casserole dish fitted with a lid. Add the macaroni and cheese mixture. Cover and bake for 20 to 25 minutes until hot.

8 Meanwhile, melt the last tablespoon of butter in a small skillet. Add the breadcrumbs and sauté over low heat, stirring constantly, until they're moistened but not browned.

(continued)

9 Remove the casserole from the oven and raise the temperature to broil. Spread the breadcrumbs evenly over the macaroni and cheese. Return the dish to the oven, uncovered, and broil for 1 to 2 minutes, or until the crumbs are crisp and browned. Serve immediately.

PER SERVING: *Calories 732 (From Fat 392); Fat 44g (Saturated 27g); Cholesterol 134mg; Sodium 743mg; Carbohydrate 55g (Dietary Fiber 2g); Protein 30g.*

Shepherd's Pie

PREP TIME: ABOUT 25 MIN	COOK TIME: ABOUT 1 HR 20 MIN	YIELD: 6 SERVINGS

INGREDIENTS

2½ pounds baking potatoes, peeled and quartered

4 tablespoons butter

About 1 cup milk

Salt and black pepper

1 tablespoon vegetable oil

1 medium yellow onion, chopped

2 large cloves garlic, peeled and chopped

1½ pounds cooked, chopped lamb (or raw, ground lamb)

1 tablespoon all-purpose flour

½ cup beef or chicken stock

1 tablespoon chopped thyme or sage, or 1 teaspoon dried thyme or sage

1 tablespoon chopped rosemary leaves, or 1 teaspoon dried rosemary

Dash of ground nutmeg

DIRECTIONS

1 Preheat the oven to 350 degrees.

2 Put the potatoes in a large pot of lightly salted water and bring to a boil. Cook, covered, until the potatoes are tender, about 20 minutes. Drain and return the potatoes to the pot.

3 Mash the potatoes along with 2 tablespoons of the butter and enough milk to make them smooth and fluffy. Season with the salt and black pepper to taste and set aside.

4 Heat the oil in a large skillet over medium-low heat. Add the onion and garlic and cook, stirring often, until the onion is soft and wilted. (Don't let the garlic brown.)

5 Turn up the heat to medium and add the lamb. Cook about 5 minutes, stirring. (If using raw ground lamb, cook about 10 minutes, stirring often, until browned.) Pour off and discard any fat in the pan.

6 Add the flour and cook, stirring often, for 2 to 3 minutes. Add the stock, thyme, rosemary, and nutmeg.

7 Reduce the heat to low and simmer, stirring occasionally, for about 15 minutes. Remove from the heat and let cool slightly.

8 Transfer the lamb mixture to an oval gratin dish (about 13 inches long). Spread the mashed potatoes over everything. Dot with the remaining 2 tablespoons of butter and bake for 45 minutes or until nicely browned. Let cool for 5 minutes before serving.

PER SERVING: *Calories 474 (From Fat 173); Fat 19g (Saturated 9g); Cholesterol 125mg; Sodium 589mg; Carbohydrate 38g (Dietary Fiber 4g); Protein 37g.*

Chapter **17**

Making More (and Better) for Less

To understand how much money the average American shopper wastes every week, just stand around any supermarket checkout counter. Instead of flipping through the intellectual journals on sale ("Lady Gaga Dresses Like a Normal Person for a Month"), take an inventory of customers' shopping carts. Even discounting the usual junky snack food, you'll find that the average cart is loaded with high-priced (for what you get) frozen dinners, sugared-up prepared sauces, prebuttered garlic bread, precut vegetables, frozen pizzas, boxed croutons (stale bread, only $3.99 a box!), and more. (It's no surprise that America has the highest obesity rate in the world — and the personal debt to match it.)

You can definitely save money by making food from scratch, or even semi-scratch. In this chapter, we introduce you to the types of food that can help you feed a family for less — in many cases, far less. Frugality is no reason to forgo class, however, as the recipes in this chapter demonstrate.

Creating Big Dishes for Small Bucks

Whether you're using inexpensive cuts of beef, stretching chicken with heaps of veggies and rice, or taking advantage of a weekly special at the supermarket, a little attention to detail and presentation can make any meal fit for a family — even one full of finicky eaters.

TIP

Here are a few guidelines for budget cooking:

>> Rice, pasta, cornmeal, dried beans, and other grains cost far less than meat yet, if prepared creatively, can deliver as much or more protein. Serve smaller portions of meat along with any of these items.

>> Soups and stews made with meat, veggies, and grains are great vehicles for getting the most out of relatively little.

>> And don't forget salads! A big bowl of salad with a little meat (or cheese or egg) costs a lot less than a big plate of meat.

All the main dish recipes in this chapter also make delicious leftovers — a blessing for busy cooks.

Crowd-pleasing chili

Few words spark gastronomic brouhaha like *chili*, whether it's rich Texas-style chili con carne, fiery Arizona-style chili, or one of the myriad variations in between. Maybe it's not a glamorous meal, but chili is a real crowd pleaser, and you'll be surprised how festive you can make it look with some thought to presentation. Plus, you can feed your whole Little League team for about 20 bucks.

Stir-fry for pennies

Stir-fry provides great nutrition for the budget-conscious. Because of all the vegetables and the rich oil, you can stretch a little bit of meat for a lot of people. You don't need a wok to make stir-fry. Just be sure that the pan is hot, the oil is hot, and you cook the vegetables just long enough to be bright and crisp. You can whip up a stir-fry whenever you like, using beef, pork, chicken, fish, or whatever you have on hand, plus whatever fresh vegetables are waiting in your refrigerator. A little oil, a little sizzle, some spices, and you have dinner. Serve stir-fry alone or over hot cooked rice or thin Chinese noodles (available in the Asian food section of your grocery store).

Be sure to check out our recipe for Pork and Noodle Stir-Fry in Chapter 18.

Dressing Up Your Meals with Super Sidekicks

Inviting side dishes are another great way to dress up your meals. Following are some ideas for inexpensive, tasty sides.

Root vegetables

Root vegetables such as potatoes, carrots, turnips, and beets are hearty, filling, super-nutritious, and — you guessed it — cheap! Root vegetables make great side dishes, including the traditional (see the recipe for Homemade Mashed Potatoes in Chapter 5) and the unusual (raw julienned kohlrabi sticks, anyone?). Root vegetables stretch a soup, stew, or stir-fry, and they can also be good raw with a dip: Try mixing equal parts nonfat plain yogurt and sour cream with some minced garlic and dill, or just dip them in ranch dressing.

REMEMBER

Potatoes can add creamy or thick texture to many dishes, and potato side dishes alone number in the dozens.

Seasonal vegetables

Using seasonal produce in your cooking is not only economical but also follows the venerable tradition of European cooking.

Since this book was first published in 1996, there has been an explosion of local farmers' markets. Chances are there is one within ten miles of your home. Thanks to the proliferation of these markets, Americans can again purchase fresh, local, and seasonal food. This opens a world of possibilities for wholesome and inexpensive cooking. Take advantage of it!

Dried beans

We find it rather amazing that Americans don't cook more with dried beans, which are inexpensive, healthful, and delicious. You can use dried beans in a side dish or as part of a main course. Whether or not you're cooking on a tight budget, becoming familiar with all kinds of legumes, each of which has a special texture and flavor, is definitely worthwhile. Table 17-1 lists several common types of dried beans.

TIP

Before cooking dried beans, sort and rinse them. Look over the beans carefully, picking out and discarding any that are withered. Rinse them thoroughly in cold water until the water runs clear, removing any beans or other substances that float to the surface.

TABLE 17-1   **Dried Beans**

Bean	Description
Black beans	Often used in South American and Caribbean dishes and mixed with rice and spices. Sweetish flavor.
Black-eyed peas	Traditional ingredient in the cooking of the American South (black-eyed peas and collard greens; black-eyed peas with ham). Earthy.
Borlotto beans	Large, speckled beans. Mostly puréed and turned into creamy dips.
Boston beans	See *White beans, small (navy and pea)*.
Chickpeas	Large, semifirm beans sold dried and canned. Used in casseroles, soups, and stews. Puréed and seasoned in Middle Eastern cuisine. Also known as garbanzo beans.
Kidney beans/ red beans	The traditional beans used in chili and other earthy casserole dishes and soups. A white kidney bean, called *cannellini,* is used in many northern Italian dishes. A staple in Mexican cooking as well. Faintly sweet.
Lentils	A tiny legume. Boiled with vegetables and other seasonings for side dishes, soups, and stews. No soaking is required before cooking.
Lima beans	Eaten as a side dish with mild seasonings. Also good in casseroles, especially with ham. Sweet flavor.
Pinto beans	The base of Mexican refried beans. Frequently used in highly spiced dishes. Earthy, mild flavor.
Split peas	Often used in soups, especially with ham. Sweet. Like lentils, no soaking is required.
White beans, large	Used in stews and casseroles. Often simmered with ham bones or other flavorful stocks. Neutral flavor.
White beans, small (navy and pea)	Foundation of Boston baked beans and the French *cassoulet.* Neutral flavor.

Many cookbooks advise home cooks to soak dried beans overnight before cooking them to reduce cooking time. We have consulted with some leading Mexican chefs, and they maintain that this step isn't necessary — in fact, soaking dried beans can leave them mushy. However, soaking them and discarding the soaking water does help with digestibility.

RECIPE ALERT

Later in the chapter, we show you how to make two great bean dishes:

>> **Lentils with Balsamic Vinegar:** The sweet edge of the balsamic vinegar performs magic on the nutty flavored lentils in this recipe. Lentils don't require soaking, and they boil tender in 20 to 25 minutes.

>> **White Beans with Tomatoes and Thyme:** White beans are among the most likable of dried beans, appealing to almost everyone, even kids. This side dish relies on bacon, onions, garlic, tomatoes, and herbs to add panache.

MONEY-SAVING KITCHEN TIPS

Being economical in the kitchen has nothing to do with cutting quality — in fact, just the contrary. Making every ounce count takes skill and respect for food. Here are some ways to begin:

- **Don't let leftovers ossify in the refrigerator.** Think ahead and use them the next day in omelets (see Chapter 11), chili, soups (see Chapter 12), stir-fries, casseroles like macaroni and cheese (see Chapter 16), and salads (see Chapter 12).

- **Don't use leftovers the same way you did the first time you served them.** Chop leftover roast chicken into a casserole or mix it with noodles in a soup. Toss leftover vegetables into a stir-fry or a pasta dish.

- **Develop knife skills.** Cutting up your own chicken and deboning your own meat saves considerable money. (See www.dummies.com/go/deboningchicken for step-by-step instructions to debone a chicken.) Plus, you have bones for making homemade soup stock, another money saver. Whole vegetables are cheaper than cut-up ones, too, and heads of lettuce are less expensive than bagged salad mix.

- **Develop delicious recipes with high-protein dried beans and economical vegetables.** Try pairing red beans with collard greens, navy beans with winter squash, kidney beans with green beans, or garbanzo beans with mustard greens.

- **Use your freezer intelligently.** Take advantage of supermarket sales. Buy ground meat, chicken breasts, steaks, and chops in bulk. Wrap and save leftovers from large casseroles such as baked lasagna (see Chapter 16), meat from a roasted leg of lamb (see Chapter 8), or a baked ham. And date everything you put in the freezer.

- **Grow an herb garden, even in a window box.** So many packaged fresh herbs go to waste because you don't use them often enough. Plus, they're expensive, and the cost adds up over time. With an herb garden, you can cut just what you need, and the rest will stay fresh until you need more. Start with some popular herbs that are easy to cultivate: basil, thyme, rosemary, mint, parsley, and tarragon.

- **Make your own versions of foods that you routinely buy in the supermarket.** You'll spend less money and get better quality. Examples include salad dressings (see Chapter 12), garlic bread, pizza (see the recipe later in this chapter), and soup (see Chapter 12).

- **Buy less-expensive cuts of meat and learn to tenderize them by braising and stewing.** See Chapter 7.

Pizza Pizazz

PREP TIME: 15 MIN | COOK TIME: 20 MIN | YIELD: 4-6 SERVINGS

INGREDIENTS

15 to 16 ounces refrigerated fresh pizza dough

2 teaspoons cornmeal flour

⅔ cup marinara sauce

Salt and black pepper to taste

¼ teaspoon crushed red pepper (optional)

6 ounces fresh mozzarella, thinly sliced and cut into ½-inch wide strips

1 tablespoon olive oil

2 ounces thinly sliced prosciutto, cut into 2- to 3-inch pieces

¼ cup fresh basil leaves

DIRECTIONS

1 Position a rack in the lower third of the oven and place a heavy 15-x-10-inch or larger baking sheet or 15- to 16-inch pizza stone on the rack. Preheat the oven to 450 degrees with the baking sheet or pizza stone in the oven. Allow the dough to stand at room temperature, covered, while the oven preheats.

2 On a lightly floured surface, roll the dough into a 14-x-9-inch rectangle (or a 14-inch circle if using a stone); pierce the dough about a dozen times all over with a fork (to keep the dough from bubbling up).

3 Carefully remove the hot baking sheet or stone from the oven and sprinkle with the cornmeal. Transfer the dough to the baking sheet or pizza stone. Bake in the preheated oven for 5 minutes.

4 Remove the partially baked crust from the oven. Spread the sauce over the crust, leaving a ½-inch border. Season with salt, black pepper, and crushed red pepper (if desired); top evenly with the cheese and brush the crust generously with olive oil.

5 Bake for 15 minutes or until the cheese melts and the crust is lightly browned. Remove from the oven; scatter the prosciutto and basil over the pizza. Cut into 6 to 8 slices and serve.

PER SERVING: *Calories 374 (From Fat 126); Fat 14g (Saturated 6g); Cholesterol 28mg; Sodium 1,346mg; Carbohydrate 47g (Dietary Fiber 1g); Protein 17g.*

VARY IT! You can omit the prosciutto and basil and add cooked chopped broccoli or eggplant or chopped black olives, anchovies, sun-dried tomatoes, or roasted peppers. You can mix up the mozzarella cheese with some grated Parmesan, or you can add some crumbled cooked sausage or sliced pepperoni. You can use whole-wheat pizza dough rather than the white flour dough. When you get the hang of this easy dish, you can make your own pizza yeast dough for even better pizza!

Curry Salmon Cakes

PREP TIME: 20 MIN	COOK TIME: 10 MIN	YIELD: 3–4 SERVINGS

INGREDIENTS

One 14.75-ounce can boneless salmon, drained

1 cup fresh, coarsely ground whole wheat or multigrain breadcrumbs

¼ cup chopped fresh parsley

2 tablespoons grated red onion (grated on largest holes of box grater)

1 egg, lightly beaten

3 tablespoons mayonnaise

¼ to ½ teaspoon curry powder, or to taste

Big dash cayenne pepper (optional)

Salt and black pepper to taste

2½ tablespoons vegetable oil

Dijon-style mustard for serving

DIRECTIONS

1 Put the salmon in a large mixing bowl; pick over the salmon and remove any small bones or cartilage. Use a fork to flake apart any large pieces.

2 Add half of the breadcrumbs, parsley, red onion, egg, mayonnaise, curry powder, cayenne pepper (if desired), salt, and black pepper to the salmon and mix until well combined. The mixture should hold together when pressed in the palm of your hand; if necessary, add 1 to 3 more teaspoons mayonnaise, 1 teaspoon at a time, to sufficiently moisten.

3 Place the remaining breadcrumbs on a large plate. Divide the salmon mixture into 6 equal portions, shaping each into a patty no more than 1 inch thick and about 2 inches across. Dredge the patties lightly on both sides in the breadcrumbs.

4 Heat 1½ tablespoon of the oil in a large nonstick skillet over medium-high until the oil starts to shimmer. Gently place 3 of the patties in the pan, without crowding them. Cook 3 to 5 minutes on each side or until lightly browned and heated through, turning once with a wide metal spatula and adjusting the heat to medium if necessary to keep them from browning and cooking too quickly. Remove them to a warm plate (or keep them warm in a 200-degree oven while you finish the second batch).

5 Add the remaining 1 tablespoon of oil to the pan and cook the remaining cakes. Serve with the Dijon-style mustard on the side.

PER SERVING: *Calories 370 (From Fat 189); Fat 21g (Saturated 3g); Cholesterol 87mg; Sodium 843mg; Carbohydrate 21g (Dietary Fiber 1g); Protein 26g.*

Lentils with Balsamic Vinegar

PREP TIME: ABOUT 20 MIN	COOK TIME: ABOUT 30 MIN	YIELD: 4 SERVINGS

INGREDIENTS

1½ cups lentils, rinsed

1 quart water

Salt

2 whole cloves

2 small yellow onions

1 bay leaf

2 sprigs fresh thyme, or ½ teaspoon dried

1 tablespoon butter

1 tablespoon olive oil

1 large carrot, peeled and finely diced

1 large clove garlic, finely chopped

1 tablespoon balsamic (or red wine) vinegar

Black pepper

DIRECTIONS

1 Put the lentils in a large pot or saucepan. Add the water and salt to taste. Cover and bring to a boil over high heat.

2 Stick the cloves into one onion and chop the other onion finely. Add the onion with cloves to the pot, along with the bay leaf and thyme. Reduce the heat and simmer, partially covered, for about 20 minutes or until the lentils are tender.

3 Carefully scoop out and reserve ½ cup of the cooking liquid. Drain the lentils. Remove and discard the onion with cloves, bay leaf, and thyme sprigs.

4 Heat the butter and olive oil in a large sauté pan or skillet over medium-high heat. Add the carrot, chopped onion, and garlic. Cook, stirring often, until the onion wilts, about 3 to 4 minutes. (Don't brown the garlic.)

5 Add the vinegar and the reserved ½ cup cooking liquid to the skillet. Cover, reduce the heat, and simmer for about 5 minutes, or until the vegetables are tender.

6 Stir the lentils into the vegetable mixture, cover, and cook over medium heat for about 2 minutes more, just to blend the flavors. Season with salt and black pepper to taste and serve.

PER SERVING: *Calories 309 (From Fat 63); Fat 7g (Saturated 2g); Cholesterol 8mg; Sodium 161mg; Carbohydrate 45g (Dietary Fiber 17g); Protein 19g.*

White Beans with Tomatoes and Thyme

PREP TIME: ABOUT 20 MIN	COOK TIME: ABOUT 1 HR 10 MIN	YIELD: 4 SERVINGS

INGREDIENTS

2 whole cloves

2 medium yellow onions

1 cup dried white beans (such as Great Northern or navy beans), rinsed

1 quart water

3 slices bacon

1 large carrot, peeled and cut in half lengthwise

1 bay leaf

Salt and black pepper

2 teaspoons butter or oil

1 large clove garlic, minced

1 teaspoon fresh chopped thyme, or ½ teaspoon dried

One 14.5-ounce can diced tomatoes, drained

2 tablespoons chopped parsley

DIRECTIONS

1 Stick the cloves into one of the onions and coarsely chop the other onion.

2 Place the beans in a large pot and add 1 quart water, the onion with cloves, the bacon, carrot, bay leaf, and salt and black pepper to taste.

3 Cover the pot and bring to a boil over high heat. Reduce the heat to medium-low and simmer, partially covered, for about one hour, or until the beans are tender.

4 Remove the bacon strips and chop into small pieces.

5 Heat the butter or oil in a large skillet over medium heat and sauté the bacon until golden brown, stirring.

6 Add the chopped onion, garlic, and thyme to the skillet and cook for about 2 to 3 minutes, or until the onions wilt.

7 Add the tomatoes to the skillet and cook for 2 to 3 minutes, stirring frequently. Remove from the heat.

8 Remove and discard the carrot, onion with cloves, and bay leaf from the pot of beans. Carefully scoop out and reserve half of the bean liquid and drain the beans.

(continued)

9   Add the beans to the tomato mixture and stir gently. If the mixture seems dry, add a little of the reserved liquid. Adjust the seasoning with salt and black pepper. Serve the beans hot, sprinkled with the parsley.

PER SERVING: *Calories 194 (From Fat 43); Fat 5g (Saturated 2g); Cholesterol 9mg; Sodium 315mg; Carbohydrate 28g (Dietary Fiber 9g); Protein 12g.*

TIP: If you prefer to soak the beans to aid with digestibility, cover them with cold water and soak overnight, or boil them for 2 minutes and let stand for 1 hour. Drain and replace water to cook.

Spanish Rice

PREP TIME: ABOUT 10 MIN | COOK TIME: ABOUT 30 MIN | YIELD: 10 SERVINGS

INGREDIENTS

1 tablespoon olive oil

2 cups converted rice

½ medium yellow onion, chopped

2 cloves garlic, peeled and minced

1 teaspoon oregano

½ teaspoon thyme

2 bay leaves

One 14-ounce can diced tomatoes

1 teaspoon salt

4 cups chicken broth

DIRECTIONS

1 In a large nonstick saucepan or Dutch oven, heat the olive oil over medium-high heat. Add the rice, onion, garlic, oregano, thyme, and bay leaves. Sauté until the rice is coated and onions are translucent, about 5 minutes.

2 Add the tomatoes, salt, and chicken broth. Bring the mixture to a boil.

3 Reduce the heat to medium-low, cover, and simmer until all the broth is absorbed, about 20 minutes. Add more broth if the rice looks dry. Remove the bay leaves and serve hot.

PER SERVING: *Calories 175 (From Fat 27); Fat 3g (Saturated 1g); Cholesterol 2mg; Sodium 683mg; Carbohydrate 33g (Dietary Fiber 1g); Protein 4g.*

VARY IT! If this dish isn't spicy enough for you, you can always stir in a few chopped jalapeño peppers or some hot red pepper flakes.

Chapter **18**

Going Global with Asian and Mediterranean Dishes

Without question, the biggest culinary trend in the United States over the past decade or more is Asian cuisine. Indeed, it has been a revolution. Not so long ago, the average home pantry was set up for two kinds of cooking: American and Italian — steak and potatoes on Wednesday, lasagna on Friday. But in the 1990s, Americans began to travel more, exploring new and exotic locations, among them Asia. They were exposed to foods they had never heard of and returned with a desire to enjoy them at home.

Restaurants heeded the call, and soon authentic Chinese and Japanese, Thai, Malaysian, Vietnamese, and Korean restaurants, to name a few, were readily available. This in turn led to a curiosity about cooking Asian-style, which, aside from being seductively delicious, is exceedingly healthful.

Similarly, the sunny and healthful food of the Mediterranean has become part of our culinary vocabulary. Based on heart-healthy ingredients like olive oil, garlic, summer vegetables, and fresh herbs, Mediterranean dishes have a secondary appeal because they require little time to prepare. Sauces, if there are any, are quick pan reductions. Furthermore, Mediterranean restaurants have opened at dizzying rates nationwide, so if you're looking for inspiration, you have plenty of places to turn.

In this chapter, we give you a sampling of the flavors and cooking techniques of Asian and Mediterranean cuisine. It will make you yearn for more.

Discovering the Asian Pantry

Asian cuisine relies on foods that are common to that area of the world. For this reason, you may be unfamiliar with some of the ingredients that Asians eat on a regular basis, and you'll probably need to do a little investigative shopping to find them. Happily, quality Asian markets can now be found in most medium-sized and larger cities. And, of course, you can find everything online. The following sections outline the most common ingredients to get you started.

TIP

Some of the ingredients in the following sections are used in the Asian recipes at the end of the chapter. If you can't find a specific ingredient at your regular grocery store, try a store that specializes in Indian and/or Asian foods.

Stocking up on Asian staples

If you want to dive into the marvelous world of Asian cooking, you need to gather a few staples to always have on hand. You'll also want to familiarize yourself with the common Asian produce, like bok choy and ginger root. Here's a rundown of products to consider, but don't think of using them only when cooking up Asian dishes. You can use the following to enhance the flavor of your favorite soups, stews, dressings, salads, and marinades. Check out the many everyday uses we provide for each product.

>> **Bok choy:** Also known as Chinese cabbage, its long white stem and dark ribbed leaves resemble romaine lettuce. A staple in Chinese cooking, it has a very mild flavor and lends a nice crunchy texture when eaten fresh. Look for firm white stalks with crisp, unblemished green leaves. Toss thinly sliced bok choy leaves and stems into chicken soup or minestrone, or sauté in olive oil with onions to garnish a serving of roasted fish.

CURRY PASTES

Making a curry sauce at home requires a lot of time and ingredients, some of which are found only in Asian markets. A great shortcut is jarred curry paste. The three versions here add a heady, complex flavor to many dishes, and not only Asian. We suggest you experiment with each of them to see which best suit your tastes and style of cooking. Curry pastes are widely available in most American supermarkets.

- **Red curry paste:** The hottest of commercial chili pastes, this is made with a complex blend of dried red chilies. But it's more than mere flame throwing. In the mix are aromatic ingredients, like lemongrass, galangal, kaffir lime, coriander, and cumin. Aside from curries, you can use it to enhance crab cakes, pork stir-fries, shellfish stews, Thai peanut sauce, and more.

- **Green curry paste:** The medium-hot paste gets its color from fresh green chilies, giving it a fresher, more vegetal flavor. It pairs well with poultry, seafood, soups, and all kinds of noodle dishes.

- **Yellow curry paste:** Sharing a heat intensity with its green counterpart, this paste gets its color from turmeric, which is slightly bitter and carries a hint of horseradish. Like green curry paste, it enlivens all kinds of sauces, soups, stews, and noodle dishes.

» **Cilantro:** Love it or hate it, cilantro is a key flavor in many Asian cuisines. Similar to parsley, its bright green leaves are extremely pungent and fragrant, so use them in moderation. Try it as a garnish as well as a kick-starter for soups and sauce.

» **Coconut milk:** Creamy and rich, canned coconut milk has a distinctive sweet and assertive flavor and contributes a smooth texture to curries, soups, marinades, and dairy-free puddings.

» **Curry paste:** A blend of ghee (clarified butter), curry powder, vinegar, and seasonings, this rich and nuanced condiment can be interchanged with the sharper dried curry powder.

» **Dried black mushrooms:** Asian cooking employs all kinds of dried mushrooms, but if you stock only one, we recommend dried black ones. Intensely flavorful, rich and earthy, they lend structure and heartiness to all kinds of soups and sauces. To rehydrate, simmer for about 15 minutes and then add them, along with the soaking water, to your favorite chili, chicken stew, or vegetable soup. Keep them cool and dry, and they'll last indefinitely.

» **Fish sauce:** Made from fermented fish and sea salt, fish sauce packs a powerful punch of flavor that you may or may not fancy. Asian chefs add it to all kinds of dishes to contribute a warm, rounded character. Try adding a small amount to stir-fry sauces, soups, and casseroles. It pairs particularly well with shellfish.

» **Ginger root:** The knobby, odd-looking little root makes up for in flavor what it lacks in pulchritude. The flavor is sharp, peppery, and faintly sweet. It isn't the same spice as ground ginger. Ginger root is used to brighten all kinds of Asian sauces, especially in India. Toss some raw into salad dressings; sprinkle it into meat or vegetable stir-fries; add thin slices to vegetables, like cauliflower florets, before roasting; shred and sauté some in oil with garlic and then add sliced cabbage and apples to the pan; you can even add coin-sized slices to pitchers of homemade lemonade, or make yourself a steaming cup of ginger tea. The skin should be greenish-yellow to white and have no dark spots.

» **Hoisin:** One of the most widespread and versatile of Asian sauces, this thick sauce is spicy and quite sweet, made from soybeans, garlic, and sun-dried chili peppers.

» **Oyster sauce:** This isn't as exotic as it sounds, but it does have subtle uses in many Asian dishes, primarily rounding out flavors in stir-fries. Oyster sauces today are usually made with a base of sugar and salt thickened with corn starch. Oyster extracts or essences are then imparted for flavor. Oyster sauce has a pleasing balance of sweet and salty with a rich, earthy undertone.

» **Rice vinegar:** Mild in flavor and less harsh than wine vinegar, rice vinegar is great for marinades, dipping sauces, and even in vinaigrettes.

» **Sesame oil:** With a characteristic toasty flavor and unctuous texture, sesame oil rounds out all sorts of dressings, dipping sauces, and marinades.

» **Soy sauce:** This should be in every cupboard. You can use it as a flavorful salt substitute in all kinds of cooking. Made from fermented soybeans, soy sauce can be thick or thin, dark or light. Many home cooks prefer the low-sodium version, which works perfectly fine. It's loaded with *umami* — a savory taste that lingers on the tongue. Add it to meat mixtures when making burgers or meatloaf and to dressings, dips, and soups.

» **Sriracha (chili garlic sauce):** You may call this the "Asian Tabasco," an all-purpose bright red hot sauce made from red chili peppers, garlic, vinegar, and sugar. It's hot and tangy with a touch of sweetness and perks up all kinds of grilled meats as well as Asian style sauces and stir-fries.

RECIPE ALERT

Don't let the long list of ingredients dissuade you from making Pad Thai. After you've chopped, measured, and set the ingredients out, *mis en place* (the French term for having all recipe ingredients prepared and ready for cooking), you can assemble the dish in minutes, just like they do on the streets of Thailand. Check out the recipe at the end of the chapter for Pad Thai with Shrimp.

Starting with the basics: Asian noodles

Asian cooking employs an endless variety of noodles, each with its own shape, texture, and flavor — and they're taken very seriously. You don't need to stock more than one or two types of noodles. Get to know the following varieties before heading in more exotic directions. Here are a few of the most popular:

>> **Lo mein noodles (Chinese egg noodles):** These are linguini-shaped noodles made with wheat flour and eggs, the base of Chinese stir-fry dishes. They're sold in both flat and round shapes and fresh and dried. If you're in a pinch and don't have lo mein noodles on hand, you can substitute with spaghetti noodles, but don't sub regular egg noodles for lo mein.

>> **Ramen:** These are dry, deep-fried noodles usually sold in cellophane bags (some contain morsels of dehydrated vegetables and broth mix). Made of wheat, ramen noodles are much thinner and longer than udon (see description later in this list) and have a slightly elastic texture. They're typically served in broth and are great soaked in homemade chicken or vegetable stock. (See the recipe for Chicken Stock in Chapter 12.)

>> **Soba noodles:** These are Japanese buckwheat noodles. In Japan, people slurp up these noodles in restaurants and street corners for breakfast, lunch, and dinner. American chefs have fallen in love with them for both their versatility and nutty flavor, so you'll encounter them in the most unlikely of places. The dried version is widely available.

>> **Udon noodles:** These big thick Japanese wheat noodles, both round and flat, are now found in many supermarkets and gourmet stores. Fresh are preferable to dried for their tender toothy texture. Because of their size, they're particularly well suited to rich, assertive flavored sauces.

Getting it right with Asian rice

There are more than 40,000 different varieties of rice worldwide, although you would do fine to memorize only about 800. Asians consume a bewildering array of rice that varies in color (white, brown, black, and red), shape (short, medium, and long), and flavor (jasmine, basmati, and more). To get you started with Asian cooking, we recommend three commonly available, highly versatile rices. Get to know these and, if your curiosity is piqued, start working your way through the other 39,997 varieties. Store rice in an airtight container, such as a mason jar.

>> **Jasmine rice:** This is a medium- to long-grain rice grown in Southeast Asia. It's favored for its earthy, nutty flavor and pleasing floral aroma when cooked. Its soft, clingy consistency (be extra careful not to overcook it) makes it well suited to fried rice dishes and preparations with sauces.

>> **Basmati:** This widely popular rice in Asia and America grows in the foothills of the Himalayas in northern India and Pakistan as well as some parts of the United States. The grain is long and almost needle-shaped and is available in white or brown. Unlike starchy Jasmine rice, Basmati remains firm and doesn't stick together. If you've had rich Indian curries from restaurants, you've probably had them with Basmati.

>> **Japanese sushi rice:** A short- to medium-grain rice, Japanese sushi rice has raw grains that are almost translucent. Although the grains separate when cooked, they become relatively sticky in comparison to Basmati — good for the chopstick-challenged! This rice is often referred to as sticky rice and is what you find at many sushi restaurants.

Exploring the World of Mediterranean Cooking

Mediterranean cuisine represents a grab bag of sunny and healthful cuisines from countries bordering the Mediterranean, including France, Spain, Morocco, Greece, Turkey, Lebanon, and Syria. That's quite a pot full, and we don't try to show you all of them in this book. Our goal is to give you a sense of some regional ingredients.

You've probably heard how the low-fat, produce-rich Mediterranean diet can help you live to 120 or older — well almost. Indeed, this regional pantry is filled with foods everyone should be eating more of: olive oil, protein-rich legumes, seafood, whole grains, pasta, cheese, and in-season produce. And a little red wine doesn't hurt, either, so say the food scientists.

RECIPE ALERT

Although the ingredients and spices may vary from country to country, Mediterranean cooking is based on simple, light, unfussy cooking, which makes it suitable for quick family dinners. Often, you can toss together a wonderful main course in less than 30 minutes (see the Shrimp Pasta with Kalamata Olives and Feta Cheese recipe later in this chapter). Sometimes all you need is some olive oil, garlic, and fresh herbs as a base for a quick pan sauce.

Meeting popular Mediterranean meats

The Spanish love ham, and that's an understatement. Go into almost any bar or restaurant, and you'll see haunches of serrano ham hanging over the bar. Serrano ham is essentially dry-cured and aged ham from a special breed of pigs. It's savored as a tapa, on a slice of bread, or in a sandwich. The most treasured of these is called *jamón Iberico* (ham from Iberia) from acorn-fed pigs. For decades, importing cured ham from Spain was illegal. That has changed, but still the easiest way to purchase it is online.

RECIPE ALERT

Made from coarsely ground pork, *chorizo,* another Spanish and Portugeuse specialty, is aggressively flavored with garlic, chili powders, and other ingredients. Salty and slightly peppery, chorizo is generally eaten as a snack. Many cooks remove the casing and add it to soups, stews, and casseroles to impart a complex, smoky flavor. See our recipe later in this chapter for Spanish Lentils with Vegetables, which uses chorizo.

Goat cheese and feta cheese

Feta cheese is most associated with Greece and goat cheese with France, although they have pretty well infiltrated the cuisine of all countries in the region.

Goat cheese, or goat milk cheese, was once found primarily in Mediterranean countries; however, it's now available in the United States in every variation: fresh, aged, semi-aged, herb-coated, pepper-coated, and more. Fresh goat cheese is creamy and mild; as it ages, it becomes more tart. It is most often eaten plain with bread or crackers. It's also popular in salads and, sometimes, in simple cold sauces.

Feta, made from sheep's milk, has a higher fat content than most goat cheeses. Feta's creamy texture and faintly tart flavor make it a great addition to all kinds of dishes. Sprinkle it on top of baked potatoes or over pizza (it pairs nicely with olives and fresh tomatoes), add it to a sandwich with some oregano, crumble it and distribute over salads, add it to pastas, serve it as a snack on crackers or bread with sun-dried tomatoes, or even use it on hamburgers.

Olives

Olives are a staple in the Mediterranean diet. People eat them raw but also cook with them. In Spain, Greece, Turkey, Italy, Morocco, and Argentina, olives find their way in numerous recipes, from the Italian pasta puttanesca to Spanish rice dishes and Moroccan-style *tagines* (a slow-cooked meat or poultry stew with vegetables and olives). In Greece they are paired with feta cheese in salads. Olives are green or black (these are tree-ripened or cured). Black olives are generally more salty.

RECIPE ALERT

Kalamata olives are almond-shaped Greek olives with a dark eggplant color. Both salty and fruity from curing in wine vinegar, they're delicious as a snack or in salads. Available everywhere, they're usually sold packed in olive oil. In Greece, they're primarily served plain as snacks. They're also the source of much Greek olive oil (for more details about olive oil, see Chapter 12). (See our recipe for Shrimp Pasta with Kalamata Olives and Feta Cheese later in this chapter.)

SAFFRON: NOT YOUR RUN-OF-THE-MILL SPICE

Saffron is called the world's most expensive spice. Derived from the dried stigmas of the purple saffron crocus, it takes anywhere from 70,000 to 250,000 flowers to make one pound of saffron. Moreover, the flowers have to be individually hand-picked in the autumn when fully open.

Fortunately, you add only a little to a dish to lend it color and aroma. Saffron isn't easy to describe. Earthy, with an aroma almost reminiscent of hay, it can be magical in dishes like paella, risotto, pilafs, and stews. It's considered essential for French bouillabaisse. You can also combine various root vegetables in a quick braised dish with saffron, cinnamon, cumin, and almonds.

Pure saffron is made up of tiny, bright-red threads. The redder the saffron, the higher the quality. The tips of the threads should be slightly lighter with an orange-red color, showing that it's not cheap saffron that has been tinted red to look expensive. Prices vary widely. A 0.06-ounce container can run from $15 and up. Don't add too much to a dish or else food will taste almost medicinal. Ground and powdered saffron are a pale and risky substitute, sometimes illegally cut with turmeric or paprika.

Preserved lemons

This easy-to-make delicacy is associated with the fragrant cooking of Morocco. Preserved lemons are a crucial ingredient in that country's famed tagines: meat and vegetable stews (we include a recipe for Chicken Tagine with Tomatoes, Olives, and Preserved Lemons in Chapter 7). Aging the fruit in salt reduces the intense bitterness of lemon rind, and the pith mellows out and develops a fresh lemony character.

Preserved lemons spark up grains, salads, salad dressings of all kinds, dips, salsas, and even some light pasta sauces. You can also eat them like a vegetable — rind and all.

RECIPE ALERT

You can find preserved lemons at almost any specialty food store, or you can make your own. See the recipe later in this chapter.

Orange–Ginger Asian Salad

PREP TIME: 20 MIN	YIELD: 4–5 SERVINGS

INGREDIENTS

½ cup fresh orange juice

1½ teaspoons grated orange peel

2 tablespoons rice vinegar

1 to 1½ teaspoons minced, peeled fresh ginger, or to taste

1 tablespoon low-sodium soy sauce

1 tablespoon plus 2 teaspoons dark sesame oil

1 tablespoon plus 1 teaspoon peanut or vegetable oil

1 teaspoon hot chile sauce (such as sriracha)

4 to 6 cups torn iceberg lettuce

1 cucumber, peeled, halved lengthwise, and thinly sliced

Salt to taste

1 carrot, peeled and grated on large holes of grater

DIRECTIONS

1 To make the dressing, add all the ingredients, except the lettuce, cucumber, salt, and grated carrot to a small bowl and whisk well to combine. Set the dressing aside to blend flavors while preparing the salad.

2 Place the iceberg lettuce and cucumber slices in a large mixing bowl. Drizzle with the salad dressing and toss well to combine. Taste and season with salt.

3 Divide the salad between four individual plates; garnish each serving with an equal amount of the grated carrot and serve.

PER SERVING: *Calories 127 (From Fat 90); Fat 10g (Saturated 1.5g); Cholesterol 0mg; Sodium 456mg; Carbohydrate 8g (Dietary Fiber 1g); Protein 1g.*

VARY IT! Add 1 clove of crushed garlic to the dressing. Let the dressing set 20 minutes to blend the flavors, and then remove the garlic before dressing the salad.

Pork and Noodle Stir-Fry

PREP TIME: ABOUT 15 MIN | COOK TIME: ABOUT 15 MIN | YIELD: 4 SERVINGS

INGREDIENTS

½ pound dried Chinese noodles, or thin spaghetti or linguini (broken in half)

2 teaspoons sesame oil

3 tablespoons light soy sauce

1 tablespoon dry or medium-dry sherry

2 teaspoons cornstarch

1 teaspoon packed brown sugar

2 cups thinly sliced cooked pork (or raw pork)

2 tablespoons vegetable oil

1 tablespoon peeled and grated ginger root

3 cups thinly sliced napa cabbage, bok choy, or green cabbage

1 cup thinly sliced or shredded carrot

½ cup chicken stock

3 thinly sliced green onions (white and green parts)

1 large clove garlic, peeled and minced

½ jalapeño or red chile pepper, seeded and chopped (optional)

Salt and black pepper to taste

3 tablespoons chopped cilantro

DIRECTIONS

1 Bring a large pot of lightly salted water to a boil; add the noodles and cook according to package directions. Drain and rinse noodles under cold water; drain again.

2 Transfer the noodles to a medium mixing bowl; toss them with the sesame oil. Set aside.

3 In a medium mixing bowl, stir together 2 tablespoons of the soy sauce, the sherry, cornstarch, and brown sugar; add the pork and toss to mix well. Set aside.

4 Place a wok or large skillet over high heat. Add the vegetable oil and heat until oil is hot but not smoking.

5 Add the ginger root to the wok and stir just a few seconds, or until it browns lightly. Add the cabbage, carrots, chicken stock, green onions, garlic, jalapeño pepper (if desired), and pork with all of the marinade.

6 Cook, tossing the ingredients often, for 3 to 5 minutes, or until the vegetables are crisp-tender.

7 Remove the wok from the heat; add the noodles and toss thoroughly. Stir in the remaining tablespoon of soy sauce. Season to taste with salt and black pepper. Sprinkle with the cilantro before serving.

PER SERVING: *Calories 444 (From Fat 134); Fat 15g (Saturated 2g); Cholesterol 56mg; Sodium 813mg; Carbohydrate 53g (Dietary Fiber 10g); Protein 29g.*

Asian Peanut and Sesame Noodles

PREP TIME: 25 MIN	COOK TIME: 6–8 MIN	YIELD: 4–6 SERVINGS

INGREDIENTS

½ cup all-natural, sugar-free peanut butter

¼ cup water

3 tablespoons rice vinegar

3 tablespoons low-sodium soy sauce

3 tablespoons toasted sesame oil

2 tablespoons minced, peeled fresh ginger

1 tablespoon dark brown sugar

2 to 3 tablespoons red chili sauce, or to taste

12 ounces linguine, or ¼-inch wide lo mein noodles

3 large scallions, both white and green parts, thinly sliced on a diagonal

1 large red bell pepper, cored, seeded, and sliced into thin 1-inch long strips

⅓ cup lightly salted peanuts, coarsely chopped

¼ cup chopped cilantro leaves (optional)

DIRECTIONS

1 Combine the peanut butter and water in a large glass measuring cup and microwave about 15 seconds, just to soften the peanut butter. Remove from the microwave and stir to combine.

2 Add the vinegar, soy sauce, sesame oil, ginger, brown sugar, and chili sauce to the peanut butter, and mix well to combine. Set the peanut sauce aside.

3 Cook the linguine or noodles until al dente, according to the package directions. Drain and place in a large bowl. Immediately pour the peanut sauce over the linguine or noodles; add the scallions and red pepper, and toss well to combine.

4 Sprinkle with the chopped peanuts and cilantro (if desired) and serve.

PER SERVING: *Calories 514 (From Fat 252); Fat 28g (Saturated 6g); Cholesterol 40mg; Sodium 820mg; Carbohydrate 48g (Dietary Fiber 8g); Protein 19g.*

VARY IT! If you can't find chili sauce, which is simply a mixture of chilies and garlic, you can substitute 1 to 2 stemmed, seeded, and finely chopped fresh chili peppers, like serrano or jalapeño, or crushed red pepper flakes to taste. You can also toss 2 cups of shredded or thinly sliced Napa cabbage into the noodles.

Pad Thai with Shrimp

PREP TIME: 25 MIN | COOK TIME: 15 MIN | YIELD: 3–4 SERVINGS

INGREDIENTS

8 ounces thin rice stick noodles

⅓ cup warm water, plus more for soaking noodles

1 tablespoon tamarind paste

3 tablespoons fish sauce

3 tablespoons packed brown sugar

2 teaspoons red chili sauce, or ½ teaspoon red cayenne pepper

4 tablespoons peanut or vegetable oil

1 pound extra-large shrimp, peeled and deveined

⅛ teaspoon salt

4 cloves garlic, minced (about 5 teaspoons)

1 small chili pepper, seeded and minced (about 2 tablespoons)

5 scallions, both white and green parts, sliced thinly on a diagonal

2 large eggs, lightly beaten

3 cups bean sprouts

⅓ cup finely chopped unsalted roasted peanuts

Lime wedges for serving

DIRECTIONS

1   Pour hot water to cover the rice noodles in a large bowl; soak until softened but not fully tender, about 10 to 15 minutes. (The noodles should be soft enough to bend easily but still a little firm and slightly undercooked; they'll finish cooking in the skillet.) Drain and set the noodles aside.

2   To make the sauce, add the tamarind paste and the ⅓-cup warm water to a small bowl and stir to combine. Add the fish sauce, brown sugar, red chili sauce (or cayenne pepper), and 1 tablespoon of the oil; set the sauce aside.

3   Heat a wok or large, 12-inch frying pan over medium-high. Add 2 tablespoons of oil and tilt the pan to swirl the oil and coat the bottom. When the oil shimmers, add the shrimp and season with salt. Cook, tossing occasionally until the shrimp are pink and opaque, 1 to 3 minutes, depending on their size. Transfer the shrimp to a plate and set aside.

4   Add the remaining 1 tablespoon of oil to the skillet. Set the pan over medium heat and when the oil shimmers, add the garlic, minced chili, and the white and pale green parts of the scallions. (Save the dark green parts to garnish the finished dish.) Cook, scraping up any browned bits on the bottom of the pan with a wooden spoon, and stir constantly, about 1 minute, or until the scallions soften slightly.

5   Add the beaten eggs and stir with a wooden spoon about 20 seconds or until scrambled but still a little moist. Add the softened rice noodles and about 3 tablespoons of the sauce and toss with two wooden spoons (two wide spatulas also work well) just until combined. Lift and turn the noodles over in the pan to help coat them in the sauce and cook evenly.

6   Pour the remaining sauce over the noodles; increase the heat to medium-high, and cook, tossing constantly by lifting and turning the noodles, for 2 to 3 minutes.

7 Add the bean sprouts and the shrimp, and continue to cook 1 to 2 minutes, tossing until the noodles are tender but with a bite. Stir in 2 to 4 tablespoons water, or more if needed, to moisten the noodles. Scrape up the browned bits on the bottom of the pan with the wooden spoon to incorporate them into the mixture.

8 Portion out onto individual plates, garnishing each with the remaining scallions, a generous sprinkling of nuts, and the lime wedges.

PER SERVING: *Calories 571 (From Fat 207); Fat 23g (Saturated 4g); Cholesterol 236mg; Sodium 1,772mg; Carbohydrate 67g (Dietary Fiber 3g); Protein 23g.*

VARY IT! The tamarind paste is an important ingredient in Pad Thai, but if you can't find it, you can substitute 2 tablespoons of lime juice combined with 2 tablespoons of water. If you're a fan of fresh ginger, add 2 teaspoons to the pan along with the garlic, chilies, and scallions.

MISE EN PLACE

The French term *mise en place* (meeze-on-plahs) translates as "everything in place" and means to have on hand all the ingredients that you need to prepare a dish. For example, onions and herbs are chopped, garlic is minced, vegetables are rinsed, ingredients are measured, and so on, all ahead of time. This preparation allows you to cook efficiently and without interruption, the way real restaurant chefs do it. Practice *mise en place* by having all your prep work completed right up to the point of cooking.

Yellow Chicken Curry

PREP TIME: 20 MIN	COOK TIME: 35 MIN	YIELD: 4–5 SERVINGS

INGREDIENTS

1¼ to 1½ pounds boneless, skinless chicken breasts, cut into 1½-inch pieces

Salt

4 teaspoons peanut or vegetable oil

2 medium shallots, chopped (about ¾ cup)

1 red bell pepper, cut into 1-inch pieces

1 clove garlic, chopped (optional)

½ cup yellow curry paste

1 teaspoon brown sugar

1¼ pounds sweet potatoes, peeled and cut into ½-inch pieces

One 13.5-ounce can unsweetened coconut milk

1¼ cups chicken broth or water

½ cup chopped fresh cilantro or basil

6 cups boiled jasmine or basmati rice for serving

DIRECTIONS

1 Sprinkle chicken lightly with salt. Heat 2 teaspoons of the oil in a large saucepan or skillet over high heat. Add the chicken and cook 6 to 8 minutes or until lightly browned, using tongs to turn once. Remove the chicken to a plate and set aside.

2 Reduce the heat to medium; add the remaining 2 teaspoons of oil to the pan. When the oil is hot, add the shallot and bell pepper; cook, stirring occasionally, until the shallot is translucent and the pepper has softened slightly, 3 to 5 minutes. Add the garlic (if desired) and cook, stirring, about 30 seconds, or until fragrant.

3 Add the yellow curry paste to the pan; sprinkle the brown sugar and cook, about 1 minute or until heated through, stirring and scraping up any browned bits on the bottom of the pan.

4 Add the sweet potatoes, coconut milk, and chicken broth or water. Raise the heat to high and bring to a boil. Reduce the heat and simmer about 15 minutes, until the sweet potatoes are nearly tender, stirring occasionally.

5 Return the chicken and any juices that accumulated on the plate to the pan and cook about 5 minutes, or until the chicken is cooked and the curry sauce is slightly thickened. Spoon onto individual plates and garnish each serving with cilantro or basil. Accompany with boiled jasmine or basmati rice.

PER SERVING: *Calories 1,088 (From Fat 216); Fat 24g (Saturated 15g); Cholesterol 120mg; Sodium 1,831mg; Carbohydrate 149g (Dietary Fiber 5g); Protein 58g.*

Preserved Lemons

PREP TIME: ABOUT 20 MIN	PRESERVING TIME: 4 WEEKS	YIELD: 16 SERVINGS

INGREDIENTS

4 medium, thick-skinned lemons

About 6 tablespoons (not iodized) salt

Juice of 4 lemons, or more if needed

DIRECTIONS

1 Scrub the lemons well. Using a sharp knife, slice the lemons into quarters, stopping about ½-inch from the end to leave the quarters attached to the fruit. Pack 1 tablespoon of salt into the center of each cut lemon. Place them in a tall 1-quart wide-mouth mason jar, fitted with a lid, and press them down so they fit snuggly.

2 Sprinkle them with one more tablespoon of salt. Add the lemon juice and press them gently into the juice as much as possible. Cover the jar and let set 3 to 4 days, turning the jar over a couple of times a day, during which time they'll soften and release their juice.

3 Press them down again and add 1 more tablespoon salt and additional juice if necessary to completely cover. Close the jar and let set for at least one month, turning the jar over every few days to redistribute the salt and juices.

4 Before using, remove and discard the pulp, and then rinse the rind well. A harmless white mold may appear on the fruit; simply rinse it off before cutting up and using the peel. After opening, preserved lemons will keep up to a year, without refrigerating. You can use the salted juice to make salad dressings or marinades.

PER SERVING: *Calories 7 (From Fat 0); Fat 0g (Saturated 0g); Cholesterol 0mg; Sodium 2,654mg; Carbohydrate 7g (Dietary Fiber 1g); Protein 0g.*

TIP: Cut up the juiced lemons and, if you have a rose garden, compost them into the soil around the roots of the plant. Roses love the acidity of lemon peel.

Goat Cheese with Honey and Fruit

| PREP TIME: 12 MIN | YIELD: 8 SERVINGS |

INGREDIENTS

32 whole-grain crackers

8 ounces goat cheese

8 dried apricots

8 dried figs

1 pear, thinly sliced

3 tablespoons honey

DIRECTIONS

1 Arrange the crackers on a serving dish. Spread each cracker with 1 tablespoon of goat cheese and top with an apricot, a fig, or a pear slice.

2 In a microwave-safe bowl, heat the honey for 30 seconds; drizzle the honey over the fruit and crackers and serve.

PER SERVING: *Calories 249 (From Fat 99); Fat11g (Saturated 6g); Cholesterol 22mg; Carbohydrate 31g (Dietary Fiber 4g); Protein 9g.*

Spanish Lentils with Vegetables

PREP TIME: 15 MIN	COOK TIME: 45 MIN	YIELD: 8 SERVINGS

INGREDIENTS

3 tablespoons olive oil

1 medium onion, diced

3 cloves garlic, mashed

4 ounces Spanish chorizo or Portuguese sausage (linguiça)

2 cups dried red lentils

1 medium tomato, diced

2 medium carrots, sliced in ½-inch rounds

1 large potato, cut in 1-inch cubes

4 cups low-sodium chicken stock

½ teaspoon ground cumin

1 teaspoon sweet paprika

1 bay leaf

Salt to taste

DIRECTIONS

1 In a 4-quart saucepan, heat the olive oil over medium heat. Add the onion and garlic and sauté for 2 minutes.

2 Add the sausage and cook for 5 minutes. Add the dried lentils, diced tomatoes, carrots, and potatoes, and sauté for 3 minutes.

3 Pour the stock over the vegetable mixture, season with the cumin, paprika, and bay leaf, and bring the mixture to a boil.

4 Reduce the temperature to medium-low and simmer the lentil mixture for 30 minutes or until tender. Season with salt to taste, remove the bay leaf, and serve.

PER SERVING: *Calories 353 (From Fat 112); Fat 12g (Saturated 3g); Cholesterol 12mg; Sodium 234mg; Carbohydrate 43g (Dietary Fiber 7g); Protein 19g.*

Lemon Asparagus with Parmesan

PREP TIME: 8 MIN	COOK TIME: 3 MIN	YIELD: 6 SERVINGS

INGREDIENTS

½ teaspoon salt

1¼ pounds asparagus

Zest and juice of 1 lemon

1 clove garlic, minced

¼ cup parsley, chopped

2 tablespoons olive oil

1 tablespoon butter, melted

¼ teaspoon salt

2 ounces Parmesan cheese

DIRECTIONS

1 Fill a 6-quart pot with water and a ½ teaspoon salt. Bring the water to a boil.

2 Meanwhile, trim tops of the asparagus and remove the outer skin of the bottom of the stalks (about 2 inches from the bottom) with a vegetable peeler. Cut the stalks into 3-inch pieces.

3 Add the asparagus to the boiling water and boil for 3 minutes; strain. Immediately place asparagus into a large bowl of ice water for 1 minute. Strain again and place in a serving bowl.

4 Combine the lemon zest and juice, garlic, parsley, olive oil, melted butter, and salt. Pour the mixture over the asparagus and toss. Peel long strands of Parmesan over the top of the asparagus and serve.

PER SERVING: *Calories 116 (From Fat 83); Fat 9g (Saturated 4g); Cholesterol 13mg; Sodium 451mg; Carbohydrate 4g (Dietary Fiber 2g); Protein 6g.*

Shrimp Pasta with Kalamata Olives and Feta Cheese

PREP TIME: 4 MIN	COOK TIME: 14 MIN	YIELD: 4 SERVINGS

INGREDIENTS

2 teaspoons olive oil

3 cloves garlic, minced

½ teaspoon red pepper flakes

2 cups frozen baby artichoke hearts, quartered

½ cup chopped pitted kalamata olives

1 cup white wine

1 pound medium shrimp, peeled and deveined

½ pound angel hair pasta

¼ cup fresh basil, cut into long strips

¼ cup crumbled feta cheese

DIRECTIONS

1 Bring 3 quarts of water to a boil. Meanwhile, coat a nonstick skillet with cooking spray and heat the olive oil over medium heat. Add the garlic and red pepper flakes, and sauté for 1 minute.

2 Add the artichoke hearts and olives and sauté for 3 minutes. Add the wine and shrimp and continue to cook until the shrimp is no longer translucent (about 4 minutes).

3 Add the pasta to the water and cook according to package instructions (2 to 5 minutes). Drain the pasta and gently toss with the shrimp sauce in a large serving bowl until well coated. Top with the basil and feta to serve.

PER SERVING: *Calories 500 (From Fat 78); Fat 9g (Saturated 2g); Cholesterol 181mg; Sodium 431mg; Carbohydrate 60g (Dietary Fiber 4g); Protein 34g.*

Osso Buco

INGREDIENTS

4 meaty slices of veal shanks cut across the bones (each about 2 inches thick; about 3½ pounds total)

Salt and black pepper

½ cup all-purpose flour

2 tablespoons olive oil

1 large yellow onion, finely chopped

2 to 3 large carrots, peeled and chopped

1 stalk celery, chopped

3 large cloves garlic, finely chopped

4 canned anchovy fillets, drained and mashed (optional)

½ teaspoon dried marjoram

2 sprigs fresh thyme, or 1 teaspoon dried

1½ cups canned crushed tomatoes

1 cup dry white wine or white grape juice

1 bay leaf

1 teaspoon finely grated lemon zest

1 teaspoon finely grated orange zest

Gremolata (see the following recipe)

DIRECTIONS

1 Sprinkle the veal shanks with salt and black pepper to taste. Roll them in the flour to give them a light coating, patting to remove excess flour.

2 Heat the oil over medium-high heat in a heavy Dutch oven large enough to hold the veal shanks in one layer with the bones upright. Brown the veal all around, turning often, about 10 minutes. Remove the shanks from the pan and reserve them on a plate.

3 Lower the heat to medium and add the onion, carrots, and celery to the pan. Cook, stirring often, until the onions wilt, about 2 or 3 minutes.

4 Add the garlic, mashed anchovies (if desired), marjoram, and thyme. Stir and add the tomatoes, wine, bay leaf, and salt and black pepper to taste.

5 Return the veal shanks to the pan with any juices that have accumulated in the plate. Cover, reduce the heat to low, and simmer for about 1 hour, or until the meat is tender. (The meat should easily separate from the bone when prodded with a fork.)

6 Remove the veal from the pan and scoop some of the vegetable mixture onto each serving plate. Sprinkle with lemon and orange zest. Place a veal shank on top of each serving, and sprinkle Gremolata over it.

PER SERVING: *Calories 447 (From Fat 125); Fat 14g (Saturated 3g); Cholesterol 195mg; Sodium 378mg; Carbohydrate 24g (Dietary Fiber 4g); Protein 54g.*

Gremolata

PREP TIME: ABOUT 10 MIN   YIELD: 3½ TABLESPOONS

INGREDIENTS

5 teaspoons grated or minced lemon peel (without the bitter white pith)

2 teaspoons finely chopped Italian parsley

1 teaspoon finely chopped garlic

1 teaspoon finely chopped rosemary (optional)

DIRECTIONS

Combine all ingredients in a bowl.

PER SERVING: *Calories 10 (From Fat 1); Fat 0g (Saturated 0g); Cholesterol 0mg; Sodium 3mg; Carbohydrate 3g (Dietary Fiber 1g); Protein 0g.*

TIP: Tightly covered, this topping will last several days in the refrigerator.

Sautéed Chicken Breasts in Red Wine Tomato Sauce

PREP TIME: 10 MIN	COOK TIME: 45 MIN	YIELD: YIELD: 4 SERVINGS

INGREDIENTS

Four 4-ounce bone-in, skin-on chicken breasts

4 tablespoons olive oil, divided

¼ teaspoon salt

½ teaspoon black pepper

1 tablespoon fennel seeds

2 celery stalks, chopped

½ medium onion, chopped

4 cloves garlic, sliced

1 teaspoon red pepper flakes

¼ cup black kalamata olives, pitted

One 14.8-ounce can tomatoes, chopped

1 cup spicy red wine, such as a red Zinfandel

2 tablespoons parsley, chopped

2 tablespoons mint, chopped

DIRECTIONS

1 Preheat the oven to 350 degrees. Rub the chicken with 2 tablespoons olive oil and season with the salt and black pepper.

2 Heat the remaining olive oil in a heavy ovenproof (preferably cast-iron) Dutch oven over medium-high heat. Brown the chicken breasts on each side for 4 minutes; remove them from the pan and set aside.

3 Add the fennel seeds, celery, onion, and garlic and cook for 3 minutes, stirring frequently. Add the red pepper flakes and olives, cook for 1 minute, and return the chicken to the pan. Add the tomatoes and stir in the wine.

4 Bake for 30 minutes. Top the chicken with the parsley and mint and serve.

PER SERVING: *Calories 343 (From Fat 175); Fat 19g (Saturated 3g); Cholesterol 50mg; Sodium 649mg; Carbohydrate 12g (Dietary Fiber 3g); Protein 20g.*

Chapter **19**

Quick Picks: Cooking with Fewer Ingredients

Much of this book is about cooking great meals with the least fuss — and least expense — possible. We guide you on stocking your pantry so you can whip up last-minute dishes based around one or two main ingredients. In this chapter, we take a slightly different approach. We present recipes that contain a minimal number of ingredients, most of which you can buy ahead of time. Many of the recipes also give you one or two optional ingredients, which if you choose to use will boost the dish's flavor.

We believe there's a big difference between feeding and cooking. Feeding, for example, is serving a box of macaroni and cheese or heating up a frozen pizza for dinner. However, this convenience comes with a price: Packaged commercial products are often loaded with sugar and fat and are short on real flavor. On the other hand, cooking delicious family meals with limited fat and salt requires a little bit more time, knowledge, and effort. The recipes and techniques in this chapter give you the basics to *cook* a satisfying dinner in about 30 minutes (and in some cases, even less time).

Whipping Up Dinner with Convenience Foods

Being able to cook well and quickly calls for knowing how to shop for tasty, healthful convenience foods. Head into any good supermarket and you'll find rotisserie chicken, frozen shrimp, Italian pork and chicken sausage, assorted cheeses — all good sources of protein that you can build a complete meal around without doing much cooking.

Most grocery stores offer ready-to-eat rotisserie chicken that you can grab on your way home from work. Once home, you can slice the chicken into servings and toss together a simple salad for a quick dinner. Or, for something a little different, take home the chicken to make any of the following dinners for four.

>> **Chicken and Grilled Vegetable Wraps:** Along with a 3½-pound rotisserie chicken, pick up about 3 cups of grilled vegetables in the deli department, such as eggplant, peppers, onions, and zucchini. Shred or cut the chicken into ½-inch cubes, discarding the skin and bones, to make about 4 cups. Moisten the chicken, according to taste, with a bottled salad dressing of your choice. Divide the vegetables and chicken among four 8- to 9-inch flour tortillas, and then fold the tortillas over the filling to enclose.

>> **Chicken Tacos:** Shred the meat from a 3½-pound rotisserie chicken, discarding the skin and bones, and divide it equally into 8 taco shells. Top each taco with your favorite store-bought salsa and grated Monterey Jack cheese. Serve with sour cream, avocado, and chopped cilantro on the side.

>> **Easy Caesar salad:** For a quick version of a Caesar salad, cut a 3½-pound rotisserie chicken into thin slices, discarding the skin and bones. Tear 2 large hearts of romaine into 2- to 3-inch pieces and place them in a large salad bowl. Toss the romaine with your favorite bottled Caesar salad dressing. Add 2 to 3 cups of store-bought croutons, several gratings of good Parmesan cheese, and black pepper. Divide the salad and croutons between four serving plates and top with the rotisserie chicken.

>> **Pasta Chicken Pesto Salad:** Slice 2 rotisserie chicken breasts, discarding the skin and bones, into ½-inch cubes. Toss into 12 ounces of cooked pasta, such as penne or medium shells, 1 package frozen and cooked peas, and enough store-bought pesto sauce to moisten to taste. Sprinkle with the grated rind of 1 small lemon and black pepper, and toss to combine.

TIP

Roast two chickens on a weekend afternoon. Serve one for dinner, and remove the meat from the other one for use in a chicken dish — salad, pot pie, hash — during the week. You'll kill two birds (meals) with one stone, so to speak, and won't have to stop to pick up a rotisserie chicken later in the week. Freeze the carcasses for later use in a stock (see Chapter 12 for a Chicken Stock recipe).

Keeping Things Simple and Delicious

We know that some nights it's tempting to hit the drive-through on your way home from work. However, when you plan ahead, you can serve cheaper and healthier alternatives to fast-food combo meals. Pick up some cheeses, fresh fish fillets, or steaks, and you can create an impressive meal with little thought or effort any night of the week.

Chowing down on cheese

Cheese platters need not be saved for parties and other special occasions. They can be constructed for casual dinners that the whole family can enjoy with little or no time spent in the kitchen.

Choosing cheeses for your platter doesn't have to be intimidating. Go to the cheese counter of any good market and ask to taste the cheese before you purchase it. Most good markets will accommodate you. Cheese does age in the store and may look perfect, but sample a piece before purchasing to make sure it hasn't over ripened. Unless you're serving other sources of protein, figure on 4 to 6 ounces of cheese per person.

Think about choosing one type of cheese made from the milk of each animal that produces cheese: cow, goat, and sheep. Or you may consider having a cheese from each of the four basic categories: aged, soft, firm, or blue. Buy what you like and what you can afford and build your platter around that.

Here are some reasonably priced cheeses for a cheese platter, commonly found in good supermarkets:

» **Gouda:** Buy the aged, yellow (not white) kind.

» **Gorgonzola:** A good blue cheese with lots of character.

» **Vermont Cheddar:** Buy aged, white cheese, as sharp as possible.

>> **Chevre (goat cheese):** For a mild fresh flavor, buy it un-aged and vacuum-packed; the aged is sharper.

>> **Supreme Brie:** Soft, without being runny, and made in France.

TIP

Make the platter more than just cheese. Include assorted seasonal fruits on the platter, like grapes, sections of tangerines, slices of apple or pear, dried apricots and dates, and pecans or walnuts. You can also set out sour or sweet pickles, green and black olives, fig preserves, and honey for drizzling on the fruit. Cheese doesn't need to be the only source of protein; you can add dried, spicy smoked and sliced sausage or prosciutto.

Cheese is best served at room temperature, so set it on the counter for at least 30 minutes still wrapped in its paper or plastic before plating and serving. Serve baguette slices, crackers, or bagel chips in a basket or bowl alongside the cheese. Set out a few cheese knives for slicing and sampling.

Serving more-substantial meals quickly

Some nights you may be in the mood to cook a satisfying meal, but you don't want to spend a lot of time in the kitchen. On those evenings, you can make a dinner in almost no time that will impress your family.

Panini is the Italian word for sandwich, and it's traditionally made with firm and often crusty bread, such as ciabatta, French bread, or slices of country white. Avoid using bread that's soft like a loaf of white Wonder Bread or so thick that you'll have a difficult time melting the cheesy filling. You can purchase a special panini press, which has a lid to hold down the sandwich as it grills. But if you don't have a press, you can use a pancake griddle pan, a flat grill pan, or even a large nonstick skillet and achieve the same effect by placing a cast-iron or other heavy skillet on top of the sandwich as it grills in the pan.

RECIPE
ALERT

When you're hankering for a hot sandwich, try the Panini with Sun-Dried Tomatoes and Ham recipe later in this chapter. After you get the hang of making paninis, you'll find many ways to create these luscious sandwiches.

RECIPE
ALERT

Do you love fish but aren't sure how to cook it at home (beyond the precooked fish sticks or fillets in your grocer's freezer)? Cooking fresh fish, even for an experienced cook, can be tricky with disappointing results. Wrapping the fish in a foil packet with tasty vegetables and aromatics steams the fish to perfection and creates a delicate butter sauce while the fish and veggies cook. It's practically a no-fail, hands-off way to prepare fish. See our recipe for Foil-Baked Fish Fillets with Lemony Vegetables later in this chapter.

RECIPE
ALERT

If you're a meat-and-potatoes kind of guy or gal, you probably appreciate a good steak. With a London broil, you can have steak any night of the week. *London broil* refers to the name of the dish and the way the meat is cooked, not to any particular cut of meat. However, boneless sirloin tip and top round steaks are often labeled "London broil," to indicate that these cuts are especially good if broiled to medium-rare and cut thinly across the grain before serving. Check out the London Broil with Garlicky Steak and Potatoes recipe later in this chapter.

Seeing the Pasta-bilities!

The one ingredient that never lets a busy home cook down is pasta. It's quick, cheap, filling, and kid-friendly and plays well with other foods.

Grated Parmesan cheese, which lends a creamy richness, is just as important to a pasta dish as its sauce. But other cheeses that mix well with pasta include creamy blues, like Gorgonzola, fresh mozzarella, ricotta, Fontina, and Pecorino Romano.

RECIPE
ALERT

Bocconcini are small mozzarella balls, 1 to 2 inches in diameter, sold packed in either water or an oil marinade and found in the cheese or dairy sections of quality supermarkets. Try the Bow Tie Pasta with Pesto, Tomatoes, and Bocconcini later in this chapter. It's particularly good served on a hot summer day at a backyard barbecue. Bocconcini also make great additions to an appetizer platter.

Consider also fresh pasta and ravioli, sold in the dairy or frozen food sections and stuffed with assorted meats, cheeses, vegetables, and fish. A jarred or fresh tomato pan sauce is all that's needed to make a meal of these convenient foods.

TIP

One secret ingredient used by many pasta cooks is to add a little of the salty, starchy hot pasta water back into the pasta after it's been drained. Simply remove about ½ cup of water before draining the pasta and add the water with the pan sauce, using enough to moisten the pasta as desired. This technique works especially well to thin a sauce that's too thick or too dry.

When it comes to combining pasta with other foods, the possibilities are limitless! Check out just some of the many ways to mix and match pasta with other ingredients for quick and easy meals:

>> Brown some sliced Italian sausage and toss it into cooked pasta with some fresh spinach and grated Parmesan cheese.

>> Roast a small head of cauliflower on a baking sheet with sliced onions, red peppers, garlic, olive oil, salt, and black pepper; toss into steaming pasta with crushed red pepper to taste and grated Parmesan cheese.

>> For Pasta Alla Gricia, combine diced, cooked bacon with linguine, grated Pecorino Romano cheese and good olive oil. Add some red pepper flakes for a little spiciness.

>> Toss steaming pasta with shrimp and sliced scallions sautéed in lemon and butter.

>> Add chopped fresh sage or parsley to browned butter and toss with ziti or penne, Parmesan cheese, salt, and black pepper.

>> Mix cooked penne or ziti with fresh ricotta, Parmesan cheese, and cooked fresh or frozen peas. Thin the sauce with a little of the pasta cooking water and season to taste with salt and black pepper.

Here are some other pasta recipes to try:

>> Pasta with Escarole, Beans, and Sausage (Chapter 13)

>> Penne with Parmesan Cheese and Basil (Chapter 13)

>> Spaghetti with Quick Fresh Tomato Sauce (Chapter 13)

>> Homestyle Macaroni and Cheese (Chapter 16)

>> Hungry Family Lasagna (Chapter 16)

Panini with Sun-Dried Tomatoes and Ham

PREP TIME: 10 MIN	COOK TIME: ABOUT 6 MIN	YIELD: 4 SERVINGS

INGREDIENTS

4 multigrain club rolls (about 4 ounces each)

8 oil-packed sun-dried tomatoes, plus oil from the jar

8 slices fresh mozzarella cheese (about 8 ounces total)

8 thin slices Virginia or black forest ham (about 4 to 6 ounces total)

16 large fresh basil leaves

Black pepper or crushed red pepper to taste

Vegetable oil

DIRECTIONS

1 Slice each of the club rolls horizontally into two halves. Hollow out some of the inside bread to make room for the sandwich filling.

2 Remove the sun-dried tomatoes from the jar and chop them coarsely. Pour ¼ cup of oil from the jar into a small bowl and drizzle it evenly over one-half of each roll (about ½ tablespoon of oil per roll). Layer the mozzarella and ham slices, basil leaves, and sun-dried tomatoes evenly over the oil-drizzled half of each roll. Season each sandwich with black pepper or crushed red pepper. Cover with the other half of the roll.

3 Heat a thin layer of vegetable oil in a large cast-iron skillet over medium heat. Add two sandwiches to the pan and lay a cast-iron skillet or other heavy pan over the sandwiches to gently press down and flatten. Cook over medium heat 3 to 5 minutes on each side or until lightly browned. (Watch the sandwiches carefully to see how they're browning after about 3 minutes, and lower the heat if necessary to keep the crust from browning too quickly.) Turn once and leave the heavy skillet on the sandwiches as they cook. Repeat with the remaining two sandwiches and serve immediately.

PER SERVING: *Calories 465 (From Fat 234); Fat 26g (Saturated 10g); Cholesterol 52mg; Sodium 840mg; Carbohydrate 39g (Dietary Fiber 7g); Protein 26g.*

VARY IT! You can substitute any type of firm sliced sandwich bread, such as country-style white or sourdough, for the multigrain club rolls; swap out two slices of cooked bacon for the ham; spread mustard or mayonnaise to taste on the rolls before layering with the filling. Try ripe sliced tomatoes in place of the sun-dried tomatoes, and use provolone or Muenster instead of mozzarella. You can also substitute cooking spray for the vegetable oil.

Bow Tie Pasta with Pesto, Tomatoes, and Bocconcini

PREP TIME: 10 MIN	COOK TIME: 10 MIN	YIELD: 4–6 SERVINGS

INGREDIENTS

12 ounces bow tie or fusilli pasta

Salt

¾ cup pesto

20 ripe cherry tomatoes, halved

20 bocconcini, packed in oil, drained and halved

Black pepper to taste

Crushed red pepper to taste (optional)

⅓ cup freshly grated Parmesan cheese (optional)

DIRECTIONS

1 Fill a large pasta pot with 4 to 5 quarts water; cover and bring to a boil over high heat. Add salt to taste. Add the pasta to the water and boil according to package directions until al dente or just tender. Drain the pasta and pour it into a large serving bowl.

2 Add the pesto, cherry tomatoes, and boconccini; toss well to combine. Taste and season with additional salt and black pepper and the crushed red pepper (if desired). Sprinkle with the Parmesan cheese (if desired), and serve.

PER SERVING: *Calories 700 (From Fat 342); Fat 38g (Saturated 18g); Cholesterol 67mg; Sodium 1,264mg; Carbohydrate 55g (Dietary Fiber 4g); Protein 32g.*

VARY IT! You can substitute 2 cups cooked, diced chicken breast for the bocconcini or use 1 package of frozen and thawed green peas instead of the tomatoes.

Sweet Potato Pancakes

PREP TIME: 15 MIN	COOK TIME: ABOUT 15 MIN	YIELD: 4 SERVINGS

INGREDIENTS

1 pound sweet potatoes, peeled

½ cup unbleached all-purpose flour

3 scallions, both white and green parts, trimmed and finely chopped

2 large eggs, lightly beaten

¾ teaspoon ground ginger (optional)

Salt and black pepper to taste

½ cup canola or other vegetable oil, or more if needed

DIRECTIONS

1 Position a rack in the center of the oven and preheat the oven to 250 degrees. Line a large rimmed baking sheet with paper towels.

2 Coarsely grate the sweet potatoes, using the large holes of a box grater. Transfer the sweet potatoes to a large mixing bowl and toss with the flour. Add the scallions, eggs, and ginger (if desired); season with salt and black pepper to taste, and stir until thoroughly combined.

3 Using a ¼-cup measuring cup, divide the potato mixture into 12 equal portions, turning out each portion onto a baking sheet. Flatten each mound into a ½-inch-thick pancake, using the back of a large metal spatula.

4 Add the oil to a large nonstick skillet. Heat the oil over medium until it shimmers. Using a large metal spatula, carefully transfer 3 or 4 pancakes to the skillet. Avoid crowding the pancakes in the pan.

5 Cook the pancakes 3 to 4 minutes per side or until browned. Adjust the heat as necessary to keep them sizzling in the pan without browning too quickly.

6 Transfer the cooked pancakes to the paper towel–lined baking sheet and place in the preheated oven to keep warm. Repeat with the remaining sweet potato–scallion mixture, adding more oil to the skillet if necessary.

PER SERVING: *Calories 427 (From Fat 270); Fat 30g (Saturated 3g); Cholesterol 93mg; Sodium 245mg; Carbohydrate 35g (Dietary Fiber 4g); Protein 7g.*

TIP: With each batch you add to the skillet, the oil will get hotter, causing the pancakes to cook more rapidly. Be sure to adjust the heat as necessary to prevent them from browning too quickly.

VARY IT! After you've made these delicious pancakes for dinner a few times, explore similar recipes for making pancakes with grated veggies, such as zucchini or carrots.

Foil-Baked Fish Fillets with Lemony Vegetables

PREP TIME: ABOUT 20 MIN | COOK TIME: 15 MIN | YIELD: 4 SERVINGS

INGREDIENTS

Four 6-ounce skinless cod fillets, 1- to 1¼-inches thick

Cayenne red pepper to taste (optional)

Salt and black pepper to taste

1 to 2 large cloves garlic, minced

12 ripe cherry tomatoes, halved

2 small leeks, white and pale green parts only, halved lengthwise, rinsed well, and thinly sliced

4 tablespoons butter

4 tablespoons fresh lemon juice

Grated zest of half a lemon

DIRECTIONS

1 Adjust an oven rack to a lower-middle position and preheat the oven to 450 degrees.

2 Cut four 12-x-14-inch sheets of aluminum foil.

3 Pat fish dry with paper towels. Place 1 fillet on top of each sheet of foil; season with cayenne pepper (if desired) and salt and black pepper to taste. Divide minced garlic, cherry tomatoes, and leeks evenly over fillets. Divide each tablespoon of butter into four pieces and distribute butter pieces evenly on top of fillets. Sprinkle fillets evenly with lemon juice and zest.

4 Fold the edges of the foil around the fish, using ¼-inch folds to make a packet that seals in juices and keeps the steam from escaping as the fish bakes. Repeat the process to wrap the three remaining fillets, and place the four packets on a rimmed baking sheet.

5 Bake for 15 minutes. Carefully open one end of the packet so the hot steam releases away from you, and gently slide the fish and vegetables onto an individual dinner plate, along with any juices. Repeat with remaining packets.

PER SERVING: *Calories 255 (From Fat 117); Fat 13g (Saturated 7g); Cholesterol 106mg; Sodium 249mg; Carbohydrate 4g (Dietary Fiber 1g); Protein 4g.*

TIP: Because you can't see the fish as it bakes, it's best to shop carefully for fillets that are between 1- and 1¼-inches thick and carefully adhere to the recommended cooking time. If your fillets are thinner at one end than the other, fold the thinner end under to create an even thickness.

VARY IT! Substitute curry powder for the cayenne. Substitute sea bass, haddock, or halibut for the cod.

TIP: If you make this dish for a dinner party, use parchment paper instead of foil, and set the pretty parchment packets on individual dinner plates for each guest to pop open.

London Broil with Garlicky Potatoes and Peppers

PREP TIME: ABOUT 15 MIN	COOK TIME: ABOUT 20 MIN	YIELD: 4 SERVINGS

INGREDIENTS

¼ cup olive oil

1½ pounds boneless sirloin or top round steak, about 1-inch thick, at room temperature

Salt and black pepper

1¼ pounds white or red-skinned potatoes, scrubbed and cut into ¾-inch pieces

2 medium red or yellow bell peppers, cored, seeded, and cut into ½-inch pieces (about 2 cups)

1 tablespoon seeded and chopped jalapeño pepper

2 large cloves garlic, peeled and chopped

DIRECTIONS

1 Set the oven rack about 6 inches from the broiler unit and heat the broiler.

2 Rub the beef with 1 tablespoon of the oil, season with salt and black pepper to taste, and place it on a rack over a broiler pan.

3 Heat the remaining 3 tablespoons of oil in a large skillet over medium heat; add the potatoes, toss them in the oil to coat, and cook about 10 to 15 minutes or until golden brown, turning them over every 4 to 5 minutes.

4 Add the bell peppers, the jalapeño, and the garlic. Toss to combine and cook another 5 minutes or until the vegetables are tender. Adjust seasoning with salt and black pepper to taste.

5 As the potatoes cook, broil the steak until an instant-read thermometer inserted in the thickest part of the meat registers 125 to 130 degrees for medium rare, turning once halfway through cooking. Plan on broiling 10 to 15 minutes for medium rare.

6 Transfer the steak to a carving board, cover loosely with aluminum foil, and let rest 10 minutes while the vegetables finish cooking.

7 Slice the steak thinly against the grain; transfer the slices to a serving platter, and pour over any juices that accumulated in the pan. Serve with the garlicky potatoes and peppers.

PER SERVING: Calories 441 (From Fat 162); Fat 18g (Saturated 4g); Cholesterol 86mg; Sodium 276mg; Carbohydrate 28g (Dietary Fiber 4g); Protein 47g.

TIP: Check the temperature of the meat after about 10 minutes of broiling to see how close it is to 125 degrees for medium rare. The more the steak cooks, the tougher it becomes, so try to avoid cooking past 130 degrees. The temperature will rise 5 degrees as the steak rests in the foil.

Pan-Sauced Chicken with Asparagus

PREP TIME: ABOUT 15 MIN	COOK TIME: ABOUT 20 MIN	YIELD: 4 SERVINGS

INGREDIENTS

Four 6-ounce skinless, boneless chicken breast halves

Juice and grated peel of half a lemon

⅓ cup Italian-seasoned breadcrumbs

2 tablespoons vegetable oil, plus more as necessary

½ cup chicken broth

1 tablespoon butter

1¼ pounds asparagus, trimmed of woody ends, rinsed and cut into 2-inch pieces

Salt and black pepper to taste

DIRECTIONS

1 Place each chicken breast half between two sheets of heavy-duty plastic wrap; pound to ¼-inch thickness, using a meat mallet or a rolling pin. Transfer the breasts to a large dish that holds them in one layer and sprinkle with the lemon juice.

2 Pour the breadcrumbs onto a large plate, and dredge the chicken in the breadcrumbs.

3 Heat the oil in a large nonstick skillet over medium-high until it shimmers. Add two pieces of chicken to the pan, reduce the heat to medium, and cook 3 minutes on each side or until the chicken is done.

4 Remove the chicken to a large serving platter and cover with foil to keep warm. If necessary, add another 1 to 2 tablespoons of oil to the pan, and repeat the cooking process with the remaining chicken.

5 Add the chicken broth and butter to the pan; stir over medium heat to scrape up any browned bits on the bottom of the pan. Add the asparagus, cover the skillet, and cook over medium heat 5 to 8 minutes or until the asparagus are still slightly crisp but tender.

6 Use a slotted spoon to transfer the asparagus to the serving platter with the chicken. Pour the pan sauce over the chicken, and sprinkle the asparagus with the grated lemon peel. Season with salt and black pepper to taste, and serve with boiled rice or buttered rolls.

PER SERVING: *Calories 435 (From Fat 153); Fat 17g (Saturated 4g); Cholesterol 152mg; Sodium 488mg; Carbohydrate 12g (Dietary Fiber 3g); Protein 58g.*

VARY IT! If asparagus isn't to your liking or is out of season, you can substitute frozen vegetables, such as 2 to 3 cups of broccoli florets or mixed vegetables.

Chapter **20**

Summertime Soirees

Summer practically *means* party. Backyard barbecues, beach volleyball bonanzas, revelry around the pool . . . from Memorial Day to Labor Day, summer is filled with opportunities for outdoor gatherings and rife with the fixin's to make them pop. Whether you're celebrating a national holiday or surrounding yourself with family and friends just for the fun of it, we have the perfect menu for a summer soiree in this chapter.

Planning the Menu

Planning a party can sometimes overwhelm even the most experienced host, but here's a secret: *It's all about the menu.* Figure out what your menu will look like and when to make what, and everything else falls into place. That's because the menu is the heart of a party. It sets the tone and sometimes even the theme of the entire affair. Although you may have some great ideas of your own, here's a perfect summertime menu to get you started. Of course, you can tweak it for any theme you prefer:

» **The Perfect Hamburger:** Juicy, meaty, and moist, these simple, savory burgers are sure to be a hit at your party. See Chapter 9 for the recipe.

>> **Barbecued Chicken:** The smoky-sweet tang of the barbeque sauce is the perfect foil for other summer foods like mellow corn, creamy salads, and sweet fruit. See Chapter 9 for the recipe.

RECIPE ALERT

>> **Summer Veggie Burger:** This is a yummy treat for the vegetarians in the crowd or those who just want to keep it light. Tasty and toothsome with black beans and vegetables, this hearty burger will satisfy any appetite without a speck of meat. Make burgers no more than 1-inch thick and grill them for just a few minutes for crispy veggie perfection.

RECIPE ALERT

>> **Grilled Corn on the Cob:** How hard can it be to cook the perfect ear of corn? Not so hard if you follow a few simple tips:

- Buy corn still in its husk, if possible, rather than the plastic-wrapped, fully shucked kind you often see in the store. It will taste fresher.

- Don't shuck the corn until close to cooking time. The silk and husk help keep the kernels moist. If you have to store corn, put it in a plastic bag and refrigerate.

- Don't overcook your corn. About 5 to 6 minutes, just until the corn is heated through, is plenty for young, tender ears. Older ears may take up to 10 minutes.

Our recipe calls for one ear of corn per person, but if you have more guests or you think your guests may eat more than one ear each, just add more to the grill. The cooking time remains the same.

RECIPE ALERT

>> **All-American Coleslaw:** Not a huge coleslaw fan? Maybe that's because you think of coleslaw as the gloppy, overly sweetened stuff so often served at the delicatessen. Give this recipe a try. Our homemade coleslaw isn't heavily coated with mayonnaise, which means the flavors of the cabbage and other vegetables shine through.

To shred the cabbage, you can use a tool called a *mandoline.* We explain what a mandoline is — and show you an illustration of how it works — in Chapter 4.

>> **A few of your favorite quick salads and dips with chips:** Here are some suggestions that highlight summer's bounty; the recipes all appear in Chapter 12:

- Tomato, Red Onion, and Basil Salad

- Cucumber-Dill Salad

- Cherry Tomato and Feta Cheese Salad

- Pasta Medley Salad

- Layered Cheese and Vegetable Salad

AS AMERICAN AS . . . CORN?

Americans in particular have always fancied themselves as corn connoisseurs. Every summer, on picnic tables across the land, culinary Olympic judges rate the current crop as if it were a high-dive competition. Soil, sun, and freshness are critical in producing superior corn for the picnic table. True corn-on-the-cob aficionados say that fresh corn should be picked as close to cooking time as possible. The sugar in corn quickly converts to starch after picking, making it lose its sweetness. However, the corn industry has made a lot of progress to develop strains of corn that hold their sweetness for several days.

Corn comes in colors ranging from almost white to deep yellow, and the ears and individual kernels can be big or small. Size and color have nothing to do with flavor. Corn in a store or market should look fresh. The husks should be green with no sign of dryness or splotching. The silk at the tip of the husk can be dark, but the silk inside should be moist.

- Grilled Vegetable Platter with Fresh Pesto
- Fruit Salsa
- Three-Berry Dessert Salad

**RECIPE
ALERT**

» **Red, White, and Blue Berry Shortcake:** With its strawberries, blueberries, and whipped cream, this patriotic cake is especially well suited for a Memorial Day or Fourth of July celebration. Not only does it look patriotic, but it's a light, refreshing dessert that won't make everybody feel weighed down in the heat of summer. You can make all the components of this cake — the berry mixture, the cream, and even the biscuits — a few hours before serving and then assemble them while someone is whisking the dinner dishes off the table. To make this recipe even easier, use easy-bake biscuits that come in a tube in the refrigerated section of the grocery store. (We won't tell.)

Mixing Fruity Drinks for Thirsty Crowds

Summer heat makes party guests thirsty! Every party needs some beverages, and if you're serving beer, wine, or fruity umbrella drinks, you also want some delicious drinks for kids and people who prefer nonalcoholic beverages.

RECIPE ALERT

Here are two great options that we provide recipes for in this chapter:

>> **Strawberry Lemonade:** Classic lemonade becomes even more exciting when flavored with other fruit purées like strawberry and watermelon. Don't feel limited by the "strawberry" in the title. This lemonade tastes great made with any kind of fresh berry, or even without berries in its unadorned, homemade goodness. People can tell that this is the real thing, not something you mixed up from a powder, so expect this recipe to be popular. Lucky for you that it's so easy to make more! (For seconds, just skip the chilling stage and serve over plenty of ice.)

>> **Sparkling Sangria:** Good red wine and juicy fruits plus a little sparkle make for the perfect grown-up summer treat. Mix this up ahead of time and add the ginger ale at the last minute for a refreshing and sophisticated offering.

Preparing in Advance for a Stress-Free Party

TIP

For the menu in this chapter, you can (and should) do a lot of the work before the party starts. That way, when the guests arrive, you can actually visit and enjoy yourself — at least for a few minutes at a time. Here, we walk you through how to handle the menu in this chapter.

Two or three days before the party:

>> Collect all your recipes. Figure out how many people you're likely to have at your party and how much of each recipe you'll need to make. For example, if a salad serves 4 and you expect 16 people, you will quadruple the recipe. If you expect 12 people, how many burgers or pieces of chicken will they probably eat? (It's always best to overestimate just a little — you won't run out of food and, at worst, you'll have tasty leftovers.)

>> Make your food shopping list based on your calculations, going through each recipe and checking to see which ingredients you need to buy.

>> Decide what you need for beverages. Do you have enough pitchers or a punch bowl? Will you supplement your homemade beverages with sodas, juice, or beer in a cooler? Will you serve drinks in glass or plastic? Will you need fruity garnishes for your drinks? What about little paper umbrellas?

>> Consider your theme. What kind of décor would work? Think of a good centerpiece for the table — flowers and flags? Glitter and poppers? A big bowl of tropical fruit? Coconuts? Make a shopping list for decorations as well as party favors (if you decide they're in order).

>> Decide whether you want music at your party, what to play, and how to play it. Make a playlist. Old-time rock 'n' roll? Calypso music? Reggae? Cool jazz? Disco? The music sets the mood.

>> Clean out your refrigerator so you have room for all the party food.

>> Go shopping and purchase everything you need: food, party supplies, décor. Don't forget ice!

The day before the party:

>> Make the All-American Coleslaw. Cover and refrigerate.

>> Make the Summer Veggie Burger mixture (but wait to shape it into patties). Cover and refrigerate.

>> Make the Strawberry Lemonade and the Sparkling Sangria (minus the ginger ale). Cover and refrigerate.

>> Make the biscuits for the shortcake. Cover.

The morning of your party:

>> Assemble all the salads except the Grilled Vegetable Platter with Fresh Pesto. (You can make the pesto, but the grilled vegetables have to wait.) Cover and refrigerate.

>> Cut the vegetables for the Grilled Vegetable Platter with Fresh Pesto.

>> Husk the corn.

>> Clean and core the fruit for the shortcakes.

>> Decorate the house, yard, and/or food table for the party.

One hour before the party:

>> Take your meat out of the refrigerator and prepare it for grilling.

>> Form the Summer Veggie Burger patties.

>> Put cans and bottles of drinks in a cooler full of ice.

>> Set out the following items on the party table: Bags of chips, platters, plates, silverware, napkins, and the centerpiece.

As guests arrive:

>> Fire up the grill.

>> Turn on the music!

>> Set out the salads, burger buns, and condiments for the burgers.

>> Grill the corn. Set out the salt, black pepper, and butter.

>> Grill the vegetables for the Grilled Vegetable Platter first, and then grill the meat and veggie burgers.

>> Assemble the Grilled Vegetable Platter with Fresh Pesto.

Right before serving:

>> Put out the pitchers of beverages, glasses, and a big bowl of ice with tongs.

>> Make the whipped cream and assemble the shortcakes.

Throughout the party:

>> Keep an eye on the table and see what needs to be replenished — Chips? Fruit? Silverware? People's drinks?

>> Smile, greet people, and have fun. It's your party, too!

Summer Veggie Burger

PREP TIME: ABOUT 25 MIN | COOK TIME: ABOUT 8 MIN | YIELD: 4 SERVINGS

INGREDIENTS

One 15-ounce can drained and rinsed black or white beans

1 medium yellow onion, peeled and minced

½ cup grated zucchini or yellow summer squash

½ cup breadcrumbs

1 egg, lightly beaten

¼ cup ketchup

1 clove garlic, peeled and minced

1 tablespoon minced fresh basil or cilantro

1 tablespoon chili powder

1 teaspoon minced jalapeño pepper (optional)

1 teaspoon mustard

½ teaspoon salt

¼ teaspoon black pepper

1 tablespoon olive oil

Whole-grain buns, for serving

DIRECTIONS

1 Put the beans in a mixing bowl and mash them thoroughly with a fork. Stir in all the remaining ingredients except the olive oil, combining well. Let the mixture sit for 5 minutes.

2 Get your hands wet and form the mixture into 4 patties. Put them on a plate and let them sit for 3 or 4 more minutes while you heat the skillet.

3 Heat the skillet on medium and add the olive oil. Put the patties in the skillet and cook for 5 minutes. Carefully flip them with a hard spatula and cook for 3 more minutes, or until the surface is golden brown and crispy. Serve warm on whole-grain buns.

PER SERVING: *Calories 311 (From Fat 76); Fat 9g (Saturated 1g); Cholesterol 53mg; Sodium 989mg; Carbohydrate 49g (Dietary Fiber 9g); Protein 12g.*

TIP: After Step 1, you can put the mixture, covered, in the refrigerator up to 24 hours. Bring the mixture back to room temperature before cooking.

Grilled Corn on the Cob

PREP TIME: ABOUT 5 MIN	COOK TIME: ABOUT 20 MIN	YIELD: 6 SERVINGS

INGREDIENTS

6 corn ears with husks

6 tablespoons melted butter, or more to taste

Salt and black pepper to taste

DIRECTIONS

1 Prepare a medium fire in a charcoal grill or heat a gas grill to medium.

2 Strip off 5 to 6 of the outer dark green corn husks, and then carefully peel back the remaining husks, leaving them attached at the base of the ear. Remove the silky threads. Pull the husks back up and wrap them securely in place with kitchen twine or a thin strip of husk.

3 Place the ears on an oiled grill grid, over medium heat, and grill for 10 to 15 minutes, turning every 5 minutes. Peek beyond the husks at the kernels to determine doneness. The kernels should be golden yellow and tender when pierced with a small knife.

4 Remove the husks, brush the ears with the melted butter and season with salt and black pepper to taste.

5 For lightly charred corn, after coating the ears in butter, place the corn back on the grill grid (without the husks) and grill for about 5 minutes, turning often until the corn is lightly charred on all sides. Serve with extra butter on the side.

PER SERVING: *Calories 179 (From Fat 117); Fat 13g (Saturated 8g); Cholesterol 31mg; Sodium 209mg; Carbohydrate 17g (Dietary Fiber 2g); Protein 3g.*

TIP: Have a spray bottle on hand and spritz the corn husks as they grill, should they char too quickly and burn.

VARY IT! Dress up butter for grilled corn and other grilled vegetables with chili powder, ground cumin, Spanish paprika, Worcestershire sauce, hot sauce, fresh herbs, and other savory seasonings. Simply sprinkle or add them to the melted butter according to taste.

All-American Coleslaw

PREP TIME: 15–20 MIN PLUS CHILL TIME | YIELD: 8 SERVINGS

INGREDIENTS

1 medium head green cabbage (about 2 pounds), tough outer leaves removed

4 carrots, peeled and grated

2 red bell peppers, cored, seeded, and diced

1 medium yellow onion, diced

1⅓ cups mayonnaise, or to taste

⅓ cup sugar

⅓ cup cider vinegar

Salt and black pepper

DIRECTIONS

1 Using a large chef's knife, halve the cabbage crosswise; cut out the hard, solid core; and then quarter the remaining chunks of leaves.

2 Slice the cabbage, starting at one end, as thinly as possible. Then chop the slices crosswise to make short lengths. (Or chop cabbage in a food processor using the shredding blade, or with a mandoline.)

3 Place the cabbage, carrots, bell peppers, and onion in a large bowl.

4 In a small bowl, using a wire whisk or fork to blend, combine the mayonnaise, sugar, vinegar, and salt and black pepper to taste.

5 Pour the dressing over the cabbage mixture and toss thoroughly to coat. Taste to see whether it needs more salt and black pepper.

6 Cover the bowl with plastic wrap and refrigerate for 2 to 3 hours before serving to blend the flavors, stirring occasionally.

PER SERVING: *Calories 360 (From Fat 263); Fat 29g (Saturated 4g); Cholesterol 22mg; Sodium 329mg; Carbohydrate 23g (Dietary Fiber 5g); Protein 3g.*

TIP: Try using low-fat or nonfat mayonnaise to lower the calorie and fat content of this recipe.

Strawberry Lemonade

INGREDIENTS

1½ cups fresh lemon juice, strained of pits (about 9 to 10 large lemons)

1½ cups sugar

6 cups water

1 pint strawberries, rinsed and hulled

Lemon slices for garnish (optional)

Mint sprigs for garnish (optional)

DIRECTIONS

1 Combine the lemon juice, sugar, and water in a large pitcher. Stir well.

2 Place the hulled strawberries in a blender or food processor; add a little of the lemonade from the pitcher, and blend until smooth.

3 Pour the strawberries into the lemonade, stir, and chill for 2 hours. Stir well before serving.

4 Pour into ice-filled glasses, garnishing each with a lemon slice or a sprig of fresh mint (if desired).

PER SERVING: *Calories 168 (From Fat 1); Fat 0g (Saturated 0g); Cholesterol 0mg; Sodium 1mg; Carbohydrate 44g (Dietary Fiber 1g); Protein 0g.*

VARY IT! To make classic lemonade, simply omit the strawberries. Or try other fruit flavors, such as watermelon (use 3 cups of watermelon chunks with seeds removed) or peaches (use 2 cups of fresh peach slices).

Sparkling Sangria

PREP TIME: ABOUT 5 MIN PLUS CHILL TIME | YIELD: 6–8 SERVINGS

INGREDIENTS

1 bottle red wine

1 orange, sliced

1 lemon, sliced

1 lime, sliced

1 cup any kind of fresh or frozen berries

2 cups ginger ale

¼ cup orange liqueur (such as Grand Marnier, Cointreau, or triple sec) or brandy

Orange slices for garnish

DIRECTIONS

1   In a pitcher, combine wine and orange, lemon, and lime slices and berries. Chill overnight in the refrigerator.

2   Just before serving, stir in ginger ale and orange liqueur or brandy. Pour into wine glasses and garnish with a slice of orange.

PER SERVING: *Calories 175 (From Fat 1); Fat 0g (Saturated 0g); Cholesterol 0mg; Sodium 14mg; Carbohydrate 20g (Dietary Fiber 2g); Protein 1g.*

VARY IT! Sangria doesn't have to be made with red wine; you can also make it with your favorite white wine or sparkling wine. If you choose red, consider a Spanish wine, such as Tempranillo, Garnacha, or something from Rioja. But any red wine you enjoy will do!

Red, White, and Blue Berry Shortcake

PREP TIME: 40 MIN	COOK TIME: ABOUT 15 MIN	YIELD: 8 SERVINGS

INGREDIENTS

2 pints strawberries, rinsed and hulled

2 cups blueberries, rinsed and drained

⅓ cup plus 3½ tablespoons granulated sugar, or more to taste

1 tablespoon Cointreau (optional)

1¼ cups heavy cream

2 tablespoons confectioners' sugar, or more to taste

½ teaspoon vanilla extract

2⅔ cups self-rising cake flour

¼ teaspoon salt

10 tablespoons chilled butter, cut into small pieces

1 cup plus 1 to 2 tablespoons milk

DIRECTIONS

1 Preheat the oven to 400 degrees.

2 Set aside the 8 best strawberries for garnish. Crush half of the remaining strawberries with a fork or the back of a spoon; cut the rest in half the long way, from core to tip.

3 In a medium mixing bowl, combine the sliced and crushed strawberries, blueberries, ⅓ cup granulated sugar, and the Cointreau (if desired). Taste the fruit mixture and add more sugar if necessary. Refrigerate until ready to assemble the shortcake.

4 In a bowl, using an electric mixer, whip the heavy cream with the confectioners' sugar and vanilla until stiff. Cover and refrigerate until you're ready to assemble the shortcake.

5 In a large mixing bowl, combine the flour, the remaining 3½ tablespoons granulated sugar, and salt. Cut the butter into the flour mixture, using two knives or a pastry blender, until the mixture resembles coarse breadcrumbs. Work quickly so the butter doesn't melt.

6 Make a well in the center of the flour mixture and add 1 cup milk. Mix gently with a fork, rubber spatula, or wooden spoon just until most of the dry ingredients are moistened. Don't overmix.

7 Drop the dough, in eight equal portions 1 to 2 inches apart, onto an ungreased baking sheet. Lightly brush the tops of the rounds with the remaining 1 to 2 tablespoons of milk.

8 Bake the biscuits on the center rack of the oven for 15 to 17 minutes, or until golden brown. Transfer to a wire rack to cool. Finished shortcakes may be served warm or cold.

9   Using a serrated knife, carefully slice the shortcakes in half crosswise. Transfer each bottom half to an individual serving plate. Spread a generous dollop of whipped cream over the bottom of each biscuit; top with about ⅓ cup of the fruit mixture. Cover with the other half of the shortcakes. Spoon over more cream and berries, and drizzle with any berry juices that have accumulated. Garnish each serving with a reserved whole strawberry. Serve immediately.

PER SERVING: Calories 522 (From Fat 269); Fat 30g (Saturated 18g); Cholesterol 94mg; Sodium 621mg; Carbohydrate 59g (Dietary Fiber 4g); Protein 7g.

» Roasting the perfect holiday turkey

» Starting things off with delicious dips

» Serving up stuffing and veggies

» Ending on a sweet note with pie and specialty drinks

Chapter **21**

Feeding Holiday Hordes: Festive Winter Menus

t's easy to lose your cool when a mob of salivating relatives comes marching your way for a holiday dinner. Don't panic. Take this approach: Rustle up only dishes you've made before (even better, several times); have on hand a generous selection of libations; and serve the meal 45 minutes late — by then they'll have lowered their threshold of satisfaction.

The challenging part of holiday entertainment is not so much the quantity of food you have to churn out, but the variety. When you consider several appetizers, four or five side dishes, a main course (in this case, turkey), and a couple desserts, it can be intimidating to say the least.

If you try to do everything at once, you're courting a disaster. Thankfully, many of the dishes in our suggested menu can be assembled beforehand. In this chapter, we show you how to tackle a holiday menu.

Planning the Menu

Just as you wouldn't serve sorbet with juicy tenderloin of beef, you shouldn't pair clashing recipes at the holiday meal. Think heavy with light, full flavored with refreshing, starchy with crisp, even sweet with sharp. Pairing foods the right way is easier than it sounds, even with a sprawling holiday spread. Here is just one suggestion for a winning menu:

» Warm Artichoke-Spinach Dip

» Roasted Turkey with Cornbread, Sausage, and Apple Stuffing

» Madeira Pan Gravy

» Fresh Cranberry-Orange Relish with Walnuts

» Green Beans with Shallot Butter

» Homemade Mashed Potatoes

» Rum-Baked Sweet Potatoes

» Praline Pumpkin Pie

» Eggnog

» Warm Red Wine and Orange Punch

Except for the Homemade Mashed Potatoes, which you find in Chapter 5, the recipes for the rest of this menu appear in this chapter.

Getting Yourself Organized

Two days of preparation should be plenty to pull off this menu, provided you don't watch too much daytime TV. Most items can be prepared in advance. In this section, we walk you through what to do and when, so you aren't too stressed when guests start arriving.

For starters, here are four items you can prepare either two or three days in advance of your holiday meal:

>> Cornbread for the stuffing

>> Fresh Cranberry-Orange Relish with Walnuts (but wait to stir in the walnuts until just before serving)

>> Rum-Baked Sweet Potatoes

>> Praline Pumpkin Pie

The day before your big meal, do these tasks:

>> Wash and trim the green beans, wrap them in a paper towel, and seal them in a plastic bag.

>> Make the shallot butter for the green bean recipe.

>> Make and chill the Artichoke-Spinach Dip.

On the morning of the dinner, do the following:

>> Make the Cornbread, Sausage, and Apple Stuffing.

>> Roast the turkey.

>> Peel the potatoes for your Homemade Mashed Potatoes and cover them with cold water.

Two hours before guests arrive:

>> Make the Eggnog.

>> Make the Warm Red Wine and Orange Punch.

>> Whip the cream for the pie.

After you remove the turkey from the oven, let it rest, covered with aluminum foil, and tackle the final tasks:

>> Make the Madeira Pan Gravy.

>> Cook the Green Beans with Shallots.

>> Make the Homemade Mashed Potatoes.

All about Turkey

Turkey is an ideal main course for entertaining a crowd, but how do you choose the right one, and what's the best method for cooking it? Here are some important turkey tips:

>> Most supermarket turkeys are frozen; fresh ones are better, so it's worth finding one. Here's why: When a turkey is frozen, its juices turn to ice crystals; when thawed, these crystals disrupt the protein cell membranes in the flesh and cause some of the juices to leak out — that's the reddish stuff you see in the packaging when you open it. A frozen turkey is never as moist as a fresh one, which is why many frozen turkeys are injected with a broth/sugar solution to replace the lost moisture.

>> If you buy a frozen turkey, let it defrost in the refrigerator; allow about 24 hours for every 4 to 5 pounds.

>> When you're trying to decide what size turkey to buy, consider that an 18- to 20-pound bird feeds 14 or more. A 25-pound bird could easily serve 20 or more. (Think roughly 1 pound of turkey per person.) Also, consider the dimensions of your oven so you don't find yourself charging the bird with a kitchen stool attempting to force it inside.

>> Basting a turkey during roasting gives the bird a nice golden skin; it doesn't, however, permeate the meat, nor does it create a crisp skin.

>> If your turkey starts to get too brown during cooking, cover it loosely with aluminum foil.

>> Check out Table 21-1 for roasting times for a fresh or thawed turkey at 325 degrees. These times are approximate and should be used only as a guide; factors that can alter cooking time include the accuracy of your oven, the temperature of the bird when it goes into the oven, and the number of times the oven door is opened during roasting. Always use a meat thermometer to be sure the internal temperature reaches 165 degrees in the inner most part of the thigh and the thickest part of the breast.

>> If you don't want to stuff your turkey, you can cook the stuffing in a casserole dish in the oven. Doing so decreases the turkey's cooking time and diminishes the chance of salmonella bacteria growing in the cavity. If you want to stuff the bird, be sure to keep the turkey well chilled before stuffing. Add the stuffing just before roasting.

>> Another stuffing tip: Pack it loosely in the turkey cavity for quicker cooking and better texture.

TABLE 21-1

Turkey Roasting Chart

Weight	Cooking Time (Unstuffed)	Cooking Time (Stuffed)
8 to 12 pounds	2¾ to 3 hours	3 to 3½ hours
12 to 14 pounds	3 to 3¾ hours	3¼ to 4 hours
14 to 18 pounds	3¾ to 4¼ hours	4 to 4½ hours
20 to 24 pounds	4½ to 5 hours	4¾ to 5¼ hours

>> Always test the stuffing for doneness. It should register 165 degrees on an instant-read thermometer. If the bird is done but your stuffing isn't, remove the turkey from the oven, spoon the stuffing into a buttered casserole dish, and continue to bake it (as the bird rests).

TIP

You can season a turkey in all sorts of ways to add flavor and color to the skin. For example, mix 2 tablespoons molasses or maple syrup with 2 tablespoons reduced-sodium soy sauce; baste the turkey with this mixture, along with the pan juices, during the last hour of cooking — but no sooner! Never baste a turkey with a sugar-based mixture for more than an hour, or the sugar will burn.

Of course, roasting a turkey means you have to carve it — a potential source of confusion for some people. Check out our illustrated instructions in Chapter 4, which walk you through the carving process, or visit www.dummies.com/go/carvingturkey to find a helpful video.

TURKEY ROASTING RESOURCES

The following organizations are available to provide information about turkey roasting — in case you need a little help around the holidays:

- **The National Turkey Federation:** Visit www.eatturkey.com for lots of recipes as well as information about purchasing, storing, and cooking a turkey. The site even gives tips for using leftovers.

- **The USDA Meat and Poultry Hotline:** Visit the USDA on the web at www.fsis.usda.gov for food and safety tips about meat, poultry, and eggs. You can also call toll-free at 1-888-674-6854.

- **Butterball Turkey:** Visit Butterball online at www.butterball.com for recipes, tips, and a list of the ten most frequently asked questions, along with the answers, of course! Or you can call 1-800-BUTTERBALL (800-288-8372).

RECIPE
ALERT

Turkey meat, especially the dryer parts from the breast, calls for a great gravy. We offer a recipe later in the chapter for Madeira Pan Gravy. *Madeira* is an earthy sweet wine from the island of the same name, which is part of Portugal. If you don't have the wine, you can substitute chicken broth.

For an attractive presentation, garnish your turkey platter with fruits and other produce. Try a heap of fresh cranberries, piles of leafy greens or fresh herbs (such as tarragon and thyme branches), a few kumquats or orange slices, or red and green grapes dusted in sugar.

Teasing the Palate with Fresh Dips

RECIPE
ALERT

As a rule, you don't serve filling hors d'oeuvres, like aged cheeses or puff pastries filled with meat, before a big meal. We favor light, tasty starters like fresh raw vegetables and dips. Later in the chapter, we present a recipe for Warm Artichoke-Spinach Dip. This classic dip is perfect to tantalize everyone's palate for the big meal. Serve it in hollowed-out round sourdough bread. Or use tortilla chips, good crackers, or thin toasted slices of French bread.

Scrumptious Stuffings and Sides

Some people like stuffing even better than the turkey. Here's some advice:

>> Whenever making stuffing for your roasted turkey, make sure that the bread you use is very dry, even stale. Two-day-old bread (left out uncovered) yields the best result; fresh, moist bread can create gummy stuffing. Just be sure to slice the bread before you dry it, or it can get too hard to work with.

TIP

To dry out fresh bread, place slices or cubes on a baking sheet and leave them uncovered a day or two, turning them now and then. Or dry out the bread on a baking sheet in a 200-degree oven, turning frequently.

>> You need about ¾ to 1 cup of stuffing per pound of bird. This amount also leaves you with delicious leftovers.

>> When making stuffing, overmixing and packing it too densely into the bird's cavity can cause it to cook more slowly and crumble when served. If you're not baking it inside the bird's cavity, bake your stuffing in a well-buttered, covered baking dish for about 45 minutes. (You can remove the cover for the last ten minutes of baking to give it a crisp crust.) Try to time the cooking so the stuffing comes out of the oven as the bird is being carved.

>> Drizzle a little chicken stock, white wine, or turkey pan drippings over the stuffing for extra flavor and moisture.

RECIPE ALERT

In our recipe for Cornbread, Sausage, and Apple Stuffing later in the chapter, we use *poultry seasoning,* which is a commercial blend of ground sage, rosemary, thyme, marjoram, savory, and salt. However, you can experiment and substitute any of your favorite herbs. Be sure the poultry seasoning — or any seasoning in a jar for that matter — is not over-the-hill. One telltale sign is a faded label with a promotional quote like "Eleanor Roosevelt's favorite!" Dried spices can lose potency within a year of opening.

Stuffing cooked separately from the turkey may need a little extra moisture. The stuffing in our recipe is kept moist with pork sausage, eggs, and an assortment of fruits and vegetables. However, if after 30 minutes in the oven the stuffing becomes a little dry, simply add a little more chicken stock or warm water and return it to the oven to finish baking.

RECIPE ALERT

Cornbread mixes and cornbread muffins are often too moist and sweet to use as a base for turkey stuffing. Our Cornbread for Stuffing recipe later in the chapter holds its shape when combined with the other ingredients. You can make it ahead of time and freeze it, or wrap it and keep it in the refrigerator for a few days.

RECIPE ALERT

Looking for another accompaniment to your roasted turkey? Be sure to check out our recipe for Fresh Cranberry-Orange Relish with Walnuts. We jazz it up by adding some Cointreau or Grand Marnier (sweet orange-flavored liqueurs), but they're optional. So are the walnuts, but they add interesting texture.

RECIPE ALERT

Don't forget the mashed potatoes (see Chapter 5) so you can use that delicious gravy. Here are two other favorites that round out the meal nicely:

>> **Green Beans with Shallots:** This recipe is simple and elegant; it also lends a nice green color to your menu, which is dominated by shades of orange. And while several of the other side dishes are sweet, this bean dish is savory. You can make it at the last minute provided you've already trimmed the beans and minced the shallots.

>> **Rum-Baked Sweet Potatoes:** Remember that bottle of dark rum you bought at the duty-free store in Barbados? If you're like us, that bottle is sitting, unopened, somewhere around the house. Well, go find it! You finally have an excuse to taste it.

   These terrific sweet potatoes can be baked very quickly — you can put them in the oven as you're removing the turkey to rest. First, you parboil the sweet potatoes (which softens them slightly and makes the second cooking much quicker) for about 15 minutes, and then you bake them for about 20 minutes.

Last Man Standing: Holiday Desserts

One American dessert that's fitting from the first blush of autumn through the chills of Christmas is pumpkin pie. On the difficulty meter, it comes in low. The most common failing is having the cooked center collapse. This simply means your pie filling wasn't thick enough. If your pumpkin mix looks too thin, beef it up by stirring in a tablespoon or more of cornstarch.

RECIPE ALERT

In this chapter, we offer a great variation on this classic: Praline Pumpkin Pie. It features a pecan layer on top of the crust that's a nice contrast to the semisweet pumpkin filling. To make this recipe, you first need a crust, of course! You have two options: Make one yourself by following our recipe and illustrated instructions in Chapter 10, or buy a frozen shell. A deep-dish pie plate is best for this recipe because the filling comes right to the top of a regular pie plate (and you want to avoid spillage). So you're better off taking the time to make your own crust.

If your dinner is for ten or more people, we suggest making two pies. Perhaps make one pumpkin and one apple; for a homemade apple pie recipe, see Chapter 10. If your family likes a wider variety of desserts, you can find plenty of choices in Chapters 10 and 15 or in *Desserts For Dummies*, by Bill Yosses, Alison Yates, and Bryan Miller, or *Baking For Dummies*, by Emily Nolan (both published by Wiley).

Warming Up with Holiday Libations

RECIPE ALERT

You're trashing your diet for the holidays anyway, so why not really blow it off with a rich, rum-laced eggnog? As you see in our recipe later in the chapter, eggnog can be made delightfully frothy by folding in beaten egg whites — without adding significant calories.

Eggnog is traditionally made with raw eggs. Because of widespread concerns over possible salmonella poisoning, we give you a great recipe for eggnog made with eggs that are cooked long enough to eliminate the problem but not the flavor. This recipe is adapted from one created by Alton Brown of the television Food Network.

RECIPE ALERT

It's a good idea to pair a rich, cool drink like eggnog with something lighter and warmer, such as our terrific Warm Red Wine and Orange Punch in this chapter. It couldn't be easier, and the combination of fruity red wine, orange, cinnamon, and clove makes for a sure holiday winner. You can serve it warm, or mix it a couple of hours in advance and chill until serving.

Roasted Turkey

PREP TIME: 15 MIN	COOK TIME: ABOUT 3 HR	YIELD: 12 SERVINGS

INGREDIENTS

1 fresh or thawed frozen turkey (about 12 pounds)

1 medium yellow onion, quartered

2 carrots, peeled and quartered

2 large cloves garlic, crushed

2 tablespoons vegetable oil

Salt and black pepper

DIRECTIONS

1 Preheat the oven to 325 degrees, with the oven rack on the lowest rung. Set a wire roasting rack in a large roasting pan.

2 Remove the giblets and neck from the turkey cavity and reserve for gravy (see the next recipe). Discard the liver. Remove any excess fat from the turkey. Rinse the turkey inside and out with cold water and pat dry.

3 Place in the turkey cavity the onion, carrots, and garlic. Tie the legs together with kitchen string. If desired, bend the wing tips back and fold them underneath the turkey.

4 Set the turkey, breast-side up, on the roasting rack. Rub the turkey all over with the oil. Season generously with salt and black pepper.

5 Add 1 cup of water to the roasting pan. If using a meat thermometer, insert it into the thickest part of the thigh, close to the body, without touching any bone.

6 Roast for about 3 to 3¼ hours, or until the internal temperature registers 165 degrees in the innermost part of the thigh and the thickest part of the breast. Add another ½ cup water to the roasting pan if it gets dry. To brown the turkey evenly, turn the pan laterally midway through the roasting. Check for doneness during the last 30 minutes of roasting, and baste with the pan drippings 2 to 3 times during the last hour.

7 Remove the turkey from the oven, transfer it to a carving board, and cover loosely with aluminum foil, letting it rest for 20 minutes while you make gravy.

8 Remove the vegetables from the cavity and discard. Carve the turkey and serve with the Madeira Pan Gravy.

PER SERVING (WITHOUT GRAVY): Calories 404 (From Fat 122); Fat 14g (Saturated 4g); Cholesterol 171mg; Sodium 206mg; Carbohydrate 0g (Dietary Fiber 0g); Protein 66g.

Madeira Pan Gravy

PREP TIME: 10–15 MIN | COOK TIME: ABOUT 35 MIN | YIELD: 12 SERVINGS

INGREDIENTS

4 cups canned chicken broth

Turkey giblets (liver discarded) and neck

1 medium yellow onion, peeled and quartered

2 carrots, quartered

2 stalks celery, quartered

1 bay leaf

Turkey pan drippings

½ cup Madeira (optional)

3 tablespoons flour

Salt and black pepper

DIRECTIONS

1 In a medium saucepan, combine the chicken broth, turkey giblets and neck, onion, carrots, celery, and bay leaf. Cover and bring to a boil. Reduce the heat to low and simmer, partially covered, for 30 minutes.

2 Strain the stock through cheesecloth or a fine sieve into a large measuring cup. You should have 1½ to 2 cups. If you have less, add water or chicken broth. Refrigerate.

3 When the broth is chilled, skim and discard any fat that rises to the surface.

4 Pour the drippings from the turkey roasting pan into a 2-cup glass measuring cup or a degreaser. Spoon off and discard all but 3 tablespoons of fat from the drippings. Reserve the fat in a small cup.

5 Strain the skimmed drippings through a fine sieve into a second 2-cup glass measuring cup or bowl. Set aside.

6 Add the Madeira (if desired) to the roasting pan and cook over medium-high heat, stirring and scraping the bottom for about 1 minute; strain this into the cup holding the skimmed pan drippings.

7 Add the 3 tablespoons of reserved fat to the roasting pan. Set two burners to medium heat under the pan and heat the fat. Add the flour to the pan and stir constantly with a wire whisk, about 1 to 2 minutes, to blend the flour into the fat. The mixture should turn golden brown.

8. Slowly whisk in the Madeira pan drippings; whisk for about 1 minute, stirring and scraping the bottom of the pan. Continue whisking and gradually add the turkey stock, 1 cup at a time. Use only enough stock to reach a gravy consistency. Season to taste with salt and black pepper.

PER SERVING: *Calories 102 (From Fat 52); Fat 6g (Saturated 2g); Cholesterol 32mg; Sodium 392mg; Carbohydrate 2g (Dietary Fiber 0g); Protein 10g.*

Warm Artichoke-Spinach Dip

PREP TIME: ABOUT 15 MIN	COOK TIME: ABOUT 20 MIN	YIELD: 12 SERVINGS

INGREDIENTS

Two 10-ounce boxes frozen spinach, thawed

2 tablespoons butter

¼ medium yellow onion, minced

2 cloves garlic, peeled and minced

2 tablespoons flour

1½ cups whole milk or half-and-half

3 tablespoons canned chicken broth

1 teaspoon freshly squeezed lemon juice

½ teaspoon Tabasco sauce

¼ teaspoon salt

½ cup grated Romano cheese

⅓ cup low-fat sour cream

⅔ cup shredded Monterey Jack cheese

1 large ripe plum tomato, cored, seeded, and chopped

One 12-ounce can artichoke hearts (not marinated), drained and coarsely chopped

DIRECTIONS

1 Preheat the oven to 350 degrees.

2 Put the thawed spinach in a colander and cover with paper towels. Squeeze to remove as much moisture as possible. Set aside.

3 In a medium saucepan, melt the butter over medium- high heat. Sauté the onion and garlic until the onion is soft and translucent but not brown, about 5 minutes.

4 Add the flour and cook, stirring, for 2 minutes.

5 Slowly whisk in the milk or half-and-half and the chicken broth. Bring to a boil and then remove from the heat. Immediately add the lemon juice, Tabasco sauce, salt, and Romano cheese. Stir to combine and then set aside.

6 Combine the sour cream, Monterey Jack cheese, tomato, artichokes, and spinach. Fold into the warm cream mixture and pour the dip into an ovenproof casserole dish.

7 Bake in the oven for 10 minutes, or until warmed through but not browned. Serve immediately.

PER SERVING: *Calories 96 (From Fat 55); Fat 6g (Saturated 4g); Cholesterol 19mg; Sodium 231mg; Carbohydrate 6g (Dietary Fiber 2g); Protein 5g.*

VARY IT! Add more spice to this dish by upping the amount of Tabasco sauce, or make it milder by eliminating the Tabasco altogether. If you do the latter, try adding ½ teaspoon dried dill or 1 tablespoon fresh, chopped cilantro leaves.

Fresh Cranberry-Orange Relish with Walnuts

PREP TIME: 10 MIN PLUS CHILL TIME | YIELD: 12 SERVINGS

INGREDIENTS

1 navel orange

One 12-ounce package fresh or frozen cranberries

1 cup sugar

2 teaspoons Cointreau, Grand Marnier, brandy, or other orange liqueur (optional)

½ cup chopped walnuts (optional)

DIRECTIONS

1 Starting at the stem end of the orange, remove the peel, working in a spiral fashion with a sharp paring knife. Take care to leave behind the bitter pith (the white layer beneath the orange peel). Set the orange peel aside.

2 Peel away and discard the white pith from the orange; coarsely chop the fruit.

3 Put the orange pieces, the orange peel, and the cranberries into the bowl of a food processor. Pulse 4 or 5 times, or until the fruit is coarsely chopped.

4 Transfer the cranberry-orange mixture to a bowl or a glass serving container. Stir in the sugar and the brandy or orange liqueur (if desired) and the walnuts (if desired). Chill until ready to serve.

PER SERVING: *Calories 85 (From Fat 0); Fat 0g (Saturated 0g); Cholesterol 0mg; Sodium 0mg; Carbohydrate 22g (Dietary Fiber 1g); Protein 0g.*

Green Beans with Shallots

PREP TIME: 15 MIN | COOK TIME: ABOUT 20 MIN | YIELD: 12 SERVINGS

INGREDIENTS

3 pounds fresh green beans, rinsed and trimmed

6 tablespoons butter

1 cup shallots, sliced crosswise into thin rounds

2 teaspoons fresh lemon juice (optional)

Salt and black pepper

DIRECTIONS

1 Place the beans in a large pot. Add cold salted water to cover. Cover the pot and bring to a boil over medium-high heat. Cook until just tender but still firm, about 10 to 15 minutes. Check for doneness after about 8 minutes.

2 As the beans cook, melt the butter in a large skillet. Add the shallots and cook over medium heat for 3 to 4 minutes, stirring often, until golden. Set aside.

3 Drain the beans well and add them to the skillet with the shallots. Stir to combine and heat briefly just before serving. Stir in the lemon juice (if desired). Season to taste with salt and black pepper.

PER SERVING: *Calories 99 (From Fat 54); Fat 6g (Saturated 4g); Cholesterol 15mg; Sodium 54mg; Carbohydrate 11g (Dietary Fiber 4g); Protein 3g.*

VARY IT! An elegant alternative for this dish is thin, French string beans, called *haricot verts.* If making this variation, reduce the cooking time to 4 to 6 minutes, or until tender.

Rum-Baked Sweet Potatoes

PREP TIME: 5–10 MIN	COOK TIME: ABOUT 45 MIN	YIELD: 12 SERVINGS

INGREDIENTS

6 medium sweet potatoes (about 3½ pounds), peeled

⅓ cup butter

1½ cups packed dark brown sugar

⅔ cup dark rum

⅓ cup fresh orange juice

¾ teaspoon ground allspice

Salt and black pepper

DIRECTIONS

1 Preheat the oven to 350 degrees.

2 Place the potatoes in a large pot of lightly salted boiling water. Cover and boil for 15 to 20 minutes, or until still slightly firm when pierced with a fork.

3 Drain and cut each sweet potato in half lengthwise and then widthwise into quarters. Place the potatoes in a single layer in a 9-x-13-inch baking pan or ceramic dish. Set aside.

4 In a large skillet, melt the butter over medium heat; add the brown sugar, rum, and orange juice. Bring to a boil, stirring occasionally to break up any lumps of sugar.

5 Reduce the heat and simmer for 7 to 8 minutes, stirring occasionally, until the sauce is thickened and slightly caramelized. Stir in the allspice.

6 Drizzle the rum mixture over the sweet potatoes. Gently turn the potatoes in the glaze to coat all sides. Season the potatoes well with salt and black pepper. Bake for 20 to 25 minutes, or until the sauce is bubbly and the potatoes are heated through and tender.

PER SERVING: *Calories 261 (From Fat 48); Fat 5g (Saturated 3g); Cholesterol 14mg; Sodium 73mg; Carbohydrate 53g (Dietary Fiber 2g); Protein 2g.*

VARY IT! Instead of rum, you can use ⅓ cup molasses mixed with ⅓ cup pineapple juice and ¼ teaspoon almond extract or rum extract.

Cornbread, Sausage, and Apple Stuffing

PREP TIME: 20 MIN	COOK TIME: ABOUT 1 HR	YIELD: 12 SERVINGS

INGREDIENTS

7 to 8 tablespoons butter

1 pound bulk pork sausage (mild or hot, to taste)

1 large yellow onion, diced

1 cup diced celery

1 large red bell pepper, cored, seeded, and diced

2 hot chile peppers or jalapeño peppers, seeded and diced (optional)

8 cups cornbread cubes (see the next recipe)

4 cups stale French bread, cut into ⅓- to ½-inch cubes

2 Golden Delicious apples, peeled, cored, and cut into small cubes

⅓ cup chopped parsley

2 teaspoons poultry seasoning, or to taste

1 teaspoon sugar

Salt and black pepper

One 14.5-ounce can chicken stock, or 2 cups homemade stock

2 eggs, lightly beaten

DIRECTIONS

1 In a large skillet, melt 2 tablespoons of the butter over medium-high heat. Add the sausage and cook until browned, about 5 minutes, stirring frequently to break it up. Using a slotted spoon, remove the sausage to a large mixing bowl.

2 Add to the skillet 4 more tablespoons of the butter with the onion, celery, red bell pepper, and the hot peppers (if desired). Cook, stirring occasionally, about 4 to 5 minutes, or until the vegetables are cooked but still a little firm. Stir the vegetables into the sausage.

3 Add the cornbread and French bread cubes, apples, parsley, poultry seasoning, sugar, and salt and black pepper to taste; toss well.

4 In a small bowl, whisk together the chicken stock and eggs; add this to the stuffing, about 1 cup at a time, stirring well. Add enough egg-broth mixture to moisten the stuffing so it holds together when lightly pressed between the palms of your hands.

5 Transfer the stuffing into a well-buttered baking dish with a lid; dot with the remaining 1 to 2 tablespoons of butter. Cover and bake at 325 degrees for 45 to 55 minutes, or until heated through.

PER SERVING: *Calories 360 (From Fat 204); Fat 23g (Saturated 8g); Cholesterol 86mg; Sodium 675mg; Carbohydrate 31g (Dietary Fiber 2g); Protein 9g.*

TIP: If you can't find bulk pork sausage, purchase sausage links and remove the casings.

VARY IT! You can substitute some white wine for some of the chicken stock to add more flavor. Instead of using poultry seasoning, substitute 2 to 3 tablespoons fresh chopped herbs, such as sage, marjoram, thyme, or any combination.

Cornbread for Stuffing

PREP TIME: 5 MIN	COOK TIME: 20 MIN	YIELD: 8 CUPS OF CUBES

INGREDIENTS

1 cup yellow cornmeal

1 cup flour

1 tablespoon plus 1 teaspoon baking powder

2 teaspoons sugar

½ teaspoon salt

1 cup buttermilk

1 egg

⅓ cup corn oil or vegetable oil

DIRECTIONS

1 Preheat the oven to 425 degrees.

2 In a large bowl, combine the cornmeal, flour, baking powder, sugar, and salt; stir to mix.

3 With a wire whisk, stir in the buttermilk, egg, and oil; beat just until the mixture is combined — don't overmix.

4 Spread the batter in a buttered 8- or 9-inch square baking pan. Bake for 20 minutes, or until the top of the bread springs back when touched. Cool in the pan on a wire rack.

5 If you're not using the cornbread right away, cut the bread into big pieces, wrap tightly, and refrigerate until ready to make the stuffing. Slice the cornbread into ¼- to ½-inch cubes for turkey stuffing.

PER SERVING: *Calories 227 (From Fat 95); Fat 11g (Saturated 1g); Cholesterol 28mg; Sodium 376mg; Carbohydrate 28g (Dietary Fiber 2g); Protein 5g per cup.*

Praline Pumpkin Pie

PREP TIME: 15 MIN PLUS CHILL TIME	COOK TIME: 50 MIN	YIELD: 8 SERVINGS

INGREDIENTS

One 9-inch pie crust (preferably deep dish), unbaked

1 cup packed light brown sugar

3 tablespoons butter

⅔ cup coarsely chopped, lightly toasted pecans

1½ cups canned pumpkin

3 eggs, lightly beaten

1 tablespoon granulated sugar

1 teaspoon ground ginger

1 teaspoon ground cinnamon

½ teaspoon ground nutmeg

One 5-ounce can evaporated milk

¼ cup whole milk

2 teaspoons vanilla extract

1 cup lightly sweetened whipped cream (optional)

DIRECTIONS

1 Preheat the oven to 375 degrees.

2 Place a piece of foil over the bottom of the pie crust and weight it down with uncooked rice or beans. Bake the crust for 20 minutes, and let it cool. Remove foil.

3 In a small pan, combine ⅔ cup of the brown sugar with the 3 tablespoons butter. Cook over medium heat for a few minutes, stirring constantly until the butter is melted and the brown sugar is dissolved. Stir in the pecans.

4 With a spatula or spoon, spread this hot mixture over the bottom of the cooled pie shell; set aside to cool to room temperature.

5 In a large mixing bowl, combine the pumpkin with the remaining ⅔ cup brown sugar. Add the eggs, granulated sugar, ginger, cinnamon, and nutmeg and beat lightly with a whisk or hand-held mixer on low speed until well blended.

6 Whisk or beat in the evaporated milk, whole milk, and vanilla extract, blending well. Pour the filling over the cooled pecan mixture in the pie shell.

7 Cover the top edge of the pie crust with foil (to prevent over-browning). Bake the pie for 30 minutes. Remove the foil and bake for another 15 to 20 minutes, until a knife inserted into the center comes out clean. Cool on a wire rack.

8 Cover and refrigerate until ready to serve. If desired, spoon lightly sweetened whipped cream over each portion before serving.

PER SERVING: *Calories 432 (From Fat 222); Fat 25g (Saturated 9g); Cholesterol 110mg; Sodium 168mg; Carbohydrate 48g (Dietary Fiber 4g); Protein 7g.*

Eggnog

INGREDIENTS

4 egg yolks

⅓ cup sugar

1 pint whole milk

1 cup heavy cream

1½ tablespoons vanilla extract

1 teaspoon freshly grated nutmeg

3 to 4 ounces dark rum

4 egg whites (optional)

DIRECTIONS

1 In the bowl of a stand-up mixer, whip the egg yolks until they lighten in color. (You can also do this step by hand with a whisk.) Slowly pour in the sugar while mixing until it's thoroughly incorporated. Set aside.

2 In a medium saucepan over medium-high heat, combine the milk, heavy cream, vanilla extract, and nutmeg, stirring frequently. Bring just to a boil and quickly remove from the heat.

3 Very slowly whisk a cup of the milk mixture into the egg yolks. Add remaining milk mixture, whisking.

4 Return mixture to a pot over medium-high heat until it registers 160 degrees on a liquid thermometer. Remove from the heat and stir in the rum. Chill thoroughly.

5 To give the eggnog a lighter texture, beat egg whites until they form stiff peaks. Fold them into eggnog and whisk for a minute before serving.

PER SERVING: Calories 304 (From Fat 187); Fat 21g (Saturated 12g); Cholesterol 207mg; Sodium 60mg; Carbohydrate 16g (Dietary Fiber 0g); Protein 5g.

Warm Red Wine and Orange Punch

PREP TIME: 5 MIN	COOK TIME: ABOUT 30 MIN	YIELD: 6 SERVINGS

INGREDIENTS

¾ cup water

¾ cup granulated sugar

1 cinnamon stick

One orange

8 whole cloves

One 750-milliliter bottle red wine (such as Merlot or Pinot Noir)

DIRECTIONS

1 In a saucepan, combine water, sugar, and cinnamon stick. Bring to a boil, lower heat, and simmer for 30 minutes.

2 Quarter the orange and squeeze the juice into the saucepan. Pierce the orange peels with the cloves and add to the pan. Stir the ingredients until syrupy.

3 Pour in the wine and heat to just below simmering. Remove oranges. Let cool for 10 to 15 minutes before serving in mugs. (Fragile glass may shatter.)

PER SERVING: *Calories 197 (From Fat 0); Fat 0g (Saturated 0g); Cholesterol 0mg; Sodium 7mg; Carbohydrate 30g (Dietary Fiber 1g); Protein 1g.*

5

The Part of Tens

Discover how to think like a chef by absorbing some classic cooking wisdom.

Uncover some common cooking myths and see how you should really handle these matters in the kitchen.

Get tips for eating for good health, including how to reduce fat, sugar, and salt in your diet without reducing taste, and how to cook for special diets.

Chapter **22**

Ten Ways to Think Like a Chef

n observing and interviewing many chefs, we found a consensus among them about how to progress as a cook. The ten points in this chapter reflect their thoughts.

Know the Basic Techniques

Cooking is so much more fun — and successful — when you approach it with confidence. Chefs say that confidence arises from knowing your techniques so well that they're second nature. Part 2 is chock-full of information about the basic techniques you need to know.

Use Only the Freshest Ingredients

Use only the freshest ingredients and buy in-season fresh fruits and vegetables. Seasonal produce offers the highest quality at the lowest price. Why make an apple pie in the summer from mealy fruit held in storage all year when you can make a pie with fresh, ripe peaches or juicy plums? Let what's fresh and available at the market help you spontaneously decide what's for dinner. And definitely seek out farmers' markets in your area.

Get It Together

So much of cooking, even for professionals, is preparation — slicing, peeling, dicing, and so on.

The French call this preparation *mise en place,* which translates to "everything in its place." Get the chopping, mincing, deboning, and washing chores out of the way to create an even, efficient flow of cooking steps. Also have in front of you all the seasonings you need for the dish. That way, when the butter or oil is hot and sizzling in the skillet, you don't need to lurch over to the cutting board to peel and mince onions.

Understand Flavor Combinations

People have innate sensitivity to five basic elements: sweet, sour, salty, bitter, and a more elusive flavor called *umami.* (Umami can best be described as a pleasant savory taste imparted by glutamate, a type of amino acid; it's very subtle and different from other basic taste elements). You pick up all of these sensitivities from taste receptors on the tongue as well as the roof of the mouth, inside the cheeks, the back of the mouth, and in the throat.

So why do you need to know all of this? Well, it makes for well-balanced dishes. Some basic food sensations naturally complement one another, sometimes in their contrast. For example, there's sweet and sour (lemonade); sweet and salty (many confections combine these two, though you may not taste it; ice cream, cake); and sweet and bitter (sweet cocktails). Bitter and sour, on the other hand, would be unpalatable.

Much of these flavor combinations is intuitive. When assembling ingredients for a meal, keep these in mind.

Think about Your Plate

Some cooks expend much effort preparing a fine meal only to diminish it by heaping ingredients onto plates chuck wagon–style. There is no excuse for doing so.

TIP

Think how food looks — its colors, its textures, its shapes — and make the most of it. This is not to say you should re-create Machu Picchu with your mashed potatoes, just that you give some thought to aesthetics. It can be as simple as fanning thin slices of steak over the plate instead of serving it in one big slab; garnishing with fresh herbs or citrus; spooning a sauce onto the plate and then arranging meat, poultry, or seafood over it; or packing cooked rice into a small cup and inverting it over the plate. When you begin thinking this way, the options will seem endless.

Plan Your Menus in Advance

Spend some time up front figuring out what a whole meal is going to look like. If the appetizer is a salad of grilled portobello mushrooms, featuring mushrooms in the entrée isn't an interesting choice. Keep the courses balanced, and don't overtax yourself. If you serve a time-consuming and complex appetizer, serve a simple entrée or one that needs only reheating.

Be Thrifty

TIP

Throw out nothing (unless, of course, it's spoiled). Nearly every morsel of food is usable for soups, stocks, salads, and so on. You can sometimes make great meals from leftovers.

Understand the different cuts of meat and how to cook them so you don't have to rely on more expensive cuts. Hone your knife skills so you can save money by purchasing whole chickens, meats on the bone, fish, and so on and then cutting them up yourself — a huge discount.

Don't Be a Slave to Recipes

Use a good, basic recipe that you like as a starting point, but don't consider it written in stone. One of the great chefs of his generation and a close friend of ours, the late Pierre Franey, had one mantra: Taste, Taste, Taste! Don't assume that the cookbook is infallible. Even if it is, each kitchen is different, ingredients vary, and so on. As you cook, continually taste.

Simplify

Too many spices spoil the broth. If you stick to two or three basic flavors in a dish, they work together to provide complexity, yet each flavor maintains its individuality. Don't load up your dishes with everything you can find. Sometimes the most perfect, delicious creations are the simplest.

TIP

Discover all you can about herbs, both fresh and dried, so you can season without always relying on a recipe. (Chapter 3 is a great place to start your education.) Chefs base some of the world's great cuisines on the combination of a few simple herbs and spices.

Above All, Have Fun

Take a cooking course, buy a cookbook, or make a new dish that you've always wanted to try. Cooking, like monster wave surfing, should be exhilarating — something you look forward to. So what if you wipe out once in a while? It's all part of the challenge. Bon appétit!

Chapter **23**

Ten Common Cooking Myths

C ooking, like medieval poetry, is suffused with myths, muddled logic, and inaccuracies. And they're passed down from generation to generation — and sometimes cookbook to cookbook — and taken for granted.

In the interest of investigative journalism, we explore ten common cooking myths in this chapter and give you the real story behind them.

Marinating Meat Tenderizes It

Marinades, even the most acidic, penetrate meat a tiny fraction of an inch below the surface. They can, however, impart flavor to the outside. You can tenderize tough cuts of beef, like chuck, brisket, shoulder, and shank, in several ways. For example, you can simply use a meat tenderizer, which is the size of a large hammer and looks like a medieval torture device. The working end is box shaped and studded with metal spikes. To use it, you hammer the meat evenly to break down the fibers. Another, but less efficient method is to take a sharp knife and score the meat crosswise over the muscles.

Searing Meat Traps in the Juices

Searing meat in a very hot pan can give meat a nice crusty texture and, if seasoned beforehand, a patina of flavor. But the fact is, meat loses moisture under any type of dry heat. The best way to retain moisture is slow cooking, as in braising, in which the meat rests in a few inches of liquid. Another way is to sear the meat and roast it at a very low temperature (around 275 degrees) for several hours or until just pink in the center (about 135 degrees). Let it rest for about 20 minutes to allow the juices to settle.

Basting Chicken Creates Crispy Skin

On the contrary, repeatedly dousing a roasting chicken with broth or liquid pan drippings can inhibit the skin from becoming crisp. In effect, you're creating skin-deflating steam. To achieve a parchment-like skin, first make sure the bird is thoroughly dry. Begin roasting in a 450-degree oven for 15 minutes, and then reduce to 350 degrees. You can baste the chicken periodically with thick fatty pan drippings (they shouldn't be watery).

Adding Oil to Pasta Water Keeps It from Sticking Together

We don't know where this myth originated. It has nothing to do with keeping pasta from separating. Adding oil to your pasta water wastes your time and money. Instead, add sauce to your pasta immediately to prevent it from sticking together. Or if you leave it out to cool or prefer no sauce, toss it with a little olive oil or vegetable oil.

Using Quality Olive Oil Is Important for Sautéing or Pan-Roasting

For confirmation about this myth, we consulted no other than superstar Italian chef Mario Batali, who says that when you use quality olive oil for sautéing or pan-roasting, "you are just wasting good oil. If you have a very good extra-virgin olive oil, use that to drizzle over finished dishes."

Superior olive oil (*read:* expensive) is meant for tasting, not cooking. Using a fine olive oil for sautéing meat or fish is like putting premium gas in a lawn mower — the difference won't be evident because the flavor will be lost in the sizzling pan. Run-of-the-mill supermarket olive oil or vegetable oil works fine. After all, its primary purpose is to prevent food from sticking in the pan.

Using a Garlic Press Extracts More Flavor

Using a garlic press breaks cloves into random bits and squeezes out oil in an uneven fashion, increasing the chances of burning in a hot pan. Evenly slicing garlic allows the oils to seep out uniformly.

Soaking Dried Beans before Cooking Improves Flavor and Texture

There are several schools of thought on this matter, but most chefs we consulted maintained that soaking beans for several hours in hot water, or overnight in cold water, is unnecessary. All it does is speed up the cooking and sometimes makes them mushy.

Adding a Potato to an Oversalted Soup or Stew Reduces the Saltiness

Chunks of potato added to an oversalted liquid merely leaves you with oversalted liquid with chunks of potatoes in it. The best way to bring down the salt level in a soup or stew is to add an unsalted liquid, like water. Some cooks add a little bit of sugar to cancel out some of the salt.

Cooking with Wine or Spirits Burns Off All the Alcohol

Not all the alcohol in pan sauces or stews cooks off. If you simmer something for hours, most of the alcohol does go away. But if you cook for 20 minutes or less, up to 50 percent can remain. (If you flambé, a small amount of alcohol evaporates.) And even less alcohol escapes during baking, because the booze is mired in the thick batter.

Rinsing Raw Mushrooms Causes Them to Absorb More Water

It's true that mushrooms contain a good amount of water, which means they give off a lot of liquid when sautéed, making them sometimes difficult to sauté and brown. But they won't absorb more water if you wash them. In fact, you should rinse or brush raw mushrooms with a vegetable brush to remove any surface dirt. If you do rinse them, drain them well in a colander or dab off any excess moisture before sautéing.

Glossary of 100 (Plus) Common Cooking Terms

Cooking and recipe writing have their own distinct language. Before you roast a chicken, for example, you need to know what *trussing* means. To make a soufflé that rises above the rim of the dish, you need to understand *whipping* and *folding* egg whites. This appendix gives you a list of basic terms. Most of them are thoroughly described elsewhere in the book.

al dente: An Italian phrase meaning "to the tooth" that describes the tender but still firm texture of perfectly cooked pasta. (See Chapter 13 for pasta recipes.)

au gratin: A dish, usually topped with buttered breadcrumbs, grated cheese, or both that has been browned in the oven or under the broiler.

bain-marie: A container partially filled with hot water that holds a smaller pan for gentle cooking.

barbecue: Any food cooked on a charcoal or gas grill over an indirect fire (as opposed to grilling, which occurs directly over the fire). Also refers to the process of cooking foods in a pit or on a spit for a long time, or is a descriptive term for the particular spicy tomato-based sauce used to baste grilled meat.

baste: To add flavor and moisture by brushing food with pan drippings, fat, or a seasoned liquid as it cooks.

batter: An uncooked, semiliquid mixture usually containing beaten eggs, flour, liquid, and a leavening ingredient, such as baking soda or baking powder, that makes the batter rise when cooked.

beat: To mix ingredients briskly in a circular motion so they become smooth and creamy. A hundred hand-beaten strokes generally equal one minute with an electric mixer, if you're the type who counts these things. (See Chapter 10 for information about beating egg whites.)

bind: To bring together a liquid mixture, such as a sauce, with a thickening ingredient, such as cream or butter.

blanch: To plunge vegetables or fruits into boiling water for a short time to loosen their skin or preserve their color (see Chapter 5).

blend: To mix or combine two or more ingredients with a spoon, whisk, spatula, or electric mixer.

boil: To bring the temperature of a liquid to 212 degrees for water at sea level, causing bubbles to break at the surface (see Chapter 5).

bone (or debone): To remove the bones from meat, fish, or poultry.

bouquet garni: A package of mixed herbs (often tied in cheesecloth) that's used to season stocks, soups, and stews to impart flavor. A typical combination is parsley, thyme, and bay leaf.

braise: To brown meat or vegetables in fat and then cook, covered, in a small quantity of liquid over low heat, usually for a long time. The long, slow cooking both tenderizes and flavors the food, especially tough cuts of meat. Braising can take place either on the stovetop or in the oven. (See Chapter 7 for braising and stewing recipes.)

bread: To coat a piece of food with crackers or breadcrumbs to seal in moisture and give it a crisp crust. The piece of fish, poultry, meat, or vegetable is usually first dipped into a liquid, such as beaten egg or milk, to make the crumbs adhere.

broil: To cook food under a hot oven coil, as opposed to grilling, in which the heat is underneath (see Chapter 9).

brown: To cook food briefly over high heat, usually in fat and on top of the stove, to impart a rich brown color to its skin or surface. Food also may be browned in a very hot oven or under the broiler.

brush: To coat the surface of food with a liquid ingredient, such as melted butter, egg, or fruit glaze.

butterfly: To split food down the center (removing bones if necessary), leaving the two halves joined at the seam so the food opens flat to resemble a butterfly.

caramelize: To heat sugar until it melts into a liquid, syrupy state that ranges from golden to dark brown in color (320 degrees to 350 degrees on a candy thermometer). Also, to cook onions and other vegetables until they become soft and brown (the sugars they contain caramelize).

chill: To put food in a cool place, typically the refrigerator, to bring it to a cold (but not frozen) state.

chop: To cut food into small pieces by using a knife or food processor.

clarify: To make a cloudy liquid clear by removing the impurities. For example, you can clarify a stock or broth by simmering raw egg whites or eggshells in it for 10 to 15 minutes to attract impurities. You then very gently strain the liquid through a sieve lined with cheesecloth.

compound butter: Butter that has been flavored with herbs or spices.

confectioners' sugar: A fine powdered sugar cut with cornstarch that's used for cake icings or to powder cakes and cookies. Also called "powdered sugar."

core: To cut out the core of a food, usually a fruit or vegetable such as an apple or pepper.

cream: To beat one ingredient, such as butter, with another, such as sugar, until soft and smooth.

crimp: To press together with your fingers or a fork and seal the rim of a double-crust pie to form a double thickness of dough that you can then shape into a decorative pattern (see Chapter 10).

crumble: To break up or crush food, such as dried herbs or crackers, into small pieces with your fingers.

cube: To cut food into ½-inch square pieces. Cubed food is larger than diced food. See also *dice.*

cure: To preserve food such as meat or fish by salting, drying, and/or smoking.

cut in: To use two knives or a pastry cutter to mix hard fat (like butter) into dry ingredients (like flour). For example, "Cut the butter into the flour until it resembles coarse crumbs."

dash: See *pinch.*

deglaze: To add liquid, usually wine or broth, to a hot skillet or roasting pan and scrape up the browned bits clinging to the bottom of the pan that pieces of sautéed meat, fish, or poultry left behind. You then *reduce* and season the pan sauce. See Chapter 6 for recipes that use this technique.

degrease: To skim the fat off the surface of a soup or gravy with a spoon. Also done by chilling the mixture, turning the liquid fat into a solid, which you can then easily lift off the surface.

demi-glace: A rich brown sauce made by boiling down meat stock until it's reduced to a thick glaze that can coat a spoon.

devein: To remove the vein from shrimp or other shellfish. (See Chapter 7 for illustrated instructions for cleaning shrimp.)

devil: To season foods with hot and spicy ingredients such as Tabasco sauce, mustard, or red pepper flakes.

dice: To cut into small (⅛-inch to ¼-inch) cubes.

dilute: To thin a mixture by adding water or other liquid.

disjoint: To sever a piece of meat at its joint, as when you separate a chicken leg from its thigh.

drain: To remove the liquid from a food, often in a colander. Also, to pour off liquid fat from a pan after you brown a food (such as bacon or ground meat).

dredge: To coat the surface of a food by dragging it through flour, cornmeal, or crumbs.

drizzle: To pour a liquid such as melted butter, sauce, or syrup over a food in a thin, slow stream.

dust: To give the surface of food a thin coating of flour or confectioner's sugar.

emulsify: To combine two liquids that ordinarily wouldn't meld on their own (water and oil, egg yolks and acid). This is achieved by combining small amounts of each while beating vigorously. Mayonnaise is one example.

fillet: As a verb, to cut the flesh away from the bones of a piece of meat or fish. As a noun, a piece of meat, fish, or poultry that has the bones removed.

flake: To peel off or form into flakes, usually with a fork, as in the process for determining whether fish is done. (When you can flake the fish with a fork, it's cooked.)

flambé: To ignite food that's drenched in alcohol so it bursts into a dramatic flame just before serving.

flute: To form into a decorative pleated groove, as in fluting a pie crust before baking.

fold: To combine a light mixture, such as beaten egg whites or whipped cream, with a heavier mixture, such as sugared egg yolks or melted chocolate, by using a gentle mixing motion. (See Chapter 10 for illustrated instructions.)

fond: A French word for "base," which refers to the browned bits left in a pan after sautéing or roasting.

fricassee: A white stew in which meat or poultry isn't browned before cooking.

fry: To cook or sauté food in fat over high heat. Deep-fried foods are submerged in hot fat and cooked until crisp.

garnish: An edible plate adornment, ranging from a simple wedge of lemon to a fancy chocolate leaf.

glaze: To coat the surface of a food with syrup, melted jelly, an egg wash, or another thin, liquid mixture to give it a glossy shine.

grate: To rub a large piece of food (such as a block of cheese) against the coarse, serrated holes of a grater.

grease: To spread a thin layer of fat, usually butter, on the inside of a pan to prevent food from sticking as it cooks.

grill: To cook food over a charcoal or gas grill, or to cook on an iron (or other) grill pan on the stovetop (see Chapter 9). Relatively high heat is used to sear food and add depth of flavor.

hull: To trim strawberries by plucking out their green stems.

indirect grilling: To create two heat sources on a grill: one directly over the fire, and the other off to the side. This allows for more controlled and slower cooking, which helps retain moisture while achieving a seared crust.

julienne: To cut foods into thin ($\frac{1}{8}$ -inch or less) strips; see Chapter 4.

knead: The technique of pushing, folding, and pressing dough for yeast breads to give it a smooth, elastic texture. You can knead by hand, with an electric mixer equipped with a bread hook, or with a bread machine.

macerate: To soak fruit in liquid — usually liqueur, wine, or sugar syrup.

marinate: To soak or steep a food such as meat, poultry, fish, or vegetables in a liquid mixture that may be seasoned with spices and herbs to impart flavor to the food before it's cooked (see Chapter 9). The steeping liquid is called the marinade.

mash: To press food, usually with a potato masher or ricer, into a soft pulp.

mince: To cut food into tiny pieces.

mirepoix: A combination of finely chopped sautéed vegetables, usually carrots, onions, and celery, that's used as a seasoning base for soups, stews, stuffings, and other dishes.

pan-fry: To cook thick cuts of chicken, pork, steak, and fish fillets at a temperature somewhat lower than that for a sauté and in a small amount of oil. This allows the interior to cook through without overcooking the surface.

pan-roast: To sear a piece of meat, poultry, or seafood in a hot pan to create a crispy surface and then finish it in the oven. This technique minimizes moisture loss.

papillote: The practice of placing food, herbs, and spices in a sealed pouch made of parchment paper or aluminum foil. This technique, which retains moisture, works especially well with seafood.

parboil: To partially cook foods, such as rice or dense vegetables like carrots and potatoes, by plunging them briefly into boiling water (see Chapter 5).

pare: To remove the skin from fruits or vegetables (see Chapter 4).

pickle: To preserve food in a salty brine or vinegar solution.

pinch or dash: A small amount of any dry ingredient (between ⅙ and ⅛ teaspoon) that can be grasped between the tips of the thumb and forefinger.

poach: To cook foods in a simmering, not boiling, liquid (see Chapter 5).

pound: To flatten food, especially chicken breasts or meat, with a meat mallet or the flat side of a large knife (such as a cleaver) to make it uniform in thickness. Has some tenderizing effect.

powdered sugar: See *confectioners' sugar*.

preheat: To turn on the oven, grill, or broiler before cooking food to set the temperature to the degree required by the recipe.

purée: To mash or grind food into a paste by forcing it through a food mill or sieve or by whirling it in a food processor or blender. Finely mashed food also is called a purée.

ream: To extract the juice from fruit, especially citrus.

reconstitute: To bring dehydrated food, such as dried milk or juice, back to a liquid state by adding water.

reduce: The technique of rapidly boiling a liquid mixture, such as wine, stock, or sauce, to decrease its original volume so it thickens and concentrates in flavor.

refresh: To cool hot food (especially vegetables) quickly by plunging it in ice water or rinsing.

render: To cook a piece of meat over low heat so its fat melts away.

roast: To cook in the dry heat of an oven (see Chapter 8).

roux: A cooked paste of flour and fat such as oil or butter that's used to thicken soups, stews, and gumbos (see Chapter 14).

sauté: To cook food quickly in a small amount of fat, usually butter or oil, over very high heat (see Chapter 6).

scald: To heat milk to just below the boiling point when making custards and dessert sauces to shorten the cooking time and add flavor.

score: To make shallow cuts (often in a crisscross pattern) on the exterior of a food (such as meat, fish, or bread) so it cooks more evenly.

sear: To brown quickly in a pan, under the broiler, or in a very hot oven (see Chapter 8).

shred: To reduce food to thin strips, usually by rubbing it against a grater.

shuck: To remove shells from shellfish, such as clams, oysters, and mussels, or to remove husks from fresh corn.

sift: To shake dry ingredients, such as flour or confectioner's sugar, through a fine mesh sifter to incorporate air and make them lighter.

simmer: To gently cook food in a liquid just below the boiling point or just until tiny bubbles begin to break the surface — at about 185 degrees (see Chapter 5).

skim: To remove the fat and bits of food that rise to the surface of a soup or stock with a spoon (see Chapter 12).

sous vide: A method of cooking (used primarily by the food industry and restaurants) in which ingredients or entire meals are cooked in vacuum-packed pouches for a long time at low temperatures and then chilled. They can be reheated and served or frozen for up to 18 months.

steam: To cook over a small amount of simmering or boiling water in a covered pan so the steam trapped in the pan cooks the food (see Chapter 5).

steep: To soak dry ingredients like herbs and spices to infuse the liquid with flavor.

stew: To simmer food for a long time in a tightly covered pot with just enough liquid to cover. The term *stew* also can describe a cooked dish (see Chapter 7).

stiff peaks: A term describing whipped egg whites at the stage when they form stiff, upstanding peaks that stay erect when the beater is lifted out of the egg whites.

stir-fry: The Asian cooking technique of quickly frying small pieces of food in a wok with a small amount of fat over very high heat while constantly tossing and stirring the ingredients. The term *stir-fry* also can refer to a dish prepared this way.

stock: The strained, flavorful liquid that's produced by cooking meat, fish, poultry, vegetables, seasonings, or other ingredients in water.

strain: To separate liquids from solids by passing a mixture through a sieve.

tenderize: To soften the connective tissue of meat by pounding or cooking very slowly for a long time. See also *braise*.

toss: To turn over food a number of times to mix thoroughly, as when a green salad is mixed and coated with dressing.

truss: To tie meat or poultry with string and/or skewers to maintain its shape during roasting (see Chapter 8).

whip: To beat air into ingredients such as eggs or cream with a whisk or electric beater to make them light and fluffy (see Chapter 10).

whisk: A hand-held wire kitchen utensil used to whip ingredients like eggs, cream, and sauces. When used as a verb, the term *whisk* describes the process of whipping or blending ingredients together with a wire whisk.

zest: As a noun, the colored, grated outer peel (the colored portion only) of citrus fruit that's used as a flavoring ingredient in dressings, stews, desserts, and so on. As a verb, the process of removing the colored, grated outer peel.

Appendix B

Common Substitutions, Abbreviations, and Equivalents

In this appendix, we list all kinds of ingredients to substitute for those you may not have on hand; we also decode the most common cooking abbreviations and give you a list of English to metric equivalencies.

Substituting in a Pinch

Say that you're making a vinaigrette dressing for a salad and suddenly realize that you're out of vinegar. But you do have lemons. Can you use them? (Yes!) You may not have whole milk for a gratin dish, but you do have skim milk. Is skim milk okay? (Yes, but the taste won't be as rich.) Situations like these are what this section is all about.

Some ingredients are almost always interchangeable. For example, you can substitute vegetable or olive oil in most cases for butter when sautéing or pan-frying; lemon juice for vinegar in salad dressings and marinades; almonds for walnuts in baked breads and muffins; vegetable stock for beef or chicken stock in soups, stews, or sauces; and light cream or even whole milk for half-and-half in almost anything.

Sometimes the substitution must be very exact. This is most often the case for baked goods, where you need to follow a formula for a cake, soufflé, pastry, or bread with the perfect height, density, and texture.

Here are some reliable substitutions for thickening soups, stews, and sauces:

>> 1 tablespoon cornstarch or potato flour = 2 tablespoons all-purpose flour. Make sure to cook the dish for at least 10 minutes after adding flour to get rid of the raw flour taste.

>> 1 tablespoon arrowroot = 2½ tablespoons all-purpose flour. See the preceding note about cooking the dish.

Different flours have different protein contents. These substitutions aren't ideal, but they'll work:

>> 1 cup minus 2 tablespoons sifted all-purpose flour = 1 cup sifted cake flour

>> 1 cup plus 2 tablespoons sifted cake flour = 1 cup sifted all-purpose flour

>> 1 cup sifted self-rising flour = 1 cup sifted all-purpose flour plus 1¼ teaspoons baking powder and a pinch of salt

For leavening agents in baked goods:

>> ¼ teaspoon baking soda plus ½ teaspoon cream of tartar = 1 teaspoon double-acting baking powder

>> ¼ teaspoon baking soda plus ½ cup buttermilk or yogurt = 1 teaspoon double-acting baking powder in liquid mixtures only; reduce liquid in recipe by ½ cup

For dairy products:

>> 1 cup whole milk = ½ cup unsweetened evaporated milk plus ½ cup water

   or 1 cup skim milk plus 2 teaspoons melted butter

   or 1 cup water plus ⅓ cup powdered milk

   or 1 cup soy, rice, coconut, or other non-dairy milk

   or 1 cup buttermilk plus ½ teaspoon baking soda

>> ¾ cup whole milk plus ⅓ cup melted butter = 1 cup heavy cream (but not for making whipped cream)

>> 1 cup skim milk = 1 cup water plus ¼ cup nonfat powdered milk, or ½ cup evaporated skim milk plus ½ cup water

>> 1 cup sour milk = 1 cup buttermilk or plain yogurt

or 1 cup minus 1 tablespoon milk plus 1 tablespoon lemon juice or white vinegar after standing 5 to 10 minutes

>> 1 cup sour cream = 1 cup plain yogurt

For eggs:

>> 2 egg yolks = 1 egg for thickening sauces and custards

>> 4 extra large eggs = 5 large eggs or 6 small eggs

For sweetening:

>> 1 cup sugar = 1 cup molasses (or honey) plus ½ teaspoon baking soda

>> 1 cup brown sugar = 1 cup white sugar plus 1½ tablespoons molasses

Miscellaneous substitutions:

>> 1 cup broth or stock = 1 bouillon cube dissolved in 1 cup boiling water

>> 1 square (1 ounce) unsweetened chocolate = 3 tablespoons cocoa plus 1 tablespoon butter, margarine, or vegetable shortening

>> 1 square (1 ounce) semisweet chocolate = 3 tablespoons cocoa plus 1 tablespoon butter, margarine, or vegetable shortening plus 2 tablespoons sugar

>> 1 2- to 3-inch piece of vanilla bean = 1 teaspoon pure vanilla extract

>> 1 tablespoon fresh chopped herbs = ¾ to 1 teaspoon dried herbs

>> 1 medium garlic clove = ⅛ teaspoon garlic powder

>> 1 cup red wine = 1 cup apple cider, cranberry juice, or beef broth

>> 1 cup white wine = 1 cup apple juice, apple cider, white grape juice, or chicken broth

Taking a Quick Look at Abbreviations

Although we spell out measurements in this book, many cookbooks use abbreviations. Table B-1 lists common abbreviations and what they stand for.

Common Abbreviations

Abbreviation(s)	What It Stands For
C., c.	Cup
G, g	Gram
kg	Kilogram
L, l	Liter
lb.	Pound
mL, ml	Milliliter
oz.	Ounce
pt.	Pint
t., tsp.	Teaspoon
T., Tb., Tbsp.	Tablespoon

Looking Up Conversions and Metric Equivalents

Cookbook writers have a penchant for practical jokes. Just when you're getting the hang of cups and tablespoons, they throw you a recipe in ounces or pounds or some other measurement. Tables B-2 and B-3 list common equivalent measures. All measurements are for level amounts.

Note: Some metric measurements are approximate. The recipes in this cookbook weren't developed or tested using metric measures. There may be some variation in quality when converting to metric units.

Tables B-4 through B-6 show you metric conversions for volume, weight, and temperature. Use them if you need to convert a recipe, but remember that these are approximate, and results could vary.

TABLE B-2   ## Conversion Secrets

This Measurement . . .	. . . Equals This Measurement	. . . Equals This Metric Measurement
Pinch or dash	less than ⅛ teaspoon	0.5 mL
3 teaspoons	1 tablespoon	15 mL
2 tablespoons	1 fluid ounce	30 mL
1 jigger	1½ fluid ounces	45 mL
4 tablespoons	¼ cup	50 mL
5 tablespoons plus 1 teaspoon	⅓ cup	75 mL
12 tablespoons	¾ cup	175 mL
16 tablespoons	1 cup	250 mL
1 cup	8 fluid ounces	250 mL
2 cups	1 pint or 16 fluid ounces	500 mL
2 pints	1 quart or 32 fluid ounces	1 L
4 quarts	1 gallon	4 L

TABLE B-3   ## Food Equivalents

This Measurement . . .	. . . Equals This Measurement
3 medium apples or bananas	about 1 pound
1 ounce baking chocolate	1 square
2 slices bread	about 1 cup fresh bread crumbs
1 pound brown sugar	2¼ cups packed
4 tablespoons butter	½ stick
8 tablespoons butter	1 stick
4 sticks butter	1 pound
6 ounces chocolate chips	about 1 cup
1 pound confectioner's sugar	about 4½ cups sifted
1 pound granulated sugar	2 cups
½ pound hard cheese	about 2 cups grated

(continued)

This Measurement . . .	. . . Equals This Measurement
1 cup heavy whipping cream	2 cups whipped cream
1 medium lemon	3 tablespoons juice, 2 to 3 teaspoons grated zest
1 pound macaroni	4 cups raw, 8 cups cooked
4 ounces nuts	about ⅔ cup chopped
1 large onion	about 1 cup chopped
1 cup uncooked rice	4 cups cooked
1 pint strawberries	about 2 cups sliced
1 large tomato	about ¾ cup chopped
3 to 4 tomatoes	about 1 pound
1 pound all-purpose flour	about 4 cups sifted

TABLE B-4   ## Volume

U.S. Units	Canadian Metric	Australian Metric
¼ teaspoon	1 milliliter	1 milliliter
½ teaspoon	2 milliliters	2 milliliters
1 teaspoon	5 milliliters	5 milliliters
1 tablespoon	15 milliliters	20 milliliters
¼ cup	50 milliliters	60 milliliters
⅓ cup	75 milliliters	80 milliliters
½ cup	125 milliliters	125 milliliters
⅔ cup	150 milliliters	170 milliliters
¾ cup	175 milliliters	190 milliliters
1 cup	250 milliliters	250 milliliters
1 quart	1 liter	1 liter
2 quarts	2 liters	2 liters
3 quarts	3 liters	3 liters
4 quarts (1 gallon)	4 liters	4 liters

TABLE B-5   Weight

U.S. Units	Canadian Metric	Australian Metric
1 ounce	30 grams	30 grams
2 ounces	55 grams	60 grams
3 ounces	85 grams	90 grams
4 ounces (¼ pound)	115 grams	125 grams
8 ounces (½ pound)	225 grams	225 grams
16 ounces (1 pound)	455 grams	500 grams (½ kilogram)

TABLE B-6   Temperature (Degrees)

Fahrenheit	Celsius
32	0
212	100
250	120
275	140
300	150
325	160
350	180
375	190
400	200
425	220
450	230
475	240
500	260

Index

A

acorn squash, roasted, 140
  recipe for, 154
alcohol, cooking with, 271, 408
Alfredo sauce, 270
All-American Coleslaw, 366, 373
All-Butter Pie Crust, 188
all-purpose flour, 187
allspice, 45
almond extract, 41
apples
  Apple Pie, 190
  Apple-Pear Crisp, 293
  Braised Cabbage with Apples and Caraway, 123
  Cornbread, Sausage, and Apple Stuffing, 394
  paring, 74–76
  storing, 50
appliances
  major, 11–17
  small, 33–35
Apricot Glaze, Smoked Ham with, 148–149
aquaculture, 59
Arborio rice, 249
artichokes, 50, 85
  Warm Artichoke-Spinach Dip, 384, 390
arugula, described, 227
Asian ingredients and dishes
  Asian Peanut and Sesame Noodles, 341
  noodles *See* noodles, Asian
  Orange-Ginger Asian Salad, 339
  overview, 331–332
  Pad Thai with Shrimp, 342–343
  Pork and Noodle Stir-Fry, 340
  rice, 335–336
  staples, 332–334
  Yellow Chicken Curry, 344
Asian pasta, 255. *See also* noodles, Asian
asparagus
  boiling, 86
  Lemon Asparagus with Parmesan, 348

Pan-Sauced Chicken with Asparagus, 364
  storing, 50
assumptions of this cookbook, 2–3
avocados, storing, 50

B

bacon
  Bacon and Cheese Strata, 211
  baking, 205
  Broccoli Salad with Warm Bacon Dressing, 241
  frying, 204–205
  Kale Salad with Bacon and Eggs, 242
  microwaving, 205
  overview, 204–206
  in turkey burgers, 108–109
bain marie, 82
baking. *See also specific baked dishes*
  cakes and quick breads, 186–187
  eggs, 178–179
  equipment, 30–33
  flours, 187
  measuring dry ingredients, 177
  measuring other types of ingredients, 178
  measuring wet ingredients, 177–178
  overview, 175
  techniques used in, 180–181
baking dishes, 26
baking powder, 41, 177
baking sheets, 31, 288
baking soda, 41, 166
baking supplies, 40–41
balloon whisk, 30
balsamic vinegar, 232
  Lentils with, 326
bananas, 51
  Chocolate Chip Banana Bread, 194
Barbecue Sauce, Country, 135
  Roasted Pork Ribs with, 146–147

escarole
  described, 227
  Pasta with Escarole, Beans, and Sausage, 266
extra-virgin olive oil, 230

F

Fabulous French Toast, 215
farmers' markets, 52–53
farro, 250
  Farro Salad, 261
feta cheese, 337
  Shrimp Pasta with Kalamata Olives and Feta
    Cheese, 349
fettuccine, 254
filé powder, 219
filet mignon, 134
fillet roast (tenderloin), 134
  Roasted Fillet of Beef, 141
fish. *See also* salmon; tuna
  Canadian Fish Rule, 89
  canned, 46
  Foil-Baked Fish Fillets with Lemony Vegetables, 362
  quick and easy dishes, 356
  sautéing, 99
  selecting, buying, and storing, 58–60
  Snapper Fillets with Tomatoes, 110
fish filleting knife, 65
fish sauce, 333–334
flat ribbon pasta, 254
flavor combinations, 402
flour, 41, 177, 187
flour sifter, 32
Foil-Baked Fish Fillets with Lemony Vegetables, 362
folding, defined, 181
fond, 98, 271
food processor, 34
fortified wines, 271
Free-Form Fresh Fruit Tart, 287, 296–297
free-range chickens, 57
free-range eggs, 199
freezer, 16, 323
French Onion Soup, 239
French Potato Salad, 245

French toast, 206
  Fabulous French Toast, 215
Fresh Cranberry-Orange Relish with Walnuts, 385, 391
Fresh Strawberry Sauce, 283
Fresh Summer Pesto Sauce, 279
freshest ingredients, using only, 401–402
frisee, description of, 227
frittata, 203
  Mushroom-Swiss Frittata, 210
fruit relish, 46
Fruit Salsa, 234
fruit smoothies, 207
  Strawberry-Mango Fruit Smoothie, 216
fruits. *See also specific fruits*
  buying and storing, 50–52
  drinks, 367–368
  Free-Form Fresh Fruit Tart, 296–297
  Goat Cheese with Honey and Fruit, 346
  pie, 190
  tropical, storing, 52
frying pans, 24
fully cooked ham, 136
fumet, defined, 219

G

garbage disposal, 17
Garbanzo Bean Toss, 234
garbanzo beans. *See* chickpeas
garlic
  Browned Butter, Lemon, and Herb Sauce, 276
  Garlic-Grilled Portobello Mushrooms, 168
  London Broil with Garlicky Potatoes and Peppers, 363
  Mashed Potatoes, 91
  mincing, 70
  Sautéed and Braised Kale with Rosemary and
    Garlic, 122
  in soup, 222
  storing, 51
garlic press, 407
gas grills, 158
gas stoves, 11–12
gelatin, 41
giblets, 132, 133

About the Authors

Bryan Miller is a food and wine writer and a former restaurant critic for *The New York Times.* He has written and cowritten 11 books. In the past 25 years, he has received numerous awards, including three writing awards from the James Beard Foundation as well as the organization's prestigious Lifetime Achievement Award. He is president of the Miller Dining Group, a restaurant consulting company.

Marie Rama grew up in the restaurant business surrounded by a large Italian family of food professionals and entrepreneurs. She has worked as a pastry chef, a recipe tester, and an account executive and spokesperson for national companies and associations such as Tabasco Sauce, the United Fresh Fruit and Vegetable Association, Korbel Champagne, and Sunkist Growers. In addition to *Cooking Basics For Dummies*, Marie also wrote *Grilling For Dummies* with John Mariani (published by Wiley) and *Bacon Nation* with Peter Kaminsky (Workman Publishing). Marie has two sons, Nicholas and William, and lives in Yonkers, New York, with her husband and literary agent, Mark Reiter.

Dedication

From Marie: To Mark Reiter, who first set me on the *Cooking For Dummies* journey.

Publisher's Acknowledgments

Senior Acquisitions Editor: Tracy Boggier
Senior Project Editor: Victoria M. Adang
Copy Editor: Jennette ElNaggar
Technical Editor: Jeff Bricker, CEC, CCE MAdEd

Production Editor: Magesh Elangovan
Cover Image: © alistaircotton/iStock.com

DIXON PUBLIC LIBRARY
DIXON ILLINOIS

DIXON PUBLIC LIBRARY
DIXON ILLINOIS

CPSIA information can be obtained
at www.ICGtesting.com
Printed in the USA
LVHW100707071020
668083LV00010B/233

9 781119 696773